ETHICS IN CRIMINAL JUSTICE

Christopher Dreisbach

Johns Hopkins University

D0730817

McGraw-Hill Irwin

Boston Burr Ridge, IL Dubuque, IA New York San Francisco St. Louis
Bangkok Bogotá Caracas Kuala Lumpur Lisbon London Madrid Mexico City
Milan Montreal New Delhi Santiago Seoul Singapore Sydney Taipei Toronto

McGraw-Hill
Higher Education

A Division of The McGraw-Hill Companies

Published by McGraw-Hill, an imprint of The McGraw-Hill Companies, Inc., 1221 Avenue of the Americas, New York, NY 10020. Copyright © 2009. All rights reserved. No part of this publication may be reproduced or distributed in any form or by any means, or stored in a database or retrieval system, without the prior written consent of The McGraw-Hill Companies, Inc., including, but not limited to, in any network or other electronic storage or transmission, or broadcast for distance learning.

2 3 4 5 6 7 8 9 0 DOC/DOC 0 9

ISBN: 978-0-07-337999-9
MHID: 0-07-337999-9

Editor-in-chief: *Michael Ryan*
Publisher: *Frank Mortimer*
Sponsoring editor: *Katie Stevens*
Development editor: *Rhona Robbin*
Marketing manager: *Leslie Oberhuber*
Production editor: *Paul Wells*
Art director: *Jeanne M. Schreiber*
Cover designer: *Laurie Entringer*
Production supervisor: *Louis Swaim*
Media project manager: *Ron Nelms*
Production service: *Scratchgravel Publishing Services*
Composition: *10/12 Palatino by Laserwords*
Printing: *45# New Era Matte by R.R. Donnelley & Sons*

Cover images © 2008 iStock International Inc.

Library of Congress Cataloging-in-Publication Data
Dreisbach, Christopher.
   Ethics in criminal justice / Christopher Dreisbach.
      p. cm.
   Includes index.
   ISBN-13: 978-0-07-337999-9 (alk. paper)
   ISBN-10: 0-07-337999-9 (alk. paper)
1. Criminal justice, Administration of—Moral and ethical aspects.
2. Criminal justice, Administration of—Philosophy.   3. Criminal justice,
Administration of—Case studies.   I. Title.
   HV7419.D74 2008
   172'.2—dc22

                                        2007052002

The Internet addresses listed in the text were accurate at the time of publication. The inclusion of a Web site does not indicate an endorsement by the authors or McGraw-Hill, and McGraw-Hill does not guarantee the accuracy of the information presented at these sites.

www.mhhe.com

*For my daughters, Abigail Dreisbach Pulcinella
and Anna Lisa Dreisbach, models of virtue*

ABOUT THE AUTHOR

Christopher Dreisbach, PhD, is Chair of the Department of Applied Ethics and Humanities for the Division of Public Safety Leadership in Johns Hopkins University's School of Education. He also is Professor of Moral Theology at the Ecumenical Institute of Theology, St. Mary's Seminary & University. He can be reached at cdreisbach@jhu.edu.

Brief Contents

CONTENTS

PART VI

CRIMINAL JUSTICE ETHICS IN THE FUTURE 301

PREFACE

This is a book for criminal justice students, criminal justice professionals, and others with an interest in the ethics of criminal justice. Criminal justice ethics has been a major topic of popular and scholarly discussion for millennia. Issues have included the purpose of law; the difference between morally good laws and morally bad laws; the purpose of punishment; the morally proper means of punishment; and the relationship among the lawmakers, law enforcers, and law adjudicators. Today's news headlines announce legislative misconduct, police misconduct, judicial misconduct, and the moral misdeeds of corrections officials. Criminal justice programs, both general and specific to a particular field of criminal justice, put a premium on moral education. Current political concerns give criminal justice professionals crucial roles to play in homeland security, roles which require strong moral character.

As one of many such books on the market, this book seeks to combine in one text useful materials and approaches that appear only partially or not at all in other individual texts. This attempt involves six premises that inform the text throughout and an organization of the text into six parts.

✦ PREMISES

First, this book builds on the strengths of morally good professionals rather than focusing on the corruption or misconduct of morally bad professionals. Too often today, the study of criminal justice ethics emphasizes corruption and other misconduct, but corrupt professionals are unlikely to become uncorrupt simply by taking a course in ethics or reading a book on it. An analogy may help here. In an episode of the TV show *King of the Hill,* the father Hank Hill examines his son Bobby's report card for a moment before exclaiming with dismay, "Bobby, you flunked English? But you speak English!" There is a significant difference between speaking English, which any native speaker can do well enough to get by in the ordinary discourse of life, and studying English academically, which is necessary to communicating well at a higher level and which may be beyond the ability of many speakers to do successfully. Similarly, there is a difference between doing ethics and studying ethics. Anyone with a moral conscience can generally distinguish good from bad and decide whether to do one or the other. But in the more difficult moral cases, one who has studied ethics will have an advantage over one who has not, because the student will have at the ready a set of tools to apply quickly to the problem and will be able to explain his or her actions if necessary. And just as one who can't speak English at all will gain little from the academic study of English, a criminal justice professional without a moral conscience will gain little from a study of ethics. The target audiences for this book, therefore, are those who can gain from such a study—namely, criminal justice students, scholars, and professionals who seek ethics in the profession.

Second, this book aims primarily at the individual moral agent rather than at the corporate body of agents. There has been a good deal of writing on the relationship between the "apple" and the "barrel" in criminal justice, with emphasis on ensuring that the barrel—the criminal justice agency—does not rot the apple—the individual professional. One of the presumptions of this book is that the responsibility for morally good character, decision making, and behavior falls first and foremost on the individual. No group or organization can corrupt an individual who is capable of moral agency, unless that individual permits it. The book, therefore, aims to help the individual exercise his or her moral muscle in the face of personal and corporate temptations to do otherwise.

Third, this book focuses on the logic of ethics rather than on the psychology or sociology of ethics. The latter two sorts of texts are useful in describing the general stages of moral development and the psychological and sociological causes of and incentives for corruption and misconduct. But they are not so helpful in offering a concise guide for dealing with the hard moral cases. One approaches these cases best through logical analyses and the use of techniques for problem solving. To this end, this book includes 59 cases, distributed among the 15 chapters. Some of these cases are real; some are imaginary. In some of the real cases, I have altered details to disguise principals in the case or to honor the request of the person who told me the case. There also are around 200 questions about those cases. At the end of each chapter are my answers to these questions—which I offer for the sake of argument and to help the readers focus their thinking about the cases—with many of those answers explicitly exhibiting their logical structure.

Fourth, this book covers various influences on criminal justice ethics. Most obvious is philosophical ethics, but the U.S. Constitution, religion, and professional ethics also figure prominently in the challenges to and resources for criminal justice ethics. The book attempts to make these influences clear and to put them in a proper balance relative to each other. Thus, for example, the U.S. Constitution is more important than religious ethics to criminal justice, because one enters the criminal justice profession by taking an oath to the Constitution, but one need not be religious to be in the profession. On the other hand, religion is important even to the nonreligious criminal justice professional to the extent that religion influences people and policies that affect the professional's work.

Fifth, this book discusses a variety of basic moral theories but focuses on Aristotle's version of virtue theory, which emphasizes acting habitually in a way that is neither excessive nor deficient and that exhibits the cardinal virtues of courage, justice, temperance, and prudence. In my 28 years of teaching ethics, I have found students routinely embracing this approach and reporting later that they found it useful in their personal and professional lives.

Sixth, this book's purpose is not to address every problem, much less solve each one, but to help the reader identify tools for solving any of them.

✦ ORGANIZATION

This book has 15 chapters distributed among six parts.

Part I, "Preliminaries," has two chapters.

- Chapter 1, "Introduction: Challenges and Tools," emphasizes the importance of accountability and integrity to criminal justice professions and lays out the working assumptions of the text.
- Chapter 2, "Moral Decision Making: The Logic of Ethics," offers a brief introduction to logic as it underlies the study of ethics.

Part II, "Philosophical Ethics," has four chapters.

- Chapter 3, "Consequentialism," examines the theory that an act is morally good if its consequences are good and morally bad if its consequences are bad. There are two basic consequentialist theories: egoism, which promotes the greatest good for the self, and utilitarianism, which promotes the greatest good for the greatest number. This chapter also discusses the basic moral controversies of hedonism versus non-hedonism, absolutism versus relativism, objectivism versus subjectivism, and free will versus determinism.
- Chapter 4, "Regularianism," examines the theory that an act is morally good if it obeys a rule and morally bad if it breaks a rule. There are all sorts of rules, such as religious commands, criminal and civil laws, social norms, and professional codes of conduct. The moral scope and limits of such rules are the primary focus of this chapter.
- Chapter 5, "Deontology," examines the theory that an act is morally good if the agent acts from duty and morally bad if the agent does not act from duty. This invites several questions: What is duty? What if one's duty is unclear? What about conflicts of duty?
- Chapter 6, "Virtue and Responsibility: An Aristotelian Approach," describes Aristotle's virtue theory and discusses his criteria for determining when someone is morally responsible for his or her actions. For Aristotle, to be fully morally responsible for an act is to know what choices the situation offers; to intend to do the act; to have full knowledge of right and wrong; and to be able to do otherwise—that is, to have free will. Although this book favors Aristotle's moral theory, the chapter will examine it with a critical eye.

Part III, "Constitutional Ethics," has three chapters.

- Chapter 7, "Law," examines three theories of law, tying each to a particular document in American history. Natural law theory, which the Declaration of Independence (1776) reflects, holds that law comes to humans from a higher power, and humans must discern and live by that law. Legal positivism, which the U.S. Constitution (1787) reflects, holds that human legislators make law. Legal realism, which the U.S. Supreme Court decision in *Marbury v. Madison* (1803) reflects, holds that the law is whatever a judge decides. Much of this chapter focuses on the moral implications of these different theories of law and the importance of keeping them distinct.

- Chapter 8, "Rights," looks at the distinctions between interests and freedoms; inalienable and conferred rights; positive rights, whose enjoyment depends on other people fulfilling certain obligations, and negative rights, whose enjoyment depends only on the rights holder being left alone; and legal rights and moral rights.

- Chapter 9, "Justice," distinguishes among distributive justice, commutative justice, and retributive (punitive, corrective) justice. Distributive justice concerns the just distribution of goods and services among the stakeholders. Commutative justice is about contracts. Under what circumstances are contracts valid, and under what circumstances are they invalid? Retributive justice is about the proper response to people who have acted unjustly, either distributively or commutatively. Should the response be punitive? Corrective? Reformative? Transformative?

Part IV, "Religious Ethics," has one chapter.

- Chapter 10, "Religious Ethics," examines ethics from the three major religions in the United States—Judaism, Christianity, and Islam. This examination works from the four basic moral authorities of each religion—scripture, tradition, reason, and experience—while focusing on a major moral issue: the possibility of just war.

Part V, "The Profession of Criminal Justice," has four chapters.

- Chapter 11, "Professions and Professional Ethics," examines the meaning of the word *profession* and the moral implications of a profession versus a nonprofessional job.

- Chapter 12, "Ethics in the Legislature," considers the ethical problems that U.S. senators and representatives face and discusses ways of handling those problems.

- Chapter 13, "Ethics in Law Enforcement," examines the moral problems of police officers and corrections officials, including probation and parole officers.

- Chapter 14, "Ethics in the Courtroom," looks at moral problems facing the judge, the lawyers, the jury, and the court reporter.

Part VI, "Criminal Justice Ethics in the Future," has one chapter.

- Chapter 15, "Criminal Justice Ethics in the Future," builds its examination on three factors: technology, demographics, and the media.

✦ INSTRUCTOR SUPPORT

To aid instructors, the author has created an instructor's manual which is available on the book's Web site, www.mhhe.com/dreisbach1e. For each chapter, the manual includes

- Objectives
- Chapter outline
- Summary
- Review of key terms

✦ ACKNOWLEDGMENTS

This book's biggest debt is to Dr. Stephen J. Vicchio, Professor of Philosophy at College of Notre Dame of Maryland and Baltimore's philosopher laureate. A friend and mentor for more than 25 years, Stephen has involved me in many of his courses, projects, and presentations, including his extensive work with ethics in public safety. This work has taken Stephen to many venues, including other universities; several law enforcement agencies at all levels; and U.S. Attorney General Janet Reno's office, where he served as the ethics adviser on a task force to foster police integrity. Perhaps Stephen's greatest lesson to me has been to celebrate the practical value of philosophy, while making use of texts from many disciplines, including literature, religion, politics, sociology, psychology, and law. People familiar with Stephen's work will recognize his influence especially in my use of cases from literature and in my treatment of Aristotle's notion of responsibility. I hope that I have done justice to Stephen's invaluable guidance.

I also owe much to Dr. Sheldon Greenberg and L. Douglas Ward, my bosses in the Division of Public Safety Leadership at Johns Hopkins University. When the division received a grant from the U.S. Department of Justice to write an ethics book for law enforcement, Shelly and Doug gave me the task, the time to perform it, and many fine suggestions for completing the book. It was the prototype for the present book.

That prototype has served as a central text in many of my ethics courses in the Police Executive Leadership program, Public Safety Aspiring Leaders program, and Fire/EMS Executive Leaders program at Johns Hopkins. The students in these courses have been extraordinarily patient and helpful in my use and refining of the text, as it has evolved into the present text. I have also used parts of the text in Hopkins' U.S. Secret Service Executive Development Program and the Masters in Intelligence Analysis Leadership Program. I thank the students in these programs for all of their help.

The prototype and its revised editions have also served as the basis of one-day ethics courses that I have offered for the U.S. Federal Law Enforcement Training Center (FLETC), the U.S. Secret Service, the U.S. Drug Enforcement Administration, the Florida Department of Law Enforcement (FDLE), the Command College of California's Peace Officer Standards and Training Commission, the Maryland State Police, Washington, DC's Metropolitan Police Department (MPD), and several county and city police agencies in Maryland. Among the many individuals I wish to thank are Malcolm Adams, FLETC; Dick Stephens, Danielle Desilet, Terry Everest, and Evan Barry, FDLE; Tom Esensten, California POST Command College; and Larry Edwards, MPD. In every case, program leaders and participants have taught me a great deal, and I hope this book serves as a testament to their wisdom.

I bring to this text 28 years of teaching philosophy and 16 years of teaching theology. Especially pertinent were courses I have taught in professional ethics, business ethics, legal ethics, medical ethics, and media ethics. The debt I have incurred to all of the students, colleagues, and administrators who enabled to me to teach and refine those courses is far too big to articulate fairly. It is also too big not to acknowledge here.

I thank my father, Frank Dreisbach, for his valuable help with Chapter 12 of this book. His leisurely visit to my home became a mentoring and editing session that helped me produce that chapter better than if I had attempted it by myself.

Thanks, too, to my daughter Anna Lisa, who generously gave up some of her time with me so that I could make the publishing deadlines. In between those efforts, Anna's company more than anybody's kept me grounded and in good humor.

Last, but not least, I must thank Katie Stevens, Executive Editor for Criminal Justice at McGraw-Hill. Her many suggestions for improvements to this manuscript were always constructive, humbling, and correct. Without her faith in me and her steady guidance, this book would not have happened.

Of course, any flaws in this text are solely my responsibility and do not reflect on the valuable help that I have acknowledged above and for which no amount of thanks will ever be sufficient.

PART I

PRELIMINARIES

CHAPTER 1

INTRODUCTION: CHALLENGES AND TOOLS

CASE 1.1

The Counterfeit Counterfeit 20s

A deputy in a small town arrests a Filipino national, Francis Juarez, for passing a counterfeit $20 bill and possessing four others. Upon receiving the bill from Juarez, a mini-mart clerk marked the bill with a special pen, as she had been trained to do; the mark turned a color that suggested the bill was counterfeit, so the clerk called the sheriff's office, which dispatched the deputy.

After the deputy tells the sheriff of the arrest, the sheriff calls the nearest Secret Service office, which is several hours away by car. The sheriff asks the duty agent whether he would like to prosecute the case or whether the local prosecutor should take the case. The duty agent decides that the local prosecutor should take the case given its simplicity. The agent asks the sheriff to keep him in the loop, and the agent takes an arrest credit. Juarez pleads guilty without a trial, serves nine months in jail, and is deported for his conviction. About a month later, the sheriff calls the duty agent again and asks what he should do with the five counterfeit 20s. The duty agent agrees to pick up the five bills and dispose of them properly. As soon as the agent sees the bills, he realizes that the bills are not counterfeit.

✦ ACCOUNTABILITY AND INTEGRITY

This case invites us to think about the moral rights and responsibilities of criminal justice professionals. These rights and responsibilities derive from a *social contract* with the community. The foundation of this contract for most criminal justice professionals is the oath to protect, preserve, and defend the U.S. Constitution. The quality of service depends on how well professionals fulfill their oath. How well they fulfill their oath is a matter of accountability and integrity.

> **Q 1.1**
>
> Did the sworn officials in Case 1.1 fulfill all of their responsibilities? Did they act in ways in which they didn't have the right to act?

Accountability is the external test by which professionals demonstrate that they are fulfilling their promise to the people. The clearest sign of success is the community's safety and comfort.

> **Q 1.2**
>
> Did the sworn officials in Case 1.1 act with full accountability? Is the community better off for their actions?

Integrity is the internal test by which professionals demonstrate to themselves that they are fulfilling their promise. To have integrity is to have integrated moral virtues into one's life. Ancient Greek ethics recognized four basic or "cardinal" virtues: courage, justice, temperance, and prudence (practical wisdom). We could identify many other virtues (honesty and tolerance, for example), and we need to explain what a virtue is and why these are examples of virtues (see Chapter 6). For now it is enough to relate the importance of integrity to doing one's job well as a criminal justice professional.

> **Q 1.3**
>
> Did the sworn officials in Case 1.1 act with integrity?

✦ Working Assumptions

This book makes five assumptions. First, its readers are ethical people who know as a rule what the moral good is and how to achieve it. This book does not offer to make unethical people ethical. Rather, it hopes to build on the moral strengths of its readers, not on the moral weaknesses of others.

> **Q 1.4**
>
> What moral strengths are immediately obvious in Case 1.1?

Second, everyone, no matter how ethical, faces situations in which the morally right course of action is not obvious. These hard cases make the study of ethics, and therefore this book, useful. The more one prepares for such situations, the better one is able to know the right response.

Q 1.5

Case 1.1 presents at least two hard cases: whether and how to make things right with Juarez, and what to do with the five $20 bills. Why are these hard cases?

Third, the tools that we use, often intuitively, to solve the easier cases are the same tools available for solving the difficult cases. This book, then, is as much a reminder as it is a new proposition.

Q 1.6

Intuitively, most people regard fairness as morally desirable. Was Juarez treated fairly in Case 1.1?

Fourth, the moral problems facing the field of criminal justice put it in the category of a profession rather than just a job. If criminal justice ethics were merely job ethics, it would only require showing up on time, following the organization's rules while on duty, and not leaving work until the shift is complete. But the rights and responsibilities of criminal justice experts, and the accountability and integrity to which the community holds them, put these experts in the professional company of doctors, lawyers, priests, and teachers.

Q 1.7

In Case 1.1, what moral challenge does the duty agent face that goes beyond merely following a rule or completing a contracted job well?

Fifth, this book will be most useful to leaders whose moral decisions affect not only themselves but also their peers, their profession, and the community. This assumption recognizes leaders in fact, not leaders in name only. Here it is useful to distinguish mere managers from leaders. It is possible to manage without leading, but it is not possible to lead without managing. In confronting moral challenges, the difference is that while mere managers may hide behind the organization's rules, assuming no other responsibility for their moral decisions, leaders exist in every rank and stand out in their ability *to know when to break a rule.*

Q 1.8

Why might appeal to rules be inadequate to solve the moral challenge of Case 1.1?

On the basis of these five working assumptions, this book focuses on real and hypothetical cases that morally challenge criminal justice professionals. It examines the cases, identifies the tools of relevant moral theories and principles, and offers the reader guidance in deciding on the best disposition of the cases.

Upon completion of this book, readers should:

- Be familiar with the fundamental moral theories and principles that underlie ethical discourse in America.
- Have an idea of the connection between the U.S. Constitution, American ethics, and moral leadership.
- Be aware of the elements and relevance of religious ethics to the solution of problems facing criminal justice professionals.
- Be able to articulate the basic relationships that criminal justice professionals have to consider when making moral decisions.
- Have identified a set of tools for confronting the difficult moral cases.

✦ THE CHALLENGE AND TOOLS OF MORAL LEADERSHIP

The challenge of moral leadership is how best to handle the hard moral cases for which there is no rule that adequately does the job. How do leaders remain accountable and maintain their integrity in the face of overwhelming moral difficulties? In practical terms, what tools are available for deciding the hard cases?

Q 1.9

Other than appealing to a rule, what might the duty agent in Case 1.1 turn to for determining the right response to his discovery?

Criminal justice professionals in America have four general sources of moral tools: philosophy, the U.S. Constitution, religion, and professional ethics.

Philosophy is the historical basis for the study of ethics. Philosophically, moral focus may rest on the consequences of an act, the rules governing the act, the motive behind the act, or various syntheses of these three. The most important synthesis for this book is Aristotle's effort at promoting the virtuous person, whose character enables him or her to know how much weight to give consequences, rules, and motives in any given circumstance.

Q 1.10

In Case 1.1, would it be fair not to notify Juarez of the mistaken conviction, since it is "water over the dam"?

Constitutionally, moral problems invoke debate about laws, rights, and justice. For example, do we receive law from a higher power, as the Declaration of Independence suggests, or is law man-made, as the Constitution suggests? Are constitutional rights inalienable, or can they be taken away? Is distributive justice a matter of every citizen receiving the goods and services of society equally, or is justice a matter of letting each person keep what is his or hers, even if others need it? Is retributive justice a matter of rehabilitating the person being punished? Is it a matter of revenge? These significant constitutional concepts of law, rights, and justice are ambiguous, and we need to understand and clear up these ambiguities before we can put the concepts to good use in solving difficult moral cases.

Q 1.11

Does Juarez in Case 1.1 have any rights that others are violating by not informing him of the mistake?

Religion offers four basic tools for moral decision making: scripture, tradition, reason, and experience. When making moral decisions, should religious people regard their *scriptures* as books of commands or simply as narratives with moral points? How should religious people deal with their disagreements over the moral meaning and values of sacred texts? What weight should a believer give the *tradition* of one's faith? If the moral decree of a powerful religious organization disagrees with the moral views of a member of that organization, how should that member proceed? What is the moral importance of distinguishing between a genuine religious *experience* and something—such as a hallucination or a dream—that one has mistaken for a religious experience, especially when someone claims to be receiving moral guidance from that experience? And given the traditional tensions between religion and *reason*, what role should reason play in discourse on religion and morality?

Many moral problems that confront criminal justice professionals arise out of the religious views of individuals and groups who oversee the professionals or require services from them. Thus, whether the professional is religious, it is important for him or her to understand the tools that religious people may use when making moral decisions.

Q 1.12

Did the deputy in Case 1.1 "bear false witness," in violation of one of the Ten Commandments? If so, does this make his action immoral?

In professional ethics, the most fundamental question is what distinguishes a profession from a mere job. We have already hinted at one answer: Professions carry greater moral responsibilities and afford the professionals greater rights. In a subsequent chapter we will consider the definition of a profession more fully. Another question in professional ethics is what relationships a professional has that may occasion moral problems. Every professional has at least a relationship with oneself; the client; colleagues—superiors, peers, subordinates, and other agencies; third parties; and the profession itself. In each of these relationships the professional has many obligations, including, for example, loyalty, honesty, candor, competence, and diligence. What constitutes each relationship and which obligations pertain to each are significant inquiries for determining the value of professional ethics to solving moral problems.

Q 1.13

What are the sheriff's professional relationships in Case 1.1?

SUMMARY

Criminal justice ethics arises from the social contract between the criminal justice professional and the community that the professional serves. Requiring both accountability and integrity, criminal justice ethics requires the professional to handle tough moral cases. This ability begins with the moral strength of the professional and builds on it through the study of ethics and the use of moral tools available from philosophy, constitutional scholarship, religion, and professional ethics.

In the next chapter we look at the logic of ethics. Logic, the basic tool of philosophical study, will serve us well as we work through the rest of the text.

Answers to Case Study Questions

Q1.1. Did the sworn officials in Case 1.1 fulfill all of their responsibilities? Did they act in ways in which they didn't have the right to act?

There is no apparent rule that the officials could have broken. But the duty agent should have questioned the sheriff's assumption that the bills were counterfeit, even if there was no policy requiring the duty agent to do that.

The biggest mystery is why Juarez pleaded guilty so quickly. Because of that, he bears some responsibility for the outcome.

Q1.2. Did the sworn officials in Case 1.1 act with full accountability? Is the community better off for their actions?

The deputy and the sheriff acted as the community should have expected them to. But again the duty agent was not as accountable as he could have been when the sheriff called for advice.

The community is no better or worse off, since there was no crime and Juarez was not a (permanent) resident of the community. On the other hand, one might object that the community, through its legal representatives, bears some of the responsibility for Juarez's unfair imprisonment and deportation.

Q1.3. Did the sworn officials in Case 1.1 act with integrity?

The virtue of justice is giving someone his due. Apparently Juarez did not deserve jail time or deportation, so he was treated unjustly. To act unjustly is to act without integrity.

An interesting problem is that no one official appears to have treated Juarez unjustly; rather a glitch in the justice system led to the unjust treatment. If so, then perhaps the *system* failed to act with integrity.

Q1.4. What moral strengths are immediately obvious in Case 1.1?

The most immediate moral strength is the sheriff's willingness to seek advice, although he might have received bad advice. There is no apparent moral weakness, although we wonder whether the prosecutor and judge challenged Juarez's guilty plea adequately.

Q1.5. Case 1.1 presents at least two hard cases: whether and how to make things right with Juarez, and what to do with the five $20 bills. Why are these hard cases?

Juarez is out of the country and is no longer under the protection of the U.S. Constitution. Therefore, any effort to make things right must come from the goodness of somebody's heart. But who should this be? The deputy? The sheriff? The prosecutor? The duty agent? And what should this person do? Fly to the Philippines, then try to find Juarez and return his $100? Or write him a letter explaining the situation and offer to help in some way? Since personally tracking Juarez down is too much to ask, should somebody go to the Philippines consulate in the United States and hand the problem over to it?

As for the five $20 bills, should these go to the consulate? To some charity?

The point is that while Case 1.1 calls for some action to set things right on behalf of Juarez, it is difficult to decide what that action would be.

Q1.6. Intuitively, most people regard fairness as morally desirable. Was Juarez treated fairly in Case 1.1?

Everyone treated Juarez fairly up to the adjudication of his case. We don't know whether the prosecutor and judge treated him fairly. Still, there is something intuitively unfair about the outcome, and the question remains whether this is any one person's fault.

Q1.7. In Case 1.1, what moral challenge does the duty agent face that goes beyond merely following a rule or completing a contracted job well?

The duty agent's problem is how to respond to Juarez's serving time for a crime he didn't commit, in part because the agent did not treat the sheriff's call with due diligence.

Q1.8. Why might appeal to rules be inadequate to solve the moral challenge of Case 1.1?

Everybody appears to have followed the rules, and yet the outcome was unjust.

Q1.9. Other than appealing to a rule, what might the duty agent in Case 1.1 turn to for determining the right response to his discovery?

The duty agent might (a) turn to a trusted adviser for help, (b) confer with others involved to see whether some collective wisdom might help, or (c) trust his own instincts and experience.

Q1.10. In Case 1.1, would it be fair not to notify Juarez of the mistaken conviction, since it is "water over the dam"?

Fairness requires a constructive response to the problem. And it would be morally good to try to contact Juarez. But at some point the effort required to locate him could be more than the situation morally demands. In the end, the fair response might be for the sworn persons involved to ensure that this problem doesn't happen again—through revised policy or training, for example.

Q1.11. Does Juarez in Case 1.1 have any rights that others are violating by not informing him of the mistake?

Juarez had constitutional rights while he was in the United States, but he has none now that he is out of the United States. On the other hand, he has the moral right to be treated with respect, but how the sworn officers should honor this right remains a challenge.

Q1.12. Did the deputy in Case 1.1 "bear false witness," in violation of one of the Ten Commandments? If so, does this make his action immoral?

The deputy did not "bear false witness." He had probable cause for arresting Juarez, even though that cause was nothing more than a positive reaction from a pen on a $20 bill.

Q1.13. What are the sheriff's professional relationships in Case 1.1?

The sheriff's professional rights and responsibilities put him in direct relationship with the suspect, the deputy, and the Secret Service agent. The sheriff has a somewhat less direct relationship with the mini-mart clerk, the prosecution, and the judge. We may also assume that by virtue of his oath the sheriff has a professional relationship with anyone under his jurisdiction; with the lawmakers, law enforcement officials, and judges of his state; and with the law enforcement profession in general.

CHAPTER 2

MORAL DECISION MAKING: THE LOGIC OF ETHICS

CASE 2.1

When Fred Shot Barney

Because Fred has good evidence to suggest that his wife Wilma is having an affair with Barney, Fred has resolved to kill Barney. Today, Fred goes to the bus stop where Barney awaits a bus. As Fred approaches Barney, Barney has his back turned to Fred. Without warning, Fred fires six shots into Barney's back; Barney slumps to the ground, and Fred drops his gun to wait for the police. When the police arrive, Fred gives up willingly, as one officer begins to take the statements of several witnesses.

At Barney's autopsy, the medical examiner is surprised to find that Barney died of a massive heart attack and was probably dead before Fred fired the first shot. Thus, under local law, Fred's only obvious crimes were desecration of a corpse and unlawfully firing a gun in the city limits.

✦ CONCLUSIONS, PREMISES, AND GOOD AND BAD ARGUMENTS

Did Fred do something morally wrong? The study of ethics gives us the chance to entertain several possible answers to this question, each of which can take the form of an argument. Consider the following examples:

Argument 1

1. Fred intended to commit murder.
2. An agent's intent determines the moral quality of the act.
3. Therefore, Fred is morally guilty of murder, even if Barney died before Fred fired a shot.

Argument 2

1. Fred did not legally commit murder.
2. The legality of an act determines the morality of an act.
3. Therefore, Fred did not morally commit murder.

Argument 3

1.   Fred illegally desecrated Barney's corpse.
2.   It is immoral to desecrate a corpse.
3.   Therefore, it was immoral of Fred to desecrate the corpse.

Argument 4

1.   Fred is a moral man.
2.   Therefore, Fred did not act immorally in shooting Barney.

Each of these represents a moral decision, and each is open to logical evaluation.

Failures in moral decision making are failures in logic. Criminal justice professionals must frequently make moral decisions. A legislator may have to choose between voting according to her conscience and voting according to the will of the majority of her constituents. A police officer may have to choose between hiding his partner's romantic indiscretions and reporting them to internal affairs. A judge may have to decide whether to recuse herself from a case involving someone she loathes. The morally right decision in each of these cases depends in part on which decision is the more logical. Thus, having an understanding of logic should help in making the decision. Students of criminal justice ethics must also have an understanding of logic in order to evaluate the moral decisions of people and positions that are the objects of study.

Because logic is so basic and useful a tool in the study of ethics, it is worth spending time learning some techniques for logical evaluation in moral decision making.

From a logical point of view, a moral decision is good when its premises support it, and a moral decision is bad when its premises fail to support it. Thus, every moral decision answers two questions:

1.   What is the **conclusion** (or decision, judgment, or thesis)? That is, what is the argument trying to prove?

Q 2.1

In each of the first three arguments, which sentence is the conclusion? How does each conclusion differ from the other two? Which of the three conclusions best captures the point of Case 2.1?

2.   What are the **premises** (or reasons, evidence, support, or justification) for the conclusion? That is, which sentences does the argument offer as proof of the conclusion?

Q 2.2

In each of the four arguments, which sentences are premises?

Every evaluation of a moral decision adds a third question:

3. Do the premises support the conclusion? In other words,
    a. Are the premises all true? If not, then they do not support the conclusion.

Q 2.3

Is it true that every illegal act is an immoral act? If not, how does this claim affect the reasonableness of each of the four arguments?

b. If true, are the premises relevant enough to prove the conclusion? If not, then they do not support the conclusion.

Q 2.4

In which of one of the four arguments is there a premise that, while true, appears not to be relevant to the conclusion?

c. Are the premises less doubtful than the conclusion? If not, then they need as much proof as the conclusion and thus do not support the conclusion.

Q 2.5

In the fourth argument, is the premise less doubtful than the conclusion?

The consideration so far gives us the following definitions:

Moral reasoning: The process of drawing a morally significant conclusion from a set of premises.

Argument: Any set of sentences in which one sentence is claimed to be proven by the other sentences.

Conclusion: The sentence that an argument claims to prove.

Premise: Any sentence that an argument offers as proof of the conclusion.

A good argument: An argument in which the premises are true, the premises are relevant to the conclusion, and no premise simply restates the conclusion.

A bad argument: An argument in which a premise is false, a premise is irrelevant to the conclusion, or a premise simply restates the conclusion.

So far our discussion of logic has been preliminary. Given the importance of logic to ethics, it is worth saying some more about the nature and value of moral arguments. We will do so next, under three major headings: deduction versus induction; truth versus validity; and fallacies.

✦ DEDUCTION VERSUS INDUCTION

From Case 2.1 we may conclude with *certainty* that Fred fired a gun in the city limits. We may also conclude that he *probably* intended to commit murder, although it's possible that he only intended to wound Barney. These two conclusions remind us that some arguments claim certainty and thus fail if they cannot prove their conclusions with certainty. Other arguments claim probability and thus fail if they cannot prove the degree of probability that they claim. Criminal justice professionals and students of criminal justice will benefit from understanding these differences and their relevance to sound moral decision making.

Arguments that claim certainty are **deductive.** They claim that because the premises are true, the conclusion is definitely true. For example,

Argument 5

1.   To desecrate a corpse is immoral.
2.   To shoot a corpse is to desecrate it.
3.   Fred shot Barney's corpse.
4.   Therefore, Fred acted immorally in shooting Barney's corpse.

This argument claims with certainty that Fred's act was immoral. Also, if the three premises are true, then the conclusion must be true. Upon initial examination, this is a good deductive argument, because the premises are true and they prove the conclusion.

Argument 6

1.   Several witnesses claimed to see Fred kill Barney.
2.   Fred confessed to killing Barney.
3.   Therefore, Fred killed Barney.

This argument also claims certainty; it does not claim merely that Fred probably killed Barney. But notice that the two premises might be true while the conclusion is false, just as Case 2.1 demonstrates. So this is a deductive argument, because it claims certainty, but it is a bad argument because it fails to prove its claim.

Arguments that claim probability are **inductive.** They claim that because the premises are true, the conclusion probably is true.

Argument 7

1.   Past observations suggest that when a living person is shot six times and falls to the ground lifeless, the shooting caused the death.
2.   Barney was alive shortly before Fred shot him and fell to the ground lifeless after Fred shot him.
3.   Therefore, Fred probably killed Barney.

This argument claims that Fred probably killed Barney. Moreover, if the premises are true, it is a pretty good bet that Fred killed Barney. Even though the medical examiner determined a different cause of death, this is a good inductive argument.

Another example:

Argument 8

1.   Just before Barney dropped to the ground lifeless, a bystander, Dino, sneezed.
2.   Therefore, Dino's sneeze probably killed Barney.

This silly argument claims that Dino's sneeze probably killed Barney, so it is an inductive argument. Our experiences and observations tell us that the sneeze is probably not the culprit, so this argument is a bad one.

As a general rule, all inductive arguments are based on past observation and can be better or worse with additional information in the premises. Suppose Argument 8 added a premise: "Dino's sneeze startled Fred, causing him inadvertently to pull the trigger on the gun that he had pointed at Barney." Now the connection between Dino's sneeze and Barney's death would be a bit more probable.

The distinction between deduction and induction is important when evaluating moral decisions, because each calls for a different kind of evaluation. The conclusions of deductive arguments are certain or they are not certain. When the premises don't prove a conclusion with certainty, even if the conclusion is highly probable, the deductive argument has failed.

Inductive arguments may be more difficult to assess, because one person's probability may be another person's improbability. Imagine that in Case 2.1 there were no witnesses to the shooting and Fred fled the scene before the police arrived. Imagine further that Fred left his gun at the scene and forensics was able to lift a fingerprint that matched a print of Fred's on nine points. The argument might be:

Argument 9

1.   Usually, if two fingerprints have at least nine matching points, then the two prints probably belong to the same person.
2.   Fred's fingerprint matches the shooter's print on nine points.
3.   Therefore, Fred is probably the shooter.

For some agencies, a 9-point match may be sufficient to implicate Fred—the conclusion is sufficiently probable based on the premises. For other agencies, perhaps, nothing lower than a 12-point match will do.

Q 2.6

Is the following argument inductive or deductive? Why?

> Judge Harlan almost always falls asleep during trials lasting more than an hour. Sleepiness during the day may indicate a sleep disorder such as sleep apnea. Therefore, Judge Harlan might want to be checked for sleep apnea.

Q 2.7

Is the following deductive argument a good one? Why or why not?

> People who fail the polygraph test are liars. Mandy failed the polygraph test.
> Therefore, Mandy is a liar.

Q 2.8

Is the following inductive argument a good one? Why or why not?

> Republican legislators tend to favor laws that protect private business. Congresswoman
> Smith is a Republican. Therefore, Congresswoman Smith probably favors laws that
> protect private business.

✦ Truth versus Validity

Good criminal justice professionals make good moral decisions. Good students of criminal justice ethics are able to evaluate a professional's moral decisions well. Both criminal justice professionals and students of criminal justice need to know how to distinguish logically good moral arguments from logically bad moral arguments. Arguments, including those that express moral decisions, are sets of sentences. A good argument is **valid,** and a bad argument is **invalid.** Individual sentences, whether premises or conclusions, are true or false.

Valid arguments are either **sound** or **unsound.** A sound argument is a valid argument with all true premises. An unsound argument is a valid argument with at least one false premise.

More formally,

Valid: If the premises are true, then the conclusion must certainly be true (in a deductive argument) or as probable as the argument claims (in an inductive argument). Argument 5 is a valid argument.

Sound: The argument is valid and all of the premises are true. If we assume that all of the information in Case 2.1 is correct, then Argument 5 is sound.

Unsound: The argument is valid, but one or more of the premises is false. Argument 2 is valid, but its second premise is false—or at least not necessarily true. Some moral acts may be illegal (protecting fugitive Jews in Nazi Germany, for instance), and some immoral acts may be legal (enforcing segregation laws in the early 1900s, for example). Therefore, Argument 2 is unsound.

Invalid: Even if the premises were true, that would not demonstrate the truth or probability of the conclusion. Argument 8 is clearly invalid. The premises could be true, while the conclusion is obviously false.

Q 2.9

Is the following argument valid? Why or why not? If it is valid, is it sound?

> Ed Richards is campaigning to be this state's attorney general, but it is a pointless campaign. Nonresidents of this state are ineligible to be its attorney general. Anyone registered to vote in another state is considered a nonresident of this state. And Richards is registered to vote in another state.

Whereas validity, soundness, unsoundness, and invalidity are fairly straight-forward notions, truth and falsity are trickier. It is necessary for a good argument to have true premises, but what is truth? Consider whether each of the following five sentences is true or false.

1.   Ordinary window glass cannot stop a .45 caliber bullet shot from a gun.
2.   The consecrated host is the body of Jesus Christ.
3.   Aspirin cures a headache.
4.   Chocolate chip cookies taste good.
5.   Jealousy is a green-eyed monster.

Sentence 1 is true, and we can verify it objectively. This exemplifies the **correspondence theory** of truth. On this theory, a sentence is true if it corresponds to the facts; a sentence is false if it is contrary to the facts; and in the absence of facts one must suspend judgment about the truth of the sentence. In Case 2.1, Fred and the witnesses at the bus stop assumed the truth of the sentence "Fred killed Barney," but the medical examiner provided facts to prove that sentence false.

A problem arises when people will not agree on the facts. What facts are available to verify or falsify sentence 2, which asserts that when a priest says the proper words over a piece of bread or communion wafer, it turns into the body of Jesus Christ? An observant Roman Catholic will assent readily to the claim that the consecrated host is the body of Jesus Christ. Observant Protestant Christians might agree that the sentence is at least symbolically true. Non-Christians and skeptics might regard the sentence as false or at least not provable. What would count as proof? Mere observation suggests that there is no difference in the communion wafer or bread before and after the priest has consecrated it. Yet it is perfectly coherent for a Roman Catholic to believe a change has occurred and for a non-Christian to believe that no change has occurred. Furthermore, it would be incoherent for an observant Roman Catholic to deny that the consecrated host is the body of Jesus Christ.

Sentence 2 exemplifies the **coherence theory** of truth. On this theory, a sentence is true of it is coherent within one's system of belief, and a sentence is false if it is incoherent within one's system of belief. This removes the problem of finding a fact on which all can agree, as the correspondence theory requires, but it raises two new problems. First, what if your system of belief (Judaism, for example) is different from my system of belief (Islam, for example), and each of us holds that his

God has ordained Jerusalem as his belief system's holy city? It is as coherent for a Muslim to claim Jerusalem for Islam as it is for a Jew to claim Jerusalem for Judaism. Therefore, mere appeal to coherence will not settle the question of whose position, if either, is true.

A second problem with the coherence theory of truth is that many people have beliefs that are incoherent with their own systems of belief. In Western culture, for example, coherence is usually a matter of logical or scientific proof, yet many people in that culture hold beliefs—religious or superstitious, for example—that defy logic and science. Consider the belief, widely held in Mediterranean cultures, that certain amulets will ward off the bad thoughts—the evil eye—of others. Although there may be no logical or scientific proof, there is strong belief that the amulets work. We see this thinking in sentence 3: "Aspirin cures a headache." Most people who answer that the sentence is true probably don't care whether there is objective proof; for them, they have a headache, they take an aspirin, and the headache goes away. Similarly, many people who find sentence 3 to be false have found that their head-ache remains after taking aspirin. In the former case, it works to believe that aspirin will cure a headache; in the latter case, it does not work to believe this.

Sentence 3, then, exemplifies the **pragmatic theory** of truth: A sentence is true if it works to believe that it is true—that is, if there is some helpful consequence to accepting the sentence as true. A sentence is false if it is harmful to believe that the sentence is true. And if there is no practical value to believing the sentence, then it is neither true nor false, but nonsense. Medieval metaphysicians might argue the truth of the sentence "Thirty angels can dance on the head of a pin." The pragmatist would argue that because believing this is neither practically helpful nor practically harmful, it is a nonsense sentence. But consider the sentence "Human beings can fly in heavier-than-air aircraft." Centuries ago, anyone who believed this and acted on it would get hurt, so the sentence was false; today, airplanes and rockets show the sentence to be true.

The pragmatic theory of truth avoids the major pitfall of the correspondence theory by avoiding the need for finding a fact on which all can agree. The prag-matic theory also avoids the major pitfall of the coherence theory—namely, that all sentences must be coherent within a given system of belief, even though there are competing systems of belief and not everyone's reasonable beliefs are consistent within one's own system. But as sentence 3 shows, the subjectivity of the pragmatic theory allows for a sentence to be true and false at the same time: If aspirin works for you and it doesn't work for me, then it is both true and false that aspirin cures a headache. This is intuitively unsatisfactory if we are to resolve disagreements.

Sentence 4, "Chocolate chip cookies taste good," exemplifies the **performative theory** of truth—the view that when one says something is true, one *performs* the act of making it true (albeit subjectively). Rather than saving the pragmatic theory from its subjectivity, the performative theory makes the thoroughly subjective claim that to regard a sentence as true is nothing more than to assent to it. Whether one answers true or false to sentence 4 depends on personal experience. How could those of us who like chocolate chip cookies prove the truth of sentence 4 to those who despise the taste of those cookies?

If the performative theory is correct, than we no longer need to debate the criterion of truth: It is not about facts, it is not about coherence, and it is not about workability. It is simply a matter of taste, about which there is no point in disputing. However, if this theory is correct, then it also entitles those of us unhappy with its subjectivity to reject it, since truth is whatever we want it to be. In other words, according to the performative theory, if I say that the theory is false, then it is. Thus, the theory becomes self-refuting.

One theory of truth remains, as sentence 5 exemplifies. This is the **metaphorical theory** of truth. When Iago says to Othello, in Shakespeare's play *Othello*, that "Jealousy is a green-eyed monster," the audience members who understand English and who have suffered jealousy might find this a much more apt description of jealousy than any that a textbook on clinical psychology offers. Yet we could not verify the sentence by appeal to objective facts—try as we might, we will not find a slithering, green-eyed reptile living in a jealous person. We need not appeal to a system of belief to determine the truth of the sentence. While it might work to regard the sentence as true, our assent to it need not prove its practical value. And the truth of sentence 5 transcends mere taste—the truth is in the inherent meaning of the metaphor, not in the hearer's assent.

The first four theories of truth, ranging from the most objective to the most subjective, do not require us to pick one to the exclusion of the others. They remind us that we regard sentences as true in different ways and that each way has its place in determining the truth. It is important, however, that we do not confuse the theories when rendering our own judgments. Whether Fred killed Barney is a matter of objective evidence, Fred's confession and the witnesses' testimony notwithstanding. To decide this as a matter of taste or of workability would be grossly unfair. On the other hand, whether someone's intent makes a difference to the moral value of one's act is not something we can determine on the basis of empirical observation. We need to consider this within the larger system of our beliefs about the moral good.

The fifth theory of truth—the metaphorical theory—reminds us that not all truth comes to us in literal, clear-cut language. "Love is blind," "I'm dying to meet her," "That exam was murder," all might be true in ways that require no further explanation. But their truth does not fit neatly into any of the first four theories of truth. It would be dumb, for instance, to declare "It's false to say that the exam was murder, since no one was killed the entire time!" This would be subjecting a metaphorical claim to the correspondence theory of truth. We must be ready, therefore, to exercise our literary and poetic muscles when deciding whether a premise or conclusion is true or false.

Q 2.10

For each of the following premises from previous arguments, decide which theory of truth it best reflects: Argument 1, premise 2; Argument 5, premise 3; Argument 7, premise 2; Argument 9, premise 1.

✦ FALLACIES

CASE 2.2

Inside Information

A superior in Dudley's law enforcement agency has been in the field investigating alleged financial fraud. Today the superior, Special Agent Franklin, returns to headquarters and casually mentions to Dudley that her investigation reveals that a company in which she holds a lot of stock is in deep trouble and will fail as soon as the information becomes public. She notes regretfully that under the inside information rule for her agency, she will have to take a heavy hit to her stock portfolio rather than sell the stock before its problems are public knowledge.

Unbeknownst to Franklin, Dudley has $30,000 worth of stock in the same company, money he has been accruing to pay for his daughter's pending college tuition. If he acts to sell the stock before the information becomes public, he will realize most of the stock's current value, but he will violate the agency's inside information rule. If he waits to sell the stock until the information is public, he will have broken no rules or laws, but he will have lost most of the $30,000, and his daughter might have to turn down admission to the prestigious college that accepted her.

Of the choices that Dudley faces in Case 2.2, which is morally better—to sell or not to sell? This chapter has focused on how to determine whether a moral decision is logically good. At its best, the argument of a moral decision will be valid and sound. For example,

Argument 10

1. It is against the law for U.S. federal law enforcement agents to sell or buy a stock based on inside information.
2. If Agent Dudley sells his stock before the company's troubles are made public, he will be acting on inside information.
3. Therefore, if Agent Dudley sells his stock before the company's troubles are made public, he will break the law.

In this argument, if the premises are true, then the conclusion must be true, so the argument is valid. And the premises—sentences 1 and 2—are true, so the argument is sound.

Less preferable but worth considering is an argument that is valid but whose soundness is in question—that is, the argument is valid, but we don't know whether the premises are all true. For example,

Argument 11

1.   If Dudley loses his daughter's tuition, she will be sad.
2.   If Dudley waits to sell his stock until the company's troubles are public knowledge, he will lose his daughter's tuition.
3.   Therefore, if Dudley waits to sell his stock until its troubles are public knowledge, then his daughter will be sad.

This argument is valid, because if the premises are true, then the conclusion must be true. But we don't know whether premise 1 is true, so we don't know whether the argument is sound.

Where the argument is unsound (it is valid but contains at least one false premise) or invalid (even if the premises were true, this would not prove the conclusion), we may dismiss the argument and look elsewhere for a better one. For example,

Argument 12

1.   Franklin is free to choose whether or not to sell her stock.
2.   Therefore, Dudley may sell his stock if he wishes.

In this argument, even if the premise were true, this would not necessarily make the conclusion true, so the argument is invalid.

Even as we hope for a good argument, sometimes it is easier to identify bad arguments. Certain types of bad argument are common enough that to know them and be able to identify instances of them will save us a lot of time when deciding whether a moral decision is a good one. Bad arguments are **fallacies.** We should pay special attention to bad arguments that, while logically incorrect, may be psychologically persuasive.

Suppose, for example, we rewrite Argument 11 slightly:

Argument 13

1.   If Dudley loses his daughter's tuition, she will be sad.
2.   If Dudley waits to sell his stock until the company's troubles are public knowledge, he will lose his daughter's tuition.
3.   Therefore, Dudley should sell his stock.

The poignancy of Argument 13 might make us sympathetic with the conclusion. But there is no logical connection between the sadness of Dudley's daughter and the claim that he should disobey the rule or violate the law.

Now consider this argument:

Argument 14

1.   Dudley does not know for sure that it is morally wrong to act on inside information.
2.   Therefore, Dudley will not do anything morally wrong if he acts on inside information.

Argument 14 suggests that as long as one doesn't know something to be the case, then it isn't the case. While such thinking might temporarily soothe Dudley's conscience, the logical absurdity of such thinking emerges more clearly in the following example.

Argument 15

1.   Franklin doesn't know that Dudley has stock in the company she mentioned.
2.   Therefore, Dudley does not have stock in the company Franklin mentioned.

These three examples represent a general type of fallacy—a fallacy of non sequitur (Latin for "it does not follow"). There are two other general types of fallacy—inconsistency and petitio principii (or circular argument). Since good moral decision making is essential to good professional practice in criminal justice and to criminal justice students' abilities to evaluate professional moral decisions, understanding these three general types of fallacies will help in assessing the logic of moral judgments. Thus, while the list of fallacies may seem daunting at first, the effort a criminal justice professional or student puts into learning them will pay off in the long run.

Each general type of fallacy is a violation of a rule for a good argument.

Rule 1: It must be possible for all the premises to be true at the same time. Otherwise, the argument commits the **fallacy of inconsistency.**

For example,

Argument 16

1.   It is always morally wrong to trade on inside information.
2.   It is morally wrong to upset one's daughter when one can prevent it.
3.   All Dudley has to do to avoid upsetting his daughter is to act on inside information.
4.   Dudley is morally obliged to do whatever he can to avoid upsetting his daughter.
5.   Therefore, Dudley should act on the inside information.

Note that premises 1 and 4 cannot be true at the same time, so this argument violates Rule 1 and thus commits the fallacy of inconsistency.

Q 2.11

Does the following argument commit a fallacy of inconsistency? Why or why not?

Execution is morally warranted in cases of premeditated murder because no one should ever take a human life, a premeditated murderer has taken a human life, the only way he can pay for his crime is with his own life, and the best way to take his life is by execution.

Rule 2: You may not use as a premise what you are trying to prove in the conclusion. Otherwise, the argument commits the **fallacy of petitio principii** (pronounced pe-TEET-i-o prin-CHIP-ee-ee) or **circular argument.**

For example,

Argument 17

1.   Dudley is an honest man.
2.   Therefore, Dudley doesn't lie.

The premise and the conclusion assert the same fact, even though the premise states it in the affirmative and the conclusion in the negative.

There are two types of petitio principii. Argument 17 is an example of **begging the question.** The question why doesn't Dudley lie is answered with the premise that he is an honest man. But we still want to know why he is honest—that is, why he doesn't lie.

A second type of petitio principii uses a **complex question** as a premise. A complex question does not permit all possible answers, thus forcing a conclusion.

Argument 18

1.   Agent Franklin, did you come across that information by deceit or by fraud?
2.   Either way, we may conclude that your obtaining that information was reprehensible!

The arguer assumes in the premise that Franklin could only have obtained the information reprehensibly. But she might have stumbled upon it by accident or through proper execution of a warrant, for example. Thus, the premise assumes the conclusion, rather than proving it.

Q 2.12

Does the following argument commit a petitio principii fallacy? Why or why not?

Ladies and gentlemen of the jury, you have the duty to find my client not guilty because she has the constitutional right to a presumption of innocence and the prosecution has failed to prove my client's guilt beyond a reasonable doubt.

Rule 3: The premises must be logically relevant to the conclusion. Otherwise, the argument commits the fallacy of **non sequitur.**

Arguments 6, 8, 12, 13, 14, and 15 of this chapter commit non sequitur fallacies. Arguments 6 and 12 are general non sequiturs, but many non sequitur fallacies fit into more specific subcategories.

There are three basic subcategories of non sequitur fallacies:

1.   Pure or formal fallacies
2.   Fallacies of ambiguity
3.   Fallacies of irrelevance

Since many errors in moral decision making commit fallacies of these sorts, it is worth considering an example of each.

A **pure** or **formal non sequitur** is a bad argument because of its structure rather than its language. Often the fallacy closely resembles a valid argument. Consider, for example, the fallacy of **affirming the consequent** versus **modus ponens.**

Modus ponens—Latin for "the mode of positioning"—is a valid argument form:

If p, then q.

p._____

Therefore, q.

Any argument with this structure is valid (although it may not be sound).

For example,

Argument 19

1. If Fred shot Barney six times, then Barney is dead.
2. Fred shot Barney six times.
3. Therefore, Barney is dead.

Here p = "Fred shot Barney six times" and q = "Barney is dead."

Argument 20

1. If Dudley loses the $30,000, then his daughter will be upset.
2. Dudley will lose the $30,000.
3. Therefore, his daughter will be upset.

Here p = "Dudley will lose the $30,000" and q = "his daughter will be upset."

In both these cases, if the premises are true, then the conclusion must be true. This is not because of Freds, Barneys, Dudleys, and daughters, but because of the structure of the argument.

Technically, the first sentence in a modus ponens is a hypothetical or conditional sentence—an "If . . . then" sentence. The first part, p, is the antecedent (because it comes first), and the second part, q, is the consequent (because it follows the antecedent). In a modus ponens, the second premise affirms the antecedent and the conclusion affirms the consequent.

The fallacy of affirming the consequent resembles modus ponens, but with a significant difference. Consider:

Argument 21

1. If Fred shot Barney six times, then Barney is dead.
2. Barney is dead.
3. Therefore, Fred shot Barney six times.

Argument 22

1. If Dudley loses the $30,000, then his daughter will be upset.
2. His daughter will be upset.
3. Therefore, Dudley will lose the $30,000.

Both these examples, as with all fallacies of affirming the consequent, have the form:

If p, then q.

q.
_____

Therefore, p.

This fallacy affirms the *consequent* in the second premise, where modus ponens affirms the *antecedent* in the second premise. In the fallacious form, it is possible for the premises to be true while the conclusion is false. Barney might not have died from the gunshot wounds, as he did not in Case 2.1. Dudley's daughter might be upset for reasons having nothing to do with her father. That is, the premises of Arguments 21 and 22 can be true while the conclusion is false.

Q 2.13

Is the following argument in modus ponens form, or does it commit the fallacy of affirming the consequent?

If Roger is a convicted felon, then Roger cannot vote in the upcoming election. Roger cannot vote in the upcoming election; therefore, he must be a convicted felon.

A second form of non sequitur fallacy that may reflect a bad moral decision is the fallacy of **ambiguity.** It occurs when something about the language of the argument is ambiguous.

For example,

Argument 23

1. For Dudley to act on Franklin's information would be morally wrong only if it was inside information.
2. But Dudley learned about the stock problems from Franklin when both were outside on the parking lot.
3. Therefore, the information was not inside information, and thus it is OK for Dudley to act on it.

This argument uses the word *inside* ambiguously. In the first premise, it means "nonpublic"; in the conclusion, it means "indoors."

There are many forms of fallacy of ambiguity, but a look at two of them should suffice for our purposes.

In **amphiboly,** the grammar of an entire sentence is ambiguous. For example,

Argument 24

If the Bloods attack the Crips, they will destroy a once mighty gang. Therefore, the
Bloods will win.

From this premise, we cannot logically conclude which gang will win, because the
premise is grammatically unclear.

In **equivocation,** a word or short phrase in the argument is ambiguous. Argument 23 is fallacy of this sort, because it equivocates on the word *inside.*

Q 2.14

Does the following argument commit a fallacy of ambiguity? If so, what wording is ambiguous?

Justice is blind. Therefore, Justice Breyer is blind.

A third form of non sequitur fallacy that may reflect a bad moral decision is
the fallacy of **irrelevance.** It occurs when the premises are logically irrelevant to
the conclusion. This chapter has included many examples of fallacies of irrelevance,
including Arguments 6, 8, 12, and 15. Note that an argument may commit more
than one fallacy. Argument 23, for instance, commits both a fallacy of ambiguity and
a fallacy of irrelevance.

The fallacy of irrelevance takes many forms. A look at eight of these should
suffice for our purposes.

Argumentum ad hominem (argument against the person) is an attempt to
refute an argument by attacking the arguer. For example,

Argument 25

The chief has ordered all of us to wear our hats while on duty. But he is just self-
conscious about his bald spot and doesn't want to be the only one to wear
a hat.

An interesting form of ad hominem argument is the **tu quoque** (pronounced
TU kwo-KWAY) or "you do it too!" fallacy. This argues illogically that someone's
argument is bad because he is hypocritical. For example,

Argument 26

Retired Police Commissioner Gordon is warning the recruits not to drink so wildly
off duty. But why should we listen to that old drunk?

Argumentum ad baculum (appeal to force or fear) is an attempt to scare
someone into accepting a conclusion. For example,

Argument 27

You should obey your sergeant's unlawful order, because he could make your
professional life unbearable if you don't.

Argumentum ad misericordiam (appeal to pity) is an attempt to refute an
argument by appealing to pity, rather than to logic. Argument 13 is an example of an
ad misericordiam fallacy.

Argumentum ad ignorantiam (appeal to ignorance) is an illogical argument
that because one does not know something to be the case, it must not be the case.
Arguments 14 and 15 are examples of an ad ignorantiam fallacy.

Argumentum ad populum (appeal to the masses) is an illogical argument that
because so many people like something, it must be the best; or because so many
people believe something, it must be true. For example,

Argument 28

A vast majority of people would take advantage of inside information if they believed
that they wouldn't get caught. Dudley does not think he will get caught if he acts
on Franklin's information. Therefore, Dudley should act on that information.

Argument 6 also commits this fallacy.

The fallacy of **false cause** is an illogical argument that because two things
occur together, one must be the cause of the other. Argument 8 is an example of a
false cause fallacy.

The fallacy of **hasty generalization** involves drawing a conclusion based on
insufficient evidence. For example,

Argument 29

I once got held up in the north part of the city. Therefore, the north part of the city
is extremely dangerous.

The fallacy of **black and white thinking** involves illogically jumping from one
extreme to another when the truth is somewhere in between. For example,

Argument 30

Officer, this is the third night this week that you have told us to stop loitering. You
must not want us to have any fun at all!

Q 2.15

Does the following argument commit a fallacy of irrelevance? Why or why not?

Ladies and gentlemen of the jury, my client is a member of a historically oppressed
minority, and the principal witness against him is a member of the ethnic group
that has historically been the oppressor. Therefore, you cannot consider the
witness's testimony against my client to be credible!

SUMMARY

Given the importance of sound moral decisions to the study and practice of criminal justice ethics, this chapter has examined the logical structure of moral decision making. It has explained the concepts of argument, premise, and conclusion. It has explained the difference between a deductive argument and an inductive argument. It has distinguished between valid and invalid arguments and between sound arguments and unsound arguments. It has discussed five theories of truth. Finally, it has defined and identified three basic types of fallacies—inconsistency, petitio principii, and non sequitur—and listed several subtypes of fallacies.

The next three chapters analyze and evaluate the three most common types of premises for arguing that an action is morally good or bad.

ANSWERS TO CASE STUDY QUESTIONS

Q2.1. In each of the first three arguments, which sentence is the conclusion? How does each conclusion differ from the other two? Which of the three conclusions best captures the point of Case 2.1?

The conclusion is the final sentence in each of the first three arguments, as the word *therefore* indicates.

It is difficult to argue that Fred committed murder at all, so the conclusion of the first argument is doubtful. We will see that some moral theories hold that moral responsibility for an act is in the intent, not the consequent, so the conclusion to the second argument is open to debate. Factually, the conclusion of the third argument is less debatable then the other two conclusions, so at least superficially, this conclusion best captures the point of Case 2.1.

Q2.2. In each of the four arguments, which sentences are premises?

In each of the four arguments, every sentence prior to the conclusion is a premise of that argument.

Q2.3. Is it true that every illegal act is an immoral act? If not, how does this claim affect the reasonableness of each of the four arguments?

It is not true that every illegal act is an immoral act. When, for example, German Gentiles hid Jews from persecution and execution in Nazi Germany, these Gentiles were violating German law but were doing a morally good thing.

Only the second argument claims that the legality of an act determines the morality of an act, so the argument's reasonableness is diminished by the falsity of this claim.

Q2.4. In which of one of the four arguments is there a premise that, while true, appears not to be relevant to the conclusion?

The first premise of the third argument claims the illegality of Fred's act, but this turns out to be irrelevant to the conclusion that Fred's act was immoral.

Q2.5. In the fourth argument, is the premise less doubtful than the conclusion?

No.

Q2.6. Is the following argument inductive or deductive? Why?
Judge Harlan almost always falls asleep during trials lasting more than an hour. Sleepiness during the day may indicate a sleep disorder such as sleep apnea. Therefore, Judge Harlan might want to be checked for sleep apnea.

This is an inductive argument because it is based on past observation and its conclusion claims probability not certainty.

Q2.7. Is the following deductive argument a good one? Why or why not?
People who fail the polygraph test are liars. Mandy failed the polygraph test. Therefore, Mandy is a liar.

This is a valid argument, because if the premises are true then the conclusion must be true. It is not true, however, that failing a polygraph test is always proof that the subject is lying. Thus, the argument is not sound.

Note that one might regard the first premise as true, because everyone lies at one time or another and thus all people taking polygraph tests are liars. But this misses the implication of the first premise that failing the test *is proof of* a lie.

Q2.8. Is the following inductive argument a good one? Why or why not?
Republican legislators tend to favor laws that protect private business. Congresswoman Smith is a Republican. Therefore, Congresswoman Smith probably favors laws that protect private business.

On its face, this is a good argument if both premises are true. The probability will vary depending on the strength of the tendency mentioned in the first premise.

Q2.9. Is the following argument valid? Why or why not? If it is valid, is it sound?
Ed Richards is campaigning to be this state's attorney general, but it is a pointless campaign. Nonresidents of this state are ineligible to be its attorney general. Anyone registered to vote in another state is considered a nonresident of this state. And Richards is registered to vote in another state.

This argument is valid, because if the premises are true, then the conclusion—that Ed Richard's campaign is pointless—must be true.

Among the questionable premises is the final one—that Richards is registered to vote in another state. Until we can verify or falsify this sentence, we cannot decide whether the argument is sound.

Q2.10. For each of the following premises from previous arguments, decide which theory of truth it best reflects:
Argument 1, premise 2

The coherence theory, because it reflects a particular system of belief about the moral good.

Argument 5, premise 3

The correspondence theory, because whether Fred shot Barney's corpse is objectively verifiable.

Argument 7, premise 2

The correspondence theory, because Barney's being alive or dead is objectively verifiable.

Argument 9, premise 1

The most tempting answer may be the correspondence theory, because we like to think of this sort of probability as objectively verifiable. But given that one person's probability may be another person's improbability, this statement may find its greatest support either in the pragmatic theory (a nine-point match is usually sufficient for determining guilt) or the performative theory (this is what the forensic expert believes and the expert's decision is final).

Q2.11. Does the following argument commit a fallacy of inconsistency? Why or why not?

Execution is morally warranted in cases of premeditated murder because no one should ever take a human life, a premeditated murderer has taken a human life, the only way he can pay for his crime is with his own life, and the best way to take his life is by execution.

Whether the word *best* in the final clause means "morally best" or "most efficient," this premise is contrary to the premise that "no one should ever take a human life." Thus, this argument commits a fallacy of inconsistency.

Q2.12. Does the following argument commit a petitio principii fallacy? Why or why not?

Ladies and gentlemen of the jury, you have the duty to find my client not guilty because she has the constitutional right to a presumption of innocence and the prosecution has failed to prove my client's guilt beyond a reasonable doubt.

This argument does not commit a petititio principii fallacy. If the argument were simply "My client is innocent because she is not guilty," then the argument would be circular. But the presumption of innocence coupled with the prosecutor's failure to prove otherwise makes the defense attorney's argument valid.

Q2.13. Is the following argument in modus ponens form, or does it commit the fallacy of affirming the consequent?

If Roger is a convicted felon, then Roger cannot vote in the upcoming election.
Roger cannot vote in the upcoming election; therefore, he must be a convicted felon.

Let p = "Roger is a convicted felon" and q = "Roger cannot vote in the upcoming election." This argument has the form

If p, then q.

q.
Therefore, p.

It affirms the consequent, thus committing a fallacy.

Q2.14. Does the following argument commit a fallacy of ambiguity? If so, what wording is ambiguous?

Justice is blind. Therefore, Justice Breyer is blind.

This argument equivocates on the word *justice* and on the word *blind*. In the first case, *justice* refers to an abstract value concept; in the second case, it is a professional title. In the first case, *blind* is a metaphor; in the second case, it refers to a medical condition.

Q2.15. Does the following argument commit a fallacy of irrelevance? Why or why not?
Ladies and gentlemen of the jury, my client is a member of a historically oppressed minority, and the principal witness against him is a member of the ethnic group that has historically been the oppressor. Therefore, you cannot consider the witness's testimony against my client to be credible!

This is fairly clear example of an ad hominem fallacy. The defense attorney seeks to attack a witness's argument by attacking the arguer instead.

PART II

PHILOSOPHICAL ETHICS

CHAPTER 3

CONSEQUENTIALISM

 ## CASE 3.1

Huck Finn and Jim[1]

Eleven-year-old Huck is friends with a slave, Jim, who has escaped from his owner, Mrs. Watson. They are on a raft sailing up the Mississippi River, with Jim hoping to escape to freedom and Huck helping him. As they near Cairo, Illinois, where Jim would become legally free, Huck begins to doubt the morality of his act:

> It hadn't come home to me before, what this thing was that I was doing. But now it did; and it stayed with me, and scorched me more and more. I tried to make out to myself that I warn't to blame, because I didn't run Jim off from his rightful owner, but it weren't no use, conscience up and said every time: "But you knowed he was running for his freedom, and you could a paddled ashore and told somebody."

When Jim declares his dream to buy his wife's and children's freedom or to steal them if necessary, Huck's doubts worsen:

> My conscience got a stirrin' hotter than ever, until at last I says to it, "Let up on me—it ain't too late yet—I'll paddle to shore at first light and tell." I felt easy and happy, and light as a feather, right off. All my troubles was gone.

To this end, Huck unties a canoe from the raft and takes it toward shore, lying to Jim that he (Huck) wants to determine their present location. On the way he meets two white bounty hunters in a skiff who are looking for escaped slaves. They ask Huck whether the man on the raft (whose faint outline is all they see) is black or white. The moment of truth has arrived for Huck:

> I didn't answer up prompt. I tried to, but the words wouldn't come. I tried for a second or two, to brace up and out with it, but I weren't man enough—hadn't the punk of a rabbit. I seen I was weakening, so I just gave up trying and says: "He's white."

✦ THREE BASIC MORAL THEORIES

Did Huck do a morally good thing? It seems so, but what sort of argument would prove this? The history of ethics offers three basic kinds of premises for such an argument, with each premise representing a moral theory.

- **Consequentialism:** the *consequences* of the act are good. For example,

Argument 1

1. An act is morally good when its consequences are good.
2. Huck's lie saved Jim from capture.
3. Saving Jim from capture was a good consequence.
4. Therefore, Huck's lie was morally good.

  - **Regularianism:** the act obeyed a *rule.* For example,

Argument 2

1. An act is morally good when it obeys a rule.
2. As a rule, one ought to help one's friends.
3. Huck's lie helped his friend Jim.
4. Therefore, Huck's lie was morally good.

  - **Deontology** (from the Greek word *deon,* meaning "from duty"): the agent
    acted from *duty.* For example,

Argument 3

1. An act is morally good when one acts from duty.
2. One acts from duty when one's motive is to do the right thing.
3. Huck's motive in lying was to help Jim.
4. Helping Jim was the right thing.
5. Therefore, Huck acted from duty.
6. Therefore, Huck's act was morally good.

Each of these theories has its strengths and its weaknesses. This chapter focuses
on the first theory, consequentialism. In our look at this theory, we will consider two
types of consequentialism: egoism and utilitarianism. Egoism comes in two forms:
psychological and rational/ethical. Utilitarianism also comes in two forms: act and
rule. As we consider psychological egoism, we will also examine four common moral
controversies: hedonism versus non-hedonism, absolutism versus relativism, objectivism versus subjectivism, and free will versus determinism.

The next two chapters examine regularianism and deontology. Once we have
considered the three theories, we will see the need for a fourth theory that exploits
the strengths of the first three while avoiding their weaknesses.

✦ CONSEQUENTIALISM

Often people say that an act is morally good because its consequences are good—that
is, "the end justifies the means."

Q 3.1

In Case 3.1, what good consequences should come from Huck's lying to the bounty hunters?

The big advantage to approaching ethics this way is that it relies on evidence that is, in principle, available to anybody. On this theory, "the proof is in the pudding." If the bounty hunters in Case 3.1 decide to verify Huck's claim about Jim, they have only to check the evidence: Jim is black, so Huck lied.

A related advantage to approaching ethics consequentially is that it does not require us to read minds. We don't know why Huck lied. Perhaps it was to help Jim; perhaps it was self-preservation. It might have been a heroic act; it might have been a cowardly act. If we want to determine the morality of Huck's act on the basis of his motivation, we may never have enough hard evidence to draw a conclusion. Consequentialism doesn't require us to speculate about motive; it requires only that we evaluate the consequences.

When deciding whether a consequentialist premise supports a moral decision, the correspondence theory of truth is most applicable among the five basic theories of truth. Recall that on this theory a sentence is true if it corresponds to the facts and false if it is contrary to the facts. For consequentialism, the alleged consequences are facts that either verify or falsify the sentence.

Argument 4

1.   Huck says that the man on the raft is white.
2.   Jim, the man on the raft, is black.
3.   A man cannot be both black and white at the same time.
4.   Therefore, Huck's sentence is false.

Argument 5

1.   To utter a false sentence is to lie.
2.   Huck uttered a false sentence.
3.   Therefore, Huck lied.

The premises are relevant to the conclusion and, if true, support the conclusion. Arguments 4 and 5, therefore, would be valid. Whether the argument is sound—that is, whether all the premises of these valid arguments are true—depends on objective verification. Again, this objectivity is consequentialism's greatest strength.

Consequentialism also has its shortcomings. First, consequences don't tell the whole story. We agree that Huck lied and that we can prove this objectively, yet we think he was morally right to lie. Perhaps we think this on the basis of a rule or duty, such as "one ought to be loyal to one's friends." In this case we would offer a regularian or deontological defense of Huck's lie, which takes us beyond the mere fact that he lied. Thus, even if arguments 4 and 5 are sound, they may not settle the moral question.

More to this chapter's point is that we could praise Huck's lie on the basis of *other* consequences. For example, Huck prevented the bounty hunters from harming Jim, which is a good consequence. The problem then becomes, Of the various consequences that a single act causes, which one is morally most significant? Huck's lie tricked the bounty hunters, rendered Huck a liar, prolonged or prevented

Mrs. Watson's retrieval of her legal property, and spared Jim. We think that sparing Jim is the most desirable consequence morally, but the bounty hunters and Mrs. Watson would disagree. So if the morality of an act depends on the consequences, we need to ask, Consequences for whom? Two types of consequentialist theories attempt an answer: egoism and utilitarianism.

✦ EGOISM

Egoism argues that the morally relevant consequences are the consequences "for me." An obvious, but weak, objection is that egoism's selfishness clashes with the intuition that selfishness is immoral. In response, the egoist might claim that although self-*interest* is paramount, it is not the same as self*ishness*. The reasonable egoist knows that life is better with friends and community support than without. Thus, the enlightened egoist will be friendly and law abiding, and appear not to be selfish. Nevertheless, there are strong objections to egoism that are more evident when egoism is divided into two types: psychological and rational/ethical.

Thomas Hobbes (1588–1679) offers a famous defense of **psychological egoism** in which he argues that human psychology is naturally egoist.[2] In other words,

Argument 6

1. The moral life is the good life.
2. The good life is a life of security and comfort.
3. Security and comfort are matters of self-interest.
4. Therefore, the moral life is a matter of self-interest.

An obvious objection is the possibility of self-sacrifice. Consider the case of Antigone (Case 3.2).

CASE 3.2

Antigone[3]

Antigone is a young woman who feels that she must choose between obeying her king and doing the right thing. On opposite sides of a military fight, her brothers Etiocles and Polyneices have recently killed each other. Etiocles was defending the kingdom, and Polyneices was fighting against the kingdom. King Creon declares that Etiocles should be given a hero's burial but Polyneices's corpse should be left unburied. Antigone disagrees with Creon's treatment of Polyneices and buries him, thus disobeying the king. Not to do so, she believes, would be to dishonor her brother by leaving his soul in a hellishly unsettled state.

Creon sentences Antigone to death, then commutes her sentence, but not before she has committed suicide.

It appears that Antigone has acted against her self-interest, putting her life at risk to honor her brother and obey the gods. As the play progresses, her selflessness is less certain, but it remains a possibility and thus a plausible objection to Hobbes's psychological egoism.

Before turning to rational/ethical egoism, this is a good place to consider some other aspects of Hobbes's moral theory, both because they are related to his egoism and because they are views we often encounter in ordinary moral decision making.

- Hedonism
- Relativism
- Subjectivism
- Determinism

Hedonism (from the Greek word *edon,* which means "pleasure") is the view that an act is morally good if it causes pleasure and morally evil if it causes pain. For Hobbes this is a given: humans determine security and comfort according to pleasure and the absence of pain. Epicurus (341–271 BCE) offers a more nuanced defense of hedonism by noting that nature gives us the means to determine right from wrong by seeking to satisfy our desires.[4] In other words,

Argument 7

1.   What is morally good is what is naturally good.
2.   By nature, we regard pleasure as good and pain as bad.
3.   Therefore, pleasure and the absence of pain are morally good.

Epicurus, however, is no epicure—a gourmand with a taste for fine food and drink. He distinguishes natural desires (those we are born with) from non-natural desires (those we learn) and argues that life is much more pleasant for those who need to satisfy only the natural desires, because such a life is the easiest to acquire. We are born desiring food, drink, and comfort. We learn to desire fancy clothes, expensive cars, and high-tech entertainment. Those who are satisfied with adequate food, drink, and comfort will be much easier to satisfy than those who seek life's luxuries. Further, Epicurus distinguishes necessary natural desires—those we need to satisfy, such as thirst and hunger, in order to survive—from unnecessary natural desires, such as sex, and recommends that we grow accustomed to satisfying only the necessary natural desires. Hobbes makes no such distinctions and recommends only that we seek a life, both personally and communally, that is most apt to provide the best opportunity for receiving pleasure and avoiding pain. Thus, Epicurus offers a more reasonable defense of hedonism than Hobbes offers.

Plato attacks hedonism in all its forms with a simple argument:

Argument 8

1.   Pleasures can be bad.
2.   Goodness cannot be bad.
3.   Therefore, pleasure and goodness are not the same thing.[5]

On its face, this argument seems reasonable. If pleasure could be something that goodness could never be, then goodness and pleasure must be different from each other. But Plato doesn't defend his first premise well. As examples of bad pleasure, Plato offers the pleasures of eating too much and drinking too much. But he fails to distinguish the pleasure from the means to the pleasure. Sam isn't satisfied until he has overeaten; Linda is satisfied with a healthy portion of food. Both Sam and Linda may feel the same satisfaction once they have finished eating, but we would condemn Sam's excess while praising Linda's restraint. Their pleasure is not in itself good or evil. Thus, it remains unclear whether Plato's first premise is true and, therefore, whether his argument is sound.

Q 3.2

In Case 3.1, could Huck's response to the bounty hunters have been hedonistic? How about Antigone's response to Creon in Case 3.2?

Another attack on hedonism simply claims that there are morally good acts for which pleasure and pain are morally irrelevant. Huck may have acted strictly from a sense of duty in Case 3.1, and Antigone may have acted strictly from a sense of duty in Case 3.2. If so, then their acts could be morally good without being based on pleasure or the absence of pain.

CASE 3.3

The State Trooper and the Injured Truck Driver

A state trooper patrolling along a lonely stretch of rural highway happens upon a recent accident. A flatbed tractor-trailer, carrying two multi-ton metal coils, has crashed into a tree. The impact of the crash has caused the front of the cab to collapse against the driver and has caused the metal coils to roll forward, pinning the truck driver from behind. The driver's hands are pinned beneath the steering wheel.

The trooper calls for medical assistance and learns that its estimated time of arrival is at least 15 minutes. The trooper grabs a fire extinguisher from his trunk and rushes to the driver's side of the cab. There he finds the driver conscious but unable to move. To make matters worse, a diesel fire has broken out in the truck's engine and has burned through to the driver's feet. The flames are working their way quickly up the driver's legs and threaten to engulf him in a matter of moments.

The trooper tries to extinguish the fire, but is unable to do so. He then tries everything he can to extricate the driver, but to no avail. The driver, suffering from severe burns, screams that he does not want to burn to death. He begs the trooper to shoot him to death, to prevent further suffering.

The trooper believes that he has only two choices: to shoot the driver or to stand by while the driver burns to death.

As Case 3.3 suggests, hedonism is present in the moral decision making of many people, including well-meaning people. Two examples stand out: proponents of euthanasia and animal rights activists. The primary defense of euthanasia is that it stops suffering. This simple argument works only if suffering is always and automatically evil, but the more reasonable proponents of euthanasia would not sanction it for just any suffering—the torment of a hangnail, for example. Usually, these proponents will qualify their position with terms like "*unbearable* suffering" or "*futile* suffering," but this shifts the discussion away from suffering and toward bearability and unbearability, or futility and non-futility.

Many animal rights activists argue that it is wrong to hunt, eat, own, or experiment on animals because doing so causes them to suffer. If suffering is automatically evil, then the activists have a point, but what about a veterinarian who operates on a dog causing some normal postoperative pain? The reasonable animal rights activists should modify their claim to condemn only unnecessary suffering, which would shift the discussion away from pain and toward necessity and unnecessity.

In short, while arguments for euthanasia and against animal exploitation appear to be hedonistic, they are reasonable only when they focus on something other than pain or pleasure, so they fail as reasonable examples of hedonism.

Q 3.3

In Case 3.3, is the truck driver's suffering reason enough for the trooper to kill him? What if the truck driver points out that the trooper may and probably would shoot an injured deer to put it out of its misery?

As a hedonist, Hobbes is a relativist. Moral **relativism** argues that there are no moral absolutes, because all of morality is relative to a culture, a time, or personal interest. **Absolutism,** on the other hand, argues that at least some things are always morally evil or morally good. Hobbes embraces a form of relativism that he ties to personal interest (see Argument 6). He argues that what we call good is what pleases us, and what pleases us at one moment may pain us the next. This notion is similar to subjectivism, which we will examine after relativism.

To refute relativism, the moral absolutist needs only one example of something that is always morally evil or always morally good. Child abuse is an apt candidate for the former. Isn't child abuse always evil? The relativist might note that to use the word *abuse* is to pass a moral judgment, but what one person considers abuse, another might consider normal discipline or normal relations. Therefore, even though the phrase "child abuse" always refers to something bad, the concept of child abuse is relative and will vary from culture to culture, time to time, or person to person.

Q 3.4

Is killing an innocent man, even in Case 3.3, always evil?

In response, the absolutist has at least three types of arguments at his disposal. First, consider examples of evil that transcend time or place. In Case 3.1, Huck helps Jim escape at a time when most Missourians thought it morally wrong to help slaves escape. A historical relativist would claim that although we regard slavery as wrong today, we must not pass judgment on a practice of more than a century ago. In Case 3.2, Antigone ignores her culture's value of obedience to the king in favor of acting honorably. A cultural relativist would claim that although such disobedience is admirable in our culture, we have no right to defend such disobedience in another culture. Yet the absolutist might want to argue that the two heroes acted ethically against the dictates of their culture and time.

This is not a strong argument against those who would accuse the absolutist of looking at the past through contemporary moral glasses. Sure, Huck and Antigone look good to us, but would we have thought so if we lived at the time and in the culture of either story?

A basic tenet of relativism is that we may not pass moral judgment on a culture or time different from ours. There is good evidence of genocide in the Darfur region of Sudan. My culture is not Sudanese. If I am a relativist, then I should refrain from condemning the genocide. But if I refuse to condemn it, am I not silently condoning it? And if I condone it, haven't I passed judgment on it after all? To the absolutist, there is no suspending judgment: Either I condemn genocide in Darfur or I refuse to condemn it, and in refusing I accept it. In short, no matter how relativist one claims to be, absolutes start creeping into one's thoughts. Some relativists might reply that one can suspend judgment in such cases, rather than condemn or condone the behavior or character of the foreign culture. The absolutist, however, has a third sort of objection to relativism.

To be a relativist is to believe that there are no absolutes. As a moral position, this is contradictory.

Argument 9

1. There are no moral absolutes.
2. There is morality.
3. Relative is the contradictory of absolute.
4. Therefore, all morality is relative.

Both premise 1 and the conclusion are absolutes. Relativism thus appears to be logically impossible.

Even with this objection to relativism, the absolutist is not home free. For one thing, what makes an absolute value absolute? Who says, for example, that child abuse is always evil? First, we may distinguish strict absolutism from loose absolutism. Strict absolutism holds that all of morality stems from one principle, which itself is absolute. Thus, St. Thomas Aquinas (1225–1274) claims,

Argument 10

1. What is morally good obeys natural law.
2. Natural law derives from the will of God.

3.   The will of God is absolute.

4.   Therefore, what is morally good is absolute.

Although this argument is a classic example of an absolutist position, it does not defend the position well. It raises many other issues, such as whether God exists, whether God makes his will known through natural law, and why the moral good depends on natural law.

Loose absolutism holds that there are moral absolutes, such as the absolute evil of child abuse or the absolute goodness of compassion, but one principle cannot be identified that makes all evils evil or all goods good. In the absence of such a principle on which all can agree, it appears to be the absolutist's word against the relativist's.

Many well-meaning people support relativism—in the spirit of "live and let live," for example. Thus, it is worth distinguishing behaviors that are relatively good or evil from behaviors that are absolutely good or evil. In some cultures, for example, it is acceptable to burp at the dinner table as a sign of having enjoyed the meal. In other cultures, burping at the table is offensive. Doesn't this support moral relativism? Not if the underlying principle in the two cultures is the same: the principle that one ought always to show respect and gratitude to one's dinner host. The principle could be absolute, while the means of honoring it could differ from culture to culture. In this case, it is useful to distinguish between etiquette, which is relative, and moral value, which may be absolute.

With a little effort it is easy to identify other values that appear to be universal, even if ways of exhibiting those values vary from time to time or place to place. Fairness and respect for human dignity come immediately to mind. It appears that every human culture values both of these, even if people do not always live up to them and even if people disagree on what is fair or dignified. More basic is the fact that every human culture finds moral value to be morally valuable! It appears, therefore, that absolutism—at least in its loose form—is more reasonable than relativism.

In addition to being a hedonist and a relativist, Hobbes is a subjectivist. Moral **subjectivism** holds that moral value is in the mind of the judge, not in the object of that judgment, as **objectivism** holds. To a subjectivist, the judgment "Theft is morally bad" means "I don't approve of theft." Note that "I," not theft, is the *subject* of the sentence. To an objectivist, "Theft is morally bad" is about theft itself, not about the person uttering the sentence. Recall that when Hobbes judges something to be good, he means only that it pleases him. Another person may have a painful experience of the same object and thus regard it as evil.

The objectivist's first challenge is to explain how moral value can belong to an object of judgment, since we cannot taste, touch, see, hear, or smell moral value. Take, for example, the proposition "Capital punishment is morally bad." To a subjectivist this means "I don't approve of capital punishment," which is a coherent and clear sentence, even for those who do approve of capital punishment. For an objectivist, the sentence "Capital punishment is morally bad" means that moral evil is among the properties of the punishing act. Consider execution by lethal injection. Among the observable factors are the condemned person; the equipment of the execution, including the gurney, the straps, the hoses, the needles, and so on; the observers; and the steps in the procedure—strapping the condemned to the gurney, a solemn nod from the warden, the growing stillness of the condemned, and the doctor's pronouncement of death. Where among these observable factors could we locate moral evil? To point to anyone of the observable factors in our example and declare "There's the moral evil!" would be strange.

Q 3.5

Does Case 3.2 present Antigone as subjective, since she disagrees with the prevailing ethic? Does the state trooper's reluctance in Case 3.3 appear to stem from the position that killing someone who is not a threat is absolutely wrong?

Rather than make the futile attempt to render a moral value observable, the objectivist might offer a refutation of subjectivism similar to a refutation we tried against relativism. Isn't child abuse self-evidently evil, whether or not someone agrees that it is evil? Isn't genocide self-evidently evil? Not, says Hobbes, for those who find pleasure in abusing a child or in slaughtering vast communities of people. For Hobbes, the objectivist argument would be nothing more than his word against ours, but subjectivism remains intuitively unsatisfactory.

The objectivist might try a logical approach instead. It appears that the subjectivist is confusing two theories of truth. As a consequentialist, Hobbes is claiming that an act is morally good if the consequences are good and that consequences are, in principle, objectively verifiable. As we noted earlier, this claim reflects the correspondence theory of truth—that a sentence is true if it corresponds to the facts. As a subjectivist, Hobbes also claims the truth of a moral proposition, such as "Capital punishment is morally wrong," is merely a matter of accepting the proposition. This claim reflects the performative theory of truth—that to say a sentence is true is to say only that one accepts the sentence as true. Logically, we can't have it both ways: To insist on the objectivity of truth and the subjectivity of truth at the same time with respect to the same claim is a contradiction.

If dealing with different theories of truth is too abstract, we might note a different logical contradiction that subjectivists commit. If morality is whatever I want it to be, then can't I decide that your morality is wrong? You say it is morally acceptable for the trooper in Case 3.3 to shoot the truck driver, and I say that it is not morally acceptable. As a subjectivist, you must allow that my position is as true as yours, but this leads to a sentence that contradicts itself: "This position is true and this position is false." Logically, a self-contradictory sentence is always false. So, subjectivism appears to lead to false conclusions.

Of course, the subjectivist might change the characterization of the disagreement to "I like the idea of the trooper shooting the truck driver and you don't." There is no contradiction here, but the sentence reduces the moral debate to a matter of taste—of likes and dislikes. In this case, moral debate becomes as meaningless as debate about whether chocolate chip cookies taste good. The objectivist response becomes

Argument 11

1.   If moral subjectivism is correct, then morality is merely a matter of taste.
2.   If morality is merely a matter of taste, then moral debate is always pointless.
3.   If moral debate is always pointless, then where we stand on certain moral issues, such as a trooper's right to euthanize an injured truck driver, will have no meaningful effect on social or personal well-being.
4.   Where we stand on certain moral issues can have a profound effect on social and personal well-being.
5.   Therefore, moral debate is not always pointless.
6.   Thus, moral subjectivism is incorrect.

Q 3.6

In Case 3.1, could the anti-slavery people, whom Huck and Jim represent, and the pro-slavery people, whom the bounty hunters represent, both be correct about the moral value of slavery?

The persistent subjectivist might insist that the value of moral debate is itself subjective. You might care about the outcome of a public policy debate over police euthanizing crash victims, but I might not care about such an outcome. In response, let's make matters more personal. Suppose Mary is an objectivist and her next-door neighbor Mark is a subjectivist. To make her point, Mary hotwires Mark's car and moves it to her driveway. When Mark angrily challenges her, she responds that her morality permits her to take other people's cars, and as a subjectivist Mark's only recourse is to note his displeasure at Mary's ethic. He cannot prove her wrong. He might be able to take his car back by force, but if morality is merely the physically stronger person's winning the argument, then moral argument becomes a series of fallacious appeals to force, rather than to logic.

Q 3.7

Since Creon was able to arrest and condemn Antigone in Case 3.2, does that mean he was right and she was wrong?

Note that subjectivism seems to say the same thing as relativism, and objectivism seems to say the same thing as absolutism. If moral value is relative, then isn't it subjective? If moral value is absolute, isn't it objective? Not necessarily. First, the debate between relativism and absolutism is about *time:* How long does the moral value last? For as long as the culture says so? For a limited period in history? Forever? The debate between subjectivism and objectivism is about *location:* Where is moral value? In the object being judged? In the mind of the judge?

A second difference between the two disagreements is that, by definition, a relativist cannot affirm the existence of absolutes, but she could affirm that moral value is objective. Consider the claim,

- Sometimes abortion in itself is morally acceptable, such as when it is necessary to save a mother's life, and sometimes it is not morally acceptable.

"Sometimes" makes this claim relativist; "in itself" makes the claim objective. Following this lead, we can imagine a claim that is objectivist and absolutist:

- Abortion *in itself* is *always* morally wrong.

subjectivist and absolutist:

- *I always* disapprove of abortion.

or relativist and subjectivist:

- *Sometimes I* approve of abortion; sometimes I don't.

Q 3.8

From Huck's point of view in Case 3.1, is the moral value of his lie absolutist or relativist? Is it objective or subjective?

In addition to being a hedonist, a relativist, and a subjectivist, Hobbes is a **determinist.** Contrary to those who believe in **free will,** where free will is the ability to do otherwise, determinists argue that something other than free will determines our actions. Hobbes, for example, sees all human decisions as resulting from the pleasure or pain one expects to result from the action. With more complexity, Hobbes offers this refutation of free will:[6]

Argument 12

1. *Free* means "absence of external impediments."
2. Only physical bodies can be impeded—for example, boxed, walled up, chained.
3. Will is not a physical body.
4. Therefore, will cannot be impeded.
5. Therefore, the concept of "free" will is absurd.

Defenders of free will could accuse Hobbes of using the word *free* ambiguously or too restrictively. When we refer to the free movement of physical bodies, we refer to absence of external *physical* impediments, but when we refer to free flow of ideas or desires, we refer to *psychological* freedom. Hobbes will argue for a reduction of the psychological to the physical, but it is enough here to note that we tend to distinguish the two in ordinary conversation.

Defenders of free will might also adapt St. Augustine's (354–430) theological argument for free will to a secular version. Here is Augustine's version:[7]

Argument 13

1. If we can sin, then we have free will.
2. We can sin.
3. Therefore, we have free will.

Here is a secular version:

Argument 14

1. If we can act morally wrong, then we have free will.
2. We can act morally wrong.
3. Therefore, we have free will.

Both versions assume a difference between acts for which we hold someone responsible, and thus punishable, and acts for which the agent is not responsible, and thus not punishable. What good are commandments, laws, or moral precepts if their recipients have no choice about whether to obey them?

Q 3.9

In Case 3.1, did Huck freely choose to lie, or was he determined to lie by some cause outside his control? In Case 3.2, did Antigone have to bury Polyneices, or could she have done otherwise?

One possible comeback is to distinguish between *hard* determinism and *soft* determinism. We have been describing the hard determinist—someone who holds that people have no free will whatsoever. The soft determinist argues that our contexts for choosing are determined—we have no control over the set of choices facing us—but within the context we have some choice. A favorite analogy of the soft determinist is the poker game: No player gets to choose which cards he gets, but he does choose how to play them; he may check, bet, raise, or fold. Proponents of free will note that once choice is a possibility, determinism loses. To say one could do otherwise, as the soft determinist concedes, is to agree that people can have more than one choice in a given situation. Proponents of free will do not need to argue that we have an infinite number of choices. As a human being, for instance, I have the present choice of typing the next word, getting a cup of coffee, or making a phone call; but I don't have the choice of flying around the room without mechanical assistance, suddenly becoming a concert-quality pianist, or changing the current presidential administration. Whichever available choice I pick, it appears that I could have picked otherwise, and thus I acted from free will.

We have yet to prove the existence of free will, but we have shown it to be as plausible as determinism. For our purposes, it is sufficient to note that further discussion about ethics will not be useful if all of our choices are made for us. And since a basic premise of this book is that the study of ethics is useful, consistency requires us to proceed as if we had free will.

In this chapter, we are considering one of the three basic kinds of premises for the conclusion that an act is morally good: consequentialism. The two sorts of consequentialism are egoism and utilitarianism. The two sorts of egoism are psychological egoism and rational/ethical egoism. So far we have considered Hobbes's ethical egoism and several other "isms" that accompany his view: hedonism versus nonhedonism, relativism versus absolutism, subjectivism versus objectivism, and determinism versus free will. Next we take a brief look at rational/ethical egoism.

Rational or **ethical egoism** accepts the possibility of self-sacrifice but holds that we *should be* egoists: we should tend only to our business and not "stick our noses" into anyone else's. Ayn Rand (1905–1982), Russian immigrant and American philosopher, is a famous proponent of this view, which is the foundation of her novels *Atlas Shrugged* and *The Fountainhead*. In defending this view, journalist Harry Browne offers a simple analogy.[8] Imagine that happiness is a red rubber ball. Rand would argue that if I have the ball, I should keep it. The contrary view would insist that I pass the ball on, but this view does not allow anyone else to keep the ball either. If no one kept the ball, then no one would be happy, even as he or she was trying to make others happy!

This analogy is persuasive but it fails in two ways. First, it ignores the possibility of morally good self-sacrifice. If self-sacrifice is *possible*, as Rand acknowledges, then might there be times when it is morally *good?* In Case 3.2, if Antigone is correct, her brother has to be buried or his soul will suffer eternally. She is willing to risk her life by disobeying the king to bury her brother. Her position is morally good, but it requires sacrifice of her own interests.

Second, Rand and Browne appear to confuse altruism with utilitarianism. **Altruism** holds that one's interests are irrelevant as long as one is serving the interest of others. Utilitarianism allows one to pursue one's interests, as long as that pursuit results in a balance of good over evil for the greatest number of people whom the pursuit affects. While the red rubber ball analogy may challenge altruism, it does not threaten utilitarianism. As long as I have enough red rubber balls to go around, or as long as my possession of a red rubber ball doesn't hurt others, utilitarianism is fine with my keeping my ball.

✦ UTILITARIANISM

Egoism in both its forms, psychological and rational/ethical, fails. This does not mean that self-interest is always bad; it means that one should not limit one's moral reasoning to self-interest. There is one other form of consequentialism to consider: **utilitarianism.**

Apparently utilitarianism is the basic moral view of the United States. Democracy is utilitarian, capitalism is utilitarian, the preamble to the U.S. Constitution sounds utilitarian, and the most common defense of public policy decisions—especially unpopular ones—is that the decision seeks the greatest good for the greatest number. Because of its importance to American ethics, utilitarianism deserves an especially close look.

British philosopher John Stuart Mill (1806–1873) is the most famous proponent of utilitarianism.[9] His basic argument goes like this:

Argument 15

1. What is good is what is desirable.
2. What is most good is what is most desirable.
3. Happiness is desired above all else.
4. Therefore, happiness is the greatest good and the more people that are happy, the better the act that produced it.

This argument invites several challenges. First, what is happiness? Mill argues that happiness is pleasure and the absence of pain. Thus, Mill's view is hedonistic and is subject to the same objections we raised against Hobbes's hedonism. Mill anticipates this in his famous observation that it is better to be Socrates dissatisfied than a pig satisfied. Mill believes that people are capable of much higher pleasures than the base physical ones. We seek psychological, spiritual, and intellectual pleasures, and even though we might settle for baser pleasures, these are not the mark of the moral life.

Q 3.10

On utilitarian grounds, did Huck do a morally good thing when he lied to the bounty hunters?

Second, as British philosopher G. E. Moore (1873–1958) notes, Mill's argument assumes that *desirable* and *desired* are synonyms.[10] This assumption underlies the purported link between the second and third premises of Mill's argument. Moore suggests that this is a false assumption. Ask a recovering alcoholic, for example, what is most desirable for him and he will answer "Not to drink alcohol." Now ask him what he desires most and he might, without contradiction, answer "A drink!" For him, the desirable and the desired directly oppose each other. Thus, even if happiness is most desired, it might not be most desirable, so Mill's argument fails.

Mill precedes this argument with the claim that no one can prove that utilitarianism is correct, since it is the basic premise by which we prove something else to be morally good or bad. If so, then one wonders why he offered an argument in the first place and why we should accept utilitarianism as a given.

Some other challenges remain to utilitarianism. First, what about the "tyranny of the majority"—a concern that America's Founding Fathers took seriously. Consider the "Rebellion" chapter from Fyodor Dostoevsky's (1821–1881) *Brothers Karamazov*.

CASE 3.4

The Rebellion[11]

Alyosha Karamazov, a monk who aspires to priesthood, is arguing with his agnostic brother Ivan about the existence of God. How, Ivan wonders, can Alyosha believe in a God who lets children suffer? Perhaps adults deserve to suffer, but surely a baby whom a cruel soldier befriends and then bayonets did not deserve so awful a fate!

Alyosha answers that his faith in God tells him that God wants everyone to be happy and that we must trust in a beneficial outcome to all of the mayhem. Ivan retorts with a question to Alyosha: "If you could make everyone in the world happy by torturing and killing just one baby, would you?" Alyosha admits he would not. Then it should not surprise Alyosha that Ivan does not want to get to heaven on the backs of tortured children. If that is his ticket to heaven, he is giving it back in rebellion.

From a utilitarian point of view, it would be a terrific bargain to sacrifice one person—even a baby—for the good of the rest. But is it always fair for a minority to suffer for the well-being of the majority? Clearly not. Mill is mindful of this objection, noting that such sacrifice would eventually harm the collective, much as a gangrenous toe, if allowed to fester, will eventually poison the whole body. This is a reasonable sentiment, but the danger of a tyrannical majority persists if utilitarianism is the ethic of choice.

Q 3.11

On utilitarian grounds alone, why would the sacrifice of one child, as Ivan describes it in Case 3.4, be immoral if everyone else in the world stood to benefit from it?

Another challenge to utilitarianism is who gets to decide what the greatest good is for the greatest number—the greatest number themselves or someone who knows better than most? If a group of urban children want to play on a city street during rush hour and the patrol officer realizes the danger to the children, whose preference should prevail? The lone officer's view is more apt to result in good than the children's view. Democracy says that the people should decide for themselves what is good for them, which is a utilitarian principle. But as Socrates asked, should something as complicated as governing people be in the hands of those who have no expertise in government?[12]

A final challenge to utilitarianism is that the greatest good isn't always available to the greatest number in a way that some lesser good might be. Imagine that law enforcement agencies around the country created a wish list of goods that every agency should have. Putting these items in priority order according to their value to the agency, we find in descending order, although not in direct sequence, an armored vehicle, bullet-proof vests, and shoulder holsters. Now suppose that a citizen wants to use her hard-earned savings to benefit a law enforcement agency and asks for utilitarian guidance. With her savings she could buy one armored vehicle, which would be available to the five-member special operations team. Or she could buy bullet-proof vests for 100 of the 500 officers in the agency. Or she could buy shoulder holsters for everyone in the agency. As the good becomes less great, the number she can help becomes greater. Should she focus on the greatest good, from which five people will benefit, or on the greatest number, which will mean distribution of a lesser good? Utilitarianism offers no definitive answer.

As we consider utilitarianism critically, we should note a distinction between **act utilitarianism** and **rule utilitarianism,** because each is open to different criticisms. Act utilitarianism holds that each act should result in the greatest good for the greatest number. On this view, we are not bound by rules that are irrelevant to a particular case, so we are free to decide each case on its own merits. Joseph Fletcher has famously referred to this as "situation ethics."[13] By what standard *do* we decide that one act is good and another, very similar act is not? The act itself does not answer this, so there must be some antecedent criterion by which to make the distinction. Rule utilitarianism offers such a criterion—a rule that is in the best interest of the greatest number.

In Case 3.4, the rule utilitarian might call for a rule that forbids the torturing and killing of a child. In general, this would be of greater benefit to humanity than a rule that permitted such cruelty. But couldn't there be a time when the rule did not apply? Suppose a 16-year-old terrorist, a child, claims to have planted a powerful explosive device timed to go off at a crowded day care center in an hour. Wouldn't the general utilitarian sensibility call for any measures necessary to get this terrorist to reveal the location of the bomb? The rule wouldn't permit it, but maybe there are exceptions to the rule. If so, then what criterion exists to decide that a rule does not apply? Act utilitarianism has an answer, "Forget the rule!," which we have seen is unsatisfactory.

Utilitarianism has its limits. This does not mean we should ignore the good of the many; it means only that we should not limit our moral reasoning to this concern. Sometimes the proper solution to a moral problem is the utilitarian solution, but not always. Sometimes, the good of the few, a proper rule, or a person's duty may be morally more important than the happiness of the people whom an act affects.

Summary

Chapter 3 has examined consequentialism, the first of three basic premises or theories for determining the moral good. There are two types of consequentialism: egoism and utilitarianism. There are two types of egoism: psychological and rational/ethical. There are two types of utilitarianism: act utilitarianism and rule utilitarianism. Each of these views is of limited value to moral decision making.

Also, in the discussion of Hobbes's psychological egoism, we paused to examine four moral controversies: hedonism versus non-hedonism, relativism versus absolutism, subjectivism versus objectivism, and determinism versus free will. This chapter argues for the superiority of the latter view in each controversy.

In the next chapter, we will examine the second of the three basic kinds of moral premises: regularianism—the view that an act is morally good if it obeys a rule.

ANSWERS TO CASE STUDY QUESTIONS

Q3.1. In Case 3.1, what good consequences should come from Huck's lying to the bounty hunters?

1. It is better for Huck and Jim to live than to die.
2. It is better for Jim to be free than to be a slave.
3. Huck and Jim stand a better chance of remaining alive if Huck lies to the bounty hunters than if he tells them the truth.
4. Jim stands a better chance of being free if Huck lies to the bounty hunters than if he tells them the truth.
5. Therefore, the consequences of Huck's lying to the bounty hunters would be better than the consequences of Huck's telling them the truth.

Two possible objections:

- Maintaining the law is more important than the welfare of two men, and Huck's lie is a threat to maintaining that law. So the premises are irrelevant to the conclusion.
- Premise 3 may be false. The bounty hunters might only return Huck and Jim to Missouri, without killing them, if Huck tells the truth.

Q3.2. In Case 3.1, could Huck's response to the bounty hunters have been hedonistic? How about Antigone's response to Creon in Case 3.2?

1. If, in Case 3.1, Huck lied to the bounty hunters because he was afraid of getting hurt if he told the truth, then his act was hedonistic.
2. Although Huck suggests that he lied out of fear, the story suggests, ironically, that it was moral courage—not fear of getting hurt—that led to Huck's lie.
3. Therefore, Huck's lie was probably not hedonistic.

Possible objection: Premise 2 is too speculative. On the narrative alone, Huck was acting out of fear, which would make premise 2 false.

1. If, in Case 3.2, Antigone's motive was to honor her brother, then she was not acting hedonistically.
2. Antigone's motive was to honor her brother.
3. Therefore, Antigone was not acting hedonistically.

Possible objection: Although this argument, in the form of modus ponens, is valid, it may not be sound. In the play, Antigone's exchange with Creon exhibits a mixture of motives—including a stubborn desire to win her argument. Thus, premise 2 may be only partially true or wholly false.

Q3.3. In Case 3.3, is the truck driver's suffering reason enough for the trooper to kill him? What if the truck driver points out that the trooper may and probably would shoot an injured deer to put it out of its misery?

The truck driver's argument appears to be this:

1. Suffering is bad.
2. Good is the opposite of bad.
3. Shooting me would stop my suffering.
4. Therefore, it would be better to shoot me than to let me suffer.

Response: Although it might be good to stop suffering, it might be better to refrain from killing someone who is not a threat. Thus, it's possible for the premises to be true while the conclusion is false, which makes the argument invalid.

Of course, the truck driver's argument might be this:

1. Nothing is morally worse than letting me continue to suffer.
2. Shooting me would stop my suffering.
3. Therefore, shooting me would be morally better than letting me suffer.

Response: This argument appears to be valid, because if the premises are true, the conclusion would have to be true. But the first premise isn't necessarily true—for example, murder may be morally worse than allowing one to suffer. Therefore, this argument is unsound.

If the truck driver argued that the trooper should shoot him because the trooper would shoot an injured deer, then the driver would have to show the strength of the analogy between a person and a nonhuman animal. At the very least there is a legal difference between the two, and it is arguable that there is also a moral difference.

Q3.4. Is killing an innocent man, even in Case 3.3, always evil?

This book assumes that killing is always wrong but may at times be the lesser of two evils. Thus, for example, if killing a terminally ill man in the final stages of death were the only way to save the lives of several innocent children, killing the man might be less evil than allowing the children to die. But this example does not justify killing the truck driver.

Q3.5. Does Case 3.2 present Antigone's view as subjective, since she disagrees with the prevailing ethic? Does the state trooper's reluctance in Case 3.3 appear to stem from the position that killing someone who is not a threat is absolutely wrong?

Case 3.2 presents Antigone's view as objective and Creon's ethic as subjective. Antigone believes that it is objectively wrong to allow one's dead brother to suffer eternal torment; Creon believes that ethics is what he says it is.

In Case 3.3, the trooper's reluctance may stem from the position that killing an innocent, nonthreatening person is always wrong, but the trooper may also be worried only about the consequences for himself. So we can't say with certainty whether the trooper's stance is subjective or objective.

Q3.6. In Case 3.1, could the anti-slavery people, whom Huck and Jim represent, and the pro-slavery people, whom the bounty hunters represent, both be correct about the moral value of slavery?

The person who is anti-slavery may take one of four stances:

> Position A1: Slavery is always wrong. (objective and absolutist)
> Position A2: Slavery is wrong in Jim's case, but it might not always be wrong. (objective and relativist)
> Position A3: I always disapprove of slavery. (subjective and absolutist)
> Position A4: I disapprove of slavery in Jim's case, but I may not always disapprove of slavery. (subjective and relativist)

Similarly, the person who is pro-slavery may take one of four stances:

> Position P1: Slavery is never wrong. (objective and absolutist)
> Position P2: Slavery is not wrong in Jim's case, but it may be wrong in other cases. (objective and relativist)
> Position P3: I always approve of slavery. (subjective and absolutist)
> Position P4: I approve of slavery in Jim's case, but may not approve of slavery in every case. (subjective and relativist)

There is a direct contradiction between A1 and P1 and between A2 and P2, so objectively speaking the anti-slavery people and the pro-slavery people cannot be right at the same time.

If the two sides are subjective (A3/A4 and P3/P4), then there is no contradiction between the two, just as there would be no contradiction between two people who said "I like cookies" and "I don't like cookies," respectively, or "Sometimes cake is a good dessert" and "Sometimes cake is not a good dessert," respectively.

For reasons that Chapter 3 articulates, subjectivism and relativism appear to be logically weaker theories than objectivism and absolutism. On this presumption, it is not possible for the anti-slavery people and the pro-slavery people to be right at the same time.

Q3.7. Since Creon was able to arrest and condemn Antigone in Case 3.2, does that mean he was right and she was wrong?

Creon's ability to arrest Antigone does not necessarily mean he was morally right. Contrary to the old saying, might does not always make right.

Q3.8. From Huck's point of view in Case 3.1, is the moral value of his lie absolutist or relativist? Is it objective or subjective?

Huck's position appears to be this:

1. It would be good to save Jim's life.
2. It would be good to save my life.

3. My lying to the bounty hunters will save our lives.
4. Not lying is more apt to put our lives at risk.
5. Therefore, it would be good to lie.

This view is objective—the value is in the lie. But Huck is not saying that a lie is always good; thus, he implies that the lie is good *relative* to this particular situation. Of course, Huck probably sees the value of saving their lives as being absolute, even if the value of the lie is not.

Q3.9. In Case 3.1, did Huck freely choose to lie, or was he determined to lie by some antecedent outside his control? In Case 3.2, did Antigone have to bury Polyneices, or could she have done otherwise?
It is tempting to answer this question as follows:

1. The narrative provides no evidence of an antecedent that forced Huck's choice.
2. The narrative provides no evidence of an antecedent that forced Antigone's choice.
3. Both Huck and Antigone speak as if they acted from free will.
4. Therefore, Huck and Antigone probably acted from free will.

Possible objection: This argument appears to be that because we cannot see any determining antecedent, there must not be one. But such an argument commits the fallacy of argumentum ad ignorantiam—appeal to ignorance.

Q3.10. On utilitarian grounds, did Huck do a morally good thing when he lied to the bounty hunters?
In the long run, Huck probably unintentionally contributed to the greatest good by participating in an act against slavery. These good utilitarian results would not have been obvious initially, however.

Q3.11. On utilitarian grounds alone, why would the sacrifice of one child, as Ivan describes it in Case 3.4, be immoral if everyone else in the world stood to benefit from it?
On utilitarian grounds, killing one child to relieve everyone else's suffering might reflect badly on the others' humanity, which could harm everyone else in the long run.

Notes

1. Mark Twain (1835–1910), *The Adventures of Huckleberry Finn* (1884; New York: Harper & Brothers, 1918), Ch. 16.
2. *Leviathan* (1651).
3. Sophocles (495–405 BCE), *Antigone* (451 BCE), trans. Elizabeth Wyckoff (Chicago: University of Chicago Press, 1954).
4. *Letter to Menoeceus,* trans. Cyril Bailey, in *Epicurus, the Extant Remains* (Oxford, UK: Clarendon Press, 1926).
5. *Gorgias,* trans. W. R. M. Lamb (London: Heineman, 1925), 499b–e.

6. *Leviathan,* Ch. 5.

7. Trans. Peter Holmes, in *Augustinus Aurelius: Works—A New Translation,* ed. Marcus Dods (Edinburgh: T. & T. Clark, 1871–75).

8. From *How I Found Freedom in an Unfree World* (New York: Macmillan, 1973); reprinted in *Vice and Virtue in Everyday Life,* 2d ed., ed. Christina Sommers and Fred Sommers (New York: Harcourt, 1989), pp. 391–7.

9. *Utilitarianism* (1861).

10. G. E. Moore, *On Defining "Good,"* in *Analytic Philosophy: Classic Readings* (Stamford, CT: Wadsworth, 2002), pp. 1–10.

11. Fyodor Dostoevsky, *Brothers Karamazov* (1880), trans. Constance Garnett (New York: Barnes and Noble, 2004), Book 5, Ch. 4.

12. *Gorgias,* 488b–491d.

13. *Situation Ethics: The New Morality* (Philadelphia: Westminster Press, 1966).

CHAPTER 4

REGULARIANISM

 ## CASE 4.1

The Judge and the Moral Problem

Mr. Kline is a retiree with a large retirement account that by law goes to his wife when he dies. Unbeknownst to Mrs. Kline, Mr. Kline has been having a sexual relationship with another man for the past 10 years. Mr. Kline recently discovered that he has AIDS and may die in a short time. He would like to will his retirement account to his male lover. In the state where he resides, having no sexual relations with one's spouse for at least a year is sufficient grounds for divorce, and the Klines have had no such relations since the beginning of Mr. Kline's affair. On those grounds, Mr. Kline sues for divorce. Mrs. Kline, a homemaker, never had a paying job and would have trouble finding one this late in life. She fights the divorce in order to retain her right to Mr. Kline's retirement account.

The case goes before Judge Johnson of the county circuit court. Judge Johnson asks Mrs. Kline whether she would like to counter-sue Mr. Kline for divorce on the grounds of adultery, which would make it possible for her to get alimony and a good portion of Mr. Kline's retirement, even if they are divorced. She answers that her religious practice forbids divorce.

Judge Johnson believes that Mr. Kline's request is immoral, because its purpose is to leave Mrs. Kline destitute in favor of an adulterous lover. The judge concedes that Mr. Kline appears to have a foolproof legal argument for his request, and the judge promises the Klines that he will have a decision in 30 days. Shortly after the trial, Judge Johnson spends his free time in the local law school library looking for a legal precedent that would allow him to find for Mrs. Kline on legal grounds alone.

What is the morally good thing for Judge Johnson to do if he can find no legal grounds for dismissing Mr. Kline's suit? Two possible and competing arguments come to mind immediately:

Argument 1

1. It would be morally bad for Mrs. Kline to lose her husband's estate.
2. If Judge Johnson finds for Mr. Kline, then Mrs. Kline will lose her husband's estate.
3. Therefore, it would be morally bad for Judge Johnson to find for Mr. Kline.

Argument 2

1. Judge Johnson has a professional duty to obey the county's laws.
2. If Judge Johnson finds for Mrs. Kline, he will disobey a county law.
3. It would be morally bad for Judge Johnson to violate his professional duty.
4. Therefore, it would be morally bad for Judge Johnson to find for Mrs. Kline.

At first blush, this looks like a genuine moral **dilemma.** Although it is common to refer to all sorts of moral problems as dilemmas, a genuine dilemma is one type of moral problem, captured by the expression "You're damned if you do, damned if you don't." That is, in a dilemma there appears to be no right answer or solution. Some ethics texts also define dilemmas as problems with more than one right solution, but making a moral decision in this situation is not a moral challenge, since any choice is a good choice. This book limits its use of the word *dilemma* to those cases for which there appears to be no right answer or good solution.

Case 4.1 presents a dilemma in appearance only. What appears to be a clash of contrary conclusions is a clash between two moral theories: consequentialism, which we discussed in the previous chapter, and regularianism, which is the subject of the present chapter. To the consequentialist, Argument 1 is a good solution to the problem: the judge should find for Mrs. Kline. To the regularian, Argument 2 is a good solution to the problem: the judge should find for Mr. Kline.

Note that even on rules alone, the choice Judge Johnson faces is between two types of rules: the law, which would enable Mr. Kline to leave his wife destitute; and the moral norm that a husband ought not to do such things to his wife. Such a conflict justifies this chapter's examination of the second of three basic moral theories: regularianism—the view that an act is morally good when it obeys a rule.

It is common for people to decide the good or evil of an action by referring to a rule. These rules come in many forms including, for example, divine command, constitutional principles, criminal law, civil law, social norms, professional codes of conduct, agency policy, general orders, rules of a game, and "house rules." Rules-based ethics has its advantages and its shortcomings. We will look at both. Then we will look at some specific types of rules, with special attention to codes of ethics. Finally, we will briefly discuss the Golden Rule.

✦ ADVANTAGES

Objectivity

The biggest advantage for rule-based ethics is its reliance on a set of premises that are in principle objective and verifiable. Take this regularian argument:

Argument 3

1. It is morally wrong to break the town's laws (a regularian assumption).
2. The law says that one may cross a street in town only at a crosswalk.
3. Smith crossed a street but not in a crosswalk.
4. Therefore, Smith acted immorally.

Premise 1 establishes the argument's regularian basis. Premise 2 is objectively verifiable: it will be easy to find whether such a law exists. If premise 3 is true—which is also objectively verifiable or falsifiable—then from a regularian point of view, the conclusion is true, and the argument is valid and sound. Of course, some might want to know why Smith crossed the street illegally, but that is not a regularian concern.

Common Starting Point

A second advantage to rule-based ethics is that its reliance on a common set of rules allows all concerned to be on the "same page." This requires that the rules be clear and obvious, and that the people have clearly or tacitly accepted the rules, but this need not be a difficult requirement. In Case 4.1, the judge and the Klines are U.S. citizens who operate under federal and local law. Citizens generally accept that a judge must settle a suit for divorce and that the judge must settle it on legal grounds. Although we may forgive the judge if he finds for Mrs. Kline, we understand that if he finds no legal precedent allowing him to find for Mrs. Kline, then he must find for Mr. Kline.

Advanced Preparation

A third advantage to rule-based ethics is that it allows people to create an objective and verifiable set of rules in anticipation of problems that may arise. When legislators enacted the law that permits a spouse to get a divorce merely for lack of marital sexual activity, chances are this was to allow a neglected spouse to get out of an unhappy situation. The original intent was not to allow someone to neglect a faithful spouse. Had the legislature been able to anticipate the Klines' case, the divorce law might have added a clause forbidding such neglect on the plaintiff's part. This would have made the judge's decision much easier.

Understanding Others

A fourth advantage to rule-based ethics is that it permits those of us who do not subscribe to a set of rules to anticipate the decisions of those who do subscribe. In certain countries, for example, it is illegal to chew gum in public. This may strike some of us as a silly law, but knowing it could save us trouble if we plan to visit such a country. This reminds us of the old—and often correct—adage that "Ignorance of the law is no excuse!"

Q 4.1

In Case 4.1, what rule does Mr. Kline appear to have broken? What rule does Judge Johnson seem hesitant to obey?

➜ Shortcomings

Bad Rules

There are some obvious shortcomings to rule-based ethics. Perhaps the most obvious is that a rule could be morally bad: it might permit or oblige someone to act in a way that is morally wrong. The "Nuremburg defense," for example, refers to the position of Hitler's henchmen who pled not guilty at their war crimes trial because they were only following orders. As they saw it:

Argument 4

1. Hitler made and published widely rules calling for the murder of Jews.
2. With devout and loyal patriotism, these henchmen obeyed Hitler's rules.
3. It is morally good for political officials to follow a superior's rules.
4. Therefore, these henchmen did nothing wrong.

These men were devout and loyal, and Hitler made those rules, but the morally strong would have seen the evil of the rules and disobeyed them. In other words, premises 1 and 2 are true, but premise 3 could be false. Disobeying Hitler would have required a sense of leadership, which the men on trial lacked. Leaders in fact, as opposed to (a) leaders in name only, (b) mere managers, and (c) mere followers, *know when to break a rule.* They don't follow others blindly into destruction and chaos, and they don't hide behind rules as an excuse not to take responsibility.

Q 4.2

In Case 4.1, would Judge Johnson be showing leadership if he ignored the law and found for Mrs. Kline?

No Rules

Another problem with rule-based ethics is that sometimes there may be no rule to guide an action, even though the moral quality of that action is clear. Consider Case 4.2, for example.

 ## Case 4.2

Towing the Boat

A police chief heading home from work sees a squad car from his agency towing a boat on a trailer. He recognizes the driver as a subordinate who is on duty. The chief pulls alongside the squad car and motions the officer to stop. The officer does so immediately.

When the chief asks for an explanation, the officer says that he is on his lunch break and using some of that time to tow his boat from the marina to his house. He assures the chief that he will finish before his lunch break is over.

When the chief asks the officer why he thinks it is OK to tow a boat with the squad car, the officer answers that there is no written order against it. The next day the chief issues a general order forbidding everyone to use squad cars to tow boats.

Q 4.3

Was the officer in Case 4.2 wrong to tow the boat, since there was no rule that explicitly prohibited it?

Conflicting Rules

A third problem with rule-based ethics is that two rules governing the same action may conflict with each other. We have seen that in Case 4.1, the judge seems torn between two rules—the law (Rule A) that permits Mr. Kline to get the divorce and a moral rule (Rule B) that says the wife should be provided for in the event of her husband's death. The judge wants to obey the law, but he also wants to protect Mrs. Kline. If the judge obeys one of the two rules, he will violate the other.

One solution to such conflicts is to appeal to another rule that gives one of the subordinate rules priority over the other. We may imagine a rule (Rule 1) that requires a judge to obey the law first and worry about consequences second; in other words, by obeying Rule 1, Judge Johnson must give priority to Rule A over Rule B. This gets the judge out of one conflict, but it sets him up for a second. There might be another rule (Rule 2)—unwritten perhaps—that requires someone to act on compassion first and the law second. As a decent human being, Judge Johnson may feel obliged to obey Rule 2 over Rule 1, thus giving priority to Rule B in finding for Mrs. Kline. The point is that we cannot easily settle conflicts of rules simply by referring to another rule. We may have to settle conflicts of rules by appeal to some other criterion, such as consequences or duties.

✦ Types of Rules

Cases 4.1 and 4.2 and the Nuremburg defense example cover several types of rules: divine command, law, social norms, and general orders. We have identified advantages and shortcomings of rule-based ethics in general. Let's next examine three particular sorts of rules: divine commands, laws, and codes of conduct.

Divine Commands

Many people ground their moral beliefs on their religious beliefs. Part IV of this book discusses religious ethics in detail, but we may observe here that a common appeal in religious ethics is to the alleged commands of God. Most claims about such commands derive from a sacred text, such as the Bible or the Qur'an, or from alleged revelations in personal or communal experience—giving rise to a claim such as "God told me to do it!" An obvious scriptural reference for moral decision making would be the Ten Commandments (Exodus 20:1–17). Many people who condemn killing, stealing, or adultery do so because there are scriptural commandments against them. But there are possible exceptions to the commandments. What if the only way to feed my starving children is to steal some vegetables from the garden of a wealthy farmer—vegetables he wouldn't miss? What about use of deadly force to protect an innocent third party or to protect oneself? Yet the commandment does not read "Thou shalt not steal, unless . . ." or "Thou shalt not kill, unless. . . ." Perhaps the exceptions rest on ambiguous English translations of the Hebrew. A common view is that Hebrew renders the prohibition against killing as "Thou shalt not *murder.*" The appropriate translation is closer to "Thou shalt not slaughter," but the point remains: The command in its original meaning may have been unambiguous, but centuries of translating it and quoting it out of context have rendered it ambiguous.

There is another problem with scriptural appeals. Some of the commands seem unambiguous, yet require immoral action. Medieval Jewish philosopher Moses Maimonides (1135–1204) identified 613 laws in the Jewish Bible—the *Tanakh* or, in Christianity, the Old Testament. Many of these laws require behaviors that to the modern mind are morally outrageous. Consider Case 4.3.

Case 4.3

The Protective Wife[1]

In Maryland, in the winter of 2002, a family emerged from a restaurant and encountered a street person asking for money. The father gave the street person some money but the street person wanted more. When the father refused, claiming that he didn't have any more cash on him, the street person produced a knife, grabbed the young son, put the knife to his throat, and demanded that the family drive to an ATM machine and withdraw more money.

In the family's van, the father took the driver's seat; the mother took the other front seat; the daughter sat behind her; and the assailant, still holding the son at knifepoint, sat behind the father. The father drove to a bank nearby, knowing that his ATM card was inactive. After parking the car, the father released his seat and slammed it into the assailant. The impact caused the assailant to release his hold on the knife and the boy, who scampered out of reach of the assailant to the back of the van. The assailant regained the knife and began to stab the father. In an effort to protect her husband, the wife grabbed the assailant's scrotum and squeezed until the assailant gave up. By now the children had run into the bank and notified security of the problem. Soon after, police and medical help arrived. The assailant was arrested, and the father received life-saving medical treatment.

A few months later, the assailant was convicted of attempted murder and given a long jail sentence.

The mother saved her husband with her quick and decisive act. Should her husband cut off her hand? This is an odd and barbaric question for us, but consider this biblical passage:

> When men fight with one another, and the wife of the one draws near to rescue
> her husband from the hand of him who is beating him, and puts out her hand, and
> seizes him by the private parts, then you shall cut off her hand; your eye shall have
> no pity. [Deut. 25:11–12 (RSV)]

If the husband in Case 4.3 were to obey this command, he would cut off his wife's hand without pity—an immoral and illegal act by contemporary American standards. The divine command in this case does not lead to a morally good act. The challenge facing those who rely on divine commands for making moral decisions is to decide which (alleged) commands are morally good and which are morally bad.

Laws

As for laws, Case 3.1, "Huck Finn and Jim," offers an example of a law that is contrary to the moral good, and Case 4.1 offers an example of a law that may be good in general, but that can lead to morally bad consequences sometimes. Laws protecting slavery and the rights of the slaveholder were contrary to the good of helping slaves escape by "stealing" them from their "owners." Laws allowing philandering husbands to leave their wives financially destitute are contrary to the moral good of a husband's taking care of his wife. Also, Hitler's law promoting the slaughter of Jews was obviously a bad law.

A contemporary, powerful challenge to law-based ethics appears in Martin Luther King's (1929–1968) "Letter from Birmingham Jail."[2] While he insists on the moral value of obeying just laws, he insists just as strongly that "one has a moral responsibility to disobey unjust laws, [because] 'an unjust law is no law at all.'" For King, the difference between a just law and an unjust law is the difference between a "law that uplifts human personality" and a "law that degrades human personality." Thus, for example, segregation laws are unjust "because segregation distorts the soul and damages the personality. It gives the segregator a false sense of superiority and the segregated a false sense of inferiority."

If justice is always morally desirable and some laws are unjust, as King argues, then some laws are not morally desirable, nor is obedience to those laws. Note that while King highlights the problem of morally bad laws, he does so by appealing to another set of laws. For him, natural law trumps man-made law whenever the two conflict. We will have more to say about this distinction when we discuss constitutional ethics.

Q 4.4

Is the law in Case 4.1 unjust? How about the general order in Case 4.2? How about the biblical command in Case 4.3?

Codes of Ethics

We have looked at rules in the forms of divine commands and laws. Laws are of obvious concern in criminal justice ethics, and appeals to divine commands can have a profound effect on professional practice in criminal justice. A third approach to rule-based moral decision making is to appeal to a code of ethics. Most criminal justice professions have a code, which may exist under different titles, such as a code of conduct or a code of professional responsibility. Many criminal justice professionals practice under more than one code. For example, a county attorney might practice under the American Bar Association's (ABA) code and the county bar association's code. Or a judge might operate under the ABA's code and a local code of judicial conduct. Codes of ethics exist for government organizations and professional associations from the international level down to the city level. Here are some examples:

- Alameda County (CA) Bar Association, *Statement of Professionalism and Civility*
- American Bar Association, *Model Rules of Professional Conduct*
- American Jail Association, *Code of Ethics for Jail Officers*
- International Association of Chiefs of Police, *Law Enforcement Code of Ethics*
- National Court Reporters Association, *Code of Professional Ethics*
- Nebraska State Bar Association, *Standards of Professionalism*
- Ohio General Assembly, *Legislative Code of Ethics*
- Philadelphia Bar Association, *Working Rules of Professionalism*
- United Nations, *Code of Conduct for Law Enforcement Officials*
- West Virginia Supreme Court of Special Appeals, *Code of Judicial Conduct*

Each of these codes differs in content and structure, but in general, a complete code will include

- A rationale
  - Why has someone written this code?
  - Why should concerned professionals adhere to it?
- Specific rules
  - Permissions
  - Obligations
  - Prohibitions
- Clear statements of
  - Whom the rules affect
  - Who is responsible for ensuring compliance with the rules
  - How management will ensure compliance
- Consequences of failure to comply
- Means for appealing an adverse decision

When the code is clear, complete, and readily available, and the rules of the code are morally good and apply to most problems the professional will face, then it can be quite useful in moral decision making. On the other hand, a code that is weak on any of these counts will be less helpful. Let's look at some of the possible weaknesses.

Lack of Clarity

A code of ethics may be unclear. It may, for example, lack a rationale, launching right into the list of rules without any preamble. It may lack sanctions, leaving unclear what will happen if someone violates a rule. Or it may fail to assign oversight to any particular office or person.

As ethicist Michael Bayles reminds us, lack of clarity may also come from a confusion of three kinds of norms: standards, principles, and rules.[3] **Standards** of virtue are general statements of moral value, widely open to discretion and evaluation. For example, a judge should be competent. Competence is a useful standard on which to build a set of rules, but by itself it is not too useful a criterion for moral decision making. What counts as competent? If a judge shows up for court on time, remains awake throughout the trial, and does nothing to cause an objection from counsel, is this sufficient evidence of judicial competence? Not necessarily. The judge may spend most of the trial with his mind on nonlegal matters, or he may have already made up his mind on the guilt of the defendant, neither of which is the mark of a competent judge. Thus, while it is necessary that a professional adhere to certain standards, it is not sufficient for a code of ethics merely to list such standards.

Q 4.5

What common standard appears to underlie the moral issues in Case 4.1 and Case 4.3?

Principles of responsibility are more specific than standards, although principles also leave room for discretion and a spectrum of evaluations. For example, in principle, a competent corrections officer will remain vigilant for illegal drugs among the inmates. If a lot of drugs are discovered among inmates under a particular officer's watch, this will be sufficient evidence of the officer's failure. But in the absence of such a discovery, how vigilant is vigilant? Perhaps the officer feels that she can determine the presence of drugs by observing certain behaviors, so she makes no other effort to detect drugs. Given that a drug user might be able to mask those behaviors, the officer's means of detection may be insufficient. Would we instead want to require the officer to make frequent sweeps of the inmates' cells? This seems excessively vigilant. In short, a principle helps explain the application of a standard in a particular professional context, but the principle does not describe its own scope or limits.

Q 4.6

What principle underlies the general order in Case 4.2?

Rules of duty are the best defined of the three types of values. Rules are specific and make it possible to decide readily whether one has obeyed or disobeyed them.

For example, court reporters may recognize a *standard* of diligence that underlies a *principle* to avoid conflicts of interest. To honor the principle, a rule might exist that requires court reporters who work for a county court system to refrain from doing freelance reporting. If, for example, the reporter accepts pay from an attorney to transcribe a deposition, then the reporter has clearly violated the rule. There is little ambiguity or room for discretion in making this judgment. In the absence of such a rule, it is not obvious that freelance reporting would violate the principle of avoiding conflict of interest or violate the standard of diligence.

In summary, a good code of ethics will distinguish clearly among standards, principles, and rules, recognizing that a clear statement of rules will be the most useful of the three for moral decision making. Of course, a statement of standards and principles should help make clear why the code contains the rules it contains.

Incompleteness

A code of ethics may be clear in what it says, but lack one or more of the necessary components we previously identified. It may lack a rationale, sanctions, or a clear statement of who is in charge. Perhaps most important, the code's set of rules may be incomplete, as in Case 4.2, in which no explicit rule forbade officers from using squad cars to tow boats.

Immorality

Finally, a code of ethics may be both clear and complete, but may require immoral behavior, as in the Nuremberg defense, or in Case 4.3, in which obeying a code would have meant cutting off a woman's hand. The challenge for regularianism on this point is how to distinguish morally good rules from morally bad rules. We have studied one answer—consequentialism: If obeying the rule will have good consequences, then the rule is morally good; if obeying the rule will have bad consequences, then the rule is morally bad. This answer is as strong or as weak as consequentialism itself, and since we are discussing regularianism as a response to the weaknesses of consequentialism, the latter is not of much help in supporting the former.

Perhaps the difference between a morally good rule and a morally bad rule is a matter of duty: A morally good rule is one that a person has a duty to obey, and a morally bad rule is one that a morally good person has a duty to disobey. This is Martin Luther King's suggestion in his *Letter from Birmingham Jail.* We will discuss this theory in the next chapter. Here it is enough to note that if we can justify a rule only by appealing to something other than rules, then rule-based ethics will not always be enough for good moral decision making.

Q 4.7

Is the general order in Case 4.2 a morally good rule?

✦ THE GOLDEN RULE

No discussion of rule-based ethics would be complete without considering the **Golden Rule:** *Do unto others as you would have them do unto you.* Sometimes, it appears in its negative form: *Do not do unto others what you would not want others to do unto you.* Whether the positive and negative formulas say the same thing is a matter of some debate, which we need not get into here, but some further discussion is worthwhile.

Ubiquity

First, this is probably the most widely held moral principle historically and geographically. Many cultures and many individual thinkers, both secular and religious, sum up their moral views with this formula. Among the many religions that support this rule are

- Christianity
- Judaism
- Islam
- Hinduism
- Buddhism
- Taoism
- Shintoism
- Jainism
- Sikhism

Among the more famous philosophers who have summed up their ethical views with this rule, or a close variation of it, are

- Socrates (470–399 BCE)
- Seneca (54 BCE–39 CE)
- Epictetus (c. 55–135 CE)
- Thomas Hobbes (1588–1769)
- John Locke (1632–1704)
- Immanuel Kant (1724–1804)
- John Stuart Mill (1806–1873)
- John Rawls (1921–2002)

Consistency

Second, an attractive feature of this rule is its appeal to consistency. Intuitively there is something fair about insisting on the same standards for oneself that one demands of others. Why should I complain about your careless driving, for example, if I drive carelessly too? Isn't it fair that if I cheat on my taxes, I should allow others to cheat on their taxes as well? To complain in the first case or to condemn other taxpayers in the second case is to be inconsistent—I'm not practicing what I preach.

While acknowledging the general strength of this point, we need to be careful to avoid the tu quoque fallacy. Recall that we commit this fallacy when we accuse someone of hypocrisy as an illogical attempt to refute his argument. For example,

Argument 5

1.   Uncle Bert tells me that I shouldn't smoke cigarettes.
2.   But Uncle Bert is a lifelong smoker who has advanced lung cancer.
3.   Therefore, Uncle Bert should not be preaching to me about the perils of smoking!

Although it is true that Uncle Bert seems not to have followed his own advice, he is an unfortunate expert on the perils of smoking and thus someone whose advice we should take seriously.

Another problem with appeal to consistency is that I could be consistent in behaving immorally and encouraging others to do the same. Suppose, for example, that I am a masochist. As someone who enjoys being beaten, I beat you in the hope that you will return the favor. Assuming that such a beating is immoral, you must admit that I have obeyed the Golden Rule, but only to foster immoral behavior. To pursue this line of reasoning any further would get us into psychological discussion and hence off track. It is enough here to suggest that a better formulation of the Golden Rule might be "Do unto others as you should want them to do unto you, if you are reasonable and morally sane." This raises additional questions: What is reasonable? What is moral sanity? The point is that, as widely held as the Golden Rule is, it is not a perfect solution to the problems of moral decision making.

Reciprocity

A third attractive feature of the Golden Rule is its appeal to reciprocity. Folk wisdom expresses this sentiment in claims such as "What's good for the goose is good for the gander" or "Tit for tat." It is at the root of the *lex talionis*—the law of retribution: "an eye for an eye; a tooth for a tooth." On this principle I deserve to have others do to me what I have done to them, and I have no right to complain if they do.

The problem is that morally it is not always clear that one deserves exactly what one has done to others. Imagine that a diabetic who has good reason to believe that his illness is under control suddenly falls into a diabetic coma while driving on the freeway. His cars veers onto the road's shoulder and hits and kills a woman standing near her stalled car. Would it be fair to reciprocate by having the diabetic driver be killed by a speeding car? Of course not! This example is an obvious oversimplification, but it makes the point that the moral value of reciprocity is debatable, and thus we cannot defend the Golden Rule as an unassailable tool for moral decision making.

Summary

In this chapter we have looked at regularianism, the view that an act is morally good if it obeys a rule. We have considered its general advantages—most notably, the objectivity and verifiability of rules. We have considered its general disadvantages—most notably, the possibility of immoral rules, the absence of rules, and the problem of conflicting rules. We have examined three specific sorts of rules: divine commands, laws, and codes of ethics. Finally, we have discussed the Golden Rule's scope and limits.

The next chapter looks at the third basic moral theory, deontology—the view that an act is morally good if the agent acts from duty.

ANSWERS TO CASE STUDY QUESTIONS

Q4.1. In Case 4.1, what rule does Mr. Kline appear to have broken? What rule does Judge Johnson seem hesitant to obey?

Mr. Kline has committed adultery, which violates a general social rule, as well as a rule in some religions. Judge Johnson seems hesitant to obey the county law that permits Mr. Kline to get a divorce.

Q4.2. In Case 4.1, would Judge Johnson be showing leadership if he ignored the law and found for Mrs. Kline?

No. A leader knows when to break a rule and when not to break a rule. We may sympathize with Mrs. Kline, but there is nothing immoral in this case about the judge obeying the law. On the other hand, it would be immoral—and therefore a failure in moral leadership—if the judge violated his duty by ignoring the law.

If the Judge is lucky enough to find a legal precedent that permits him to rule in Mrs. Kline's favor, then he will have stayed within the law while refusing Mr. Kline's plea. This would be a mark of leadership on the judge's part.

Q4.3. Was the officer in Case 4.2 wrong to tow the boat, since there was no rule that explicitly prohibited it?

Yes. There may be other agency rules or practices that prohibit private use of government property. Even if there weren't such rules, common sense suggests that using a police car—especially while on duty—to tend to one's private business of towing a boat amounts to theft of public funds.

Q4.4. Is the law in Case 4.1 unjust? How about the general order in Case 4.2? How about the biblical command in Case 4.3?

The law is not unjust in Case 4.1, even if the consequences of following the law might at times seem unjust. Think of the many times this law has allowed a neglected spouse to get out of an unhappy marriage. The general order in Case 4.2 is just, because its prohibition is just. The officer was acting unjustly when he used a government vehicle for this private task. The biblical command in Case 4.3 is clearly unjust by today's standards. One wonders why someone ever considered such a command to be just, but that is a question for historians or theologians.

Q4.5. What common standard appears to underlie the moral issues in Case 4.1 and Case 4.3?

Fairness is a common and basic standard in moral practice. Case 4.1 and Case 4.3 raise a question of fairness. Mr. Kline appears to be treating Mrs. Kline unfairly in Case 4.1. It also would be unfair for Judge Johnson to deny Mr. Kline his legal rights. In Case 4.3 it would be grossly unfair of the husband to cut off his wife's hand, especially since this would punish her for saving him.

Q4.6. What principle underlies the general order in Case 4.2?
A basic principle underlying the general order in Case 4.2 is that a police officer must not use government property for personal advantage.

Q4.7. Is the general order in Case 4.2 a morally good rule?
Yes. It is just. It is fair. And it honors the principle that a police officer must not use government property for personal advantage.

Notes

1. Dennis O'Brien, "Gardenville Man Pleads Guilty to Armed Carjacking and Kidnapping of Family," *Baltimore Sun,* 7 August 2002, p. 7B.
2. Reprinted in King, *Why We Can't Wait* (New York: Signet, 1963).
3. *Professional Ethics,* 2nd ed. (Belmont, CA: Wadsworth, 1989), pp. 25–8.

CHAPTER 5

DEONTOLOGY

 ## CASE 5.1

The Guilty Client

M arion Motley, Esq., a public defender, is defending Kyle Acton against a charge of first-degree murder. Acton has confessed his guilt to Motley, but has pleaded not guilty in court. In his confession to Motley, Acton has described stalking the victim, a 10-year-old girl, for some time before deciding to kidnap and kill her. He has also described the crime in vivid detail, including how he snatched her from her bike, threw her in the back of his van, took her to a secluded spot, strangled her, and buried her body. He has included in his detail the location of the little girl's corpse.

As the parents of the girl await Acton's trial, they have appeared in public interviews pleading for information about their daughter's whereabouts. While they hold some hope that she is alive, they wish at the very least to find her body so they can give her a proper burial.

Upon hearing the parents' plea, Motley, also the mother of a 10-year-old girl, feels so much empathy for the parents and so much loathing for Acton that she asks the trial judge to release her from defending Acton. In her court system, only the judge can release her from defending Acton once she became the attorney of record in the case. Under her professional code of ethics and the community's laws, she cannot tell the judge about Acton's confession or about the location of the girl's body. Not satisfied with what Motley does tell him, the judge demands that Motley continue to defend Acton to the best of her professional ability because, the judge claims, that is her duty.

Should Motley follow the judge's order? A consequentialist might encourage her to find a way out of defending Acton, so she does not lose her job for defending him poorly. Another consequentialist might tell her to obey the judge for the same reason—to avoid losing her job. Consequentialism, then, isn't much help, since the same consequence could be used to draw contradictory conclusions—that she should and that she should not defend Acton.

A regularian might cite the rules of the American Bar Association or the community's laws as the reason she should continue to defend Acton. To the regularian, Motley's feelings and the possible consequences of her decision are morally irrelevant. Non-regularians, on the other hand, might regard her feelings or the possible consequences as relevant. It is easy to sympathize with her, and it would be a shame if she were to lose her job because of so unsavory a fellow as Acton. This might be one of those occasions where it would be morally good to break or ignore a rule, so regularianism does not have the final word here.

We have a third basic moral theory to consider: deontology—the view that an act is morally good if the agent acts from duty. Case 5.1 presents the judge's position as deontological: Motley should continue to defend Acton because that is her duty. Whether and when this is a reasonable approach to moral decision making is the topic of this chapter. In it we will examine some of the advantages and shortcomings of deontology, paying special attention to the deontology of German philosopher Immanuel Kant (1724–1804).

Q 5.1

Is the judge correct in declaring it Motley's duty to defend Acton? Why, or why not?

→ ADVANTAGES

One advantage of deontology is that duty, by definition, cannot be immoral. One's duty is what one ought to do, and one ought always to do the morally good or right thing. Although it might be one's duty to avoid certain *morally bad consequences* or to disobey an *immoral rule,* it could never be one's duty to fail to do that duty. Thus, in situations where we can agree that someone has done her duty, we can reasonably conclude that what she did was morally good. Of course, there may be disagreements about what one's duty is and whether one has fulfilled a duty, but we will consider these possibilities later.

Deontology also has the advantage that it completes the story that consequentialism fails to complete. Imagine a situation in which police arrive at the scene of a shooting where the suspect gives up without a fight and confesses to the shooting. Without knowing why the suspect fired, the police cannot pass moral judgment on him, since there is a moral difference among shooting with malicious intent, shooting someone by accident, and shooting in self-defense. Deontology would ask one question: Did the shooter act from duty? If so, then he acted morally; if not, then he acted immorally.

Deontology also has some of the same advantages as regularianism, since duty-based ethics is similar to rule-based ethics. Duty is in principle objective, available to anyone capable of discerning it, and thus available for deciding whether one has done one's duty. Duty allows for advanced preparation. We can anticipate a problem before it happens, identify the duty relevant to that problem, and thus determine a proper response in the event the problem should arise. Duty offers a common starting point. And given that people often act on what they think their duty is, we can understand the moral positions of different cultures and different historical periods by identifying the alleged duties that underlie those positions.

We said that duty-based ethics is similar to rule-based ethics. Some ethics texts consider them so similar that the texts claim one to be a category of the other. For example, some hold that duty-based ethics is a form of rule-based ethics that relies on a universal or absolute rule. Common understanding of duties and rules, however, helps us distinguish between the two sorts of moral foundations. Although it might be one's duty to disobey an immoral rule, there could never be a rule that commanded one to disobey an immoral duty, because by definition a duty can never be immoral.

Now let's look at some of deontology's shortcomings.

Q 5.2

In Case 5.1, does Motley appear to be acting from a duty to remove herself from the case?

✦ SHORTCOMINGS

To a deontologist, an act is morally good if and only if the agent acts from duty. The phrase "from duty" invites at least four questions, which we can raise in a preliminary way before addressing them further. First, what is a duty? Second, how do we distinguish between a duty and an alleged, but false, duty? Does a sense of duty justify *any* act, whether moral or immoral? Might Hitler, for example, have felt that he was doing his duty in leading the assault on Jews, even though such assault was immoral? Third, what if there is a conflict of duties? How does the imperative "Do your duty!" settle the conflict? And fourth, if acting from duty is a necessary condition for all moral acts, isn't it difficult to be moral, since we rarely pause to think whether our motive for what we are about to do is duty? It is useful to address these questions against the backdrop of the case of Billy Budd (Case 5.2).

 CASE 5.2

Billy Budd[1]

It is 1797 and 21-year-old Billy Budd has recently been "impressed" into naval service aboard HMS *Indomitable.* By all accounts, Billy is a virtuous person, and so is the ship's captain, Captain Vere.

Although Billy is virtuous, he has three defects. First is his inability to speak when startled by an unexpected confrontation. Second, he has the reputation of having once responded to being startled by "letting fly" his right arm and flattening a bigger man who had been teasing him. Third, his innocence has blinded him to the vices on the ship.

While Billy and Vere represent virtue, Master-at-Arms Claggart represents vice, and he despises Billy's innocence. Vere has called Billy to Vere's cabin, where Claggart stands having falsely accused Billy of planning a mutiny. Vere asks Claggart to repeat the charges to Billy's face. Billy is so startled by the accusation that he involuntarily strikes out at Claggart—a single blow with the right arm—killing Claggart instantly.

British martial law calls for subordinates to be executed if they kill superiors. Obedience to the law is especially important to Vere, because two mutinies have recently occurred on British ships. So Vere establishes a drumhead court to try Billy for Claggart's murder. Since Vere is the only witness, he appoints three other officers to try the case. Vere admits that he does not believe Claggart's accusation, nor does he believe that Billy intentionally hurt Claggart. But the law requires that the court only determine whether Billy violated the law and, if so, that the proper punishment be administered.

To the court's inquiry about whether there might be an alternative to hanging Billy, Vere replies that the court must proceed under the Mutiny Act, even though Billy did not mean to mutiny or to kill anybody. Any other sentence, says Vere, would set a bad example for others who might be considering mutiny.

Billy is convicted, and his last words before being hanged are a heartfelt "God bless Capt. Vere!"[2]

→ WHAT IS DUTY?

The first question Case 5.2 evokes is, What is duty? German philosopher Immanuel Kant, the foremost proponent of deontology, proposes an answer to this question, as well as our other questions about duty, so we will continue our inquiry in the light of his thought.[3]

Q 5.3

Vere claims to be acting from duty, but he also claims to be setting an example for the other sailors and to be regarding only the consequences (not the intention) of Billy's act. So is Vere acting as a deontologist or a consequentialist?

Kant's basic defense of deontology goes like this:

Argument 1

1.   An act is morally good if and only if it is done from good will.
2.   An act is done from good will if and only if it is done from duty.
3.   Therefore, an act is morally good if and only if it is done from duty.

Kant sets up this argument by presuming the existence of moral law. As a law, says Kant, it never changes. In that regard it is similar to the laws of physics or the laws of thought (logic). Kant, therefore, is an absolutist and an objectivist, contrary to the relativism and subjectivism of Thomas Hobbes, discussed in Chapter 3. If there is no moral law, then Kant's argument is on shaky ground. But if Chapter 3's criticisms of relativism and subjectivism are reasonable, then so is the possibility that we can formulate moral value into a law or lawlike statement.

> ### Q 5.4
>
> Is Vere being an absolutist in Case 5.2? Is he being an objectivist?

Argument 1 is valid: If the premises are true, then the conclusion must be true. But is the argument sound? That is, are both premises true? Consider each premise more closely.

In premise 1, Kant presumes that when we regard someone as having behaved morally, we mean at least that he acted from good will. If I gave a street person a dollar because it is my duty to help my fellow man, then I acted from good will. If I gave him the dollar because I didn't want to talk to him, or because I hoped he would buy something toxic and poison himself, or because I didn't want to feel guilty hoarding my dollar, then I did not act from good will. The act was the same in both cases—donation of a dollar to a street person—but the motive was different in each case.

> ### Q 5.5
>
> Was Motley in Case 5.1 acting from good will in refusing to defend Acton? Was Vere acting from good will in Case 5.2 in refusing to make an exception for Billy?

Premise 2 of Kant's argument is the conclusion of another argument:

Argument 2

1. To act from good will is to will to do what's good.
2. To will to do what's good is to act from moral law, which defines the good.
3. To will to act from moral law is to will to do what one ought to do.
4. To will to do what one ought to do is to will to do one's duty.
5. Therefore, an act is done from good will if and only if it is done from duty. (Note that this is premise 2 of Argument 1.)

So Kant's basic answer to our first question—What is a duty?—is that it is what we ought to do if we wish to obey moral law. But how do we determine that law? Kant's answer to this question also answers our second question above, to which we now turn.

⇥ Genuine Duty versus Alleged, but False, Duty

We have two ways of detecting anything, Kant notes: reason and sense experiences. Since we cannot taste, touch, see, hear, or smell a law, we must grasp it by reason. One way reason grasps laws is by formulating them as imperatives—for example,

"Don't steal!" "Don't cheat!" "Tell the truth!" Since moral law is absolute, its imperatives must be absolute, or "categorical." We may distinguish categorical imperatives from hypothetical imperatives. Hypothetical imperatives call for an action only if the agent desires a certain consequence: "If you want it to be less noisy, then shut the door." "If you want your coffee to taste sweet, then put sugar in it." "If you want to go to the island, then go by boat." If one were to receive these commands out of context, they would make no sense. Imagine a police sergeant during roll call announcing the latest general order: "Put sugar in it!"—an odd and meaningless directive.

But remember that Kant has no interest in consequences, so for him moral imperatives will not be hypothetical. For him the only relevant criterion for a morally good act is that the agent does it from duty. Hypothetical imperatives are not moral (or immoral) imperatives, but merely practical ones. Categorical imperatives, on the other hand, do not depend on any particular context. "Don't kill!" "Don't steal!" and "Don't commit adultery!" make sense as they stand, and they offer no exceptions. It is our duty not to steal, even if we have no desire to steal. It is our duty not to commit adultery even if we find the would-be partner to be attractive.

Rather than derive an endless list of specific categorical imperatives, Kant offers this basic formula for a **categorical imperative:**

Act only according to that maxim [the principle behind one's act] *whereby you can at the same time will that it should become a universal law.*[4]

This sounds like the Golden Rule: "Do unto others as you would have them do unto you." But the difference is that, for Kant, one should do unto others only what one could argue logically that each person should *always* do. Updating one of Kant's examples, consider the following scenario: My wife needs a lifesaving drug immediately. At first, the druggist won't give it to me unless I pay him for it. I don't have the money on me, but I promise to get the money from my bank account first thing tomorrow and to bring the money to the druggist shortly thereafter. He gives in, warning me that he will hold me to my promise. It's a false promise; I have no bank account and no money. Didn't I do a morally good thing, because I acted to save my wife's life? In defending my position, I seem to be offering as the maxim of my act, "One must make a promise one intends to break." Kant would note that such a law would be logically impossible to obey, because there is no such thing as a promise that one intends to break. There can be no universal duty to do something that is impossible; therefore, my lie was immoral.

Q 5.6

Could Vere logically claim to be acting from duty in Case 5.2 when he refuses to give Billy a break?

For Kant, it is not enough to do one's duty; duty must be the motive. Here Kant distinguishes acting *contrary* to duty, acting *according* to duty, and acting *from* duty. For example, if it is a shopkeeper's duty not to cheat a customer, then he acts *contrary* to duty if he cheats the customer. He acts *according* to duty if he treats the customer fairly but for selfish reasons—for example, the desire not to be sued. He acts *from* duty if he treats the customer fairly just because it is his duty to do so.

✦ CONFLICTS OF DUTY

So far, Kant has answered our first two challenges to deontology. He has defined duty, and he has argued that because the duty must be categorical, it is not morally sufficient merely to believe that one has a duty to do something. But given Kant's explanation, the other two challenges are especially bothersome.

Our third challenge is what we should do about conflicts of duty. Consider the case of Sophie's Choice (Case 5.3).

CASE 5.3

Sophie's Choice

In William Styron's novel *Sophie's Choice,* Sophie, her 7-year-old daughter, Eva, and her 10-year-old son, Jan, are prisoners in Auschwitz, a German concentration camp.[5] A camp doctor orders her to give up one of her children, or he will take both of them. Sophie understands that whichever child she gives up will be killed. With seconds to decide, Sophie gives up her daughter, thus sparing her son.

What is Sophie's duty in Case 5.3? She has a duty to protect her daughter, and she has a duty to protect her son. To protect her son, she must give up her daughter. To protect her daughter, she must give up her son. If she refuses to choose, she fails to protect either child. Is there some higher duty that tells us when to choose among such competing duties? Kant says no, because he believes that there can be no conflicting duties. For him, if a duty is absolutely right, then its contrary will always be absolutely wrong. For example, if it is my duty to tell the truth, then it can never be my duty not to tell the truth. Although this sounds logical, the evidence, as in Case 5.3, suggests otherwise.

British philosopher W. D. Ross (1877–1971) supported deontology, but he acknowledged the challenge of competing duties.[6] His solution was to distinguish *prima facie* duties from actual or concrete duties. All else being equal, says Ross, we have several intuitively obvious duties. These include fidelity, reparation, gratitude, noninjury, prevention of harm, beneficence, self-improvement, and justice. We recognize at once the moral value of each of these. But Ross admits that these duties may conflict. In Case 5.3, to prevent harm to her son, Sophie subjected her daughter to harm. To remain faithful to his charge and to promote justice, Vere subjected Billy to harm in Case 5.2.

Although Ross answers our third challenge to Kant's deontology, the challenge of conflicting duties, Ross's view has two problems. First, the rules he identifies as intuitively obvious may not be obvious to many well-meaning people. For example, many hardworking people may have no sense of the duty to improve themselves as long as they can improve their children's lot. Second, Ross tips the scales toward consequentialism, even though he is trying to defend deontology. Sophie's decision in Case 5.3 would not have been as reasonable if she hadn't weighed the consequences of her choice. Similarly, with any conflict of duties, the better choice may be so because it promises the better consequences. Third, it is not clear why one should choose one conflicting duty over another.

→ Is Acting from Duty the Only Way to Be Morally Good?

This brings us to our fourth and final challenge to deontology. If we must always act *from* duty—that is, we must always act only because we are conscious that it is our duty and that is what we will to do—then what hope is there for being moral on a regular basis? How many times in the course of a day do we do the right thing, but not *from* duty? Suppose you have killed no one today. Ordinarily we would regard this as morally good. But suppose further that it never occurred to you to kill someone today, so that your motive for not killing anyone had nothing to do with your sense of duty. Kant would say that you deserve no moral credit for not having killed anyone, since duty was not your motive.

Kant pushes this point when he suggests that one who acts from duty contrary to one's inclinations is morally superior to one who acts from duty consistently with one's inclinations. Suppose you hate Smith and would kill him in a heartbeat if you could justify doing so, but you acknowledge your duty not to kill Smith and, on that basis alone, refuse to kill him. Suppose I like Jones a lot and would hate to see anything bad happen to him, but I also acknowledge a duty not to kill and I refrain from killing him primarily because of my duty. Kant would claim that in this scenario you have a morally superior position, because your motive is purely duty, while my motive is a mixture of duty and affection! This is contrary to common sense.

In short, Kant's demand that one act always and only from duty is impractical. John Stuart Mill, the utilitarian, agreed with this objection and offered the principle of utility—"the greatest good for the greatest number"—as a practical alternative. As we have seen, that moral theory also has its shortcomings, but it is useful to think of each of the three basic moral theories as a check and balance against the other two. That is, for each flaw we find in one theory, we may find a remedy in either of the other two.

Summary

We have discussed the three basic theories that operate as premises for the conclusion "This act is morally good." Consequentialism holds that an act is morally good if the consequences are good. Regularianism holds that an act is good if it obeys a rule. Deontology holds that an act is morally good if the agent acted from duty. We have identified the strengths as well as the shortcomings of each theory. It is because of these shortcomings that we should consider attempts to take the best that each theory has to offer while avoiding its pitfalls. In the next chapter, we consider Aristotle's theories of virtue and responsibility, which offer a useful synthesis of the theories we have considered so far.

Answers to Case Study Questions

Q5.1. Is the judge correct in declaring it Motley's duty to defend Acton? Why, or why not?

It is *a* duty of Motley's, although she may have other duties that clash with this one.

Q5.2. In Case 5.1, does Motley appear to be acting from a duty to remove herself from the case?

No. Motley appears to be acting from self-interest.

Q5.3. Vere claims to be acting from duty, but he also claims to be setting an example for the other sailors and to be regarding only the consequences (not the intention) of Billy's act. So is Vere acting as a deontologist or a consequentialist?

Vere is acting deontologically, even though he is defending his sense of duty by invoking possible consequences.

Q5.4. Is Vere being an absolutist in Case 5.2? Is he being an objectivist?

Vere is acting as an absolutist and an objectivist. He believes that he has an absolute duty to uphold the law and that the law has no exceptions. He also believes that the law itself confers the duty, regardless of his subjective feelings.

Q5.5. Was Motley in Case 5.1 acting from good will in refusing to defend Acton? Was Vere acting from good will in Case 5.2 in refusing to make an exception for Billy?

According to Case 5.1, Motley is acting from revulsion. In general, this is not the same as acting from good will. Vere, on the other hand, appears to want to do the good at all cost. Hence, he appears to be acting from good will.

Q5.6. Could Vere logically claim to be acting from duty in Case 5.2 when he refuses to give Billy a break?

Vere's argument appears to be this:

1. A ship's captain has a duty always to enforce the maritime law of his land.
2. British maritime law calls for the execution of a sailor who kills a superior officer.
3. Billy, a sailor, killed a superior officer.
4. Therefore, Captain Vere must see to Billy's execution.

The argument is logically valid; that is, if the premises are true, then the conclusion must be true. But it is not clear whether one could logically hold as a universal maxim that a captain must always enforce the maritime law of the land (premise 1). Suppose, for example, the law had conflicting commands. Then it would be impossible to enforce both and hence to have such enforcement as a duty. Therefore, it appears that Vere's argument is unsound.

NOTES

1. Herman Melville (1819–1891), *Billy Budd and Other Tales* (1924; New York: New American Library, 1979).
2. Ibid., p. 80.
3. Immanuel Kant, *Grounding for the Metaphysics of Morals* (1785), trans. James Ellington (Indianapolis, IN: Hackett, 1981).
4. Ibid., p. 30.
5. William Styron, *Sophie's Choice* (New York: Random House, 1979).
6. W. D. Ross, *The Right and the Good* (1930; London: Oxford University Press, 2002).

CHAPTER 6

Virtue and Responsibility: An Aristotelian Approach

 ## CASE 6.1

The Hit and Run Son

Chief Paulson is second in command of his police agency. He is at home late one night when his teenage son, Jerry, returns from a baseball game. Jerry, reeking of alcohol, tells his father that, driving home from the game, Jerry hit something with his car but he was too startled to stop.

After examining the damage to the car, Chief Paulson drives Jerry to the site of the accident, where police are on the scene. The chief immediately drives back to the house and calls the police station to find out what happened at the scene. The officer who answers the phone tells the chief that a man has died in a hit-and-run accident. The chief thanks the officer and hangs up.

After Jerry has had a chance to sober up, the chief drives Jerry to the police station where Jerry turns himself in.

We have seen that none of the three major moral theories is exclusively best for making moral decisions. Consequentialism does not take means or motive seriously enough and may sometimes sanction immoral consequences. In Case 6.1, Jerry and his dad might prefer the consequences of hiding the facts, but legitimate rules demand otherwise. Regularianism takes neither consequences nor motive seriously enough and may sometimes sanction immoral rules. As a rule, a father ought to be loyal to his son, but the chief in Case 6.1 would be wrong to keep his son's act a secret. Deontology emphasizes motive and never sanctions an immoral duty. But it does not take consequences seriously enough, it does not help settle conflicts of duty, and it sets an impractically high standard for morality. The chief in Case 6.1 appears to have more than one duty: to bring his son to justice and to protect his son's interests.

If we think of each theory as a tool to help us make moral decisions, we see that like all tools, each of these is useful in some respects but not in others. We would like a tool that takes the best of each theory while avoiding its shortcomings. This fourth theory would provide a synthesis to use in circumstances in which the moral alternative is not clear. As Aristotle (388–322 BCE) observed, most of us have survived many moral challenges, so we may assume that this fourth tool already exists in our moral toolbox.[1] Aristotle describes the tool in terms of virtue and responsibility. This chapter looks at each of these in turn.

✦ Theories of Virtue

> **Q 6.1**
>
> In Case 6.1, if the chief were concerned only with consequences, should he have made Jerry turn himself in?

Rawls's Synthesis

Aristotle's view is not the only plausible theory that offers a synthesis of the three basic moral theories. Two other syntheses stand out, which we will examine before turning to Aristotle's view.

Many find that John Rawls's (1921–2002) theory of justice offers a good synthesis.[2] Rawls equates justice with fairness and sees fairness as the foundation of ethics. For Rawls, promoting justice means properly balancing concerns about duties and consequences. He offers a technique for this, the **veil of ignorance,** behind which we should stand while invoking the Golden Rule to make morally significant decisions. That is, we should do unto others as we would have them do unto us while pretending that we do not know who we are until we have acted.

Imagine that I am about to vote on a proposed hike in the city property tax. Proponents argue that the hike is necessary to fund local public schools adequately; opponents argue that it will burden homeowners unfairly. In one sense, my choice is simple: vote yes or vote no. Matters become more complex as I step behind the veil of ignorance: Which vote is more apt to please me whether I am white or black, rich or poor, young or old, male or female, a property owner or not, and a parent or not? Rawls claims that my duty is to come up with the fairer answer, and that the possible consequences should guide my fulfillment of that duty.

The emphasis on fairness is appealing, but for Rawls we also operate from self-interest. Behind the veil I am asking, for each of the demographic categories, which would be the better choice if I represented that category? In theory, once I have considered all the possibilities, I should be able to make the choice that is more apt to please me no matter who I turn out to be. One objection to this approach is, Why should I step behind the veil of ignorance if my motive is self-interest? If I have no property to tax, then I will suffer less from the tax hike than if I have valuable taxable property. Why should I care about the outcome for the wealthy property holder?

Rawls's answer seems to be that on other occasions I hope the wealthy property owner will care about the effects that public policy will have on me. But I have no reason to count on this if everyone acts from self-interest.

Rawls's theory has other practical flaws, which we will consider when we examine theories of justice.

Q 6.2

In Case 6.1, should Jerry have turned himself in before he sobered up?

The Feminist Synthesis

Another contemporary synthesis of basic moral theories comes from feminist scholarship. Many feminists offer an **ethic of care** as an alternative to the ethics of justice. Carol Gilligan (1936–), a well-known proponent of the ethic of care, claims that men approach moral problems more analytically and individually than women, and seek to conquer such problems in the name of justice.[3] Men ask, What are the parts of the problem? How can I fix it? What is the most just solution? Women, Gilligan contends, tend to approach a moral problem holistically and collegially, seeking to resolve the problem in the most caring way. Women ask, What is the larger context of the problem? How can we solve it together? What is the most caring approach?

Q 6.3

In Case 6.1, would it have been morally right for Mrs. Paulson to urge the chief not to have their son turn himself in?

Gilligan offers her theory as an objection to her teacher, Lawrence Kohlberg (1927–1987), who claimed that there are stages of moral development, ranging from the child's orientation toward parental reward and punishment to the individual's internalized sense of moral right.[4] Each of these stages involves a level of intellectual awareness about good and evil, and one's moral development parallels one's intellectual development.

Kohlberg's mistake, Gilligan argues, was limiting his subjects to males and focusing on reason to the exclusion of emotions or feelings. Had he also interviewed a sufficient number of females, he would have seen that moral behavior in women takes emotions more seriously and, contrary to the male ethic of justice, focuses on care and attachment.

Q 6.4

Does Case 6.1 suggest that the chief's interest in justice is uncaring?

Kohlberg's and Gilligan's work is sociologically and psychologically interesting and may help ethicists target their audiences more specifically. For example, talking to young children about ethics may require a different approach from talking to adults about ethics. But such work is largely descriptive, telling us what they observed, rather than prescriptive, telling us how to solve moral problems. Also, both Kohlberg and Gilligan generalize their findings, whereas observation reveals variations in how individuals develop morally and how they approach moral problems. Many men appear to be more interested in care than in justice, and many women tend to be more interested in justice than in care. Thus, neither Gilligan nor Kohlberg promises as useful a synthesis as we seek.

CASE 6.2

The Harassing Legislator

Fred Thornton is a freshman United States Representative who represents a morally conservative district in his state. His campaign emphasized his 35-year marriage and his commitment to "family values."

Nearing the end of the first legislative term, Thornton has developed a reputation among congressional pages and staff as a "dirty old man" who leers at the younger women, makes sexually suggestive remarks about their appearance, and frequently invites them to dinner at his place. Most of these women have made it clear to him that they find his attitude and invitations offensive. They have also complained to senior staff and other representatives about Thornton's behavior, but to no avail.

Yesterday a story appeared in *The Washington Post* and *The Washington Times* about a 16-year-old page, a frequent object of Thornton's advances, who told her mother about Thornton's behavior and showed her sexually suggestive e-mails that Thornton had sent to the page. The mother called the news desks at both Washington papers and told them of her daughter's plight. Both papers assigned reporters to the story, and both were able to verify the page's charges and to obtain similar stories from other pages. Today the lead editorials in both papers call for Thornton's resignation.

With his campaign for reelection well under way, Thornton announces that he has "made some mistakes" in his treatment of pages and staff but that his behavior was due to problems with alcohol, to which he is finally facing up by joining Alcoholics Anonymous. He declares his intention to "stay the course" in his campaign, refusing to resign.

✦ ARISTOTLE ON VIRTUE

As we think about Case 6.2, we continue to seek a theory that permits a synthesis of the three basic theories: consequentialism, regularianism, and deontology. Neither Rawls's theory nor feminist ethics is adequate to the task. So we turn to Aristotle.

Teleology

Consider first Aristotle's assumption that everything in nature has a purpose unique to its species and that to understand anything is to understand its purpose. The Greek word for purpose is *telos*. This is often translated as "end," as in "The end justifies the means." For this reason, some scholars refer to consequentialism as **teleology**. This is imprecise, however, since not all teleologists are consequentialists. For Aristotle, moral behavior is making proper use of one's abilities and of all other objects that one's actions involve. Morality is not merely about achieving good consequences. Thus, for example, a teleologist might argue that the proper purpose of human reproductive organs is reproduction. Any action that subverts this purpose, such as homosexual activity, must therefore be immoral, even if everyone the activity affects likes the consequences.

Q 6.5

In Case 6.2, did Thornton subvert the purpose of his office by harassing pages?

There have been many challenges to Aristotle's teleology, as well as to teleology in general. Why, for example, must there be a purpose to everything in nature? And why must there be only one purpose for each kind of object? Also, regularianism and deontology are obvious challenges to teleology—rules or duty matter, not fulfillment of purpose. But it is worth mentioning Aristotle's view because it is the historical foundation of natural law theory, which we will discuss in detail in a chapter on law, and which many contemporary moral positions imply. His view also leads naturally to his virtue theory and his account of responsibility.

Q 6.6

In Case 6.2, if no page or staff member suffered more than annoyance from Thornton's advances, should Thornton resign anyway?

Virtue, Wisdom, and Happiness

For Aristotle, the study of ethics is the study of good human character—virtue—and bad human character—vice. Virtue and vice must occur relative to the agent's particular purpose. Fulfillment of that purpose must be good, and failure to fulfill that purpose must be bad. Moreover, we call the ultimate aim of human behavior happiness, so happiness must be the result of morally good human behavior. But what is humanity's unique purpose?

For Aristotle, human happiness has to do with human life, since we have never observed a happy dead person. Soul is, by Aristotle's definition, the principle of life, so what is unique about the human soul? Every living thing has a *vegetative* soul—an impetus to live—so that cannot be the unique function of the human soul. All living things that can feel pleasure and pain also have an *appetitive* soul—a desire for pleasure and an aversion to pain—so that cannot be the unique function of the human soul. The human soul also has an intellective function, which, Aristotle claims, distinguishes humans from all other living things. Therefore, human happiness depends on fulfillment of the intellective function.

The intellectual part of the human soul has two primary functions: to control the nonrational parts of the soul, the vegetative and the appetitive, and to seek the truth. **Moral virtue,** which we examine more closely below, is the ability to control the nonrational soul; **intellectual virtue** is the ability to find the truth. There are two kinds of truth: changeable (e.g., the current temperature is 68° Fahrenheit) and unchangeable (e.g., 9 is the square root of 81). **Practical wisdom** is the capacity to grasp changeable truth; **theoretical wisdom** is the ability to grasp unchangeable truth. The wiser we are, the more virtuous we are. The more virtuous we are, the more we fulfill our unique purpose in nature. The more we fulfill our unique purpose in nature, the happier we are. Therefore, the more virtuous we are, the happier we are.

Incidentally, the Greek word for theoretical wisdom is *Sophia,* and there is no higher human aspiration, says Aristotle, than to achieve Sophia. Greeks call one who longs for Sophia a lover of wisdom. The Greek word for this sort of love is *philia.* Put this all together and you have Aristotle's claim that no one is happier than the *philosopher!* On this premise, we have done well to begin our study of ethics philosophically, before looking at ethics constitutionally and religiously.

Q 6.7

On Aristotle's theory, can we regard the legislator in Case 6.2 as unhappy?

Many points in the previous paragraph invite objections. Is intellect unique to human beings? Don't other higher-level mammals exhibit creativity and understanding and thus intellect? Also, are there no other uniquely human functions, such as our capacity for evil? These are fair questions, but they do not refute Aristotle's claim that ethics is a matter of virtue, and virtue is a matter of moral self-control and intellectual growth. As we shall see, his detailed account of moral virtue holds its own, whatever the objections might be to his teleology or to his reasoning that gets him there.

CASE 6.3

The Tipsy Judge

At 8:00 a.m. on Monday, Judge Hanrahan excused himself from the poker game that had been going on since early Sunday evening. He had joined his poker companions in heavy drinking and only stopped a short while ago when he realized that he had court in an hour. He managed to drive to court without incident and at 8:30, when he entered his chambers, his clerk noticed the judge walking unsteadily and slurring his words. When the clerk asked him to postpone the 9:00 trial, given the judge's condition, the judge said no, adding that that he was an old pro at hiding his condition from court observers and that he would read all transcripts of the trial thoroughly before he rendered any judgments. The clerk concluded that the judge was in no condition to enter the courtroom and begin the trial.

Virtue and Habit

Judge Hanrahan does not strike us as virtuous. For Aristotle, virtue is *the ability habitually to know the good and to do the good.* This definition is useful to the study of ethics in many ways. First, it reminds us that no one is morally good on the basis of a single act. A morally bad person can do a good deed or have some desirable traits. For example, Hitler was kind to animals—a kind disposition of a generally unkind man. Morality is a matter of character, and character is a matter of habit. The more one is in the habit of knowing and doing the good, the more one is virtuous.

> ### Q 6.8
>
> In Case 6.3, why doesn't the judge come across as virtuous?

To clarify this point, Aristotle uses the analogy of an archer. An excellent archer habitually finds the bull's-eye and hits it. A good archer understands the principles of aiming and usually hits the bull's-eye, but not often enough. A poor archer either does not know how to aim or understands how to aim but tends to miss the bull's-eye anyway. If, after 500 unsuccessful tries, the poor archer should hit the bull's-eye, he does not suddenly become a good archer. Similarly, an occasional good act does not make a person virtuous. By the same token, an excellent archer does not become a bad archer with one errant shot, just as a virtuous person does not automatically become vicious on the basis of one misdeed.

> ### Q 6.9
>
> Does the clerk's attitude in Case 6.3 suggest that he is a virtuous person?

Ethics and Morals

A second point that emerges from Aristotle's definition of virtue comes from the fact that "habitual" in Greek has its root in the word *ethos*, and in Latin has its root in the word *mos*. From *ethos*, English gets the words *ethic, ethics,* and *ethical*. From *mos*, English gets the words *moral, morals,* and *morality*. Etymologically, then, *moral* and *ethical* are synonyms, and we speak redundantly when we say, for example, "That is both immoral and unethical." While some ethics texts note that specialized use of these terms may render them distinct from each other—as in the mafia ethic, which is immoral—the basic meaning of the terms allows us to use them interchangeably.

Sin

A third point that emerges from Aristotle's definition of virtue concerns sin—the basic unit of immorality in Judaism, Christianity, and Islam. In these religions, the word *sin* and its counterparts in Greek (*hamartia*), Hebrew (*'chata*), and Arabic (*khata*) mean "missing the mark." The mark is God's will. So to sin is to disobey God's will, either because we do not know what it is or because we know what it is but fail to do it anyway. Failure to know the good is a sin of ignorance; failure to do the good is a sin of weakness. In both cases, sin is essentially lack of virtue.

> ### Q 6.10
>
> Does it make sense to think of the judge's behavior in Case 6.3 as a sin?

This chapter offers Aristotle's virtue theory as a useful synthesis of the three basic moral theories. Virtue theory is useful (1) in directing our attention to moral character rather than individual actions, (2) by explaining the synonymy of *ethical* and *moral,* and (3) by giving us insight into the concept of sin. But how do we put virtue theory to use when trying to solve a moral problem?

> ### Q 6.11
>
> Does the clerk in Case 6.3 have a moral problem that virtue theory might help him solve?

The Good and the Golden Mean

The answer lies in Aristotle's definition of the good. Good, he notes, is a species of perfect. The better something is, the closer to perfect it is. The less good something is, the farther away from perfect it is. Something is perfect if it lacks nothing and has nothing in excess. In other words, something is perfect if adding anything to it or taking anything away from it would make it worse. Therefore, good must be the mean between the extremes of deficiency and excess. History has come to call this the **golden mean,** although Aristotle probably never used this term.

Q 6.12

In Case 6.3, what would be the most deficient response the clerk could offer? The most extreme?

When struggling with a moral decision for which appeal to consequences or rules or duty will not suffice, the virtuous person looks at the alternatives and chooses the one that is at once the least deficient and the least excessive. Justified use of deadly force is a good example. We say that deadly force is justifiable when that force is neither excessive nor deficient. If we are unsure, we need to consider the alternatives to that force, and identify and eliminate the extreme alternatives. Suppose Officer Crane has shot and killed a knife-wielding assailant who has lunged toward a child. Crane could have done nothing to protect the child, but this would have been a deficient response to the assault. Crane could have fired his gun wildly, hoping that one of the shots would find its right target, but this would have been an excessive response to the assault. Somewhere between these two extremes is the most justifiable alternative. Now suppose further that Crane could not have reached the assailant in time, that there was no one else available to stop the assailant, and that Crane had no other, less lethal weapons to use. Given the set of remaining options, Crane's use of force was the most moderate, and hence justified.

Also, notice that sometimes one may have to settle for getting close to a mean without hitting it dead on, just as with archery, it may sometimes suffice to get near the bull's-eye. So in looking for the mean between extremes as the right choice among the alternatives, if we cannot identify a perfect choice, we should accept the option that is the least extreme, even if it is more deficient or excessive than we would have preferred.

Cardinal Virtues

To help us think even more practically about virtue theory, Greek ethics identifies four basic or **cardinal virtues:**

The Cardinal Virtues

Deficiency	Mean (The Virtues)	Excess
Cowardice	**COURAGE**	Foolhardiness
Consuming too little	**TEMPERANCE**	Consuming too much
Giving one less than one is due	**JUSTICE**	Giving one more than one is due
Acting on insufficient knowledge	**PRUDENCE** (or practical wisdom)	Failing to act in the face of sufficient knowledge

---

Q 6.13

Which of the cardinal virtues does the judge appear to lack in Case 6.3?

Integrity

These details of Aristotle's theory help us to understand the concept of **integrity.** *Integrity* is a common but ambiguous word. Strictly speaking, to have integrity is to have integrated the virtues into one's life. One can act ethically and still lack integrity. For example, it may be true that a person of integrity is courageous and just, but if a courageous and just person lacks temperance and prudence, then he does not have integrity. In other words, courage and justice are morally desirable, but they are not enough to give a person integrity.

Q 6.14

In Case 6.3, does the clerk appear to be acting with integrity?

Integrity is not limited to the cardinal virtues. There are many more virtues than the four cardinal virtues. Honesty, loyalty, and reliability—when neither deficient nor excessive—are also characteristics of a virtuous person. But anyone who is habitually courageous, just, temperate, and prudent is virtuous, even if not perfectly so.

Q 6.15

In Case 6.3, is the judge lacking any virtues besides the cardinal virtues?

So far we have seen that virtue theory helps us understand ethics by highlighting the value of character over specific acts; the synonymy of *moral* and *ethical;* the relationship of virtue theory to concepts of sin; the good as the golden mean between extremes; and the cardinal virtues of courage, justice, temperance, and prudence.

Virtue theory also explains how to make the best of the three basic moral theories—consequentialism, regularianism, and deontology—each of which has limited usefulness otherwise. A virtuous person will give the proper weight to each of these considerations. In Case 6.3, for example, the easiest resolution might be for the clerk to keep silent and hope that the judge gets through the trial, but such an easy consequence ignores the rules for a fair trial. On the other hand, if duty called for the clerk to turn in the judge, the consequences might have been unhappy for all concerned—the destruction of the judge's career, bad morale among the court staff, and the media's tarnishing of the judiciary's image, for example. A person of virtue would be mindful of each basic theory's shortcomings, and would act to minimize their misuse and maximize their moral guidance. The clerk's decision to keep silent might have been the most moderate response, if the alternatives were worse.

Another advantage of virtue theory is its assistance in putting some of the basic moral controversies in perspective. Concerning hedonism versus non-hedonism, virtue theory denies that all moral goodness is a matter of pleasure and all moral evil is a matter of pain. But unlike regularians and deontologists, the virtue theorist would warn us not to excessively dismiss the value of pleasure. And unlike hedonists, the virtue theorist would warn us not to focus exclusively on the pleasure of an act.

Q 6.16

In Case 6.3, does the judge appear to be a hedonist?

Concerning absolutism versus relativism, virtue theory applies an absolute principle—seek the mean!—but allows for different circumstances. Thus, deadly force is appropriate sometimes and inappropriate other times, depending on the alternatives in the case. Whereas the relativist paradoxically denies absolutes absolutely but correctly sees the moral relevance of a specific time or place, virtue theory allows for the "floating mean" of cultural or historical situation without giving up the underlying absolute of morality.

Q 6.17

Is there any situation in which the judge's action would have been virtuous in Case 6.3?

Concerning objectivism versus subjectivism, virtue theory is essentially objective, because the measure of moderation is not merely in the mind of the beholder. But virtue theory offers a crucial role to the person making the moral judgment, because only someone capable of reason can see the moral value of the mean between extremes.

Q 6.18

In Case 6.1, did the son's fear absolve him of moral responsibility for not stopping at the scene of the accident?

Concerning free will versus determinism, virtue theory assumes the agent's free will—the ability to do otherwise—as a factor in the morality of the act and recognizes as moral the person who habitually chooses the good. The situation may determine the mean between extremes, but the agent is free to aim for that mean or not, and we are to judge the agent on whether or not he habitually knows and hits the mean.

Q 6.19

In Case 6.2, Thornton's colleagues disregarded the pages' complaints. Did those colleagues, therefore, cause Thornton's subsequent harassment of the pages and staff?

The freedom of moral agents invites the question, What about people who are constitutionally incapable of doing otherwise, whether because of age, mental incapacity, or coercion? There must be times when an agent is not morally responsible for his act because he is an infant, severely mentally disabled, or under extreme duress. Since this precludes the agent's being virtuous, does this mean the agent is vicious? Aristotle would answer that virtue and vice apply only to those who are morally responsible for their acts. People who are not morally responsible for their acts are neither virtuous nor vicious. So, let's take a look at Aristotle's notion of responsibility, its place in his virtue theory, and its usefulness in solving moral problems.

✦ RESPONSIBILITY

 ## CASE 6.4

The Double Dipper

With his agency's approval, police Sgt. Hawkins has a thriving private security business with a virtual monopoly on providing security for events at the city arena. This evening Hawkins is on patrol duty when he receives a call from one of his employees. Three security people, including a supervisor, who were assigned to tonight's rock concert at the arena, have not shown up, and the crowd is getting increasingly raucous.

Hawkins goes to the arena and begins supervising the security operations. He receives a call from police dispatch and asks dispatch to call someone else. He gives no reason for his request, but dispatch agrees.

Hawkins's police agency has clear rules against engaging in secondary employment while on police duty.

Has Hawkins acted ethically in Case 6.4? Criminal justice ethics is a matter of accountability, integrity, and responsibility. To be accountable is to be answerable for one's actions. When one is answerable, others have the right to pass moral judgment concerning one's success or failure at meeting expectations. In terms of the criminal justice profession's social contract with the community, accountability is the means by which the professional shows that he is keeping his end of the bargain. Integrity, the means by which the professional shows himself that he is upholding his end of the bargain, is a matter of integrating virtues into his life, whether or not there is anyone holding him accountable. To say that one is responsible for one's act is to say that one is the cause of the consequences of that act. Let's look more closely at the notion of responsibility.

Q 6.20

In Case 6.4, should Hawkins be held responsible for his double dipping when it is not his fault that some of his employees didn't show up?

We begin by distinguishing mere **causal responsibility** from **moral responsibility**. A baby who vomits on a passerby is causally responsible for soiling the passersby's clothing, but not morally responsible; the baby had no control over its actions, one shouldn't expect the baby to have such control, and the baby deserves no moral blame for its actions. Still, the baby did the vomiting. In contrast, if the vengeful passerby decides to vomit on the baby, the passerby is responsible both causally and morally for the resultant mess.

Q 6.21

In Case 6.4, are the agency's rules against double dipping responsible for Hawkins's doing something wrong?

Aristotle's View of Responsibility

Aristotle's view of responsibility complements his virtue theory. More recently, existentialism has offered a forceful account of responsibility, driving home its wide scope and deep implications. We will consider both views.

Aristotle suggests four conditions for being morally responsible for one's actions. First, the agent must know the situation and the choices that it offers. The vomiting baby probably did not know what was happening. Sgt. Hawkins knew that he was on duty and that his agency prohibited working at secondary employment while on duty. Note that even if Sgt. Hawkins did not know either of these things, he *should have* known them. Thus, Hawkins meets this condition for moral responsibility, but the baby does not.

Aristotle's second condition for responsibility is that the agent must know the difference between right and wrong. Assuming that it is wrong to vomit on a passerby, the baby did not know this, nor should we have expected him to know it. Thus, we may not hold him morally responsible for his act. On the other hand, the passerby knew or should have known that it is wrong to vomit on the baby; thus, he would meet this second condition for moral responsibility if he decided to retaliate.

Q 6.22

In Case 6.4, if the agency had never published or announced its rule against double dipping, would it be wrong for Hawkins to attend to his secondary business while on duty as a police officer?

Aristotle's third condition is that the agent must have acted from free will. That is, he must have been able to do otherwise. Perhaps the baby could have turned its head or vomited at a different time and thus missed the passerby. But this isn't what Aristotle means by the ability to do otherwise. For Aristotle it means being able to choose between alternatives and to act on that choice. The baby was not able to choose whether to vomit. The passerby could have chosen not to vomit on the baby, just as Sgt. Hawkins, in Case 6.4, could have chosen not to go to the arena, in spite of the personnel problems facing him. Thus, the passerby and Sgt. Hawkins satisfy Aristotle's third condition for moral responsibility.

Determinists argue that no one ever acts from free will. If this is true, then either free will cannot be a condition of moral responsibility or there is no moral responsibility. If there is no moral responsibility, then there is no point in discussing ethics. If we can't choose our actions, what difference does it make to us whether or not we know the difference between the morally good and the morally bad? Since Chapter 3 looks closely at the debate between determinism, as Hobbes defends it, and free will, we need not say anything more about it here.

Q 6.23

We are inclined to judge Hawkins harshly for his actions in Case 6.4. Is the determinist correct to suggest that we are not free to judge Hawkins differently?

Aristotle's fourth condition for moral responsibility is that the agent must have intended to act as he did. He may not have intended the results, as in Case 6.4, where Hawkins probably did not intend to get caught double dipping. Hawkins did intend to choose one alternative over another.

CASE 6.5

The Coerced Cop

Cpl. Kelly is the first to arrive at an elementary school whose silent alarm went to the police station. Although he enters the school cautiously, he is overpowered by a man whose partner is holding a classroom of young children hostage.

The man takes Kelly to the classroom and hands him a gun with one bullet in it. The man tells Kelly to shoot one child or his partner will shoot all the children. As Kelly sees it, he has only a few options: shoot a child, shoot himself, shoot one of the two hostage takers, or not fire the gun at all. He believes that any option but the first will result in his death and the death of many children.

How responsible is Kelly for his predicament in Case 6.5? As with virtue, moral responsibility is a matter of degree for Aristotle. If the agent knew the circumstances well, knew the difference between right and wrong, was free to do otherwise, and fully intended to act the way he did, then he would be fully morally responsible for his act. But there may be mitigating circumstances that make the agent only partially responsible. In Case 5.3, a concentration camp doctor forces Sophie to choose which of her two children to hand over to be killed. She may choose to give up one or both of her children, or she may refuse to give up either child, which will result in their both being killed. In William Styron's story, Sophie gives up her daughter because Sophie believes the son has a better chance of surviving the camp's horrors and trials. She knows the circumstances, she knows the difference between right and wrong, she could choose otherwise, and she intends to give up her daughter over her son. But the choice is forced on her; if her will were wholly free in this case, she would have given up neither of her children. Also, it is a stretch to say that she intentionally gave up her daughter. Anything she did in response to the officer would have resulted in the death of at least one of her children, and it is a safe bet that she never intended for either of her children to die.

Q 6.24

In Case 6.5, would Kelly be morally responsible for the death of the children if he refused to shoot a child and the hostage takers carried out their threat?

Aristotle's account of responsibility is straightforward: it entails proper knowledge, intent, and freedom to choose. Also, his account sheds light on his notion of virtue and its usefulness in solving moral problems, because one must assume responsibility for knowing and doing the good. We cannot overstate the importance of responsibility to a morally healthy community. Existentialism highlights this importance, so it is worth a closer look.

Existentialism's View of Responsibility

Existentialism is a loosely knit group of theories that agree on the individual's responsibility for who he is and what he does. Existentialists disagree on whether or not there is a God, the extent to which one's choices are limited, and the proper form of society for promoting individual responsibility. Existentialists agree that, in Jean-Paul Sartre's (1905–1980) words, "existence precedes essence."[5] This means that humans are not born preprogrammed or already defined before they have had a chance to develop. On the contrary, says the existentialist, who we are at any moment is a result of our own choices; thus, we cannot blame or praise anyone else for who we are. We are, in short, responsible for ourselves.

Q 6.25

In Case 6.5, does Kelly have anyone to blame but himself for getting caught by the hostage taker?

For Sartre, choice is not merely desire but the act of choosing. Thus, we define who we are through our actions. By our actions, we also define who we would like others to be. This is a variation on the Golden Rule: as we do unto others, so are we declaring how we want others to do unto us. For moral agents, every act is a choice, and by choosing it we give it value. In giving it value, we say this act is preferable to the alternative, and we imply, in the sense of Kant's categorical imperative, that if it were up to us we would prescribe this action for everyone. On Sartre's view, therefore, our capacity for responsibility is awesome.

Sartre summarizes his view with two declarations. We are "condemned to be free" and we are "alone without excuses." We are condemned to be free, because we have no choice whether to be born, but once we are born, we face a lifetime of choices, we are defined by those choices, and we are responsible for the consequences of those choices.

Two objections come to mind. First, we often end up in situations that we would not have chosen. In Case 6.5, Cpl. Kelly did not choose the dilemma of shooting a child or risking the deaths of many children. In Case 5.3, Sophie didn't choose to have to sacrifice the life of one of her children. Sartre would agree, but he would also note that had Kelly made different choices in the first place—not to answer the call, not to go into the building, not to become a police officer, to kill himself before today—then he would not be in this fix. Similarly, if Sophie had made different choices—to flee Germany before she was imprisoned, to commit suicide at the sound of approaching soldiers, not to have children—then she would not face the unpleasant choice between her children. Existentialism does not expect us always to know in advance the consequences of our actions; it says only that whatever those consequences are, they follow from previous choices we have made and for which, therefore, we are responsible.

A second objection to Sartre is that his view appears to let everyone but the agent off the hook. If Cpl. Kelly and Sophie are in their present circumstances because of their own choices, does this mean that the hostage takers in Case 6.5 and the concentration camp doctor in Case 5.3 are not morally responsible for putting Kelly and Sophie, respectively, in those situations? No, says Sartre, the instigators are as responsible for their choices as any agent is responsible for his or her choice. The instigators behaved immorally and deserve the appropriate punishment.

Are we "alone without excuses"? If an excuse is a reason for not holding someone responsible for the consequences of his actions, then Sartre denies the possibility of an excuse.

Recall the four conditions of Aristotle's view of responsibility:

- The agent must know the facts of the situation.
- The agent must know the difference between right and wrong.
- The agent must have intended to do what he did.
- The agent must have been able to do otherwise.

Under these conditions and using as an example a speeding motorist whom a trooper has stopped, we can imagine four sorts of excuses:

- "I didn't know the speed limit was only 45."
- "I didn't know it is wrong to speed when there is no one else on the highway."
- "I didn't intend to speed."
- "I had no choice: I had to go to the bathroom, so I had to speed."

Since the conditions for moral responsibility apply only to moral agents—people capable of being virtuous—the four types of alleged excuses would apply only to moral agents. As we have admitted, infants, people with severe mental impairments, and people in persistent vegetative states fail to meet the conditions for responsibility. In these cases, it makes little sense to speak of the excusability of their actions, just as it would be nonsense to excuse a tree for blowing over in a hurricane or to excuse a lion for killing the antelope. The actions of nonmoral agents do not require moral considerations, such as whether or not to excuse their acts.

Q 6.26

Are the children in Case 6.5 responsible for their predicament?

Moral agents, on the other hand, are able to meet or fail to meet Aristotle's conditions for responsibility. When someone says "I had no choice," the existentialist insists that we always have choices. This does not mean that at any moment we have an infinite number of choices; as human beings, there are limits to what we can do. I cannot fly around my office as a fly might, for example. Nor could I choose to be an Olympic swimming champion before suppertime tonight. But as long as I am alive, at any moment I have at least two choices: to continue or to kill myself. Thus, if I find myself in a predicament I dislike, no one can absolve me of responsibility for landing there. I have had any number of choices over my life, the aggregate result of which is this particular predicament.

Q 6.27

What other choices did Hawkins have in Case 6.4 that would have been better than the choice he made?

Once we eliminate the possible excuse that the agent had no choice, we eliminate the three other possible excuses. "I didn't know the speed limit" doesn't entail "therefore you can't hold me responsible for my choice." "I didn't know it was wrong to speed on a deserted highway" doesn't entail "therefore you can't hold me responsible for my choice," especially since a driver should know that speeding is wrong. And "I didn't intend to speed" can only mean "I didn't intend to get caught"; it can never mean "I didn't intend to make that choice," because we convey our intentions in our choices, which in turn are conveyed through our actions.

For Sartre, to act is to choose that action. If I stand before you smoking a cigarette and insist that I would rather not smoke, Sartre would point out that by my actions my comment is a lie. Proof of what I would rather do is in what I end up doing. When I claim that I would prefer a world other than the one I have chosen, I am guilty of self-deception, lying to myself, or "bad faith." Bad faith and failure to honor the freedom of others to choose for themselves are the two worst wrongs we can commit, according to Sartre. On the contrary, the fully morally responsible person will be honest with herself about who is responsible for her, and she will recognize the freedom of others to be responsible for their actions.

Q 6.28

In Case 6.4, did Hawkins lie to the dispatcher?

Sartre's rejection of excuses speaks to each of the three basic moral theories. The consequentialist lets the act's consequences, not the agent's virtue, decide the moral matter. If the consequences are good, then the act is good, whatever the agent intended. But as Sartre points out, there would have been no such consequence if the agent had made a different choice, so the agent is responsible for the consequence. The regularians, in principle, allow for the Nuremburg defense: "I was only following orders," said each of Hitler's henchmen on trial for crimes against humanity. But it would be more accurate to say "I *chose* to follow orders." Thus, the order did not force the agent to make one choice over another; the agent is responsible for the act. The deontologists agree that acting from duty is a choice and that an agent may choose instead to act contrary to duty or merely according to duty. Still we can imagine Sgt. Kelly, in Case 6.5, or Sophie, in Case 5.3., saying "It was my duty to act as I did; I had no other choice." If they mean this as an excuse, then it is false. Clearly, Kelly and Sophie could have done otherwise, even if they saw the alternative as contrary to duty. In short, when the agent acts on the basis of anticipated consequences, or according to a rule, or from a sense of duty, the agent, not the consequence, rule, or duty is responsible for that choice.

Q 6.29

In Case 6.4, did Hawkins have a duty to honor his contract with the arena?

If there is no such thing as an excuse, then we should *dis*suade ourselves and others from seeking excuses, and we should *per*suade ourselves and others to accept responsibility for our actions. Imagine a world in which typically one's first response to a misdeed was to accept responsibility for it, take whatever punishment the misdeed merits, and resolve to try harder not to make the same mistake again. This is a different, more desirable world than one in which we typically find misdoers trying to excuse their way out of taking responsibility for their actions.

Q 6.30

In Case 6.4, if Hawkins is on the whole a virtuous person, would he keep quiet about his double dipping if no one asked him about it?

Summary

If being moral is a matter of being virtuous, as we have argued in the first part of this chapter, and one cannot be virtuous without acknowledging responsibility for one's actions, as the second part of this chapter has argued, then we have the synthesis necessary to making the best of other moral theories in identifying the moral good.

So far we have examined the structure of moral decision making; the three basic moral theories—consequentialism, regularianism, and deontology; and Aristotle's virtue theory and theory of responsibility. Along the way, we have discussed hedonism versus non-hedonism, absolutism versus relativism, objectivism versus subjectivism, and free will versus determinism. We have also considered Rawls's and feminism's attempts to synthesize the basic moral theories. While we have established the foundation for the study of ethics, we have not considered all the possible authorities to which we appeal when making moral decisions. Next, we will consider the roles of the U.S. Constitution and of religion in moral decision making.

Also, so far the emphasis has been on the virtue of the individual. Frequently the agent acts on behalf of an organization, such as a government or a police agency. In police ethics, for example, this distinction often appears as "the apple" versus "the barrel." To what extent is the barrel able to be a moral agent—that is, to be virtuous and responsible? We need, therefore, to think about organizational ethics, which this book's subsequent discussion will facilitate.

ANSWERS TO CASE STUDY QUESTIONS

Q6.1. In Case 6.1, if the chief were concerned only with consequences, should he have made Jerry turn himself in?

The short-term consequences might have been good for the chief and Jerry if Jerry did not turn himself in, but

1. The possible long-term consequences, for the chief and for Jerry, could be bad if anyone ever found out.
2. The mere threat of this discovery would probably make life unpleasant for the chief and for Jerry.
3. Therefore, even on the basis of consequences alone, Jerry should have turned himself in.

Objection: Premise 1 is highly speculative; the possible long-term consequences might be OK. Therefore, premise 1 may not be true.

Q6.2. In Case 6.1, should Jerry have turned himself in before he sobered up?

A. 1. If Jerry caused the accident while drunk, he should be justly punished for that.
  2. Jerry caused the accident while drunk.
  3. Therefore, Jerry should be justly punished for that.

B. 1. If Jerry sobers up before he turns himself in, then he will avoid just punishment for driving drunk.
  2. Jerry sobered up before turning himself in.
  3. Therefore, Jerry avoided just punishment.

C. 1. It is better to receive just punishment than to avoid it.
   2. Therefore, Jerry should have turned himself in before he sobered up.

Objection: Jerry could still confess to having been drunk, and he was probably better able to handle his arrest once he was sober.

Q6.3. In Case 6.1, would it have been morally right for Mrs. Paulson to urge the chief not to have their son turn himself in?

1. Jerry has a moral obligation to turn himself in, and his parents ought to support him in that decision.
2. Therefore, if the mother fails to support that decision, she is not doing the morally right thing.

Objection: A mother's duty to protect her son trumps her duty to turn him over to the authorities.

Q6.4. Does Case 6.1 suggest that the chief's interest in justice is uncaring?

1. If the chief's interest in justice is uncaring, then he neither cares about the victim's receiving justice nor cares about his son's atoning for his wrong.
2. But the chief cares about the victim's receiving justice and about his son's atoning for his wrong.
3. Therefore, the chief's interest in justice is caring.

Objection: Premise 2 may be false. The chief may care only about protecting his job, for example.

Q6.5. In Case 6.2, did Thornton subvert the purpose of his office by harassing pages?

1. To act outside the boundaries of legislative ethics is to subvert the purposes of one's legislative office.
2. Thornton acted outside those boundaries, even if no one was seriously hurt.
3. Therefore, Thornton subverted the purpose of his office.

Q6.6. In Case 6.2, if no page or staff member suffered more than annoyance from Thornton's advances, should Thornton resign anyway?
Yes. Thornton has shown an inability to focus on the job he was elected to do. That the intended victims haven't succumbed to his advances is no positive reflection on him.

Q6.7. On Aristotle's theory, can we regard the legislator in Case 6.2 as unhappy?

1. In Aristotelian terms, failure to control oneself causes unhappiness.
2. The legislator gave in to the urge to do something wrong—harass the pages—rather than act in accord with reason.
3. To give in to an urge to do a wrong rather than act in accord with reason is to fail to control oneself.
4. Therefore, the legislator is unhappy in Aristotelian terms.

Q6.8. In Case 6.3, why doesn't the judge come across as virtuous?

1. If the judge were virtuous, he would have known the good and done the good.
2. Showing up drunk for the trial was not good.
3. Therefore, either the judge did not know the good or he knew the good but failed to do it.
4. Therefore, the judge does not come across as virtuous in Case 6.3.

Q6.9. Does the clerk's attitude in Case 6.3 suggest that he is a virtuous person?

Yes. The clerk's objection to the judge's state suggests temperance. The clerk shows courage in confronting the judge. The clerk recognizes that postponing the trial would be prudent under the circumstances. And the clerk exhibits interest in a just trial. Any other attitude toward the judge would be deficient.

Q6.10. Does it make sense to think of the judge's behavior in Case 6.3 as a sin?

1. To a Christian, Jew, or Muslim, drunkenness is a sin.
2. In Case 6.3, the judge got drunk.
3. Therefore, from the Christian, Jewish, and Muslim points of view, the judge sinned.

Q6.11. Does the clerk in Case 6.3 have a moral problem that virtue theory might help him solve?

1. In Case 6.3, the clerk has the moral problem of deciding how much loyalty to show the judge.
2. Virtue theory suggests a balance of interests, consequences, rules, and duties.
3. A correct balance of interests, consequences, rules, and duties would promote the clerk's telling on the judge, rather than letting the trial begin.
4. Telling on the judge is the right solution to the clerk's problem.
5. Therefore, virtue theory can help the clerk solve his problem.

Q6.12. In Case 6.3, what would be the most deficient response the clerk could offer? The most extreme?

The most deficient response would be to do nothing. The most extreme response would be to kill the judge. The clerk's proper response is the mean between these two extremes.

Q6.13. Which of the cardinal virtues does the judge appear to lack in Case 6.3?

All four. His act was foolhardy rather than courageous, since he seemed overly confident in his ability to get away with it. His drinking was intemperate. By arriving drunk at the trial, he failed to give the parties to the trial their due, which was unjust. And he exhibited sufficient knowledge about the situation to realize he could undermine the trial, which was imprudent.

Q6.14. In Case 6.3, does the clerk appear to be acting with integrity?

The clerk will have acted unjustly if he doesn't tell on the judge before the trial begins. But the clerk recognizes what needs to be done, so if he follows through, he will have acted with integrity.

Q6.15. In Case 6.3, is the judge lacking any virtues besides the cardinal virtues?
The judge appears to lack respect for the parties to the case, he lacks common sense, and he lacks faithfulness to his position and his profession. Each of these is a lack of virtue.

Q6.16. In Case 6.3, does the judge appear to be a hedonist?
Yes. His primary concern seems to be for his own pleasures. His clerk appears to be acting from duty.

Q6.17. Is there any situation in which the judge's action would have been virtuous in Case 6.3?
Although it is difficult to imagine how the judge's act might be virtuous, it is logically possible that a fair trial depended on his holding the trial at once—to honor the defendant's right to a speedy trial, for example—and that no other judge was available to take the bench. It might also be possible that the judge would be able to hold himself together to the satisfaction of everyone whom the trial affected. Under these circumstances, if the judge had failed to hold the trial he would have been acting deficiently.

Q6.18. In Case 6.1, did the son's fear absolve him of moral responsibility for not stopping at the scene of the accident?
1. When one chooses to drink and drive, one assumes responsibility for the consequences of the drinking and driving.
2. In Case 6.1, the son chose to drink and drive.
3. One consequence of his drinking and driving was his leaving the scene of the accident that he caused.
4. Therefore, the son's fear did not absolve him of moral responsibility for leaving the scene of the accident.

Q6.19. In Case 6.2, Thornton's colleagues disregarded the pages' complaints. Did those colleagues, therefore, cause Thornton's subsequent harassment of the pages and staff?
No, because Thornton was free not to harass anyone.

Q6.20. In Case 6.4, should Hawkins be held responsible for his double dipping when it is not his fault that some of his employees didn't show up?
Yes. First, he chose to moonlight. Second, he chose to hire and thus to rely on the employees who didn't show up. And third, he chose to go to the arena while on police duty. Note: This doesn't let the absent employees off the hook.

Q6.21. In Case 6.4, are the agency's rules against double dipping responsible for Hawkins's doing something wrong?
No. By joining the agency, Hawkins is responsible for choosing to follow the rules of his agency. He should have obeyed those rules and avoided the double dipping. That he did otherwise is not the rules' fault.

Q6.22. In Case 6.4, if the agency had never published or announced its rule against double dipping, would it be wrong for Hawkins to attend to his secondary business while on duty as a police officer?

Yes. Even if the police agency did not promulgate its rule against double dipping, when one is receiving a salary to be doing a certain job at a certain time, one should be professionally devoted to doing that job and no other.

Q6.23. We are inclined to judge Hawkins harshly for his actions in Case 6.4. Is the determinist correct to suggest that we are not free to judge Hawkins differently?

No. Experience and common sense suggest that we may decide to charge him harshly or decline to do so. If this is not true, the heavy burden of proof is on the determinist. It's possible, though, that once we are aware of and understand Case 6.4, we are *forced* to make a judgment—even if the sort of judgment is up to us.

Q6.24. In Case 6.5, would Kelly be morally responsible for the death of the children if he refused to shoot a child and the hostage takers carried out their threat?

No. He does not know that his shooting the child will save the other children, so he is responsible only for shooting the child or not shooting him. If the hostage takers shoot the children, the moral responsibility is theirs, not Kelly's.

Q6.25. In Case 6.5, does Kelly have anyone to blame but himself for getting caught by the hostage taker?

Kelly may have acted irresponsibly by making himself so vulnerable to the hostage taker, but the ultimate wrongdoing is the hostage taker's. He initiated the event, and he could have chosen to do otherwise.

Q6.26. Are the children in Case 6.5 responsible for their predicament?

No. They had good reason not to expect the predicament they are in, so they should not be expected to have foreseen it. The hostage takers are immediately responsible for the predicament, although further investigation might also find fault with school security and police tactics and strategies.

Q6.27. What other choices did Hawkins have in Case 6.4 that would have been better than the choice he made?

Hawkins probably had several better choices. One would have been to have a backup plan in case his employees didn't show up. Another might have been to stay out of the security business in the first place.

Q6.28. In Case 6.4, did Hawkins lie to the dispatcher?

Hawkins lied by omission to the dispatcher. He did not want the dispatcher to know that he was breaking the double-dipping rule, so he managed his language to direct the dispatcher's attention away from that fact.

Q6.29. In Case 6.4, did Hawkins have a duty to honor his contract with the arena?
Yes, but he put himself in a fix by also having a duty to his police agency. Had his employees shown up as scheduled, he would have had no conflict of duty. But as it stands, the conflict of duties was his responsibility.

Q6.30. In Case 6.4, if Hawkins is on the whole a virtuous person, would he keep quiet about his double dipping if no one asked him about it?
No. If he kept quiet about his double dipping, he would be displaying insufficient courage and an intemperate exploitation of the agency's trust and good will. A virtuous person would be more courageous and more temperate by admitting his problem to his superiors and taking the proper hit for it.

Notes

1. Aristotle, *Nicomachean Ethics,* trans. H. Rackham (New York: Putnam, 1926).
2. John Rawls, *A Theory of Justice* (Cambridge, MA: Harvard University Press, 1971).
3. Carol Gilligan, *In a Different Voice* (Cambridge, MA: Harvard University Press, 1982).
4. Lawrence Kohlberg, *The Philosophy of Moral Development* (New York: Harper and Row, 1981).
5. Jean-Paul Sartre, "Existentialism Is a Humanism," trans. Walter Kaufman, reprinted in *Existentialism from Dostoyevsky to Sartre,* ed. Walter Kaufman (New York: Meridian, 1946), pp. 345–68.

PART III

CONSTITUTIONAL ETHICS

CHAPTER 7

LAW

CASE 7.1

The Abortion Clinic

When Colburn became a county judge in 1970, abortion was illegal in her state. As an observant Roman Catholic, Colburn agreed with this law, believing that abortion is the murder of an innocent child.

After the U.S. Supreme Court's 1973 decision in *Roe v. Wade,* an abortion clinic opened in Colburn's jurisdiction. One day abortion protesters surrounded the clinic, verbally haranguing young women entering the building. At the clinic's director's request, Colburn issued a restraining order, prohibiting protesters from coming within 100 feet of the clinic. The order made clear that anyone violating the order would be arrested.

At the end of her workday, Colburn went to the clinic to join the protesters. One of them violated the restraining order by closely following a young woman as she neared the clinic and yelling at her to turn back. Colburn felt that the protester was morally right, but legally wrong.

As an officer of the court, did Judge Colburn do something morally wrong by protesting a legal act? Criminal justice ethics rests on the social contract between criminal justice professionals and the people they protect. Central to this contract is the U.S. Constitution, which every sworn professional promises to protect. As the supreme law of the United States, the Constitution confers civil rights and establishes the American system of justice. Therefore, a criminal justice professional's success entails enforcing the law, respecting people's rights, and promoting justice.

Moral success is virtue—habitually finding and hitting the mean between the extremes in any given case. A virtuous criminal justice professional enforces the law, respects rights, and promotes justice in a way that is neither deficient nor excessive. To uphold slavery law might be excessively legalistic (see Case 3.1, "Huck Finn and Jim"). To protect a son from a DUI conviction may be irresponsibly deficient (see Case 6.1, "The Hit and Run Son"). To exact revenge in the name of justice, without mercy or charity, might be excessively heartless (see Case 5.2, "Billy Budd"). These examples depend on what we mean by *laws, rights,* and *justice.* We use these words ambiguously, and if we don't resolve the ambiguities, then we can't render a fair judgment of the criminal justice professional's success at fulfilling her constitutional duty. To resolve these ambiguities, this chapter and the next two examine laws, rights, and justice, respectively.

Q 7.1

In Case 7.1, is Colburn's participation in the protest a virtuous act for a judge?

American criminal justice professionals promise to protect, defend, and preserve the Constitution of the United States of America. The Constitution defines itself as "the Supreme Law of the Land,"[1] but Americans confuse three different theories of law at the cost of clear thinking about the law's nature and scope. **Natural law theory** holds that some power higher than humans—God or nature—gives us our law. **Legal positivism** holds that human legislatures make law. **Legal realism** holds that judges make law. America's prime examples of each are, respectively, the Declaration of Independence (1776), the U.S. Constitution (1787), and Chief Justice John Marshall's decision in *Marbury v. Madison* (1803).

Q 7.2

Does Colburn's struggle in Case 7.1 appear to involve conflicting views of the law?

✦ NATURAL LAW THEORY

In natural law theory, the oldest of the three, a power higher than humans gives us the law; our task is to discern it, publicize it, and live by it. Its most famous American expression is in the Declaration of Independence:

> We hold these truths to be self-evident, that all men are created equal, that they are endowed by their Creator with certain unalienable Rights, that among these are Life, Liberty and the pursuit of Happiness. —That to secure these rights, Governments are instituted among Men. . . . That whenever any Form of Government becomes destructive of these ends, it is the Right of the People to alter or to abolish it, and to institute new Government.[2]

Writing these words, Thomas Jefferson applied John Locke's (1632–1704) natural law views, but the text also reflects the older, more theological brand of Thomas Aquinas (1225–1274), who put a Christian spin on Aristotle's (384–322 BCE) teleology.

Q 7.3

Could Colburn use the Declaration in defense of her stance against *Roe v. Wade?*

Aristotle agrees that moral principles come from nature. Theologically, he suggests that God is the perfect being toward which every other being strives, but God has no interest in us.[3] Thus, says Aristotle, human interaction with nature and its laws need not go beyond sound science and rational thought.

St. Thomas Aquinas, a Roman Catholic monk, embraced Aristotle's ethics, but more theologically. Whereas Aristotle's God has no interest in human morality, Thomas's God is the first cause of everything, including nature and its moral laws.[4] For Thomas, nature acts according to laws, and God is their legislator; therefore, we can discern God's will by understanding those laws, which we have a duty always to obey.[5] We discern those laws through reason, says Thomas, which supports Aristotle's virtue theory. Thus, Thomas combines Aristotle's teleology, his virtue theory, natural law, and Christianity into one package.

In Thomistic fashion, Judge Colburn in Case 7.1 objects to abortion because of her Roman Catholic upbringing, which promotes a reverence for human life "from conception." With Thomas as its premier philosopher, Roman Catholicism declares that abortion is contrary to natural law because abortion subverts the purpose of pregnancy, which is to produce life. Also, abortion is a vicious, not virtuous, response to the problems that abortion is supposed to solve, because abortion is excessive relative to the alternatives. Adoption, for example, would be a more moderate response, where the mother's health is not at risk.

Thomas combines belief in natural law with the belief that governments are naturally or divinely appointed.[6] If government enacts a law that is contrary to natural law, the human law is "no law at all."[7]

CASE 7.2

The Supportive Rookie

Officer Carlson is a rookie riding in a patrol car with a senior sergeant, Minnelli. They pull over a car for having an expired tag. Minnelli tells Carlson to call in the tag number while Minnelli confronts the driver.

While Carlson is on the radio, he sees Minnelli approach the driver from the driver's side of the car. The rear passenger door on that side of the car flies open, and Minnelli yells "gun." Carlson hears a gunshot from inside the car, and Minnelli begins to fire his gun through the opened door.

Carlson jumps from the squad car, runs to the other car, and begins to fire his gun through the open door. When the shooting stops, a gun-wielding passenger is dead, another gun-wielding passenger is wounded, and the driver has given up without incident.

Based on the investigation into the shooting, Minnelli receives praise for his valor in a clean shooting, and Carlson receives a severe reprimand for not having verified the threat before he started shooting.

Did Carlson get an unfair deal in Case 7.2? A natural law theorist might focus on the natural will to survive and a natural sense of loyalty to one's mentor, allowing Carlson off the hook. Someone more interested in keeping the social order, such as a social contract theorist, might argue that Carlson should have known the rules if he was going to enjoy the rights of a police officer; thus, his punishment was just.

Social contract theorists believe that people create governments by contracting with each other to recognize a sovereign—a monarch, a group of aristocrats, or a democratic body—and to agree to a set of laws. Jefferson says this in the Declaration: "to secure these rights, Governments are instituted among Men, deriving their just powers from the consent of the governed." He takes his cue from Locke and Thomas Hobbes (1588–1679). Hobbes and Locke believe in natural law, but they also believe that people, not nature, create governments, and that governments create law through human legislation. Thus, Hobbes and Locke develop legal theories consistent with legal positivism, but they do so on a foundation of natural law.

> **Q 7.4**
>
> Was Carlson's reaction in Case 7.2 a natural reaction? If so, was it morally right, even if it violated policy?

Social contract theory recognizes three possible social conditions: a state of nature, a state of war, and a political state. A state of nature has no government—it is "every man for himself." Hobbes and Locke disagree on why we move from a state of nature to a political state. For Hobbes, a state of nature is terrible, because in it humans are equal. Humans have equal desires and fears, and there is no law to prevent them from acting on those desires or fears. Without law, individuals in the state of nature have the right to do whatever they can to survive and to seek comfort. Thus, says Hobbes, a state of nature is a state of war in which everyone is the enemy of everyone else and life is "nasty, brutish, and short."[8] But, says Hobbes, human reason and human emotion incline us to form a strong government to keep us from killing each other. Although we have the innate right to do anything we can to survive, exercising that right without restraint will keep us in the state of war, from which fear of death drives us. Reason tells us that there are certain rules we must obey to survive; these rules, says Hobbes, are natural laws.[9]

Q 7.5

In the Hobbesian sense of "war," were the passengers in Case 7.2 in a state of war with Minnelli and Carlson?

Hobbes identifies many such laws, plus a summation. It will be enough here to consider his first three laws of nature and the summation. The first law is to seek peace. The second law is to give up some natural rights in return for a secure environment. There are three ways to give up a right: by renouncing it, by contract, or by covenant. Hobbes does not believe that anyone would simply renounce a right, since nothing is gained in return. In a contract, each party fulfils its promise immediately. For example, in the state of nature I may have exclusive access to fresh water, while you have exclusive access to the meat supply. We might from time to time contract to exchange supplies, with my giving you some water and you immediately giving me an equally valuable selection of meats. In a covenant, one party promises to fulfill his part of the contract in due course. For example, I have given you a barrel of water, and you promise to repay me with several pounds of meat tomorrow.

The third law of nature is that a person keep his covenants. But, warns Hobbes, in a state of war why trust each other to keep a promise? Since each person has the right to do anything he can to survive, I cannot trust you to give me the meat some other time. Nor can I trust you not to kidnap me or kill me at the time of the agreement. Thus, a contract or covenant with only two parties is invalid.[10] The contract needs a third party strong enough to force the other two to keep their promise. The government's primary purpose is to act as this third party.

Q 7.6

How does a rule under which Carlson was punished in Case 7.2 promote the interests of the community?

Hobbes offers a negative version of the Golden Rule as a summation of natural law: "Don't do unto others what you would not want others to do unto you."[11] In a state of nature, which is a state of war, this rule directs us to form a government for protection. In a political state, this rule directs us to obey the government's laws in order to ensure its health and its ability to protect us.

Q 7.7

If you were Minnelli, wouldn't you have wanted Carlson to come to your aid as he did in Case 7.2?

   To form a government, according to Hobbes, is to unite in the state of nature and agree with each other to give up certain rights to a sovereign.[12] As an egoist Hobbes doesn't think that the sovereign exists for us. The best form of government, for Hobbes, is a monarchy, because the king's or queen's personal and public interests are the same. Everyone wants sufficient power to survive and be comfortable. Monarchy offers this power in great abundance, but it depends on the subjects' support, so it is in the monarch's best interest to treat the people well. On the other hand, a member of a large governing body, such as a senate, might have personal interests that conflict with his public duties, so he might leave those duties to the other senators while he tends to his interests. Also, senators with conflicting interests might stymie the progress of government, whereas a monarch cannot "disagree with himself out of spite or envy."[13] In short, says Hobbes, monarchy is the best government because it is the most efficient; but any government is better than none at all, because no social condition is worse than the state of war.

Q 7.8

If in Case 7.2 the sovereign had given the police permission to shoot all suspects on sight, would this have justified Carlson's act?

   There are some problems with Hobbes's theory, beyond the problems with his consequentialism, which Chapter 3 considers. First, are people by nature as evil as Hobbes claims? If no, Hobbes asks, then why lock your doors and guard your possessions?[14] Locke's view of human nature is more optimistic, which entails a different function of government.

   Second, since people in a state of nature distrust each other so much, how could they unite to form a government? If in that state I am called to a convention to pick a sovereign, I have no reason to trust the call—this could be a life-threatening ruse. Hobbes offers no answer. Locke argues that the people are the legitimate government, so there need not be a conflict among their reasons for assembling.[15]

   Third, if government is a social contract that is invalid without a third party strong enough to hold the other two parties to their word, what third party exists to force the sovereign and the subjects to keep their ends of the bargain? In Hobbes's terms this is a trick question, because the sovereign makes no contract with the subjects.[16] The contract is among the subjects only. They agree with each other to recognize the sovereign. The sovereign makes whatever laws and punitive measures it wants;

thus, it is above the law. Hobbes assumes that anyone would want sovereign power, so the subjects do not need to offer extra inducements, and the sovereign's desire to keep its power will be a sufficient check on the sovereign's behavior toward its subjects.

Q 7.9

Since police in some sense enforce the sovereign will, weren't Minnelli and Carlson above the law in Case 7.2?

History and intuition challenge Hobbes's confidence in the sovereign's beneficence. The monarch may lack the wisdom or moral strength to resist the temptations of limitless political power. If human nature is as selfish as Hobbes describes, then won't the sovereign take whatever advantage it can? For Locke, government should operate according to the people's will, and the monarchy that Hobbes promotes becomes a state of war when the sovereign's interests invariably clash with the subjects' interests.[17]

Hobbesian thought appears in America's legislative history, as in the concepts of sovereign immunity (protecting the government from citizens' lawsuits) and eminent domain (allowing a government to take private property without the owner's consent), but Hobbes's greatest influence is indirect. His defense of monarchy prompts Locke to argue for a democratic form of government, a social contract closer to the American ideal.

Jefferson saw Locke as one of the three greatest men in human history (along with Isaac Newton and Francis Bacon).[18] This explains Lockean elements in the Declaration of Independence. The key ideas are that "All men are created equal"; we are endowed by the creator with the "unalienable" rights of "life, liberty, and the pursuit of happiness"; and we have a right to revolt against any government that fails to protect these rights. In Locke's formula, the three rights are to life, liberty, and *property*. Property, for Locke, means ownership of oneself and the fruits of one's labor. American slaveholders would not agree that all people have property rights, hence the substitution of "pursuit of happiness." The next chapter explores the concept of rights, including inalienable rights. In the present chapter, our next step is to consider Locke's concept of property as it anchors his move from natural law theory to legal positivism.

 CASE 7.3

The Pot-Smoking Grandmother

Eighty-six year-old Mabel Murdock has glaucoma. Her doctor believes that smoking marijuana can ease the debilitating pressure of the disease, but he cannot prescribe marijuana because doing so is illegal in their state.

Mabel obtained some marijuana seeds and grew several plants in her back yard, so that she has what she needs to get through the day.

Officer Smith, on her first patrol in Mabel's neighborhood, sees Mabel's plants, recognizes them, knocks on the back door, and identifies herself as a police officer. Neighbors up and down the block come out to see what's going on.

When Mabel confirms Smith's suspicion that the plants are Mabel's, Smith asks her to step outside, where Smith arrests her, handcuffs her, and begins walking her to the patrol car parked a block away. Smith's agency has a rule that officers must handcuff everyone they arrest.

Does the law in Case 7.3 have any moral flaws in it? Hobbes would grant the sovereign the right to make any laws it wishes. Locke would require the sovereign to make laws that represent the will of the people. Thus, Hobbes would have no problem with how Smith handled the case, although Locke might object. Locke agrees with Hobbes that everyone is equal in a state of nature. But Locke does not equate a state of nature with a state of war. God, says Locke, has given humans the property rights of ownership of their persons and the fruits of their labor. God has also given us the natural resources we need; there is enough for everybody. Natural law orders us to protect those rights, both our own and others'. A state of war exists when one violates this law.[19]

Q 7.10

Since, in Case 7.3, Mabel grew and smoked the marijuana only on her own property, did she have the moral right to do so?

Unlike Hobbes, Locke believes that most of us in a state of nature would go about our business without harming others, but two kinds of disputes can arise. First, some people are not content with tending their own gardens and prefer to exploit the efforts of others. Honest people need protection against these dishonest people. Second, two well-meaning people might dispute land ownership. For example, seeing an apparently unclaimed piece of land, I have planted my apple seeds, confident about my right to those apples when they mature. Learning of my planting, you claim to have planted barley in the same location, assuming as I did that the land was unclaimed. The land can't sustain the growth of both crops at the same time—one of us will have to give up his claim on the property, but which one? Whoever came first? How do I know that you came first? Whoever has the more important crop? Whoever has the more convincing proof of ownership? If we cannot resolve this dispute ourselves, then we need a third party who can. Because of these two types of disputes, we need an "umpire" whom we both trust to settle them. Government is this umpire. Legitimate government has no other interest than the protection of natural property rights.[20]

Like Thomas Aquinas, but unlike Hobbes, Locke holds that legitimate man-made law is consistent with natural law. For Hobbes, once people agree to a government, the sovereign may make any laws it wants.

Q 7.11

Suppose the law in Case 7.3 prescribed life in prison for possessing as much marijuana as Mabel had. Would sending Mabel to prison be morally proper, since Mabel lived under the rules of that state?

Like Hobbes, but unlike Thomas Aquinas, Locke believes that governments are man-made. Further, the government exists solely to protect people's rights, and the government should move according to the people's will. Since the people's will can change, the legislature must be able to change, enacting laws appropriate to the time. Thus, while Locke's legal theory is grounded in natural law theory, his defense of the social contract favors legal positivism, to which we turn next.

 CASE 7.4

The Abusive Stepfather

Officer Gunther is lifelong friends with Mack. Mack has been divorced for a few years and has been estranged from his children since his wife won full legal custody, remarried, and made it difficult for Mack to exercise his visitation rights.

Mack tells Gunther that there is good reason to suspect that the stepfather is abusing Mack's children. When Gunther hears the reasons, he agrees that they are compelling but notes that they fall short of probable cause for arrest.

Honoring Mack's plea for help, Gunther notifies the proper social service agencies, each of which tells Gunther that there are too many active cases for agency workers to investigate a purely speculative charge. Gunther's superior agrees.

✦ LEGAL POSITIVISM

In Case 7.4, does Gunther, as a police officer, have any further legal responsibility to help Mack? Legal positivism holds that human legislatures—people in the right *position*—make the law. In contrast with natural law, legal positivism holds that (1) law is man-made, (2) lawmakers can abolish the law, and (3) there is no necessary connection between law and morality.

Q 7.12

Since the law doesn't appear to be helping Mack and Gunther in Case 7.4, does Gunther have a moral duty to take matters into his own hands?

In the United States, legal positivism's most famous exemplar is the Constitution (1787)—the centerpiece of American criminal justice ethics. In contrast to the Declaration of Independence, the Constitution makes no mention of natural law or inalienable rights. In its preamble, the Constitution justifies itself "In order to form a more perfect union." The federal legislature determines the law within the guidelines that the Constitution establishes, and the Constitution allows amendment of those guidelines.[21]

Q 7.13

Does the constitutional right to due process protect the stepfather in Case 7.4 rather than the children?

Two influential legal positivists are John Austin (1790–1859) and H. L. A. Hart (1907–1992). Their views shed light on the concept of legal positivism and the positivist aspects of the Constitution.

Austin argues that positive law, not natural law or positive morality, is the proper subject of jurisprudence. He defines natural law as God's law and as the basis for much of human morality. Positive morality comprises the habits and etiquette that society deems acceptable.[22]

Q 7.14

Is Gunther's legal duty in Case 7.4 contrary to his moral duty?

According to Austin, positive law is a political superior's command to a political inferior—a sovereign to a subject.[23] Commands express desires that others must fulfill.[24] Laws are commands that create general obligations for groups of people, not just a particular command for a particular person. For example, instructions to a babysitter may involve commands, but would not count as laws. On the other hand, a society's prohibition of children under 13 years old from babysitting would count as a law.

For Austin, the law's force is in the punishment that one can expect if one breaks the law. In other words, this punishment *sanctions* the law.[25] The sanction must promise an evil—something the would-be lawbreaker would rather avoid. If the sanction were a reward, Austin argues, then the legislative act would confer a right, not an obligation.[26] For example, U.S. law encourages charity by offering the donor a tax deduction. Legally, one has a right to give to charities, but no one has a duty to do so.

Sovereign and subjects are defined by their relationship to the law. A sovereign makes and enforces law; a subject obeys that law or faces punishment for disobedience. Like Hobbes, Austin believes that this puts the sovereign above the law.[27]

Q 7.15

If the law permitted Gunther, in Case 7.4, to execute on sight the allegedly abusive stepfather, would doing so be morally right, according to Austin?

So far, constitutional law's resemblance to positive law is slight. Both are man-made, rather than derivations from natural law, and both make no claim to morality. In fact, some elements of the Constitution protect *im*morality. The First Amendment protection of speech is necessary only to protect the minority who might utter words offensive to the majority. The amendment does not limit free speech to morally inoffensive speech, nor do many Supreme Court cases about free speech issues.[28] Of the 27 amendments, only the Second Amendment offers anything like a moral justification: "A well regulated Militia, *being necessary to the security of a free State,* the right of the people to keep and bear Arms, shall not be infringed [emphasis added]." And the Preamble to the Bill of Rights sets out the first 10 amendments "in order to prevent misconstruction or abuse of [the Constitution's] powers" and to "extend . . . the ground of public confidence in the Government, [in order to] best ensure the beneficent ends of its institution."

Beyond the view that law is man-made and that law and morality are distinct, Austin's view of law disagrees with the Constitution's in at least three ways. First, under the Constitution the sovereign and the subjects are one: the law's purpose is to allow the union to govern itself. Second, therefore, the sovereign is as obliged as the subject to obey the law. Third, some laws in the Constitution are not commands, contrary to Austin's definition of a positive law. Some constitutional laws, for example, create offices (e.g., Art. 1, sec. 2, which establishes the House of Representatives); establish processes for creating laws (e.g., Art. 1, sec. 7); abolish earlier laws (e.g., Amendment 21, repealing prohibition); or confer rights, without obliging any one person or threatening disobedience with sanctions (e.g., the First Amendment).

Q 7.16

If the stepfather in Case 7.4 is guilty, is he violating the Constitution?

Austin calls this distinction between laws that command and laws that don't command a distinction between perfect laws and "imperfect laws."[29] Any law that we can express as an imperative is a perfect law; any purported law that we cannot express as an imperative is an imperfect law. For example, the Constitution declares that "Each House may determine the Rules of its Proceedings, punish its Members for disorderly Behaviour, and, with the Concurrence of two thirds, expel a Member."[30]

But Austin begs the question, Why must all laws be commands sanctioned by evil? Austin answers with a stipulative definition: because a command not sanctioned by evil is not a law. H. L. A. Hart disagrees and offers a theory of positive law that has more nuances and comes closer to the constitutional ideal.

Hart agrees with Austin that society's laws are man-made and have no necessary connection to morality.[31] But he questions Austin's definition of law as a command from a superior that obliges an inferior under threat of punishment. First, concerning obligation, Hart offers a scenario in which a gunman orders a victim to hand over his money and threatens to shoot him if he disobeys. At the moment, the gunman is superior in force to the victim, who may feel obliged to hand over his money to avoid being killed. But the victim has no *legal* duty or obligation to comply. That the victim feels obliged to comply is a psychological fact; that the gunman has an obligation not to rob the victim is a legal fact.[32] Austin's explanation of law does not permit this distinction.

Q 7.17

Would Hart's distinction between psychology and law help explain Gunther's dilemma in Case 7.4?

Hart also notes the logical possibility of a small, close-knit community operating under a set of rules that functions as law, but does not require a legislative body.[33] Somebody may have created these rules generations ago, but no community members today recall any legislative activity. Still these rules serve as the law of the land, even though no one knows where they came from. Thus, the need for a sovereign, especially a sovereign who is above the law, is less crucial to law than Austin suggests.

Hart acknowledges that legal matters are more complex in larger communities, where it is not enough to obey the rules without being conscious of them or having a legislative body at the ready. To live like the small community is to risk three legal defects.[34] The first defect is *uncertainty* about the existence or meaning of certain alleged laws—hence the need for a system that clears up these uncertainties. Second, the small community's rules are *static* in the absence of a legislative system that responds to the need for legal change. Third, the tacit or subtle rules of the small community are *inefficient* as a means for promoting community well-being. There is no system to deal with alleged violations of the law or to clarify the law. In short, says Hart, the system of primary rules or laws that may be sufficient in small communities needs a system of secondary rules to establish the scope and limits of primary rules.

Q 7.18

What secondary rules exist constitutionally that would invalidate any law that permitted Gunther in Case 7.4 to torture the stepfather into a confession?

Larger communities need three types of secondary rules.[35] First are "rules of recognition" that specify when a rule is a legitimate law. Second are "rules of change" that prescribe criteria and methods for changing the law. Third are "rules of adjudication" that specify who adjudicates legal disputes and violations, and how the judges should adjudicate these cases.

All three types of secondary rules are in the U.S. Constitution, giving it, in Hart's terms, the dual purpose of establishing primary and secondary rules for the Union. The main rule of recognition is the Constitution's claim that it is the supreme law of the land. Article 5, which describes the process for amendments, is the main rule of change, and Article 3, which establishes the judiciary, is the main rule of adjudication. Although there are primary rules in the Constitution, such as the prohibition of treason, which is "levying War against [the United States], or in adhering to their Enemies, giving them Aid and Comfort,"[36] the Constitution is largely a collection of secondary rules.

The two key claims of legal positivism are that government is man-made and that there is no necessary connection between law and morality. History proves the first claim, but the second claim is controversial. If it were true and the Constitution is a positivist document, then there would be no necessary connection between it and morality. Since our task is to think about criminal justice ethics and since the Constitution is the centerpiece of criminal justice's moral responsibility, how can we reconcile the legality of the Constitution with its morality? Two critics of legal positivism's second claim may help here.

Lon Fuller (1902–1978) and Ronald M. Dworkin (1931–) argue that the business of legislation and adjudication is a moral business. Each offers several reasons for this claim, but there are three general reasons.

First, Fuller claims that there is an "internal morality of law," because amoral law would put the society at moral risk.[37] Law should guide government and citizen behavior in a morally good direction, rather than a morally bad direction or no direction at all. Successful law, says Fuller, is inherently moral on this count. For example, good law makes it difficult for immoral judges to hide behind the law. If the law had no moral value, a judge might use "the law is the law" as an excuse to condemn an innocent person unfairly. Or law without moral value might benefit the legislators, but unfairly hurt a minority that has no legislative representation.

Appeal to fairness in the previous two examples leads to the second critical point. As Fuller puts it, Hart's secondary rules—rules governing legislation—are rules of morality that cover both legislation and adjudication. Good law and the adjudication of it should be fair and just, which are moral values. In Dworkin's words, secondary rules reflect principles or policies for making law and adjudicating legal disputes.[38] A policy is "a kind of standard that sets out a goal to be reached, generally an improvement in some economic, political, or social feature."[39] A principle is "a standard that is to be observed, not because it will advance or secure an economic, political, or social situation deemed desirable, but because it is a requirement of justice or fairness or some other dimension of morality."[40] Social desirability, justice, and fairness are moral concerns to which good law is subordinate.

The third critical point against positivism's separation of law and morality emphasizes the moral implications of adjudication, rather than legislation. Fuller notes the positivist's concern that a Roman Catholic judge might be torn between a papal pronouncement against abortion and a legal pronouncement protecting abortion.[41] The positivist would remove from the judge all responsibility for making moral decisions, limiting him to legal ones. Fuller argues that this Roman Catholic judge faces two moral pronouncements: the papal prohibition of abortion and the legal permission of abortion. The judge cannot avoid this dilemma by declaring the legal pronouncement morally neutral.

Agreeing with Fuller, Dworkin emphasizes **judicial discretion.** Legal positivists agree that judges have discretion, but the positivist meaning is that laws don't adjudicate themselves or that judges have the final authority in a judicial proceeding; there is no necessary moral implication.[42] Dworkin argues that judicial discretion means that the judge is "not bound by standards set by the authority in question," and where he is not bound by the rules, he should "act with fairness and justice in mind."[43] Since fairness and justice are moral matters, morality plays a central role in adjudication.

Dworkin offers *Riggs v. Palmer* as an example of his position. This 1889 decision by the Court of Appeals of New York refused to let Elmer Palmer inherit his grandfather's estate, because Elmer had murdered his grandfather in order to hasten the inheritance. Dissenting justices noted, in the spirit of legal positivism, that the law was unambiguous in granting the inheritance to Elmer; but the majority of justices acted, in Dworkin's words, on the moral principle that "No man may profit from his own wrong."[44]

So far this section has (1) identified the Constitution as America's premier example of legal positivism; (2) articulated Austin's and Hart's versions of legal positivism, noting especially the points of agreement between Hart's version and the Constitution; and (3) described Fuller's and Dworkin's criticisms of positivism's view that law has no necessary connection to morality. Positivism is correct that law is man-made, but positivism may be wrong in denying a necessary connection between morality and the law. Fuller and Dworkin make a good case for thinking morally about law and for the moral challenges legislators and adjudicators face, but Fuller and Dworkin have not proved conclusively that a law is illegitimate if it is amoral. In Austin's terms, the force of constitutional law is in the sovereign's ability to enforce it, not in any inherent morality. Two historical examples that support Austin's point are Justice Taney's 1857 *Dred Scott* decision, which declared that African Americans have no constitutional rights, and the U.S. Supreme Court's decision in *Plessy v. Ferguson* (1896), which supported the segregationist policy of "separate but equal." Both decisions were legally binding; neither was morally good, since neither was fair or just. Although these decisions were eventually overturned, we have already noted that the Constitution protects certain types of immorality, such as offensive speech. So is there no necessary connection between constitutional law and morality?

Following Fuller's and Dworkin's lead, we might change the question. Criminal justice professionals must use discretion in their legal work; they are not merely to follow the laws mechanically, contrary to the regularian view of ethics. So what is the criminal justice professional's moral responsibility in relation to the Constitution?

Criminal justice professionals should obey the Constitution, unless there is a morally compelling reason not to. They are professionals because of an oath they took to the Constitution. To fulfill this oath is to enforce the law, promote justice, and protect citizens' rights. Still, as noted above, uncritical obedience to the Constitution could lead to excessive legalism, deficient prevention of wrong, or excessive heartlessness. So virtuous professionals must do more than merely obey the Constitution. There are at least three circumstances in which professionals' moral duty might be at odds with their constitutional duty.

First, criminal justice professionals may have to decide whether to enforce a law that appears to be unconstitutional. Police officers, for example, rarely have to refer directly to the Constitution for professional directions; these come instead through the community's laws, court decisions, and general and special orders. Consider a law in 1955 Montgomery, Alabama, that required Rosa Parks to give up her bus seat to a white person. Ms. Parks refused and was arrested. This law was unfair and unjust, and as courts would eventually decide, unconstitutional. Imagine the problem facing Officers Day and Nixon who were supposed to arrest Ms. Parks, but might see the unconstitutionality of the law.[45] Their first duty is to protect the Constitution, not to enforce the law, even if their superiors and the community don't see it this way, and even if the consequences for themselves are undesirable. In Aristotelian terms, an officer would be using insufficient discretion or excessive force in arresting Ms. Parks. Since this case does not pit the morally good act against the Constitution, but only against laws, orders, or court decisions that someone has incorrectly derived from the Constitution, this isn't the most challenging type of moral problem for the criminal justice professional.

A second and stronger challenge pitting the professionals' constitutional duty against their moral duty is a law that is constitutional on its face but appears to permit an act that the Founding Fathers did not anticipate, as in Case 7.1, "The Abortion Clinic."

A third sort of challenge is an act that the Founding Fathers probably would have protected but that the professional finds immoral. For example, consider the debate over the banning of assault weapons versus a citizen's Second Amendment right.

There is no easy solution to these conflicts. Virtuous criminal justice professionals—those who are courageous, just, temperate, and prudent—will balance their constitutional duties with concern for justice and rights, and may occasionally find that the most moderate alternative is to opt for the latter and hope for understanding, forgiveness, or exoneration.

Three more observations may indicate how virtuous criminal justice professionals could manage conflicts between their constitutional duty and their moral duty.

First, sometimes the professional has to choose between the lesser of two evils—there is no clear mean, but one alternative may be closer to the mean than another alternative. In Case 7.1, for example, Colburn had to choose between protecting a protester at an abortion clinic and having the protester arrested for violating Colburn's restraining order. Neither was an ideal choice for Colburn, but in her professional capacity, having the protester arrested was a less deficient response than not protecting her. And letting the client be verbally assaulted by the protester would have been excessively aggressive.

Second, no criminal justice professional is alone in the justice system. At times, acting constitutionally may seem to be a bad option, but the virtuous choice is to fulfill the duty and hope that the system will set things right. For example, a poor person's theft of food from the unoccupied kitchen of a rich person is a crime for which the arresting officer might feel sympathy. Constitutionally, it would be proper for the officer to arrest the thief and hope that the prosecutor, jury, or judge will exercise proper discretion in going easy on the defendant.

Third, as Martin Luther King, Jr., notes, the justly disobedient must be ready for punishment.[46] When virtuous criminal justice professionals must choose between the constitutional option and the morally right option, the professionals should choose the latter, knowing that the consequences for them may be unpleasant.

In promoting the morality of law, Fuller's and Dworkin's challenge to legal positivism changes the perspective from the legislator to the judge, calling for the judge to interpret the law fairly and justly. Focusing on this perspective invites us to consider legal realism.

✦ LEGAL REALISM

CASE 7.5

A Speeder Gets a Break

Sid is driving on a road where the speed limit changes from 40 mph to 30 mph. Sid missed the change and is stopped by a county police officer for going 42 in a 30-mph zone.

As soon as the officer explains Sid's violation, Sid offers to plead guilty and sign the speeding ticket. But the officer suggests that Sid take the case to court, where the judge is apt to give Sid a break, assuming his driving record is clean otherwise. Sid thinks that the more honest choice would be to take the hit and try to be more observant in the future, but the hit would include not only the fine for speeding but also a large increase in his car insurance premium. To avoid that premium, Sid decides to go to court.

As Sid stands before the judge, waiting for the chance to speak, the judge says "On your behalf, I am entering a plea of not guilty, since you've taken the trouble to come to court, and I'm granting you probation before judgment, since your driving record is clean." Sid has avoided the fine and the increased insurance premium.

The arresting officer, witnessing Sid's trial, feels that justice has been done in his case.

Has justice been done in Case 7.5? The Constitution calls itself the law of the land and requires the legislature to make all law. But that doesn't always happen in practice. Much of American law is the result of judicial decisions. The theory that recognizes this is legal realism—the view that the law is whatever the final judge in the matter says it is.

Q 7.19

In Case 7.5, would Sid have broken a law if the judge found him not guilty of breaking that law?

Legal realism's most famous defense is a 1930 essay by Judge Jerome Frank (1889–1957).[47] Justice Oliver Wendell Holmes (1809–1894) had already endorsed the idea in his essay "The Path of Law."[48] And America first sees legal realism in Justice John Marshall's (1755–1835) decision in *Marbury v. Madison* (1803).

In 1803, William Marbury sued the Jefferson administration for failing to honor John Adams's appointment of Marbury as a justice of the peace in Washington, DC. Marbury had not received the official commission before the end of Adams's presidency, and Jefferson refused to recognize the commission under his new presidency. As Jefferson's secretary of state, James Madison was the defendant in Marbury's suit. The case went before the U.S. Supreme Court, and Justice Marshall rendered the Court's decision. Marshall argued that the Court was the wrong venue for the suit, because the Constitution authorized the Court to hear such suits only on appeal and there had been no earlier case for Marbury to appeal. Historically more important was Marshall's claim, as part of the decision, that the Supreme Court had the right to review any legislative or executive act for its constitutionality. In effect, the Supreme Court would have the final say about the validity of a law. This audacious usurping of legislative power persists to the present. If there was any protest against Marshall's claim, the protest was unsuccessful.

> ### Q 7.20
>
> In Case 7.5, did the judge's decision make the speeding law invalid as it applied to Sid?

In 1897, Oliver Wendell Holmes defended legal realism, without calling it that, in his argument that all law is merely a prediction of what the judge will decide. Until that decision, the law is not settled.

> ### Q 7.21
>
> If the officer in Case 7.5 believed that the judge would cut Sid a break, what legal value is there to giving Sid a ticket?

In 1930, Jerome Frank firmly established legal realism with his fictional case of the Blue & Gray Taxi Cab Company. The company is unhappy with its state's decision in a lawsuit that the company has filed against another cab company and the railroad. Blue & Gray's lawyer suggests that the company re-incorporate in another state and re-sue the organizations, so that the case may come before a federal court. The federal court's decision is favorable to the company. The law in the first suit—the decision of the state court—has been overturned by the law in the second suit—the decision of the federal court—without any legislative involvement.

The consequences of legal realism for virtuous criminal justice professionals are profound. Professionals promise to uphold the law under the Constitution, but their efforts are for naught if a judge's decision ignores or abrogates the law. For example, decisions such as the *Dred Scott* case and *Plessy v. Ferguson* affirmed the legality of segregation, which in practice obliged police to uphold those laws, even though the Court would eventually admit that all segregation laws were unconstitutional. An officer whose moral insight was ahead of his time would be stuck between the judicial law and constitutional law, with community practice favoring the former.

Today the debate in the United States between the legal positivists and the legal realists presents itself as a debate between **strict constructionists** and **judicial activists.** The former argue that judicial decisions should rest on the intent of the framers of the Constitution and that their intent came from absolute and thus unchangeable values. The latter argue that the Constitution is a living document that judges must interpret in the context of contemporary values and that the framers intended the Constitution to be adaptable to change. There is a distinct absence of Aristotelian moderation in this debate. To limit all judicial decisions to the values of 1787 (as if all framers espoused the same values!) is excessively dogmatic. To render the Constitution irrelevant in the face of judicial decision making is deficiently respectful of the Constitution as the law of the land.

The mean between these extremes lies in the constitutional amendment process prescribed in the Constitution.[49] As an antidote to irrational dogmatism, the Constitution allows for all but one proposal for change: Congress may not consider a proposal to deprive a state of its representation in Congress. Congress may consider any other amendment to the Constitution, including a dismantling of the Constitution itself, and if two-thirds of Congress and three-fourths of the states ratify the amendment, it becomes law.

For people in a hurry to change the law, the amendment process is long and cumbersome. Some 10,000 amendments have come before Congress; Congress has approved only 33 of them; and the states have ratified only 27 of them, with the 27th taking more than 200 years to ratify![50]

If consequences were all that mattered, we might be glad that at times that the Court has made law, thus circumventing the amendment process. For example, the Supreme Court's decision in *Brown v. Board of Education* (1954) set the civil rights movement on the proper track, which might not have happened if the matter were put to Congress as a proposed amendment. But this cuts both ways; for example, *Brown v. Board* was necessary to undo the injustice of earlier Court decisions, including *Dred Scott* and *Plessy v. Ferguson*. Considering only consequences, while ignoring constitutional law, would be excessively narrow-minded.

If rules were all that mattered, then the virtuous criminal justice professional's duty would be to obey the most recent rule governing the decision. But this would subordinate criminal justice ethics to judicial whim and leave other criminal justice professionals with insufficient discretion and responsibility for their decisions.

If duty were all that mattered, then virtuous criminal justice professionals could simply ignore constitutional and judicial dictates to the extent that they determined it was their duty to do so. This extreme reliance on individual discretion could lead to anarchy in the profession.

As we have been saying all along, the virtuous criminal justice professional should obey the Constitution, unless there is a more moderate alternative in a given case. Unfortunately, the criminal justice professional cannot always rely on the courts to interpret constitutional law correctly, or on the community to operate on the Constitution's dictates rather than the Court's command. Fortunately, the criminal justice professional is also a private citizen and in that capacity may work to promote fair and just law.

Summary

Recognizing the constitutional duty of the criminal justice professional to enforce the law, promote justice, and protect rights, this chapter has discussed the three basic theories of law in America—natural law theory, legal positivism, and legal realism. These theories collectively explain why the term *law* can be ambiguous in American debate, which is why this chapter has also identified implications of this ambiguity for criminal justice ethics. The next chapter looks at the variety of American views about rights.

ANSWERS TO CASE STUDY QUESTIONS

Q7.1. In Case 7.1, is Colburn's participation in the protest a virtuous act for a judge?

1. A virtuous response is neither deficient nor excessive relative to the situation.
2. Case 7.1 offers no indication that Colburn acted deficiently or excessively in joining the protest.
3. Therefore, Colburn's participation is virtuous.

Q7.2. Does Colburn's struggle in Case 7.1 appear to involve conflicting views of the law?

1. Colburn's disapproval of abortion stems from her natural law beliefs.
2. Colburn's sense of professional duty stems from her positive law beliefs.
3. Colburn struggles with the conflict between her moral disapproval and her professional sense of duty.
4. Therefore, Colburn's struggle in Case 7.1 involves conflicting views of law.

Q7.3. Could Colburn use the Declaration in defense of her stance against *Roe v. Wade*?

1. If Colburn can use the Declaration in a legal defense of her stance against *Roe v. Wade*, then the Declaration must carry sufficient legal weight in court.
2. The Declaration has no legal weight, because it contains no laws and predates the U.S. Constitution by 11 years.
3. Therefore, Colburn cannot use the Declaration in a legal defense of her stance against *Roe v. Wade*.

Note that Colburn wishes to defend her stance on moral rather than legal grounds. If there is an inalienable right to life, as the Declaration insists, then Colburn might invoke this to make her moral argument.

Q7.4. Was Carlson's reaction in Case 7.2 a natural reaction? If so, was it morally right, even if it violated policy?

In Case 7.2, Carlson's reaction may have been a natural and understandable one. But it clearly violated morally reasonable department policy.
Objection: It's possible that the first Carlson knew of this policy was after the traffic stop.
Response: In this case, ignorance is no excuse.

Q7.5. In the Hobbesian sense of "war," were the passengers in Case 7.2 in a state of war with Minnelli and Carlson?

The passengers in Case 7.2 were in a Hobbesian state of war with Minnelli and Carlson, because Minnelli and Carlson represented the sovereign authority of the community and the passengers refused to recognize that authority.

Q7.6. How does a rule under which Carlson was punished in Case 7.2 promote the interests of the community?

In Case 7.2, the rule under which Carlson was punished protects the community by requiring an officer to establish just cause for using deadly force.

Q7.7. If you were Minnelli, wouldn't you have wanted Carlson to come to your aid as he did in Case 7.2?

In Case 7.2, it is easy to imagine Minnelli's wishing and being grateful for Carlson's coming to the rescue. But Minnelli's wish or gratitude is irrelevant to Carlson's legal duty. Since his duty is not unreasonable in this case, it appears that he had a moral duty as well not to shoot before verifying the threat.

Objection: It is unreasonable to oblige someone in Carlson's position to determine so immediate a threat before defending his partner.

Q7.8. If in Case 7.2 the sovereign had given the police permission to shoot all suspects on sight, would this have justified Carlson's act?

If in Case 7.2 the sovereign was either the legislator or had legislative authority to grant police permission to shoot all suspects on sight, then Carlson's act would be legally justified. This would not necessarily make it morally justified, however.

Q7.9. Since police in some sense enforce the sovereign will, weren't Minnelli and Carlson above the law in Case 7.2?

Case 7.2 assumes that the officers were in the United States. If so, then they are governed by the U.S. Constitution, which puts no one above the law.

Q7.10. Since, in Case 7.3, Mabel grew and smoked the marijuana only on her own property, did she have the moral right to do so?

1. A moral right to break a law requires the law to be unjust or the moral cause to be greater than blind obedience to the law (e.g., taking a severely injured person to a hospital and not waiting for a red light to change to green).
2. In Case 7.3, the law forbidding Mabel from growing marijuana does not appear to be an unjust law.
3. In Case 7.3, Mabel's cause does not appear to be morally stronger than her duty to obey the law.
4. Therefore, the moral burden of proof is on Mabel.

Q7.11. Suppose the law in Case 7.3 prescribed life in prison for possessing as much marijuana as Mabel had. Would sending Mabel to prison be morally proper, since Mabel lived under the rules of that state?

In Case 7.3, a life sentence for Mabel's illegal act would be an excessive response and thus a vicious one.

Q7.12. Since the law doesn't appear to be helping Mack and Gunther in Case 7.4, does Gunther have a moral duty to take matters into his own hands?

In Case 7.4, there may be legal ways for Gunther to pursue a remedy privately. Thus, the law's failure to help Mack and Gunther does not necessarily morally oblige Gunther to take matters into his own hands.

Q7.13. Does the constitutional right to due process protect the stepfather in Case 7.4 rather than the children?

If the stepfather is guilty, the right to due process appears to be of greater advantage to the stepfather than to the children since the children are in no legal trouble.

Q7.14. Is Gunther's legal duty in Case 7.4 contrary to his moral duty?

1. In Case 7.4, Gunther has a moral duty to help Mack and Mack's kids.
2. In Case 7.4, Gunther's legal duties appear to prevent his helping Mack and Mack's kids.
3. Therefore, Gunther's legal duty appears to be contrary to his moral duty.

Q7.15. If the law permitted Gunther, in Case 7.4, to execute on sight the allegedly abusive stepfather, would doing so be morally right, according to Austin?

According to Austin, the legal right to shoot the stepfather on sight would not necessarily give Gunther the moral right to do so since Austin argues that a valid law does not have to be morally good.

Q7.16. If the stepfather in Case 7.4 is guilty, is he violating the Constitution?

Technically, individuals who do not represent a government agency can violate only the 13th Amendment (against slavery) or the 21st Amendment (by transporting alcohol illegally across state lines). So the stepfather in Case 7.4 would not be violating the Constitution. It would be easy, though, to show that the stepfather is breaking the law, which we presume to be sanctioned by the Constitution.

Q7.17. Would Hart's distinction between psychology and law help explain Gunther's dilemma in Case 7.4?

Hart's distinction between psychology and law would enable us to see that Gunther's predicament in Case 7.4 is not a legal dilemma, because the law is clear on the matter. Rather, his psychological state clashes with his legal responsibility. This is not, strictly speaking, a dilemma, but a difficult choice—to go "with his gut" or to obey the law.

Q7.18. What secondary rules exist constitutionally that would invalidate any law that permitted Gunther in Case 7.4 to torture the stepfather into a confession?

The Constitution guarantees due process to a suspect and allows him not to incriminate himself. These secondary rules would constitutionally invalidate any law that permitted Gunther in Case 7.4 to torture the stepfather into a confession.

Q7.19. In Case 7.5, would Sid have broken a law if the judge found him not guilty of breaking that law?

Legally, someone who is not proven guilty is presumed innocent. Therefore, in Case 7.5, Sid would not have broken the law if the judge found him not guilty.

Q7.20. In Case 7.5, did the judge's decision make the speeding law invalid as it applied to Sid?

In Case 7.5, the judge's decision did not invalidate the speeding law as it applies to Sid; Sid is still legally bound not to speed again.

Q7.21. If the officer in Case 7.5 believed that the judge would cut Sid a break, what legal value is there to giving Sid a ticket?

In Case 7.5, the officer was bound to respond properly if he believed that Sid was speeding. Leaving the punishment up to the judge was the right separation of professional responsibilities.

Notes

1. Art. 6, clause 2.
2. From Jefferson's autobiography. Reprinted in *Social and Political Philosophy: Readings from Plato to Gandhi,* ed. John Somerville and Ronald E. Santoni (Garden City, NY: Doubleday, 1963), pp. 239–45.
3. Aristotle, *Metaphysics,* trans. G. Cyril Armstrong (Cambridge, MA: Harvard University Press, 1935), 1072a21–1073a12.
4. *Summa Theologica,* Question 2, Article 3, trans. Fathers of the Dominican Province (London: Burns Oates & Washbourne, 1920), vol. 1, pp. 24–6.
5. Ibid., I, ii, Q. 91, art. 1.
6. Ibid., I, Q. 103–119. Cf. Romans 13.
7. Ibid., I, ii, Q. 91, art. 1; Cf. Martin Luther King, Jr., "Letter from Birmingham Jail," in *Why We Can't Wait* (New York: Signet, 1963).
8. *Leviathan* (1651), Ch. 13. Many editions available.
9. Ibid., Ch. 14.
10. Ibid.
11. Ibid., Ch. 15.
12. Ibid., Ch. 17.
13. Ibid., Ch. 19.
14. Ibid., Ch. 13.
15. *Second Treatise of Government* (1690), Ch. 9. Many editions available.
16. *Leviathan,* Chs. 17 and 26.
17. *Second Treatise of Government,* Ch. 3.
18. Fawn McKay Brodie, *Thomas Jefferson: An Intimate History* (New York: Norton, 1998), p. 98.
19. *Second Treatise of Government,* Chs. 2 and 3.
20. *Second Treatise of Government,* Ch. 9.
21. Art. 5
22. John Austin, *The Province of Jurisprudence Determined* (1832), Lecture 1. Selections from Lectures 1 and 6 reprinted in *Philosophy of Law,* 6th ed., ed. Joel Feinberg and Jules Coleman (Belmont, CA: Wadsworth, 2000), pp. 33–44.
23. Ibid.
24. Ibid.
25. Ibid.
26. Ibid.
27. Ibid., Lecture 6.
28. *Cohen v. California,* 1971, for example, recognized Paul Robert Cohen's right to wear publicly a jacket that says "Fuck the draft."
29. Austin, Lecture 1.
30. Art. 1, sec. 5, clause 2.
31. H. L. A. Hart "Positivism and Separation of Morals," *Harvard Law Review* 71 (1958). Reprinted in Feinberg and Coleman, pp. 59–75.
32. H. L. A. Hart, *The Concept of Law* (Oxford, UK: Oxford University Press, 1961). Selection reprinted in Feinberg and Coleman, pp. 45–59.
33. Ibid.
34. Ibid.
35. Ibid.

36. Art. 3, sec. 3.
37. Lon Fuller, "Positivism and Fidelity to Law: A Reply to Professor Hart," *Harvard Law Review* 71 (1958). Reprinted in Feinberg and Coleman, pp. 76–90.
38. Ronald M. Dworkin, "The Model of Rules," *University of Chicago Law Review* 14 (1967). Reprinted in Feinberg and Coleman, pp. 130–47.
39. Ibid.
40. Ibid.
41. Fuller, "Positivism and Fidelity to Law."
42. Dworkin, "The Model of Rules."
43. Ibid.
44. Ibid.
45. Their comment to Ms. Parks was simply "the law is the law." http://www.black-collegian.com/african/rosaparks.shtml
46. "Letter from Birmingham Jail," in *Why We Can't Wait* (New York: Signet, 1963).
47. "Legal Realism," in *Law and the Modern Mind* (New York: Brentano's, 1930), pp. 46–52. Reprinted in Feinberg and Coleman, 7th ed., pp. 125–7.
48. *Harvard Law Review* 10 (1897), pp. 457–68. Reprinted in Feinberg and Coleman, 7th ed., pp. 120–24.
49. Art. 5.
50. Jerome Agel and Mort Greenberg, *The U. S. Constitution for Everyone* (New York: Penguin, 1987), p. 64.

CHAPTER 8

RIGHTS

CASE 8.1

The Handcuffed Candidate[1]

On July 27, 2003, Officer Kenneth Lane arrested Baltimore mayoral candidate Andrey Bundley for "failing to obey a lawful order, placing advertising on vehicles without the owners' permission and placing prohibited circulars." Bundley had been placing campaign handbills on car windshields in a city parking lot, touting his experience as a high school principal. Bundley was challenging Baltimore Mayor Martin O'Malley in the Democratic primary, arguing that O'Malley hadn't done enough for the public schools. Lane put Bundley in handcuffs until a police sergeant released him without charges.

According to Bundley, he had placed a couple of handbills on windshields when he heard Lane shout "Stop that!" When Bundley replied, "Stop what?" and continued to place handbills on windshields, he was cuffed without any initial explanation. Once the handcuffs were on, Lane told Bundley of his offenses and gave Bundley "a one-page letter under the letterhead of the city's Office of Promotion & The Arts stating that organizers of the farmers' market held [in the parking lot] Sunday mornings were having problems with trash and cars left overnight on the lot by . . . patrons [of a nearby nightclub]."

In response to Bundley's complaint about "aggressive policing," Baltimore Police Commissioner Kevin Clark defended the officer, citing Article 19, Section 1-3, as the city ordinance relevant to Bundley's arrest.

Political consultant Arthur Murphy claimed that he had never seen an arrest in Baltimore for violating this ordinance, and he had been practicing in the city since 1979. But "the city's public works department recently issued 79 civil citations—carrying at least a $100 penalty each—to Bundley's campaign for illegally placing campaign signs on utility poles and public property." At the same time, "City workers have cited O'Malley's campaign twice for illegal campaign signs, leading Bundley to complain that he was being unfairly targeted—a charge denied by the public works department." City councilman Kieffer Mitchell defended Bundley on the grounds that all city elected officials have violated the ordinance without being arrested. Bundley's campaign strategist, Julius Henson, claimed, "Being black in America is the only thing he did wrong." O'Malley is white. Commissioner Clark, also an African American, denied that Officer Lane was discriminating against anybody.

Did Officer Lane show a disregard for Bundley's rights in Case 8.1? A criminal justice professional's moral success entails enforcing the law, respecting people's rights, and promoting justice in ways that make the community feel safe and secure. The previous chapter discussed the law, this chapter discusses rights, and the next chapter discusses justice.

A **right,** for our purpose, is the freedom to do something or refrain from doing something. For example, the *Miranda* warning tells arrested people of their right to counsel; they have no obligation to seek counsel. This contrasts with a duty, responsibility, or obligation to do something or refrain from doing something. If people come to trial and testify, they have the obligation to tell the truth—they have no right to perjure themselves.

Q 8.1

In Case 8.1, did Officer Lane violate Bundley's First Amendment right to free speech?

➔ FREEDOMS AND INTERESTS

American moral discourse makes much of rights, but the concept is ambiguous. This chapter has sidestepped one ambiguity by limiting the meaning of *rights* to "freedoms." Some people might use the term to mean "interests" instead. Ethicist Peter Singer, for example, holds that because animals can suffer, they have an interest in not suffering, and thus have the right not to suffer.[2] It would be odd to interpret this as meaning that the animal has a *freedom* not to suffer. Limiting ourselves to rights as freedoms, however, will be sufficient for exploring the virtuous criminal justice professional's duty to respect rights.

Q 8.2

In Case 8.1, does Mitchell's "everybody does it" defense of Bundley prove Bundley's right to distribute the fliers?

There are three other types of ambiguities to consider in this chapter: inalienable rights versus conferred rights; positive rights versus negative rights; and legal rights versus moral rights. This consideration will yield at least eight different meanings of *rights,* as we shall see.

➔ INALIENABLE RIGHTS VERSUS CONFERRED RIGHTS

An **inalienable right** is one that no one can take away or give away. The Declaration of Independence lists three; the U.S. Constitution lists none. The Declaration accepts as self-evident that "the Creator" has endowed us with the "unalienable" rights of life, liberty, and the pursuit of happiness, but this notion of inalienability has problems. First, if one does not believe in a divine creator, then one denies a fundamental premise of the Declaration. Even if one believes in a creator, one would find it hard to prove that the creator has endowed humans with these inalienable rights. The Declaration avoids proof by declaring this endowment to be self-evident, but Jews, Christians, and Muslims, for example, will not find anything in their sacred texts that suggests God has given us these rights as inalienable. So it is not self-evidently true that "the Creator" has endowed us with inalienable rights.

Q 8.3

In Case 8.1, does Article 19, Section 1-3, of the municipal code appear to violate Bundley's inalienable right to liberty?

What's more, these rights appear self-evidently *not* to be inalienable. For example, police officers appear able to revoke a citizen's right to life, to liberty, and to the pursuit of happiness. If in a justified shooting an officer kills a perpetrator, hasn't the officer alienated the person's *right to life?* It would be a contradiction to object that the person's right was inalienable, even though the officer took it away—that is, alienated it. It would be dogmatic to object that the person retained the right even though he lost his life. And it would be of no help to argue that the right to life is an interest, which no one can take away, rather than a freedom, since the perpetrator in our case appears to have renounced that interest by acting so recklessly.

The *right to liberty* faces the same challenge. Doesn't any lawful arrest of somebody remove that person's right to liberty? Or does the person lose the liberty, but retain the right? If the person retains the right, what value is there to a right that the person cannot exercise?

The *right to pursue happiness* is even vaguer. What if someone's pursuit of happiness interferes with another's? And what if this interference is illegal or immoral? A person might consider himself happy only when shooting at passing motorists. The motorists might deem essential to their happiness driving without being targets of a sniper. The sniper and the drivers cannot pursue their happiness at the same time, so their right to do so appears not to be inalienable. Moreover, the officer who prevented the sniper from shooting would be acting legally and morally.

Q 8.4

In Case 8.1, who has the greater claim to the right to pursue happiness—Bundley, the organizers of the farmers' market, or neither?

So much for inalienable rights. Now consider the alternative: **conferred rights.** A conferred right is one that somebody with sufficient authority confers on another.

If this authority rescinds the right or the authority loses its ability to confer that right, then that right no longer exists. All constitutional rights and court-decided rights are conferred and thus may be taken away. The Second Amendment, for example, confers the right to bear arms, but the U.S. government and citizenry could rescind this right through another amendment. The U.S. Supreme Court case *Roe v. Wade* (1973) confers on women the right to an abortion, but the Court has the power to overturn that decision.

✦ POSITIVE RIGHTS VERSUS NEGATIVE RIGHTS

CASE 8.2

The Warrant That Wasn't

Officers Tong and Kelly show up to search a house for drugs, believing in good faith that a warrant is en route. The homeowner is not the suspect, but she agrees to let the officers in once they convince her that they will have the warrant in short order.

After a quick search, the officers find the drugs, call the district attorney responsible for the warrant, and learn from her that there will be no warrant. When she spoke to the officers earlier, she was confident that the judge would sign the warrant, but he refused.

The officers explain this to the homeowner, who declares that she would not have let the officers in if there was no warrant. She promises to use any legal means necessary to prevent the drugs from making it to court as evidence.

Case 8.2 offers a chance to consider another distinction about rights. In addition to classifying rights as inalienable or conferred, we may classify them as positive or negative. Isaiah Berlin makes this distinction in his essay "Two Concepts of Liberty."[3] A person has a **positive right** when someone else has a duty to help him exercise that right. If you and I enter into a legally binding contract for you to buy my house, your legal right to my house is directly connected to my duty to give you that house within the specified time, provided that you fulfill your part of the contract. In other words, you have a positive right to my house, and you can legally force me to help you exercise that right.

Q 8.5

Is the Fourth Amendment right not be subjected to unreasonable search or seizure, as it applies to Case 8.2, a positive right?

A person has a **negative right** to the extent that no one else may interfere with the exercise of that right. In Berlin's terms, these are liberties *from* coercion that interfere with the opportunity to exercise the right. Assume that in certain circumstances I have a right to brush my teeth. When I do have this right, no one may interfere with my brushing my teeth, but this does not oblige anyone to give me a tooth brushing.

Q 8.6

If the officers in Case 8.2 had a warrant, would their right to search the house be a positive right or a negative right? Would it be conferred or inalienable?

The rights that the Declaration of Independence enumerates appear to be negative. No one may interfere with my right to life, liberty, or the pursuit of happiness, but no one has to help me live, help me retain liberty, or help me pursue happiness. The Declaration does claim that government has an obligation to protect these rights, but only in the sense of preventing others from interfering with them.

Court-conferred rights may be positive or negative. *Roe v. Wade* does not oblige anyone to give a woman an abortion "on demand." It only prevents anyone from interfering with the woman if she seeks an abortion through the 24th week of her pregnancy. No doctor in the country will violate a woman's negative right to an abortion if that doctor refuses to give the woman an abortion; thus, the right to an abortion is a negative right. On the other hand, *Miranda v. Arizona* (1966), in conferring on an arrested person a right to counsel, obliges the police agency to provide counsel if the person cannot afford one otherwise. Thus, an accused person's right under *Miranda* is a positive right.

The Constitution also confers both negative and positive rights. For example, the First Amendment right to exercise one's religion is negative: government may not interfere with it, but government need not and cannot take steps toward establishing religion. On the other hand, the Sixth Amendment right to face one's accuser in court is a positive right. It obliges the prosecution to make the accuser available for public examination by the accused.

Q 8.7

For each right that the Bill of Rights enumerates, decide whether it is mainly a positive right or a negative right. Explain your answer. Note that in some cases the answer may be both, depending on the government's role in protecting that right.

Amendment I

- To establish a religion
- To exercise a religion
- To speak

- To establish a press
- To operate a press
- To assemble "peaceably"
- To "petition the government for a redress of grievances"

Amendment II

- To keep arms
- To bear arms

Amendment III

- To deny a soldier "quartering" in one's house during times of peace
- To deny a soldier quartering in one's house during times of war, except "in a manner prescribed by law"

Amendment IV

- From unreasonable search and seizure of one's
  - Person
  - House
  - Papers
  - Effects
- To require from a government official a warrant
  - Showing probable cause
  - Supported by oath or affirmation
  - Describing the particular
    - Place to be searched
    - Person or thing to be seized

Amendment V

- From trial for a capital "or otherwise infamous crime" without "presentment or indictment of a grand jury"
  - Except if one is in the military "when in actual service in time of war or public danger"
- From double jeopardy
- From self-incrimination
- To due process of law
- From having "private property be taken for public use, without just compensation"

Amendment VI

- "To a speedy and public trial"
- To a trial by a jury that is
  - "Impartial"
  - From "the state and district wherein the crime shall have been committed"

- "To be informed of the nature and cause of the accusation"
- To be confronted with the witnesses against you
- "To have a compulsory process for obtaining witnesses in [your] favor"
- "To have assistance of counsel for [your] defense"

Amendment VII

- To trial by jury in civil suits exceeding twenty dollars
- From appeal of a jury decision, except "according to the rules of the common law"

Amendment VIII

- From excessive bail
- From excessive fines
- From cruel and unusual punishment

Amendment IX

- To exercise rights other than those the Constitution enumerates

Amendment X

- (For states and individuals) to exercise "powers not delegated to the United States by the Constitution, nor prohibited by it"

✦ LEGAL RIGHTS VERSUS MORAL RIGHTS

CASE 8.3

"Coke Can!"

Police bearing a warrant legally enter a house looking for a suspect. A resident claims that the suspect is in the back bedroom. When the police enter the dimly lit bedroom, a figure lying in bed screams "Get out of here!" and kicks off his covers, revealing a metallic object in his hand. Thinking it is a gun, the officers shoot and kill the man. It turns out that there were two back bedrooms, the officers entered the wrong one, and the person they shot was not the suspect. The metallic object was a soda can.

After a proper and thorough investigation of the incident, the officers received no penalties for the shooting.

Did the officers in Case 8.3 violate any rights? A right is either inalienable or conferred, and it is either positive or negative. It may also be legal or moral. Although the Supreme Court has declared that women have a legal right to abortion, there is disagreement about a woman's moral right to abortion. In other words, although abortion is legal, it may not be moral. The First Amendment confers the negative right to free speech, including speech that might be morally offensive. In Case 8.3, one might argue that what the officers did was legally permissible, even though it was morally wrong in that it caused the death of an innocent man.

✦ The Multiple Meanings of Rights

Because of the ambiguities of the word *rights,* there are at least eight logically possible meanings, when we regard rights as freedoms rather than interests:

1. *Inalienable, positive, and legal.* On natural law theory, one might argue that we have an innate duty to help people in certain life-threatening circumstances. If so, such people would have an inalienable, positive, and legal right to assistance. The Declaration of Independence suggests no such right, and the Constitution and the Courts confer no inalienable rights at all.
2. *Inalienable, positive, and moral.* One might also argue that the right identified in #1 is moral, especially to the extent that what is legal under natural law is also moral.
3. *Inalienable, negative, and legal.* According to the Declaration of Independence, the rights to life, liberty, and the pursuit of happiness are inalienable, legally binding, and, by implication, negative.
4. *Inalienable, negative, and moral.* Since the Declaration is a natural law document, what it regards as legally binding is also morally binding.
5. *Conferred, positive, and legal.* The right to counsel that the *Miranda* warning articulates is conferred, positive, and legal.
6. *Conferred, positive, and moral.* Strictly speaking, neither the Constitution nor the courts confer rights that are explicitly moral. But one might argue, for example, that the Americans with Disability Act confers on the disabled the right to reasonable accommodations because of their moral value.
7. *Conferred, negative, and legal.* As noted previously, the First Amendment right to freedom of religion is at once conferred, negative, and legal.
8. *Conferred, negative, and moral.* Perhaps sexual harassment laws, which are clearly conferred and for the most part negative, also confer the moral right of someone not to be harassed.

These eight types refer to rights as freedoms. But they could also refer to rights as interests. Thus, there are at least 16 possible meanings of *rights.*

What does all of this mean for the virtuous criminal justice professional? The professional has a duty to protect rights, but which rights? And whose rights? Not the rights that the Declaration of Independence enumerates. The American colonies broke away from England because King George III failed to respect or protect the "unalienable" rights of life, liberty, and the pursuit of happiness. But a criminal justice professional's duty frequently requires him or her to alienate these rights when apprehending a suspect. Moreover, criminal justice professionals do not swear an oath to the Declaration; they swear an oath to the U.S. Constitution, which enumerates no inalienable rights. From a strictly professional point of view, therefore, the criminal justice professional is not concerned with the first four types of rights in our list of eight possible types. Also, as a document of positive law, the U.S. Constitution confers legal rights, but not necessarily moral rights. So from a strictly professional point of view, the criminal justice professional is not concerned with the sixth or eighth type of right. This leaves the fifth and seventh types—both conferred and legal, one positive and the other negative.

✦ CHALLENGES FOR CRIMINAL JUSTICE PROFESSIONALS

In spite of their obvious duty to respect rights, virtuous criminal justice professionals face at least three challenges concerning this duty. First, rights may legally conflict, and the professional will have to choose which to honor and which to violate. For example, what if a court decision obliges an officer to act in ways that he or she deems unconstitutional? The officer has taken an oath to the Constitution, not to the courts. Justice Taney's *Dred Scot* decision (1857) held that African Americans have no constitutional rights. An astute officer who has read and understood the Constitution might see the logical flaws in the decision and feel duty-bound to protect a black person's rights anyway. Or detaining a suspect in violation of his Sixth Amendment rights to a speedy trial and to know the charges against him might be necessary to prevent harm to others. At present, this issue underscores debate about the detention of terrorist suspects at Guantanamo Bay, Cuba, and about the value of torture.

Second, legal rights and moral rights may conflict, forcing the criminal justice professional to choose one at the expense of the other. If the professional played only one role in the community, the choice would be obvious: protect the legal right. But these professionals wear other community hats; they are members of the human race, citizens, and colleagues. These relationships impose duties that go beyond respecting constitutional rights. The *Dred Scot* case, which exemplifies conflicting decisions about legal rights, also exemplifies the possible conflict between a legal right and a moral right. One might argue that in 1857 a person had a *legal* right not to treat a certain group—African Americans—as persons, even though these persons had the *moral* right to be treated as equals of other groups of persons, including European Americans.

Third, the virtuous human, citizen, and colleague may face a conflict of moral rights and have to choose one at the expense of the other. Whether the rights to life, liberty, and the pursuit of happiness are inalienable, they certainly are desirable, all else being equal. Thus, one should honor them, unless there is a compelling reason not to. For the virtuous criminal professional, a compelling reason would be that in a given circumstance, respecting the right is a deficient or excessive response when compared with abolishing that right. We have already seen the example of a justified shooting: Although it deprives the deceased of his right to life, liberty, and the pursuit of happiness, this deprivation is necessary to protect the rights of the innocent.

Criminal justice professionals have a duty to respect rights, but which rights? Because the concept of rights is so ambiguous, there is no easy answer. Virtuous professionals, however, will habitually respond to the challenge with courage, temperance, justice, and prudence, among other virtues, seeing to it that the choices they make are the most moderate for the given situation.

Q 8.8

Is there any conflict of rights in Case 8.3?

SUMMARY

A criminal justice professional's constitutional duties include enforcing laws, respecting rights, and promoting justice. This chapter has explored the challenges of respecting rights. One challenge comes from the ambiguous meaning of *rights*. Rights may be inalienable or conferred, positive or negative, legal or moral, and freedoms or interests.

Another challenge comes from conflicting rights. A legal right and a moral right may conflict, for example, forcing the criminal justice professional to decide which right to protect.

The concept of justice also has it challenges. We turn to those challenges next.

ANSWERS TO CASE STUDY QUESTIONS

Q8.1. In Case 8.1 did Officer Lane violate Bundley's First Amendment right to free speech?

Not directly, because Lane was simply enforcing the law prohibiting placing advertising on vehicles without the owners' permission. Whether that law violates the First Amendment is an interesting question, however.

Objection: Officer Lane was representing the law, and the law prohibiting placing advertising on vehicles violates the First Amendment. Therefore, Officer Lane was directly violating Bundley's First Amendment Right to free speech.

Q8.2. In Case 8.1, does Mitchell's "everybody does it" defense of Bundley prove Bundley's right to distribute the fliers?

No. This defense commits a logical fallacy, argumentum ad populum—unreasonable appeal to the masses.

Q8.3. In Case 8.1, does Article 19, Section 1-3, of the municipal code appear to violate Bundley's inalienable right to liberty?

There may be no inalienable right to liberty, the Declaration of Independence's claim notwithstanding. Thus, Article 19, Section 1-3, in Case 8.1, may not violate such a right in Bundley's case.

Q8.4. In Case 8.1, who has the greater claim to the right to pursue happiness— Bundley, the organizers of the farmers' market, or neither?

It is unclear whether the debate has anything to do with pursuit of happiness. If, however, it is a matter of Bundley's happiness versus the happiness of the organizers of the farmers' market, then the organizers have the stronger claim on utilitarian grounds. And their claim is not defeated on regularian grounds, deontological grounds, or virtue theory.

Q8.5. Is the Fourth Amendment right not be subject to unreasonable search or seizure, as it applies to Case 8.2., a positive right?

No, it is a negative (and conferred) right.

Q8.6. If the officers in Case 8.2 had a warrant, would their right to search the house be a positive right or a negative right? Would it be conferred or inalienable?

It would be a positive right, because the occupant would have a duty to let them in. It would be a conferred right, because the local legislature could take it away.

Q8.7. For each right that the Bill of Rights enumerates, decide whether it is mainly a positive right or a negative right.

Amendment I

• To establish a religion

Negative: No one has to help anyone else establish a religion.

• To exercise a religion

Negative: No one has to help anyone exercise a religion.

• To speak

Negative: No one has to help anyone speak.

• To establish and operate a press

Negative: No one has to help anyone establish or run a press.

• To assemble "peaceably"

Negative: No one has to help people assemble.

• To "petition the government for a redress of grievances"

Positive: The government must present itself for such a petition.

Amendment II

- To keep arms

Negative: No one has to help anyone keep arms.

- To bear arms

Negative: No one has to help anyone bear arms.

Amendment III

- To deny a soldier "quartering" in one's house during times of peace

Negative: A homeowner has the right to enjoy the privacy of his home without interference from anyone—including soldiers.

or

Positive: In peacetime, soldiers must not occupy private dwellings without the owners' permission.

- To deny a soldier quartering in one's house during times of war, except "in a manner prescribed by law"

Positive: Legislators must define the legal circumstances under which a soldier may occupy a private dwelling without the owner's permission. Soldiers must obey the law when occupying a private dwelling without the owner's permission

Amendment IV

- From unreasonable search and seizure of one's
  - Person
  - House
  - Papers
  - Effects

Negative: People have the right to enjoy these without government interference.

or

Positive: Government has an obligation to refrain from unreasonable searches and seizures.

- To require from a government official a warrant
  - Showing probable cause
  - Supported by oath or affirmation
  - Describing the particular
    - Place to be searched
    - Person or thing to be seized

Positive: Government has an obligation to obtain a warrant before searching or seizing a private place, person, or thing.

Amendment V

- From trial for a capital "or otherwise infamous crime" without "presentment or indictment of a grand jury"
  - Except if one is in the military "when in actual service in time of war or public danger"

Positive: A prosecutor must obtain a grand jury indictment to try someone for these sorts of crimes.

- From double jeopardy

Positive: The government must refrain from trying the same person twice for the same crime.

- From self-incrimination

Positive: The government must refrain from forcing the accused to incriminate himself.

- To due process of law

Positive: The government must provide the accused with due process.

- From having "private property be taken for public use, without just compensation"

Positive: The government must provide just compensation for private property taken for public use.

Amendment VI

- "To a speedy and public trial"

Positive: The government must provide the accused with a trial that is both speedy and public.

- To a trial by a jury that is
  - "Impartial"
  - From "the state and district wherein the crime shall have been committed"

Positive: The government must provide the accused with a jury that meets these criteria.

- "To be informed of the nature and cause of the accusation"

Positive: The government must provide this information.

- To be confronted with the witnesses against you

Positive: The government must facilitate this confrontation. Witnesses must present themselves if requested.

• "To have a compulsory process for obtaining witnesses in [your] favor"

Positive: The government must provide such a process. Witnesses must present themselves if requested.

• "To have assistance of counsel for [your] defense"

Positive: The government must provide an attorney to the accused if the accused requests it.

Amendment VII

• To trial by jury in civil suits exceeding twenty dollars

Positive: The government must provide a jury under these circumstances, if either party requests it.

• From appeal of a jury decision, except "according to the rules of the common law"

Positive: Everyone must refrain from appealing a jury's decision, except where common law allows such an appeal.

Amendment VIII

• From excessive bail

Positive: The government must refrain from assigning excessive bail.

• From excessive fines

Positive: The government must refrain from levying excessive fines.

• From cruel and unusual punishment

Positive: The government must refrain from inflicting cruel or unusual punishment.

Amendment IX

• To exercise rights other than those the Constitution enumerates

Negative: The government does not have to help anyone exercise these rights, other than to ensure that one is left alone to enjoy them.

Amendment X

• (For states and individuals) to exercise "powers not delegated to the United States by the Constitution, nor prohibited by it"

Negative: The government does not have to help anyone exercise these rights, other than to ensure that one is left alone to enjoy them.

Q8.8. Is there any conflict of rights in Case 8.3?

Yes. The police had the legal right to be in the house because they had a valid warrant to be there. They had a moral right, if not a duty, to look for the suspect where the person answering the door said the suspect was. The person in bed had a legal and moral right not to be shot in his bed, but the police had a right to defend themselves. This was a tragic mixture of clashing rights that led to an unhappy ending.

NOTES

1. Johnathon E. Briggs, "Bundley Briefly Detained in Leafleting Incident," *Baltimore Sun*, 28 July 2003, p. 1B.
2. Peter Singer, *Animal Rights and Human Obligations* (Englewood Cliffs, NJ: Prentice-Hall, 1976).
3. Inaugural Lecture, 1969. In *Four Essays in Liberty* (Oxford, UK: Oxford University Press, 1969). Reprinted in *Readings in Social and Political Philosophy,* ed. Robert M. Stewart (Oxford, UK: Oxford University Press, 1986), pp. 92–9.

CHAPTER 9

JUSTICE

 CASE 9.1

"Give Me the Gun!"[1]

Following standard operating procedure for their department, two police officers—Luke and Marx—arrest a suspected drug dealer, but offer to let him go if he can give them a gun. As Luke explains, in minor drug arrests, police serve a greater good by removing guns from the street than from processing an arrest that will probably go nowhere in the courts.

Case 9.1 invites us to consider the role of justice in criminal justice ethics. A criminal justice professional's moral success entails enforcing the law, respecting people's rights, and promoting justice, in ways that make the community feel safe and secure. The previous two chapters discussed law and rights; this chapter discusses justice.

Q 9.1

Does Case 9.1 exemplify a just use of police discretion?

Typically the "justice" in American criminal justice refers to the system of *legal* justice: a system in which elected representatives of U.S. citizens make law; police and other members of the executive branch of government execute the law; and judges preside over an adversarial system of adjudication in criminal and civil legal complaints. All of this is supposed to occur within the restraints of the U.S. Constitution. Although the emphasis here is on legal justice, our primary interest in this text is in the *moral* implications of justice. In this sense, justice is the cardinal virtue of giving people their due, and it is the mean between giving people less than they deserve and giving people more than they deserve. One way to think about justice is to divide it into three complementary types: distributive, commutative, and retributive. Using the example of an apple pie, let's look at each of these three types.

✦ Distributive Justice

Suppose I made an apple pie using only my ingredients. I grew the apples. I purchased the flour, sugar, and cinnamon. I used my own mixing bowl and pie tin. And I baked the pie in my oven, which is in my home, which sits on my land. Who has a right to some or all of this pie? This is a question of **distributive justice.** There are three theories of distributive justice: libertarianism, utilitarianism, and egalitarianism.

Libertarianism claims that since I made the pie, I can do whatever I want with it. No one—not even a starving person—has a moral or legal claim to a piece of this pie. This is John Locke's position (see Chapter 7), when he claims that humans have a natural right to property, which is the right to oneself and the fruits of one's labor. The Declaration of Independence, under Locke's influence, sounds libertarian in declaring people's inalienable right to life, liberty, and the pursuit of happiness. More recently, Robert Nozick, a well-known American philosopher and libertarian, defended this view in his example of the star basketball player: Imagine that every professional basketball player gets the same salary, but that fans may contribute extra money to any player they wish by placing money in a container with the player's name on it.[2] Imagine further that one player, Wilt Chamberlain, far exceeds all other players in the amount of extra money he receives. Doesn't justice demand that all that extra money go to Chamberlain, since he made it by pleasing the fans more than any other player? Wouldn't it be unjust for the coach to demand that Chamberlain distribute his extra money equally among the other players?

Q 9.2

In Case 9.1, is it just that a gun-owning drug dealer might remain free by giving up the gun while a suspected drug dealer without a gun might be forced to give up his freedom?

Similarly, libertarians would argue that government has no right to tax my earnings or draft me into the military against my will, since these mean taking my property for the purposes of others.

Opponents of libertarianism note that, for example, Chamberlain wouldn't have earned a penny playing basketball unless a society allowed players to play and earn money, and allowed fans to watch and to pay money. Similarly, I would not have been able to make and enjoy my pie without community support that includes, for example, laws that protect property and provide public safety officials such as firefighters. As John Stuart Mill puts it, "Everyone who receives the protection of society owes a return for the benefit."[3] Thus, I owe something to others for the privilege of making what I wish to make.

In this spirit, **utilitarianism,** which we first encountered in Chapter 3, claims that I must distribute my pie so as to ensure the greatest good for the greatest number of stakeholders. But how many people deserve a piece of the pie? Theoretically I could break down the pie into thousands of crumbs and distribute one crumb per person. Since no measurable good would come from this, it can't be what the utilitarian has in mind. So what is the smallest piece of pie that would constitute a good enough piece? How many pieces of that size can I produce? And who among the many claimants has "first dibs" on those pieces? Utilitarianism has no ready reply, which makes ensuring this sort of justice difficult. However, this may not mean that utilitarianism is wrong.

Q 9.3

In Case 9.1, is Luke correct that the greater justice is in removing a handgun from the street than in arresting a drug dealer who might not be imprisoned?

Egalitarianism, as John Rawls (see Chapter 6) represents it, would claim that everyone with an interest in the pie has an equal right to a just serving. All else being equal, a just serving would be of equal size no matter who is to receive it. Rawls offers his theory in part as a solution to the problems of utilitarianism, but he has not solved the problem of deciding who gets pieces if there are more deserving people than there are adequately sized pieces.

Virtue theory addresses the shortcomings of each theory of distributive justice by insisting that in any given case we must distribute the pie in a way that is neither deficient nor excessive. If one child is starving and all other eligible recipients have full stomachs, then it would be intemperate of these others to demand a share equal to the amount the child should receive. If in seeking out others to receive pieces of the pie, I must engage in a life-threatening quest with no guarantee that the pie will be edible by the time I find a recipient, then it would be imprudent of me to set out on such a quest. It would be more prudent for me to eat the pie myself. No single theory of distributive justice can cover all possible cases virtuously.

A criminal justice professional's direct interest in distributive justice is twofold. First is to distribute his or her talents and services fairly. A textbook example finds the police officer having to choose between helping a wounded victim and chasing the assailant. Which is the more just distribution of the officer's time and effort? To do what will most benefit him? To do what will result in the greatest good? To treat all parties equally? Virtue theory would have the police officer assess the severity of the wound. If it is not life threatening and the victim is otherwise safe, then the officer should chase the assailant. If the wound is life threatening or the victim is exposed to other dangers, then the officer should tend to the victim first. Again, this is a question of avoiding deficient and excessive responses.

A second interest of criminal justice professionals in distributive justice is to enforce the community's laws concerning distribution. For example, it is against the law to steal someone else's property. Distributive justice requires that people be protected from theft of their property, that stolen property be recovered if possible, and that victims be compensated for the loss. To these ends, criminal justice professionals promote distributive justice by making laws that protect property, being vigilant for violations of law, discouraging violations through the police presence, responding to complaints about violations, and adjudicating formal charges of property rights violations.

Case 9.2

Homeless but Harmless[4]

Sgt. Parks orders Officer Rhodes to arrest a homeless man who is looking for shelter in a parking garage. Rhodes refuses, arguing that the man isn't harming anyone and his alternative is being outside in the frigid weather.

Parks suspends Rhodes for 30 days for failing to obey an order. Rhodes appeals to the city court, and is given one year of probation for the same offense.

✦ Commutative Justice

Commutative justice is about formal and informal contracts. In one influential view, "commutative justice calls for fundamental fairness in all agreements between individuals or private social groups."[5] Suppose you have offered me five dollars to make an apple pie, and I have agreed to your offer. I made the pie with gala apples, but you would have preferred granny smith apples, although you didn't say this until the pie was finished. Since I didn't make the pie that you wanted specifically, do you still owe me the five dollars? Suppose upon making the pie, I decide to keep it and not to charge you for it. Does justice demand that I give you the pie anyway, even though I would rather have the pie than the money? On one theory of commutative justice, "a deal's a deal." If two parties have agreed to a transaction, and each is able to fulfill its end of the bargain, then justice demands that each do so. I must sell you the pie unless we both agree to cancel the transaction. On another theory of commutative justice, a deal may be invalid in light of other considerations. When I offered to make and sell you a pie for five dollars, there was no one in greater need of the pie. But now, there is a starving street person at my door and I know you to be well fed and to have a fully stocked kitchen. Isn't the more virtuous decision to give the pie to the street person, thus sacrificing my profit and your pie? But who am I to be charitable with what rightly belongs to you?

> **Q 9.4**
>
> In Case 9.2, if Rhodes's social contract with the community calls for him to protect private property from trespassers, is he acting unjustly by refusing to arrest the homeless man?

One example depicting the urgency of these questions much better than the pie example is the case of Baby M.[6] Mary Beth Whitehead entered into a contract

with William and Elizabeth Stern for $10,000. She agreed to be artificially insemi-
nated with William's sperm and to be a surrogate mother for a baby that would
belong solely to the Sterns upon its birth. After giving birth, Whitehead decided to
keep the baby and to forego the $10,000. She claimed that her maternal instincts got
the better of her. The Sterns sued for breach of contract. A lower New Jersey court
found for the Sterns on the ground that the contract was legally valid; the New Jersey
Supreme Court found that the contract was "illegal, perhaps criminal, and potentially degrading to women." In the wake of this decision, paid surrogacy is now illegal
in Michigan and Florida, and five other states have declared surrogacy contracts to
be legally unenforceable.

For criminal justice professionals, commutative justice rests primarily on the
social contract they have made with the community through their oath to the Constitution and to the laws of the community. Under this contract, it would always be
unjust for a criminal justice professional to act unconstitutionally. Thus, for example,
the U.S. Supreme Court declared unconstitutional a New York ordinance permitting wiretaps in an attorney's office for 60 days.[7] In this case, the part of the contract
that required a New York police officer to enforce that law was invalid, and the
officer should have disobeyed it. The community must also fulfill its part of the contract, and it fails to do so when it impedes criminal justice professionals' attempts to
do their duty. This may happen, for example, when a close-knit community hides a
fugitive from police officers seeking to arrest him.

✦ RETRIBUTIVE JUSTICE

 ## CASE 9.3

Improbable Cause

Officer Yerkes, patrolling his usual beat, sees what to his expert eyes appears to be a drug
deal between a customer and a notorious drug dealer, Charles, who keeps beating the
legal system. As Yerkes approaches the scene, the party in the car speeds off, and Charles runs
down the street. Shortly after Charles rounds a corner, Yerkes rounds the same corner and
sees a plastic bag with a white powder in it lying on the sidewalk in plain view. Yerkes scoops
up the bag and continues to pursue Charles until he catches him. Guessing correctly that the
plastic bag contains cocaine, Yerkes arrests Charles for possession. When Charles protests
that the bag isn't his, Yerkes smiles and says, "It's your word against mine!"

Case 9.3 invites the question, If someone acts in a manner that is distributively or commutatively unjust, as Yerkes appears to have acted, what is the proper

recourse? This is a matter of **retributive justice.** Suppose the law says that I must give 10 percent of my apple pie to a food bank in order to help feed the poor, but on libertarian grounds I refuse to obey the law. Do police have the right to force me to give up a piece of the pie? If I have eaten the pie, does the government have the right to force me to make another one? Or suppose someone with no legal or moral claim to my pie has stolen it from the windowsill where it was cooling. Does that person owe me another pie? The monetary equivalent of that pie? Should that person be jailed or have a hand amputated for the offense? Or suppose I agree to make a pie for you but fail to produce one by the deadline upon which you and I have agreed. You are out no money, and your physical well-being is none the worse. Should the law intervene and force me to compensate you in some way?

How one feels about retributive justice depends on what one believes is the proper purpose of punishment. In the United States, we often speak as if the proper purpose were rehabilitation, although our penal system often works against rehabilitation and the public seems content just to have the offender off the streets. Other purposes that punishment might serve include preventing the offender from offending again, revenge, restitution, deterring others from committing a similar offense, or various combinations of these purposes.

Q 9.5

In Case 9.3, does the prospect of Charles's receiving punishment justify Yerkes's lie? If not, what would be a just punishment of Yerkes for the lie?

Some theorists have suggested alternatives to retributive justice, including restorative justice and transformative justice. Restorative justice—for example, community service—seeks to restore the community to its higher quality of safety and security before the crime. Transformative justice—for example, probation before judgment—rests on the hope that the offender won't offend again and that his victims won't seek revenge. Strictly speaking, these two theories fall under the more general heading of retributive justice, since they also attempt to answer the question, How do we respond to someone who has acted in a manner that is distributively or commutatively unjust?

Virtue theory recognizes justice as giving someone exactly what he deserves—no more and no less—but how do we determine what someone deserves retributively? A stark example of this issue is the debate over capital punishment. For most people who believe that capital punishment is always wrong, such punishment is an excessive response to the crime. Interestingly, some people object to capital punishment for outrageous crimes on the ground that it is a *deficient* response. Thus, we hear comments such as "Killing is too good for him!" or "Let him spend the rest of life in jail so he can think about what he's done!" The virtue theorist who wants to defend capital punishment would have to show how it can be the response that is not only just, but temperate, courageous, and prudent. This is a tall order, but not self-evidently impossible.

✦ THE CRIMINAL JUSTICE PROFESSIONS

Although all criminal justice professionals have a stake in all areas of justice, we may distinguish each field of criminal justice in part by the area of justice that it empha- sizes. For example, police officers are primarily responsible for enforcing distributive justice, not enacting retributive justice. When a police officer has arrested someone, the officer must prepare and present her case as well as she can to the judicial system, whose role it is to determine whether there has been a violation requiring retributive justice and, if so, how to exact that justice. Of course, in emergencies, police may have to act to prevent injustice to themselves or to innocent third parties, and this act of prevention may be in the form of retributive justice.

In administrative matters, police have a more direct interest in retributive justice—as a superior, a peer, or a subordinate—in situations where officers have violated policy, law, or orders. Here the people involved must determine and justify the purpose of the retributive response and must respond justly.

This example of police and justice shows that, in a preliminary way, we may acknowledge the following primary responsibilities in different areas of criminal justice.

- *Legislative:* Lawmakers are directly involved in all three areas of justice— distributive, commutative, and retributive—because laws are supposed to express the will of the people and put that will into action. The legislature, however, is not responsible for carrying out retributive justice, except among its members through censure or removal from office. To the extent that government's task is to protect citizens' liberties, laws should emphasize the freedom of individuals to acquire and enjoy property and to enter freely into contracts. To the extent that the government's task is to keep citizens secure, laws should emphasize prevention of violation of contracts or property rights. Both of these emphases reflect distributive and commutative justice, with retributive justice as a last resort.
- *Executive:* Law enforcement is the most public face of the executive area of criminal justice. Law enforcement professionals are responsible primarily for distributive justice and commutative justice, leaving retributive justice to the judicial branch. Assuming that the laws governing distributive and commutative justice are constitutionally valid, police officers, sheriffs, and federal law enforcement officials must encourage and enforce those laws, prevent people from breaking those laws, and arrest or otherwise appropriately deal with people who have broken those laws.
- *Judicial:* The judiciary is primarily responsible for retributive justice, but as a means for promoting and restoring distributive and commutative justice.

Note that corrections officials, key participants in the criminal justice pro- fession, are in a unique position relative to the distinctions we have just made. When we compare the professional responsibilities of corrections officials with the responsibilities of legislators, police officers, and judges or lawyers, corrections officials most resemble police officers. Yet corrections officials are most concerned with carrying out retributive justice, rather than promoting and protecting distributive or commutative justice. There will be more to say about this when we examine the various criminal justice professions more closely in the final part of this book.

SUMMARY

Criminal justice professionals' constitutional duties include enforcing laws, respecting rights, and promoting justice. This chapter has explored the concept of justice, dividing justice into three main types: distributive, commutative, and retributive.

Among the various theories about distributive justice, three stand out: Libertarianism holds that no one has a right to distribute my goods to anyone else without my permission. Utilitarianism holds that we should distribute the goods of the community in a way that promotes the greatest good for the greatest number of stakeholders. Egalitarianism holds that we should distribute the goods of the community equally among all stakeholders, except where giving a larger portion to someone would be fairer.

Commutative justice is about contracts. When are they valid? What constitutes unjust violation of a contract? Retributive justice is about punishment. What constitutes just punishment and how should it be carried out?

ANSWERS TO CASE STUDY QUESTIONS

Q9.1. Does Case 9.1 exemplify a just use of police discretion?

No. Although the arrest may not go anywhere in the courts, that is not sufficient reason for the officers to waive the arrest in favor of obtaining a gun. Rather, that is cause for the courts to be more forceful in prosecuting the case. Note, too, that drug dealers may keep a cache of guns just to get them out of arrests. Thus, the officers may not be acting for the greatest good after all.

Q9.2. In Case 9.1, is it just that a gun-owning drug dealer might remain free by giving up the gun, while a suspected drug dealer without a gun might be forced to give up his freedom?

No.

A. 1. Both the gun-owning drug dealer and the drug dealer without a gun are committing the same crime—drug dealing.
   2. By carrying a gun, the gun-owning dealer is also committing a second crime.
   3. If the purpose of arrest is to prevent the suspect's further criminal action, then a suspect who is committing two crimes deserves to be arrested—forced to give up his freedom—more than a person who is committing only one of those two crimes.

4. Therefore, the gun-owning drug dealer deserves to be arrested even more than the other dealer.

B. 1. Justice is giving someone what he deserves.
2. Injustice is failing to give someone what he deserves.
3. Therefore, it would be unjust for officers to let the gun-owning drug dealer go free while arresting the other dealer.

Q9.3. In Case 9.1, is Luke correct that the greater justice is in removing a handgun from the street than in arresting a drug dealer who might not be imprisoned?

No. As noted in answer to Q9.1, there is no proof that removing the handgun will result in a greater good than arresting the drug dealer (a utilitarian concern). Nor is it clear that anyone will be safer for the exchange (a libertarian concern). Thus, Luke is wrong on both utilitarian and libertarian grounds.

Q9.4. In Case 9.2, if Rhodes's social contract with the community calls for him to protect private property from trespassers, is he acting unjustly by refusing to arrest the homeless man?

Yes.

1. If Rhodes wants to justify his allowing the homeless man to stay on the property without the owner's approval, his justification must be libertarian, utilitarian, or egalitarian.
2. From a libertarian point of view, it is unjust for the homeless man to trespass on private property.
3. From a utilitarian point of view, police generally serve the greater good by protecting private property from trespassers than by allowing trespassing.
4. From an egalitarian point of view, trespassers should be treated equally under the law.
5. Thus, it is unjust for the police officer to allow the homeless person to remain on the property without the owner's approval.

Objection: From an Aristotelian point of view, arresting the homeless man may be an excessively strict alternative. For example, there may be some way to get the homeless man off the property and into a shelter.

Q9.5. In Case 9.3, does the prospect of Charles's receiving punishment justify Yerkes's lie? If not, what would be a just punishment of Yerkes for the lie?

1. Yerkes is bound constitutionally and morally to follow certain procedures for arrest.
2. Failing to have probable cause in Case 9.3 violates that procedure.
3. Yerkes's lie constitutes failure to follow the procedure.
4. Therefore, nothing justifies Yerkes's lie constitutionally or morally.

We may assume that there is a procedure for addressing an officer's false report and that Yerkes's superior would be just in following that procedure.

NOTES

1. Inspired by an article by Ryan Davis, "An Arresting Offer: Guns for Freedom," *Baltimore Sun,* 25 October 2004, pp. 1A, 4A.
2. Robert Nozick, *Anarchy, State, and Utopia* (New York: Basic, 1974), 161–163.
3. *On Liberty* (1859), Ch. 4.
4. Based on Tom Hays, "New York Police Officer Gets Probation for Refusing to Arrest Homeless Man," Associated Press. Retrieved 28 October 2004 from www.officer.com.
5. U.S. Catholic Bishops, *Economic Justice for All: Pastoral Letter on Catholic Social Teaching and the U.S. Economy* (Washington, DC: United States Catholic Conference, 1986).
6. In *Moral Issues in Business,* 9th ed., ed. William Shaw and Vincent Barry (Belmont, CA: Wadsworth, 2004): 82–84.
7. *Berger v. New York,* 1967.

PART IV

RELIGIOUS ETHICS

CHAPTER 10

RELIGIOUS ETHICS

 CASE 10.1

The Marriage Counseling Police Officer

It is New Year's Eve. Tonight and for the past three New Year's Eves, Officer Smith has responded to a domestic disturbance involving the same drunken husband and wife physically assaulting each other. In the first three calls, Smith followed departmental procedure by arresting and jailing the husband. In each case, the wife refused to press charges and the husband was released once he had sobered up.

This fourth time, Smith tries a different approach. First he asks them whether they love each other, to which they both answer yes. "Then why," wonders Smith, "do you beat the stuffings out of each other every New Year's Eve?" The couple agrees that alcohol makes them irritable toward each other, but that they want to stay married. Smith's next question is whether they have had marriage counseling. They have not.

Smith learns that they are lapsed Lutherans who would welcome affordable marriage counseling. Smith offers not to arrest the husband and to find a marriage counselor for them. In a few days, Smith tells them that he has found a nonprofit Lutheran counseling service that can take them right away and that charges little. Sometime later, Smith hears from the grateful couple that the counseling is going well.

When Smith tells his supervisor, Lt. Jones, what has transpired, Jones scolds Smith for violating protocol and for "practicing psychology without a license." Jones notes that Smith could face penalties, but because of Smith's clean record, past successful work, and lack of harm from this incident, Jones offers to let it slide this one time. Smith acknowledges his breach of protocol, but defends his action as good community policing.

Case 10.1 reminds us of religion's pervasive role in America's moral, social, and political life. This contrasts with Thomas Jefferson's famous claim that the First Amendment's freedom of religion clause creates "a wall of separation between Church & State."[1] Despite this separation, criminal justice professionals should understand religious moral views for at least four reasons. First, nonreligious professionals often deal with religious people and work under policies and laws that religious people enact. Second, a professional's duties may clash with her religious beliefs. Third, religious beliefs may cause conflict between professional co-workers. Fourth, competing religious beliefs among the citizenry may cause a conflict requiring the professional's intervention.

Q 10.1

Did Smith fail to do his duty in Case 10.1? Why, or why not?

The three major religions in the United States are Christianity, Judaism, and Islam. They have much in common, but they also disagree in important ways that matter to criminal justice ethics. This chapter examines these religions on three points: their foundations; their moral views; and their positions on the possibility of just war. This discussion about war pertains to our study of criminal justice ethics because, as social ethicist Ralph B. Potter notes, what one thinks about war reveals one's basic moral views and foundations, especially concerning justice, rights, the role of government, and the use of force.[2]

✦ FOUNDATIONS

Christianity, Judaism, and Islam claim a connection to God through Abraham as their common ancestor: Christianity and Judaism through Isaac, Abraham's son with his wife Sarah; and Islam through Ishmael, Abraham's son with Sarah's maid Hagar. We can identify similarities and differences among the three religions, first through a brief historical account of each and then through identification of some basic tenets.

History

Judaism

 # CASE 10.2

Taking Sides

A Neo-Nazi group has a parade permit from the mayor to march through a Jewish neighborhood whose residents include survivors of Nazi concentration camps. The neighbors have threatened the marchers, so the mayor orders the police to protect them. Capt. Green, who commands the district that includes this neighborhood, challenges the mayor's order on three grounds: (1) Green's grandmother, a camp survivor, lives in that neighborhood, and Green sympathizes with the neighbors. (2) The potential violence from this march would overwhelm the small police department's resources. (3) On her oath to protect the Constitution, Green believes that the First Amendment does not protect the marchers, because their intentions go beyond speech, and the First Amendment protects the neighbors' right to assemble peacefully, which the marchers' incitement will threaten.

Case 10.2 illustrates the challenges that religious conflicts can pose to criminal justice professionals, especially when dealing with age-old prejudices. Judaism is the oldest of the three religions. It claims the world was created around 3950 BCE, after which God entered into a series of covenants with humankind. In each covenant, God promises to protect the people in return for their obedience and worship. The first covenant was with Adam at the creation.[3] Because he and his descendants failed to fulfill their part of the agreement, God destroyed the world in a flood and made a new covenant with Noah, around 2800 BCE.[4] This covenant covered all people, but as human populations grew and people took sides against each other, God took sides too, making a more specific and personal covenant with Abraham, around 2000 BCE.[5] Around 1450 BCE, God focused his attention on the Israelites, descendants of Abraham, promising to take them from Egyptian bondage to a free land. In exchange, the Israelites were to obey Moses, the Ten Commandments that he received from God, and the other laws as God pronounced them.[6]

There is debate over when the term *Jewish* came into being and how it relates to the Israelites. A common view is that the Jews are Israelites who established a kingdom in Jerusalem around 1060 BCE, under the sovereignty of King David.[7] The Romans destroyed this kingdom around 70 AD. After that, the Jewish population dispersed among many nations, often facing persecution and exile, which came to an awful head in World War II with the holocaust in Nazi Germany, which ended in 1945. In 1948, with U.S. and British support, Jewish leaders declared the state of Israel their rightful home. Today, the largest Jewish populations are in Israel and the United States.

Q 10.2

In Case 10.2, is the neighbors' Jewishness morally relevant to the question of whether Green should obey the mayor's order?

This history is important to criminal justice professionals in the United States because of the important roles Judaism and Jewish leaders play in the American criminal justice system. Of special importance is Judaism's claim to be God's chosen people and Judaism's commitment to obeying just law.

> ### Q 10.3
>
> In Case 10.2, does Capt. Green appear to hold that for Jews, Jewish law trumps the town's law? If so, why is she correct or incorrect?

Christianity

 # CASE 10.3

Speech Unbecoming

While conducting roll call, Sgt. Gleason uses the name *Jesus Christ* as an expletive. Chief Larkin, recently appointed and new to this agency, has been listening secretly to Gleason from the hall. At the end of roll call, when everyone has left the room but Gleason, Larkin confronts him and tells him that he will be reprimanded "for using the Lord's name in vain." Larkin shows no interest in Gleason's protests, including the claim that this sort of language is in common use among the police in this agency and that, as chief, Larkin has no right to impose his religious morality on his subordinates because they are public servants and the Constitution demands separation of church and state.

As Case 10.3 reminds us, Jesus Christ is an important and provocative figure in America. As the term *Common Era (CE)* suggests, Christianity begins with Christ's birth, traditionally set at 2007 years ago but probably four years earlier. Jesus was a Jewish carpenter who at age 30 gathered a small group of disciples and traveled around the area that is now Israel and Palestine, preaching that the kingdom of God was at hand.

> ### Q 10.4
>
> In Case 10.3, does Gleason have the constitutional right to "use the Lord's name in vain"?

Christians believe that Jesus was God in human form. Judaism teaches that one can atone for one's sins by sacrificing something of suitable value. Christianity teaches that humankind became so sinful that no sinner's sacrifice would be adequate. Thus, God chose to sacrifice himself in the person of his son, Jesus Christ. Christians believe that this sacrifice took place when the Romans crucified 33-year-old Jesus for vaguely defined political crimes, and that Jesus subsequently rose from the dead.

After Christ's crucifixion, Christianity spread throughout the Middle East, Asia Minor, North Africa, and Southern Europe, but was treated as a peculiar cult by most political powers, especially the Roman Empire. This changed in 313 when the Roman Emperor Constantine, in his Edict of Milan, announced toleration for Christianity, because he believed that the Christian God had helped him keep his power in a decisive battle in 312. Over the next two decades, Constantine would give more and more authority to Christianity, converting to Christianity himself in his old age.

Since its political legitimization in 313, Christianity has had a major influence in world politics and religion, and has been the primary religious influence in America. It is impossible to understand well the scope and limits of criminal justice ethics in the United States without appreciating the historical and contemporary influence of Christianity.

Q 10.5

Given the traditional "separation of church and state," did Larkin in Case 10.3 have the right to work his religious beliefs into his supervision of public officials?

Islam

CASE 10.4

The Beard[8]

Wickoren, a veteran of the Newark, New Jersey, police department, recently converted to Islam and grew a beard as a sign of his commitment to Islam. This was in keeping with the Muslim tradition of men wearing beards to avoid looking effeminate. Also recently, the Newark city council banned city public safety officials from wearing beards except in documented medical cases where shaving would be harmful. Wickoren claims religious discrimination and is suing Newark to let him to keep his job and his beard.

Case 10.4 highlights a clash between Muslim culture and Western culture. If Western culture understood Islam better, there might be fewer clashes. Islam developed as a religious and political force soon after the Arabic prophet Muhammad (570–632) declared God's final revelation complete. *Islam* means "Submission to the will of Allah ["the God"]" in Arabic. *Muslim* means "one who submits." To become a Muslim, one declares, "I testify that there is no god but Allah and Muhammad is his messenger."

According to Islam, God revealed his will through 124,000 prophets, most notably Moses and Jesus Christ.[9] Islam reveres them, but insists that their audiences failed to listen. Thus, God made one final attempt to reveal his will through Muhammad.

Q 10.6

In Case 10.4, is there any merit to the claim that if one has a moral right to wear a beard for medical reasons, then one has the right to wear a beard for religious reasons?

Muslims believe that in 610 Muhammad was in a cave near his home in Mecca, Arabia, praying and meditating, when he received a divine revelation to preach God's word. Muhammad obeyed this order, receiving and preaching the word over the next 22 years, until his death. The Qur'an ("The Recitation"), the Muslim holy book, is a record of these revelations. Muslims also accept the sayings (*hadith*) and practice (*sunnah*) of Muhammad as authoritative, but less so than the Qur'an.

Muhammad faced many political challenges as he preached, developing political power as he met each challenge. After his death, his successors parlayed this power into a dominant force throughout the Middle East, Asia, Africa, and Southern Europe. The succession of Muslim empires flourished until World War I (1914–1918), when European forces overthrew Muslim forces, putting many of them into British protectorates.

On September 11, 2001, terrorists claiming to be Muslims doing the will of God attacked American landmarks, killing several thousand people. Since then, interest in and misinformation about Islam have skyrocketed. There is no doubt that some Muslim groups, such as al-Qaeda, hate the United States. There is no doubt that criminal justice professionals are major defenders against terrorists. Also, there is no doubt that most Muslims in America have no interest in performing terrorist acts, although cultural differences pose problems for American criminal justice professionals when dealing with Muslims. Therefore, these professionals need at least a basic understanding of the Muslim mind, the ethical challenges Islam poses for American criminal justice, and the importance of handling professional–Muslim relations with finesse and respect.

Let's now consider fundamental tenets of the religions of Abraham.

Fundamental Tenets

Judaism, Christianity, and Islam challenge criminal justice. Arguably, criminal justice professionals' first task is to secure citizens' liberties. Often these liberties conflict with religious teachings to the point where believers seek government restraints on those liberties, as in Case 10.2. Deeper understanding of the basic tenets of each religion may help professionals confront these conflicts with more sensitivity and finesse.

Similarities

Judaism, Christianity, and Islam have many theological and secular beliefs in common. Among the common theological beliefs are:

- There is only one God.
- God is all-knowing, all-good, and all-powerful.
- God created the world.
- God has revealed his will through prophets and scripture.
- God's will can be summed up in one word: *shalom* (Hebrew), *salaam* (Arabic), or *concord* (English). Often translated as "peace" in English, the idea has more to do with everything being in its right place and everyone being happy and healthy.
- Moral goodness is a matter of obeying God's will.
- God has made a covenant with his people through Abraham to protect them in return for their worship.
- There is life after death.
- There will be a final day of judgment.
- People who accept God's covenant will have eternal happiness.

Among the common secular beliefs that are relevant to our study, each of the three religions believes that

- All people are created equal.
- Human rights are important, especially the right to property, security, and freedom to worship God.
- Peace is preferable to war.
- Justice is a fundamental moral value.

Differences

Judaism's most significant difference from Christianity and Islam is that Judaism is ethnic as well as theological. Most Jews claim to be a race with ancestral roots going back to Abraham, although people from other ethnic groups may convert to Judaism.[10] Neither Christianity nor Islam considers itself to comprise a single race of people.

The key tenet for Judaism is the exhortation:

> Hear, O Israel: The LORD our God is one LORD. And thou shalt love the LORD thy God with all thine heart, and with all thy soul, and with all thy might.[11]

This love is best expressed by obedience to God's commandments, especially the Ten Commandments or "Decalogue":[12]

- I am the Lord your God.
- Thou shalt have no other gods before me and Thou shalt not make for yourself an idol.
- Thou shalt not take the name of your God in vain.
- Remember the Sabbath and keep it holy.
- Honor thy Mother and Father.

- Thou shalt not kill.
- Thou shalt not commit adultery.
- Thou shalt not steal.
- Thou shalt not bear false witness.
- Thou shalt not covet thy neighbor's house or thy neighbor's wife.

Many Americans, including many criminal justice professionals, regard the Ten Commandments as the basis of American ethics. Yet many people don't know the commandments, don't understand their historical or religious context, or choose to ignore one or more of them. The presumption about the sanctity of the commandments and the failure to understand them fully have caused much friction between criminal justice professionals and nonprofessionals, as well as between criminal justice professionals.

Christianity reveres these tenets of Judaism, but offers a different emphasis:

> And Jesus answered him, The first of all the commandments is, Hear, O Israel; The Lord our God is one Lord. And thou shalt love the Lord thy God with all thy heart, and with all thy soul, and with all thy mind, and with all thy strength: this is the first commandment. And the second is like, namely this, Thou shalt love thy neighbour as thyself. There is none other commandment greater than these.[13]

Q 10.7

If the neighbors in Case 10.2 were Christian, would they be morally bound by their scripture to take the marchers' abuse peacefully?

The greatest difference between Judaism and Christianity is that the latter acknowledges Jesus Christ as the Messiah, whereas Jews who believe in a messiah believe that he has not come yet, or—in some rare cases—that he is someone else.

Another difference between Judaism and Christianity concerns grace. Christian history sometimes characterizes this as a clash between two principles: salvation through works and salvation through faith. For Jews, people can satisfy God and receive God's salvation by doing good works—that is, by obeying God's laws. For Christians, no human act, no matter how good, is enough to satisfy God. Only through God's gratuitous sacrifice of his son and people's faith in that sacrifice can people receive salvation.

Islam, like Christianity, regards its message as universal and exclusive. For Islam, God wants the whole world to be Muslim—that is, to accept the Qur'an's message. Like Judaism, Islam emphasizes God's law more than Christianity does. Also, Islam recognizes Jesus Christ as a prophet and a messiah, but not the son of God.[14]

Islam's basic tenets appear in the Qur'an, Muslim worship, and the "Five Pillars" of Islam. We will consider the Qur'an later in the chapter, in our discussion of moral theology. Here let us consider the Muslim concept of worship and the Five Pillars of Islam.

Worship

CASE 10.5
Lawful Entry

Police officers in an American city chase a robbery suspect into a mosque. Without removing their shoes or making ablutions, the police enter the mosque and close in on the suspect, who is darting in and out among the praying faithful. After arresting and cuffing the suspect, the police take him from the mosque without saying a word to the startled onlookers.

The mosque administrators sue the police for civil rights violations because the officers ignored protocol for entering a mosque, which includes removing one's shoes and washing one's hands, feet, face, and neck before entering.

Case 10.5 reflects the fact that worship, *ibadah* ("slavery to Allah"), is central to the life of every Muslim. It consists of four parts: good deeds (*ihsan*); faith (*iman*) in God, angels, scriptures, prophets, and the final day of judgment; action (*amila*) to live according to this faith; and striving (*jihad*) against the world's evils.[15]

Note that *jihad* in its broadest sense means struggle, especially in fulfilling God's will. Often the Qur'an refers to a personal, internal struggle against self-love and against the world (*dunya*). In the rare cases where the Qur'an refers to jihad against others, the Qur'an forbids fighting to gain personal or national glory.[16] Today, it is common to define *jihad* as "holy war," similar to the Christian crusades of the 10th and 11th centuries against Islam. Although this gives the word *jihad* strong rhetorical power to Muslim terrorists and to their opponents, keeping the word in its proper historical and theological perspective may permit more rational discourse about Muslim views on criminal justice.

Q 10.8

In Case 10.5, suppose the mosque supports Iranian revolutionary principles, although no known member of the mosque has been in legal trouble. Given Iran's contempt for America, do the police have the right to ignore mosque protocol?

The Five Pillars of Islam [17]
Muslims recognize five basic duties:

- Bearing witness (*shahadah*) that there is no God but Allah and Muhammad is his messenger.[18]
- Prayer (*salah*). Allah orders five daily prayers: *fajr* (morning between dawn and sunrise); *zuhr* (just after the noonday sun); *asr* (afternoon); *maghrib*

(just after sunset); and *isha* (during darkness).[19] Muslims must not pray precisely at sunrise, noon, or sunset, since such timing corresponds to pagan rituals. Although individuals must pray all five prayers each day, the only congregational prayer that is required in the mosque is the Friday *asr*. In the mosque, the imam leads the prayer, which is his primary function. He does not have the same sacred role as a priest.

- Payment of a religious tax (*zakah*).[20] This is not for the sake of charity or sympathy, but to recognize that all one has comes from God and that one should give some back in appreciation.
- Fasting (*sawm*) during Ramadan, the ninth month.[21] Tradition holds that God first revealed the Qur'an to Muhammad on the 27th day of Ramadan.
- Pilgrimage (*hajj*) to Makkah (Mecca), the holiest site in Islam, at least once in a lifetime.[22] One who is unable to make the Hajj because of exigent circumstances—ill health or poor finances, for example—is excused but should consider helping someone else make the Hajj instead.

Q 10.9

In Case 10.4, would it be fair for the authorities to argue that since wearing a beard is merely a tradition among Muslim men and not one of the five basic duties, banning beards does no harm to Muslim practice?

We have looked at the historical background and the basic tenets of Judaism, Christianity, and Islam. We turn now to a discussion of their specific approaches to ethics—the subject of moral theology.

✦ MORAL THEOLOGY

Moral theology, the study of religious ethics, considers how to live as an adherent to one's God. John Wesley (1703–1791), founder of Methodism, a Christian denomination, offered a useful framework for studying moral theology. In 1964, author Albert C. Outler named this framework the **Wesleyan Quadrilateral,** because Wesley recognized four sources of religious moral authority: scripture, tradition, experience, and reason.[23]

The following examines the moral views of Judaism, Christianity, and Islam in terms of each authority.

Q 10.10

Of the four authorities on the Wesleyan Quadrilateral, which does Smith seem to be emphasizing in his handling of the situation in Case 10.1?

Scripture

The primary source of religious ethics is a sacred narrative, either a body of oral tradition or written scripture. The Christian scripture is the Bible containing the Old and New Testaments; the Jewish scripture is the Tanakh, containing the same books as the Protestant Old Testament, but in a different order; and the Muslim scripture is the Qur'an.

There are different ways to use scripture in making moral decisions; two ways stand out. First is to regard the text as a set of laws to obey without question; this is the regularian approach. Second is to regard the text as a narrative containing morals in the way that fables or parables contain them. This second way emphasizes the character of the person, so it emphasizes a virtue approach. Consequentialists and deontologists can also find support for their moral approaches in the Tanakh, Bible, and Qur'an.

A problem with the regularian approach is that many of the so-called laws or commands work against moral behavior because they are outdated, irrational, or immoral. Recall Case 4.3, about the wife who grabbed the genitals of her husband's assailant. According to Deuteronomy 25:11–12, in the Old Testament or Tanakh, that husband should cut off his wife's hand without pity. Today this command strikes us as brutal and unjust, but it might once have made sense because people incorrectly regarded the human scrotum as the sole biological source of human life; woman's role in procreation was merely to act as a vessel for the growing seed. This biological view, coupled with a strong Jewish reverence for life, would make the helpful wife's act disrespectful toward life. Our understanding of biology has changed since then, and with it our sense of the proper response to a woman trying to save her husband. We wonder, therefore, how to distinguish between biblical commands one should follow and those one should ignore.

The second approach to using scripture as moral authority is to regard scriptural narrative as a set of morally guiding stories. Biblical parables are an example. Consider the Parable of the Prodigal Son.[24] A son takes his inheritance before his father has died, runs off, loses the money, and crawls back to his father, begging the father to let him return, if only as a slave. The father, overjoyed by his son's return, calls for a celebration. This story is neither a historical report nor an explicit set of commands. But there appears to be a moral point: the power of a loving father's grace over human notions of justice, and the analogy one should draw to the Christian God as a God of grace.

Since scriptures contain both clear imperatives and literary narratives, criminal justice professionals who seek to understand scriptures' role in guiding moral behavior must recognize any scripture as a combination of different kinds of writing. These professionals will then acknowledge the challenges of interpreting the writings correctly. Thus cautioned, let's consider the role of scripture for each religion specifically.

Judaism and Scripture

Jewish ethics focuses on law. Jewish law, or *halakha* (Hebrew for "the way to go"), permeates all four sources of Jewish morality—scripture, tradition, reason, and experience—but the primary written source for *halakha* is the Tanakh, the Jewish Bible. *Tanakh* is a Hebrew acronym for the three main divisions of the Bible: *Torah,* the teaching or law; *Neviim,* the prophets; and *Ketuviim,* the writings, such as Psalms, Proverbs, and

Ecclesiastes. The Tanakh has the same books as the Protestant Old Testament, but in a different order. Also, the Protestants divide these into 39 books, while the Jews divide them into 24. Roman Catholicism and Orthodox Christianity add 6 more books, which the Protestants refer to as "the Apocrypha" (Greek for "the hidden").

A particular aspect of Jewish law that summarizes Jewish morality is the **lex talionis,** or law of retaliation, which we first encountered in our discussion of regularianism:

> If any harm follows, then you shall give life for life, eye for eye, tooth for tooth,
> hand for hand, foot for foot, burn for burn, wound for wound, stripe for stripe.[25]

The point is not that one *must* take an eye for an eye, but that if one seeks retaliation, the punishment must be proportional to the crime. This is related to the Golden Rule: "Do unto others as you would have them do unto you." Its basic expression in the Tanakh is Leviticus 19.18b: "You shall love your neighbor as yourself." More famously and tellingly, Rabbi Hillel's commentary in the Talmud says, "What is hateful to you, do not do to your neighbor. This is the whole Torah; all the rest is commentary."[26]

Christianity also embraces the Golden Rule,[27] but its take on lex talionis appears to contradict Jewish teaching:

> You have heard that it was said, "An eye for eye, and a tooth for tooth." But I tell
> you, Do not resist an evil person. If someone strikes you on the right cheek, turn to
> him the other also.[28]

Q 10.11

In Case 10.2, would the Golden Rule justify the neighbors' hurting the marchers, since the marchers advocate harm to the neighbors?

As we identify the relevance of religious ethics to criminal justice ethics, consider the relevance of the debate about lex talionis to the debate over capital punishment. Many Christians, for example, support capital punishment, but how can a Christian reconcile this support with the Christian command to "turn the other cheek"?

Strictly speaking, Torah is oral law, which eventually appeared in the first five books of the Bible—the "five books of Moses" —Genesis, Leviticus, Exodus, Numbers, and Deuteronomy. For much of its history, Judaism transmitted Torah along with oral tradition, until it was recorded in Mishnah, Midrash, and the Talmud. *Mishnah,* Hebrew for "repetition," is the first recording of oral law, including all Jewish law up to 200 CE. Midrash and the Talmud attempt to connect Mishnah with Torah. Midrash is a way of explicating biblical text. *Talmud* means "written law" in Hebrew. Containing biblical commentary, it expands on Mishnah and Torah, and is the basis for later Jewish law.

For most observant Jews, Torah and Talmud are the primary textual authority. Some Jews also regard the Kabbalah, dating back to the 13th century, as authoritative. In Hebrew, *Kabbalah* means "that which is received" and allegedly contains divine revelations to a group of saints.

Criminal justice professionals will benefit from understanding the role that these Jewish texts play in guiding Judaism's moral and political thought. One benefit will be to better understand public or legal clashes between Jews and non-Jews. Another benefit will be to better understand such clashes among Jews from different denominations.

Scriptural authority also is of great importance to Christians, but with an emphasis that differs from Judaism, as we will see next.

Christianity and Scripture

Q 10.12

In Case 10.1, Smith defends his action as good community policing. Would his argument be stronger if he used the Bible to defend his act?

Of the three religions of Abraham, Christianity focuses least on scripture as a set of laws. Christians don't believe they can be sufficiently obedient without God's intervention, so merely obeying the laws is morally insufficient. Nevertheless, Christians take scripture seriously as a source of moral guidance.

The Christian Bible contains the Old Testament and the New Testament, comprising 27 books. The first five books of the New Testament, including the four Gospels and Acts, offer a history of Christ's ministry and the early church. Twenty-one books consist of letters, most from the Apostle Paul to churches he had founded or worked with. The final book, *Revelation,* purports to describe the end of the world and the second coming of Jesus Christ.

The Bible passage that is arguably both most central and unique to Christian moral teaching is Christ's "Sermon on the Mount."[29] In the beginning of the sermon, Jesus offers the "beatitudes" or "blessings." Here he declares that God has blessed the poor in spirit, the mournful, the meek, those who seek righteousness, the merciful, the pure in heart, the peacemakers, and those who are persecuted for the sake of Jesus Christ.[30] This emphasis on God's preference for the poor, the meek, and the persecuted sets a tone that distinguishes Christianity from Judaism and Islam, although neither of the latter two would deny God's concern for the downtrodden. In the rest of the sermon, Jesus lays out several principles that distinguish Christianity even more clearly from Judaism and Islam:

- Jesus has come to fulfill the law of the Old Testament.[31]
- It is not enough to obey the commandments in deed; we must also obey them "in our hearts." Thus, for example, to lust in one's heart is to commit adultery.[32] Note how deontological this sounds.
- Rejection of the lex talionis, the law of retaliation, as we saw above, and the command to love our enemies as well as our friends.[33]
- All who want to go to heaven must go through Jesus.[34]
- We are judged by the fruits of our acts.[35] Note how consequentialist this sounds, making it apparently inconsistent with the claim that it is morally sufficient for us to be judged if we have acted "in our hearts only."

In short, Christian scripture calls for a high degree of virtue, which includes an extraordinary degree of kindness toward others. As many people in the criminal justice field—students, professionals, and citizens—claim to be embracing and acting on Christian values, one wonders how people can do this without falling short of the tough moral goals that scripture sets for Christians. This is especially challenging in a political and economic system that emphasizes individualism and material success.

Take, for example, the debate over how far to extend the public's charity as opposed to giving someone only what he is due. Recall our discussion of distributive justice, in which we distinguished libertarians from egalitarians. Libertarians argue that it is unjust to take what is rightfully theirs without their consent. On this view, consider the federal welfare system that taxes people who have money and gives the money to those who do not have enough to get by. In libertarian terms, this is a forced act of charity, and hence unjust. Egalitarians, on the other hand, argue that justice requires everyone getting "an equal share of the pie." On this view, the public welfare system is both an act of charity and an act of justice, assuming that the system effects a more equal distribution of goods than existed otherwise. Many people who claim that the United States is a Christian nation or built on Christian principles also embrace libertarianism. From the scriptural passages we have just considered, egalitarianism seems to be closer to the Christian ideal. This is yet another tension worth the consideration of people interested in criminal justice ethics.

We turn now to the Islamic approach to scripture as a moral guide.

Islam and Scripture

In terms of the Wesleyan Quadrilateral, Muslims' moral decision making comes mainly from scripture and tradition, although many Muslim scholars have argued for these authorities on the basis of reason and experience. Note, for example, that the Qur'an purports to be a record of Muhammad's *experience* with receiving a revelation from God.

The basic authority of Islam is the Qur'an ("recitation" or Holy Book), which the prophet Muhammad recited intermittently from 610 to 632. The authority of the Qur'an depends on the veracity of Muhammad's claim to have had a spiritual experience. Unlike the Bible, which consists of different books, the Qur'an is a single book transmitted by a single person. It contains 114 *suwar*, or chapters, not in chronological order, with all but the ninth *surah* (the singular form of *suwar*) beginning "In the Name of Allah, the Most Compassionate, the Most Merciful." It contains 6,616 *ayats,* "signs" or verses, comprising 78,000 words in Arabic.

According to Islamic scholar Ruqaiyyah Maqsood, the Qur'an has nine basic teachings:[36]

- *Tawhid* (one-ness), the unity of God. To break this unity is *shirk.* The Christian doctrine of the Trinity, for example, is shirk because it declares that God is three persons: Father, Son, and Holy Spirit. In the Qur'an, Allah never refers to himself as "Father" (*Abb*).
- The love and compassion of Allah.
- Three sorts of beings between God and humanity: angels, jinn, and the devil. Angels are God's servants; each person has two angels who guard

the person and record the person's good and bad deeds. Jinn ("genies") are nonphysical beings with free will to do good or evil. The devil (*Shaitan* or *Iblis*) is the chief of the jinn.

- Human beings are the highest physical beings created by Allah, through Adam and Eve. Each human has an allotted life span; each is to be God's deputy (*khalifa*) on earth; and each is created equal, but becomes unequal through exercise of free will.
- This life is a test of the life to come.
- The authenticity of revelation (*Risalah*). Muslim tradition claims that there were 124,000 prophets before Muhammad, the final prophet. Twenty-six of these prophets are named in the Qur'an, including Noah (Nu), Abraham (Ibrahim), Moses (Musa), John the Baptist (Yunis ibn Zakriyah), Jesus ('Isa), and others. Some of these prophets were *nabi*, prophets who taught but never wrote; others are *rasul*, prophets who wrote books. Four of these holy books are mentioned in the Qur'an: Torah (*Tawrat*), revealed to Moses; Psalms (*Zabur*), revealed to David; the Gospel (*Injil*), revealed to Jesus; and the scrolls (*Sahifa*) dictated to Abraham.
- Jesus was a great prophet whom God rescued from death, but he is not the son of God, since that would be *shirk*.
- There is life after death, including heaven (*Jannam*) and hell (*Jahannah*), and there will be a day of judgment.
- Creation is predestined. God controls everything, even though humans have free will. This paradoxical claim that we have free will but that all of our acts are predestined also appears in some denominations of Christianity, especially those influenced by French-born Swiss reformer John Calvin (1509–1564).

Q 10.13

In Case 10.4, is it reasonable for city authorities to argue that since Muslims believe in fate, it must be God's will that the authorities ban local police officers from wearing beards?

Tradition

 ## CASE 10.6

No Women Police Officers, Please[37]

New York detective Anna Jensen is investigating a murder in a Hasidic community in New York. Hasidism is an ultra-orthodox community that discourages women from professional work that might put them in a leadership role over men, including police work.

Det. Jensen, who is unfamiliar with Hasidism, faces the rebbe, the Hasidic community's leader, who refuses to acknowledge her police authority and who demands to speak with a male officer. Jensen replies that she is an excellent investigator, that no one else is available to take the case, and that if the rebbe continues this way, Jensen will arrest him for obstructing justice.

Case 10.6 reminds us that tradition is another source of religious moral authority alongside scripture. Tradition may be formal or informal. Formal tradition includes official dogma—church teachings that are irrevocable—as, for example, Roman Catholicism, Orthodox Christianity, and Orthodox Judaism articulate, promote, and obey it. Informal tradition is simply the attitude, conscious or not, that "this is how we've always done it" and that this is why we should continue to do it.

In Roman Catholicism, for example, women cannot become priests because of the tradition that Jesus Christ chose only men as disciples. To people who don't embrace that teaching, this may seem old-fashioned, yet we cannot expect an organization that relies heavily on tradition to change its position readily just because of current trends or mores.

An interesting example of informal tradition is the Southern Baptist Convention's position that preachers must be men. The Baptist denomination developed in part as a rejection of tradition's authority, in favor of scripture as the sole authority. Recently, the Southern Baptists banned women from preaching, partly because the preaching had been fine for years without women in the pulpit. In effect, the organization decided to exclude women as ministers because its *tradition* showed there was no need for them.

One way to examine Jewish, Christian, and Muslim thinking about tradition is to identify the denominations within each one. Two of the most basic distinguishing characteristics among denominations are (1) how seriously each denomination takes tradition as a moral authority and (2) the traditions that are specific to that denomination.

Q 10.14

As a resident of the United States, should the rebbe in Case 10.6 be more accepting of Jensen's role and authority?

Judaism and Tradition

Case 10.6 highlights a strict form of Orthodox Judaism, but Judaism has three other major denominations as well. Orthodox Judaism, the most traditional and fundamentalist, follows Jewish law, *halakha,* and resists modern approaches to study and to history. Among the more visible signs of Orthodox Jewish practice in contemporary America is the believer's strict *kosher* dietary practices—no mixing of meat and dairy, no consumption of pork, and no consumption of shellfish, for example. Another visible sign is the believer's refusal to work on the Sabbath, which runs from sunset on Friday to sunset on Saturday. In the Orthodox tradition, which puts a premium on human life, one may break the Sabbath only if it is necessary to save a life.

Q 10.15

Having taken an oath to protect the U.S. Constitution, should Jensen in Case 10.6 honor the rebbe's First Amendment right to practice his religion as he sees fit, even if it interferes with her doing her job?

Conservative Judaism, which developed in the 19th century, is non-fundamentalist and less traditional than the Orthodox. While Conservatives follow *halakha* as a rule, they also embrace modern approaches to study and to history.

Reform Judaism is more comfortable with modernity than its more traditional counterparts. It emphasizes personal autonomy over *halakha*.

Reconstructionist Judaism has a strong positive attitude toward modernity, but it puts a higher premium on the community than does Reform Judaism.

An implication of this variety of denominations for the criminal justice professional is that Judaism is not as monolithic or single-minded as many non-Jews believe. To understand Judaism well, therefore, requires understanding this variety of beliefs.

Christian Denominations

Christianity includes many denominations and sects, each with its own moral slant. In the United States, the most basic denominational distinction is between Roman Catholics and Protestants. For the first 1,000 years of Christianity, Roman Catholicism had a monopoly on the faith. Then, major theological and political disagreements caused a schism between the Roman Church in the western part of the Christian world and a collection of Eastern churches that are broadly classified as "Orthodox" Christian churches. Around 1500, there was a major schism in the Western church as well, with Martin Luther, a German monk, and John Calvin, a French-born Swiss theologian, leading protests against the Roman church leaders—especially the pope—and founding new churches and new religious movements that together constituted the Protestant Reformation. For much of America's history Protestants were in charge, often with open disdain for Catholics and non-Christians. A major political change came with the election of John F. Kennedy, the first Roman Catholic president, in 1960. Since then, public disagreements between Catholics and Protestants, especially as these disagreements might concern criminal justice ethics, have been much less significant.

Today, many non-Catholic, non-Orthodox churches reject the label "Protestant," so we should regard the distinction we have just made as superficial but adequate for our purposes. One difference among the denominations is the weight that each gives to the four theological moral authorities. For example, as we saw, Roman Catholics value tradition as a moral authority much more than Baptists do. Different denominations also disagree about proper church governance. For example, Episcopal churches (Roman Catholic, Anglican, Methodist) have a hierarchical system, with bishops as the central authority. Congregational churches, such as the Baptists and the United Church of Christ, place political and decision-making authority in the congregants of each church. Presbyterians put church leaders called "elders" in charge.

Another distinction centers on specific theological issues, such as whether the consecrated bread or wafer is the body of Jesus Christ, as the Roman Catholics hold; merely symbolic of the body of Jesus, as the Methodists hold; or simply a memorial to the death of Jesus, as some other Protestant churches hold.

These different authorities, political practices, and theological beliefs affect believers' attitudes and behaviors. Some believers might have greater respect for the law, because of greater comfort with hierarchical church authority. Other believers might feel that no human is superior to any other and would-be authorities must earn their respect.

Criminal justice professionals may have to intervene in clashes between Christians over moral disagreements. Some denominations support women's right to abortion, while others condemn abortion in all instances. Some denominations permit smoking and alcohol consumption, while others forbid both. Some denominations believe that Christians have a duty to "render unto Caesar what is Caesar's," while others believe that Christians have a moral duty to disobey unjust laws.[38] Professionals who are sensitive to these differences will have an advantage when protecting the community.

Muslim Denominations

CASE 10.7

The Sniffing Dog[39]

A Muslim woman from the Middle East, having just passed through customs in a U.S. airport, is approached by a police officer and a drug-sniffing dog. As the dog nears the woman's purse, she yanks it away, refusing to let the dog get closer. The officer tells her to stand still or he will arrest her for obstructing justice. She claims that she has a copy of the Qur'an in her purse and it would be sacrilegious for a dog to touch it.

As Case 10.7 reminds us, religious traditions that are not an ordinary part of a culture can cause moral problems for criminal justice professionals and their clients. Thus, it would help to become familiar with those traditions before a problem arises. One step toward that familiarity is to understand the basic differences among the Muslim traditions. Islam is in principle so committed to a unitary front, in the guise of the *ummah* or Muslim community, that it plays down the notion of denominations.

All denominations of Islam are in fundamental agreement about the validity of six basic authorities. First, as we have seen, is the Qur'an. Second is the example of the prophet Muhammad, as described in the *hadith* (his sayings) and in the *sunnah* (his practice).

Third, in time and authority, are "The Rightly-Guided" *caliphs* (successors) or *rashadin*. These include Abu Bakr (632–634), Umar (634–644), Uthman (644–656), and Ali (656–661), son-in-law of the prophet and rightful heir, according to Shi'i Islam.

Fourth, as anthropologist and theologian David R. Smock notes, are the jurists (*'ulama*), who mediate Muslim tradition in much the same way as Talmudic rabbis mediate Jewish tradition.[40]

Beyond the *hadiths* and *sunnah*, Muslim tradition expresses itself, fifth, through *Shariah*, which is Islamic law ("the way of Islam"), and sixth, through *din*, which is the faith of Islam.[41] *Shariah* covers ways and modes of worship, standards of morals and life, and laws that allow and prescribe. *Shariah* can be amended, but *din* cannot.

Q 10.16

In Case 10.7, is the police officer morally bound to respect the woman's religious position, given our legal separation of church and state?

Islam includes two major denominations. The larger denomination is Sunni, which comprises mainstream Muslims.[42] Sunnis recognize the authority of the hereditary caliphate, they regard the consensus of the community (*ummah*) as authoritative, and they believe that Allah predestines human action.

A significant and radical Sunni sect is Wahabbism, which Muhhamad ibn Abdul Wahhab founded in the early 1700s in Arabia.[43] Although Wahhabism has been around for 300 years, it became well known outside the Middle East around 1980, when Osama bin Laden, one of its adherents, became a public figure through the terrorist acts of his organization, al-Qaeda (Arabic for "the foundation" or "the base"). Wahhab made three changes to basic Muslim teaching. First, he made *jihad*, a war against others, a first resort, whereas Muslim orthodoxy makes it a last resort. Second, he changed the status of Christians and Jews from "people of the book"—that is, fellow recipients of God's revelation—to idolaters (*mushrikun*). Third, he accused most Muslims of being impure.

Given tensions between al-Qaeda and the United States, American criminal justice professionals should recognize al-Qaeda as a fringe group that does not speak for the much larger number of law-abiding Muslims who live peacefully in the United States.

Q 10.17

In Case 10.7, suppose the woman's repugnance over the dog is a matter of religious tradition rather than a principle from the Qur'an. Would this hurt her claim to protection from the sniffing dog?

The Shi'ites form the smaller denomination of Islam. They believe that Muhammad wanted Ali to be his immediate successor, rather than the fourth caliph in line. They believe that Allah does not predestine human action. And they believe in the authority of the imam, as a direct descendent of Ali, rather than in the consensus of the community (*ummah*). A well-known recent example is Imam Ruhollah Khomeini, who ruled Iran from 1979 to 1989. Contrary to Sunni practice, Shi'ite Muslims venerate shrines and tombs of the imams.

Contemporary news reports make a great deal out of the hatred between Sunnis and Shi'ites, especially in certain areas of the Middle East. This should not mislead criminal justice professionals into regarding this as the normal relationship between Sunnis and Shi'ites. Most of the world's Muslims treat this difference much like that between Lutherans and Methodists or Conservative and Reform Jews—a difference that is far less significant than the religious similarities and one that does not justify hurting each other.

Q 10.18

In Case 10.5, suppose the robber is a Sunni Muslim and the mosque is Shi'ite. Doesn't the moral blame for violation of mosque protocol rest with the robber's disrespect for mosque protocol?

We have looked at the role of scripture and tradition in the moral decision making of Judaism, Christianity, and Islam. Of the four elements of the Wesleyan Quadrilateral—scripture, tradition, reason, and experience—scripture and tradition are the two most prominent. Thus, we will work through the other two in a more cursory fashion.

Experience

Case 10.8

The Religious Police Lieutenant

Sgt. Cary is a veteran New York policeman but is new to Washington, DC's Metropolitan Police Department. This evening he is the watch commander for his district. He receives a call that some of his subordinates are involved in a sniper situation in another district. He rushes to the site to investigate.

When he arrives at the site, he quickly discerns that the patrol officers who responded are managing well. The site is in the front of a detached home, from a first-floor window of which the sniper is reported to have fired some gunshots. One of the officers quickly brings Sgt. Cary up to date: There have been no further gunshots since the original report to 911; the officers have secured the perimeter and no civilians outside the house appear to be in danger; the officers have made no contact with the alleged sniper in the house, although they have seen the silhouette of an adult male behind a curtain that covers the window from where the shots allegedly came; and there is no indication of how many other people might be in the house.

As the officer is finishing his report to Cary, the watch commander for that district, Lt. Rusk, pulls up in front of the house. Without a word to the officers forming the perimeter or to Cary, Rusk heads up the sidewalk toward the front door of the house. Cary protests loudly to Rusk, first asking what he is doing and then, receiving no response, telling Rusk to come back. As Rusk reaches the front door, Cary decides to back him up; he runs to Rusk just as Rusk throws open the front door, which wasn't locked. As Cary and Rusk enter the house, they look to the right and see the alleged sniper with his hands raised and a rifle lying at his feet. Cary and Rusk subdue and arrest the sniper without further incident.

After officers have removed the suspect from the scene, Cary asks Rusk why he acted in a way that violated protocol for handling sniper situations. Rusk answers, "On the way over here, God spoke to me and told me that if I acted expeditiously and without fear, then everything would turn out all right—and it did!" Cary, an avowedly religious man, is stunned: "God told you? What about your safety? What about the safety of the officers on site? You were a 'sitting duck' on that sidewalk, not to mention the possibility of being ambushed when you entered the house. And what example is that to set for the other officers?" Rusk's response: "I answer first to God and then to others."

Soon after Cary and Rusk part, Cary makes an appointment to meet with Rusk's captain, Capt. Andrews. As Cary explains the situation to Andrews, Cary fully expects Andrews to react with surprise and disbelief. Instead Andrews responds, "That's old news. There is nothing I can do about it. If you think you can do something by going over my head, please feel free to take the shot; I won't hold it against you." Cary decides that there is no point in taking this further.

Case 10.8 highlights religious experience as a moral authority. As an Anglican priest, John Wesley accepted the church's "three-legged stool" of authority—scripture, tradition, and reason—but he felt that the stool was missing one leg: experience.

For Wesley this meant experience of the Holy Spirit, which comes through revelation. For many moral theologians, experience also refers to a scientific collection of empirical data.

When alleging a spiritual experience to support a moral position—concerning Rusk's violation of professional protocol in Case 10.8, for example—a major challenge is determining how one knows whether the experience is spiritual rather than, for example, merely psychological. British philosopher Thomas Hobbes notes this in his attack on belief in divine revelation: "For to say that god hath spoken to him . . . in a dream, is no more than to say he dreamed that god spake to him."[44] This is a good point: It is difficult to prove that one has had a divine revelation rather than a mere dream or hallucination.

As for scientific experience, it may challenge religious teaching as often as it enhances such teaching. Consider the debate between "creationists" and "evolutionists." The latter argue that empirical data show the world to be much older and more slowly developed than the account of creation in the biblical book of Genesis. Some scientists have tried to find a compromise between the two views by offering the hypothesis of "intelligent design"—the theory that while science refutes Genesis's timeline, science enhances the likelihood that a divine intelligence created this complex and orderly world.

Reason offers the greatest challenge to claims of spiritual experience, and reason often underlies attempts to work scientific experience into religious moral decision making. We turn now to reason as the fourth element in the Wesleyan Quadrilateral.

Q 10.19

Is there any moral similarity between Case 10. 1 and Case 10.8? If not, why not?

Reason

CASE 10.9

The Chaplain

Three officers in a small police agency are Muslim. For years the agency has had a Christian chaplain, who receives a salary to be on call 24 hours a day, and a Jewish chaplain, whom the city government pays by the hour when the agency requests his services. The local Muslim community has been growing steadily over the past several years and is now larger than the local Jewish population, although the number of Jews on the police force has remained steady at three. When the Muslim officers ask the police chief to hire a Muslim chaplain, the chief declines, arguing that there is no money in the budget for such a hire. However, the chief notes that he would welcome a volunteer Muslim chaplain.

Sometimes issues of fairness are issues of reasonableness, as in Case 10.9. Reason is the fourth religious moral authority. Recall that to use reason is to argue that if one accepts certain premises then one must accept a certain conclusion. For example, one could imagine the Muslim officers in Case 10.9 arguing as follows:

Argument 1

1. The police department should manage its chaplaincy fairly.
2. Department chaplains are there for officers and for the community.
3. There should be chaplains for each of the three major religions that the department and community represent: Christianity, Judaism, and Islam.
4. The support for each chaplain should be in proportion to the number of people the chaplain represents.
5. There are as many Muslim officers as Jewish officers, and there are more Muslim citizens than Jewish citizens.
6. The Jewish chaplain receives an hourly wage.
7. Therefore, the Muslim chaplain should receive an hourly wage, and it should be at least as much as the Jewish chaplain gets.

The chief's argument appears to be simpler:

Argument 2

1. The department can afford only what it has in its budget.
2. There is no money in the budget for a Muslim chaplain.
3. Therefore, the department cannot afford to pay a Muslim chaplain.

It is hard to tell the more reasonable argument. Argument 1's fourth premise is controversial: Why should support for each chaplain be in proportion to the number of people he represents? What, for example, entails this representation? The Muslim chaplain's role may be different enough from the Jewish chaplain's role to justify giving each different types and amounts of support.

Argument 2 is valid, but its second premise may not be true. There may be ways to fix the budget to provide money for a Muslim chaplain. Our point is not to declare a winning argument but to acknowledge the role of reason in a religiously charged debate.

Q 10.20

In Case 10.9, would it be morally reasonable for the department to reject the idea of a Muslim chaplain on the grounds that Christianity and Judaism traditionally don't express enmity toward the United States, in contrast to the rhetoric and practice of many Muslims?

In moral theology, reason's focus is philosophical ethics, which we considered in Part I. The philosophical views of consequentialism, regularianism, and deontology pertain to religious ethics as well. Religious ethics tends to focus on the character of the agent, so consequences would generally be insufficient for judging an act's morality. If the agent's "heart is in the right place," the act might be morally good regardless of the consequences. The example of the protective wife (Case 4.3) shows that the regularian faces the same problem as anyone who takes scripture as a set of rules to obey blindly. What if the rule demands immoral behavior or makes no sense?

Q 10.21

In Case 10.9, if the police department hires a Muslim chaplain, should it be allowed to preclude chaplains with al-Qaeda sympathies?

Deontology fits nicely with religious ethics, because both demand that people do their duty. But how do we determine our duty? By following scripture blindly? By doing "as the spirit moves us," as in the case of the religious police lieutenant (Case 10.8)? What about conflict of duty? Judaism, Christianity, and Islam tell us to obey our secular authority—to "render unto Caesar what is Caesar's"—but what if that authority demands an act that contradicts our religious duty? "Go to war," says the ruler. "Thou shalt not kill," says the sixth commandment. Is it possible to obey both commands at the same time?

Q 10.22

Does Smith's argument for the morality of his act in Case 10.1 appear to rest mostly on consequences, rules, or duty?

As in philosophical ethics, virtue theory offers an approach to religious morality that makes the best of the other theories while avoiding their shortcomings. Recall the relationship between virtue theory and the concept of sin—the worst sort of wrongdoing from a religious point of view. Aristotle uses the analogy of the archer. An excellent archer knows how to aim at the bull's-eye and hits it routinely. A good archer understands the basics of aiming, but misses the bull's-eye more than he would like. A poor archer either does not know how to aim, or knows how to aim but still tends to miss the bull's-eye. Similarly, a person of high virtue usually knows the good and does it as a matter of habit. A virtuous person with considerable room for improvement usually knows the good but does it less often than he should. A vicious person either fails to know the good, even though he should know it, or knows the good but tends not to do it.

In Case 10.1, is there an alternative that is more moderate than Smith's choice for handling the situation? If so, what is that alternative, and why is it both less deficient and less excessive than Smith's choice?

In Judaism, Christianity, and Islam, this Aristotelian idea applies to sin. The Greek word for sin, *hamartia*, means "missing the mark." A Hebrew word for sin, *chata*, means the same thing, as does an Arabic word for sin, *khati'a*. The mark is the will of God. We miss the mark when we fail to know it, which is a sin of ignorance, or we know it but fail to hit it anyway, which is a sin of weakness.

Another aspect of Aristotle's virtue theory, the idea of balance between extremes, applies to moral theology. The Wesleyan Quadrilateral notes the four basic sources of religious moral authority: scripture, tradition, experience, and reason. Virtue theory tells us always to look for the mean between the extremes—to choose the option that is at once the least deficient and the least excessive relative to the situation. From a religious point of view, we might focus too much on one source and not enough on the others. In Case 10.8, for example, the religious police lieutenant puts too much credence in his alleged *experience* of talking to God and not enough credence on the *rationality* of protocol. A proper approach to religious moral decision making would be to use the right balance of scripture, tradition, experience, and reason in coming to a decision. The question remains, however, What constitutes the right balance?

So much for moral theology in general. Let's now look at each of the three religions' views about war. As noted previously, this should prove useful to students of criminal justice ethics because such an examination brings out moral views that are especially relevant to criminal justice. Chief among these relevant views are those regarding justifiable violence. When, if ever, is war justified? Against whom is it justified? Who gets to decide? What are participants' rights and responsibilities in war?

✦ THE MORALITY OF WAR

 ## CASE 10.10

The Reluctant Sniper

Anderson County police have cornered a carjacker, who remains in the car with his victim. A hostage negotiator is on the scene, and two police snipers are on a roof nearby. When the carjacker slits the throat of the victim, leaving her alive but seriously wounded, the commander tells the negotiator to forget negotiations and try to position the carjacker so he is an easy target for the snipers. The commander also gives the snipers permission to shoot when they have a clear shot.

The negotiator convinces the carjacker to open the door and accept a bottle of water, which gives the snipers the clear shot. Sniper #1 fails to fire; Sniper #2 fires and kills the carjacker, permitting emergency medical officials to get the victim to the hospital in time to save her life.

When the commander asks Sniper #1 why he didn't take the shot, he explains that he suddenly realized that his Christian faith did not allow him to kill another human being. He resigns from the agency soon after and becomes a minister.

Case 10.10 invites the question, When, if ever, is violence morally good from a religious standpoint? Given the especially violent nature of war, we may address this question with war in mind. Central to religious views about war is the debate over **just war.** Can war ever be just, and if so, what constitutes just war? Two of the more influential thinkers on this issue, Catholic theologians Augustine (354–430) and Thomas Aquinas (1225–1274), argued for the logical possibility and moral propriety of just war.[45] For them, it is just to go to war when the call to war meets six criteria:

- There is a *just cause* for the war.
- The declarer is the *right authority.*
- The warriors have the *right intention.*
- War is a *last resort* to fix the problem it is meant to fix.
- There is a strong *prospect for an emergent peace.*
- There promises to be a *proportionate balance of good over evil.*[46]

This constitutes *jus ad bellum,* a Latin phrase referring to just reasons for declaring war. Once war has begun, the concern is for *jus in bello,* justice in war, for which just war theory identifies two criteria:

- *Discrimination* between combatants and noncombatants
- A *proper proportion of evil to the good* achieved

Q 10.24

In Case 10.10, is Sniper #1 discouraging violence by refusing to take the shot?

Let's examine the various ways to think about war and peace. Then let's look at concepts of war within each of the three religions.

War and Peace

Today, war means a "hostile contention between groups by means of armed force"; its etymology begins with the Old High German *werra,* meaning broil, confusion, or strife.[47]

Peace may mean inactivity;[48] concord and harmony, not just absence of war;[49] or, theologically, *shalom* (Hebrew) or *salaam* (Arabic). Shalom/salaam, however, comprises more than peace; it is the opposite of chaos, and regards God as righteous, compassionate, and sovereign. In this sense, war transforms shalom into chaos.[50]

Philosopher Duane Cady describes a continuum from radical pacifism to radical "warism."[51] At the pacifist end are absolute pacifists, who avoid violence at all costs. Quakers, for example, refuse to harm people because Quakers believe there is "that of God in every man" and to hurt a person is to hurt the divine. Next on the spectrum come people who believe that nonlethal force is OK, but not lethal force. Then come people who believe that individuals may have to treat each other violently at times, but collections of people should not, because the prospect for unfair harm is too great. Some promote pacifism because of the position that we don't know enough about the intended adversaries to justify our hurting them. Finally on the pacifist side of the spectrum come those who would refrain from war because modern technology makes it potentially too destructive.

Just war theorists would put their subject in the middle of this spectrum, arguing that war is just when a pacifist response would be deficient but war that violates a just war criterion would be excessive.

Warists defend war as a first resort or war for the sake of war and occupy the farthest end of the spectrum opposite absolute pacifism.[52] Today it is not seemly to defend such a position. Of course, some Muslim radicals have been condemned for waging a holy war, which they refer to as *jihad*. Also, Christians have the Crusades and the Puritans in their history, both of which mark a willingness to use war as a first resort, confident in the belief that God is behind the decision. So, the concept of holy war is not foreign to the religions of Abraham.

We have laid the foundation for a consideration of just war from the religious perspective. Let's next look more closely at the three religions and their thoughts on war.

Pacifism

Judaism and Pacifism

 ## CASE 10.11

"NYC Rabbi Organizing Armed Patrols Draws Anger"[53]

"Rabbi Yakove Lloyd, president of the right-wing Jewish Defense Group, called a news conference Sunday to explain details of his patrols, which were planned to begin Sunday night with groups carrying shotguns, baseball bats, pipes, cellular phones and walkie-talkies."

Lloyd claimed that these patrols were necessary to protect heavily Jewish neighborhoods against terrorist threats from Muslims who have called for harm to Jews.

Jewish and non-Jewish community and political leaders condemned this plan for giving the community a bad name, for possibly inciting violence, and for putting innocent lives at unnecessary risk. Police Commissioner Raymond Kelly went farther, calling the patrols vigilantes and threatening to arrest any armed member of the patrol.

Lloyd countered that the patrol members had permits to carry firearms and thus could not be arrested simply for patrolling the neighborhood.

Case 10.11 raises the question of appropriate use of violence by Jews in self-defense. Since *halakha,* Jewish law, often permits or requires violence, Judaism forbids quietism—the view that one should do nothing in the face of aggression.[54] However, individuals, such as pregnant women, may be excused from fighting if their death will "cause a clear incompleteness in the impending life cycle" or if their conduct would hurt army morale. Preference for life drives much of Jewish moral theology and challenges the righteous person to balance concern for life against justified use of violence.

Q 10.25

In Case 10.11, is Rabbi Lloyd's plan a morally proper response to *halakha's* prohibition of quietism?

In addition to forbidding quietism, Judaism limits pacifism, allowing it only as a practical social strategy to prevent war, but never beyond the point of self-defense.

The Tanakh contains 281 references to peace and 192 references to war.[55] Prooftexting—that is, selectively "cherry-picking" verses from the Bible—yields apparently contradictory positions on war. Isaiah 2:4 and Micah 4:3 call for beating swords into plowshares; Joel 3:10 calls for beating plowshares into swords. We can resolve this apparent contradiction by locating these imperatives at different times in Jewish history. This shows that we must not take brief biblical moral statements out of context, if we wish to understand their moral import today.

Three basic Jewish principles about war tip the scales somewhat toward pacifism.[56] First, Jews must avoid misuse of religious authority in making war: "God is on my side" does not justify violent acts against others. Second, justified war is at best the lesser of two evils, because it involves taking human life. Third, Jewish victors in war must avoid triumphalism, because war is too terrible to celebrate, even in victory.

Christianity and Pacifism

Unlike most Jews and Muslims, many Christians are pacifists, calling for nonviolence at all costs. Christian pacifism is of two types:[57] *Obedient/fiduciary* pacifism—the

Mennonites' view, for example—holds that being a disciple of Jesus Christ entails obedience to Christ, and Christ requires peace.[58] *Empathetic/compassionate* pacifism—the Quakers' view, for example—holds that disciples of Christ must love their enemies.[59]

In terms of the Wesleyan Quadrilateral, Christian pacifists offer these justifications. *Scripture* says that the kingdom of God is imminent, so we should be living peaceably and prayerfully. Also, Christ's central teaching is the Sermon on the Mount (Matt. 5–7) in which he declares, "Blessed are the peacemakers." In its earliest *tradition,* Christianity was generally pacifist, believing that Christians may be in the world, but they are not of it. This posed an interesting problem for Roman soldiers who converted to Christianity but chose to remain in the military. Further, it stands to *reason* that love of neighbor, which Christ demands of everyone, is contradictory to violence. Finally, *experience* shows that war hurts everyone involved.

It is evident that two areas of criminal justice are especially challenging to Christian pacifists: self-defense that requires some form of aggression, and punishment that may require harm to the punished. In the world today, both self-defense and severe punishment appear to be potentially proper responses, but not on pacifist grounds.

Islam and Pacifism

Islam's attitude toward war is like Judaism's. It forbids quietism and requires all able-bodied believers to engage in a war of self-defense if necessary.

In sum, of Judaism, Christianity, and Islam, only Christianity makes room for defense of pacifism. All three make room for just war theorists, which we consider next.

Just War

Judaism and Just War

There are three types of just war in Jewish history, but only two today.[60] For an *optional* war, the Jewish fighters must have a moral reason and the enemy must have violated universal moral law. War is *obligatory* when necessary for immediate self-defense. In the time of Joshua (c. 1440 BCE), God permitted war of conquest against the Canaanites.

Smock notes the following concerning Judaism on just war:[61] There is *just cause* when Jews must defend themselves, and there is no alternative or when a victim of aggression needs help. After World War II, it became especially important to save Judaism and Jewry. To ensure that the *good outweighs the evil* of going to war, Jewish law requires pursuit of justice and avoidance of wanton destruction. Scholars disagree about whether Judaism has a principle of *last resort,* with some arguing that Jewish law requires only that people make a good faith effort at avoiding war. In any event, Judaism calls for giving the enemy a chance to surrender or flee before taking military action. Any enemy who stands fast is an enemy combatant.[62] Because of the law's importance to Judaism, its notion of *right authority* is clearer than Christianity's; the New Testament offers no precise rules for engaging in war. Although Judaism has no interest in *proportionality*, it distinguishes between permissible and impermissible wars, and demands that combatants not harm the environment unnecessarily.

Concerning *jus in bello*, just action once the war is on, legal scholar Michael J. Broyde notes the following principles from Jewish law:[63] Soldiers may not use civilians as pawns. No one may kill an innocent third party to save a life. No one may force another to risk his life to save someone else's. And no one may kill a pursuer as punishment after his evil act has ended.

Concerning nuclear war in particular, Broyde notes that the Talmud forbids war when the casualty rate would exceed one-sixth of the population, so it appears to forbid the use of nuclear strikes. Nevertheless, contemporary Jewish jurists have concluded that it is permissible to use the *threat* of nuclear strikes.

The virtuous criminal justice professional should understand Jewish ethics to the extent that the community includes Jews, the professional has Jewish colleagues, or the professional is Jewish. To that end, our look at Jewish law and Jewish attitudes toward violence has revealed four points. First, in light of the Jews' special covenant with God and the many persecutions of Jews, Jews must act to keep Judaism alive and prospering. Second, Jewish acts should show a preference for life. Third, Jews must follow the Golden Rule. And fourth, where retaliation is appropriate, even to the point of violence, it must be in proportion to the offense; excessive force is never morally right.

Q 10.26

In Case 10.11, Rabbi Lloyd appears to hold that the neighbors have an obligation to defend themselves, given Muslim terrorists' verbal threats against them. Is the threat immediate enough to justify the rabbi's plan morally?

We turn next to Christianity on just war.

Christianity and Just War

For Roman Catholic Saints Augustine and Thomas Aquinas, war is just when, in Aristotelian terms, it is virtuous—that is, when it is the mean between extremes and any other response would be deficient or excessive.

Important to Roman Catholic just war theory is the **principle of double effect,** which many Protestants reject. On this principle, when doing something right requires doing something usually considered wrong, that wrong becomes right. Consider the example of a father finding his young daughter under attack by a grown man. The father has two choices: let the assault continue or intervene to protect his daughter. The latter choice is obviously better, but the father has to kill the assailant to stop him. Although it is wrong to kill, the principle of double effect justifies this killing because the father's primary object was, laudably, to protect his daughter. Had the father used this opportunity to kill a person, with no interest in protecting his daughter, the Church would condemn the killing. Roman Catholic proponents of just war use the principle of double effect in a similar way. For them, although killing is wrong as a rule, sometimes war may be necessary to stop a greater evil, in which case the war becomes a just response.

Contrary to the principle of double effect is the Protestant reformer Martin Luther's (1483–1546) notion of **"sinning bravely."** Whereas Roman Catholicism teaches that God always leaves a right path open to us, Protestantism teaches that people may mismanage things so badly that the subsequent choices are all undesirable; that is, whatever one does next will be morally wrong. Here the agent must choose the lesser of two evils, sinning bravely with the faith that the agent is operating under an umbrella of God's grace. Thus, a Protestant might agree with a Roman Catholic on the need for war, but whereas the Catholic might consider the war just, the Protestant might regard the war as unjust but less so than the alternative. Note that some Catholics do not believe in just war and some Protestants do, so we must not be too restrictive in distinguishing between the principle of double effect and the notion of sinning bravely.

Christian just war theory is of two types: the Augustinian and the Thomistic.[64] For Augustine, one may kill while being guided by *love,* somewhat in the spirit of "tough love." Protestants Martin Luther and John Calvin (1509–1564) agree with Augustine that there are two kingdoms: the kingdom of man and the kingdom of God.[65] For them, the evils of man sometimes require violence, but there will be no need for violence when the Kingdom of God is all that exists. Thomas Aquinas emphasizes the *natural order* in God's kingdom and the *natural justice* of doing what is necessary to restore that order when it is harmed, even if war is the only means of restoration.

In terms of the Wesleyan Quadrilateral, Christian just war theorists offer these justifications. First, the Old Testament *scripture* has many positive references to war as necessary to carrying out God's plans. Also, the Bible claims that the Kingdom of God is not imminent and that in its absence war may sometimes be necessary. This distinction between the two kingdoms also underlies the *tradition* that just war theorists invoke for moral support. Appeals to *reason* in defense of just war include the Augustinian analogy to loving punishment and Thomas's claim that natural law is a dictate of human reason, sometimes calling rational beings to war to preserve the natural order. Finally, there is the Christian *experience* of the depravity of human nature, which reminds us that sometimes war is the best response to acts of depravity.

We have considered the just war theories of two Abrahamic religions: Christianity and Judaism. We turn now to Islam.

Islam and Just War

There is no single Islamic theory of war, but we can make some general observations about Islamic war theory, and thus about Islam's attitude toward violence.[66] First, there are two basic types of war, according to Islam: *jihad* (Islamic war), "a war fought in accordance with the purpose and limits determined by God"; and *harb,* "every other kind of war."[67] Since much is made these days about jihad, it is worth examining more closely. There are two classical types of jihad: internal—the jihad of the Qur'an—and external.[68] Externally, Islam distinguishes dar al-Islam—the world of Islam—from dar al-harb—the non-Islamic world. Islam teaches that the whole world must become dar al-Islam for there to be lasting peace.

According to theologian James Turner Johnson, there are two general situations in which external jihad—war against non-Muslims—is appropriate. A caliph (Sunni) or imam (Shi'ite) with sufficient authority could declare offensive war, but today there is no caliph or imam to call such a war. External jihad is also appropriate in an emergency where no milder form of self-defense will suffice. According to Johnson, this occurs when dar al-harb crosses the border into dar al-Islam. Smock claims that emergency jihad is prescribed in only three cases: to eliminate oppression, to protect human life, and to uphold Islamic principles.[69] Theologian Ruqaiyyah Maqsood agrees with Johnson and Smock, noting that Islam calls for war in defense of Allah, to restore peace and freedom of worship, and to fight tyranny.[70] Maqsood goes on to note the limits of jihad: It excludes wars of conquest, aggression, or ambition. War should not be a response to border disputes or tribal squabbles. War must be fought only until everyone lays down arms. War should not harm the old, the young, the sick, women, trees, or crops. And war should never be a means to force people to accept a faith they don't believe.

Osama bin Laden, leader of the terrorist organization al-Qaeda, has a radically different view from his more moderate colleagues on when war is appropriate.[71] Bin Laden has four basic assumptions. First, dar al-Islam includes any territories whose population is mainly Muslim and which were part of the historical dar al-Islam. Second, aggressors include anyone who supports a non-Islamic presence. Third, since this jihad is based on an emergency, there are no limits on jihad. And fourth, all Muslims must fight. Bin Laden's stand is contrary to Muslim faith and history, because bin Laden leaves no room for toleration of "people of the book," or for different interpretations of God's will. Also, bin Laden's war is an offensive war disguised as a defensive war.[72]

We may summarize the foregoing concerning Islam and just war theory. First, Islam promotes peace and love over hate and war,[73] but it rejects pacifism, because it believes that complete peace will occur only when the whole world is dar al-Islam.[74]

Second, only jihad can be a just war; *harb* can never be just. A special case of jihad is war between Muslims. An important resource here is the "Judgment of the Tyrants," which Muslim jurists declared in the eighth century. The guidelines are stricter than for wars of Muslims against non-Muslims. Following Ali's lead, the jurists prohibit chasing someone who is fleeing, killing Muslim prisoners of war, killing the wounded in battle, enslaving women and children, and confiscating the property of Muslims.[75]

Third, in all war, Muslims must maintain the integrity of the *ummah* (family of Islam).[76]

Fourth, mainstream Islamic just war theory agrees with Christian just war theory in three ways: the value of international law; the requirement for a right authority to make war; and the aim of the common good, but never in terms of repression or intolerance.

Having considered pacifism and just war from the viewpoint of the three religions, we turn now to holy war.

Holy War

Judaism and Holy War

Judaism appears to accept violence more readily than Christianity, yet Jewish history has nothing so violent as the Christian crusades.

Even as Judaism embraces lex talionis and the Golden Rule, each denomination may interpret these differently, so the virtuous criminal justice professional must be open to such differences when dealing with Jewish people or with his or her own beliefs.

Christianity and Holy War

The basic point of holy war theory is that war is a *first* resort in defense of religious tenets. To holy war advocates, there is no need to try less drastic methods first because the enemy has brought this aggression on itself. Today, fringe groups calling themselves Christians promote holy war—against other races or "godless" government agents, for example—but mainstream Christianity has no contemporary influential proponent of holy war. This was not always true, however. The Christian Crusades are the most obvious example of Christian support for holy war.[77] Popes Urban II (c. 1095) and Innocent II (c. 1145), with the support of church leader Bernard of Clairvaux (1090–1153), called for a holy war against the Muslims to protect Jerusalem for the Christians.[78]

In terms of the Wesleyan Quadrilateral, Christian holy war theorists offer these justifications. First, *scripture* recognizes the Lord as a warrior (Exod. 15:3; Isa. 42:13; Ps. 137:8) and contains God's command to "destroy them all" (Josh. 6:21; 1 Sam. 15:2–3). To holy war proponents, Christian *tradition* recognizes God as a God of war. For them, it stands to *reason* that infidels are contradictory to Christianity and, therefore, are outside the order of Christendom.[79] *Experience,* says the holy war proponent, shows that only violence can get our land (Jerusalem) back.

Since Christianity influences American legislation, public policy, and community affairs, and since Christians vary in their attitude toward violence, the virtuous criminal justice professional—the professional who is courageous, just, temperate, and prudent—will be sensitive to this influence in all of its nuances, and will operate accordingly.

Islam and Holy War

Although the West often refers to jihad as holy war, as do some Muslims terrorists, there is no defense of this position in Islamic scripture, tradition, reason, or experience.

Nevertheless, we note three points here. First, Muslims tend not to separate their theology from their morality, contrary to the American principle of separation of church and state. Second, Islamic morality in its strictest form clashes with the more pluralist and permissive morality of American society. Third, for Muslims, there is a presumption of resistance to violence, but they stand ready to meet perceived threats to Islam by whatever means necessary to remove the threat. This may help explain current concerns about terrorist threats from a small but dangerous group of Muslims.

SUMMARY

This chapter has discussed ethics from the perspectives of America's three most populous religions: Christianity, Judaism, and Islam.

After identifying the foundations of each religion, this chapter introduced the Wesleyan Quadrilateral as a useful framework for discussing moral theology—the study of religious ethics. Using that framework, we looked at the moral authority of scripture, tradition, reason, and experience for each of the three religions.

Finally, we looked at each religion's views on war, noting the relevance of this study to criminal justice ethics, because one's views on war say much about one's views on issues important to criminal justice, such as use of force, the limits of government intervention, and the scope of a government leader's authority to require violence.

The next chapter examines criminal justice ethics from a professional point of view.

ANSWERS TO CASE STUDY QUESTIONS

Q10.1. Did Smith fail to do his duty in Case 10.1? Why, or why not?

No. He had discretion in handling the case, so the question is whether he fulfilled his duty to use his discretion well. Since he knew the couple, he believed they were sincere, and the result was good, it appears that he fulfilled his duty in this case.

Q10.2. In Case 10.2, is the neighbors' Jewishness morally relevant to the question of whether Green should obey the mayor's order?

No.

1. If the mayor's order is legal and consistent with Green's professional duties, then Green should obey that order.
2. The mayor's order is legal and consistent with Green's professional duties.
3. Therefore, Green should obey the mayor's order.

Objection: It is immoral for the Neo-Nazis to aim their hate at a Jewish neighborhood. Response: The First Amendment, which Green has sworn to uphold, protects the Neo-Nazis' right to assemble and to spout their hate.

Q10.3. In Case 10.2, does Capt. Green appear to hold that for Jews, Jewish law trumps the town's law? If so, why is she correct or incorrect?

No. None of her arguments appeals to Jewish law. Rather, she appears to be pitting commonsense morality against the town's law.

Q10.4. In Case 10.3, does Gleason have the constitutional right to "use the Lord's name in vain"?

Yes, in civilian life. But police departments may—without violating the Constitution—impose restrictions on officers that governments cannot impose on civilians. Gleason has a stronger case by appealing to precedent, especially if there is no formal departmental rule to the contrary.

Q10.5. Given the traditional "separation of church and state," did Larkin in Case 10.3 have the right to work his religious beliefs into his supervision of public officials?

No. But he might have argued on procedural terms—for example, citing conduct unbecoming an officer.

Q10.6. In Case 10.4, is there any merit to the claim that if one has a moral right to wear a beard for medical reasons, then one should have the right to wear a beard for religious reasons?

No. A medical right implies nothing about a religious right. Any argument that rests on an analogy between the two would be a weak argument.

Q10.7. If the neighbors in Case 10.2 were Christian, would they be morally bound by their scripture to take the marchers' abuse peacefully?

Yes. But this is not the same thing as taking the marchers' abuse—there may be ways to avoid the abuse without treating the marchers violently.

Q10.8. In Case 10.5, suppose the mosque supports Iranian revolutionary principles, although no known member of the mosque has ever been in legal trouble. Given Iran's contempt for America, do the police have the right to ignore mosque protocol?

No.

1. The First Amendment protects Iranian religious practice in general, even if it does not protect every possible Iranian act.
2. The police officers' first duty is to protect the Constitution, including the First Amendment.
3. Therefore, the police officers have a duty to protect Iranian religious practice in general—or at least a duty not to interfere with it.
4. If the police simply ignore mosque protocol in entering the mosque, then they fail in their constitutional obligation to protect the religious practice in the mosque.
5. Thus, the fact in Case 10.5 that the mosque supports Iranian revolutionary principles would not justify the police's ignoring mosque protocol.

Q10.9. In Case 10.4, would it be fair for the authorities to argue that since wearing a beard is merely a tradition among Muslim men and not one of the five basic duties, banning beards does no harm to Muslim practice?

No. The five basic duties are not the only principles governing Muslim practice. In every religion's practice, tradition can play a significant role.

Objection: Many observant Muslim men do not wear beards, so wearing a beard is not essential to a Muslim's religious identity.

Q10.10. Of the four authorities on the Wesleyan Quadrilateral, which does Smith seem to be emphasizing in his handling of the situation in Case 10.1?

Smith emphasizes reason and experience over scripture and tradition.

Q10.11. In Case 10.2, would the Golden Rule justify the neighbors' hurting the marchers, since the marchers advocate harm to the neighbors?

The Golden Rule makes the marchers vulnerable, because on that rule preachers of violence and hate would have to accept violence and hate in return. Further, lex talionis would let the neighbors respond to violence with violence. However, since the neighbors would like to be treated with respect and nonviolence, the Golden Rule would require them to remain respectful and nonviolent. Note that the Golden Rule may not be the best moral principle here, because it puts the neighbors in an uncalled-for difficult moral position.

Q10.12. In Case 10.1, Smith defends his action as good community policing. Would his argument be stronger if he used the Bible to defend his act?
No. His argument is based on good community policing, defined in terms of the specific community and its norms, which is a more relevant premise than the Bible.

Q10.13. In Case 10.4, is it reasonable for city authorities to argue that since Muslims believe in fate, it must be God's will that the authorities ban local police officers from wearing beards?
No. This would be a frivolous argument. Both sides could argue from fatalism, which renders fatalism a useless premise.

Q10.14. As a resident of the United States, should the rebbe in Case10.6 be more accepting of Jensen's role and authority?
Yes. If the rebbe wants police protection, then he should accept that service no matter what the officer's gender is. In other words, the public principle of nondiscrimination in this case trumps the rebbe's principle of discrimination.
Objection: Police should respect the religious beliefs of the community, unless those beliefs are harmful to the community.

Q10.15. Having taken an oath to protect the U.S. Constitution, should Jensen in Case 10.6 honor the rebbe's First Amendment right to practice his religion as he sees fit, even if it interferes with her doing her job?
No. The rebbe's right does not impose on Jensen the duty to avoid doing her job. If she continues on the rebbe's case, she is not violating the rebbe's religious freedom; thus, she is not infringing on the rebbe's First Amendment right.

Q10.16. In Case 10.7, is the police officer morally bound to respect the woman's religious position, given our legal separation of church and state?
The police officer is morally bound to respect the church/state limits set by the Constitution. But this does not necessarily preclude him from searching the woman's purse, since he could do so respectfully.

Q10.17. In Case 10.7, suppose the woman's repugnance over the dog is a matter of religious tradition rather than a principle from the Qur'an. Would this hurt her claim to protection from the sniffing dog?
Yes. If it is a matter of tradition, rather than a Qur'anic principle, then she stands on shakier moral ground. Tradition's authority is more ambiguous in Islam than the Qur'an's authority.

Q10.18. In Case10.5, suppose the robber is a Sunni Muslim and the mosque is Shi'ite. Doesn't the moral blame for violation of mosque protocol rest with the purse snatcher's disrespect for mosque protocol?
If the robber is a Muslim, then he merits moral blame for his violation of mosque protocol because he ought to know that entering the mosque as he has is against

Muslim teaching—Shi'ite or Sunni. This does not let the police officers off the hook, however. Their duty to respect mosque protocol is independent of the robber's duty to do so.

Q10.19. Is there any moral similarity between Case 10.1 and Case 10.8? If not, why not?

No. In Case 10.8, the lieutenant's main premise is his belief that God told him to act in a certain way. In Case 10.1, Officer Smith's main premise is that his act constituted good community policing. Smith's premise is thus more relevant than the lieutenant's premise to good policing. That Officer Smith's solution included a religious marriage counselor is irrelevant to whether his act constituted good community policing.

Q10.20. In Case 10.9, would it be morally reasonable for the department to reject the idea of a Muslim chaplain on the grounds that Christianity and Judaism don't express enmity toward the United States, in contrast to the rhetoric and practice of many Muslims?

No. To assume that a Muslim chaplain would follow the abhorrent teachings of a radical few Muslims would be to commit the fallacy of hasty generalization.

Q10.21. In Case 10.9, if the police department hires a Muslim chaplain, should it be allowed to preclude chaplains with al-Qaeda sympathies?

Yes. The police department does not have to hire the first Muslim cleric to apply. The department could demand that the chaplain honor the mission of the department—that is, protection of the community—and the department could note correctly that al-Qaeda sympathies are antithetical to that mission.

Q10.22. Does Smith's argument for the morality of his act in Case 10.1 appear to rest mostly on consequences, rules, or duty?

Consequences—his success in getting the couple into counseling and the more general good result for the community.

Objection: Smith may feel a religious duty to act as he did, regardless of the outcome.

Q10.23. In Case 10.1, is there an alternative that is more moderate than Smith's choice for handling the situation? If so, what is that alternative, and why is it both less deficient and less excessive than Smith's choice?

Smith might have arrested one spouse, thus doing his legal duty by separating the couple for a cooling-off period. While the suspect was under arrest, Smith could use his own time to look into marriage counseling. This would be a less excessive use of discretion and a less deficient response to his duty to take some legal action.

Objection: If Smith was so sure that his plan would work out, then it would be a waste of time to go through the trouble of an unnecessary arrest.

Q10.24. In Case 10.10, is Sniper #1 discouraging violence by refusing to take the shot?

No. The carjacker's acts were already violent, and not trying to save the victim would have exacerbated that violence.

Q10.25. In Case 10.11, is Rabbi Lloyd's plan a morally proper response to *halakha's* prohibition of quietism?

No. Common sense suggests that Lloyd's vigilantism is an excessive response to the threat and thus an excessive response to *halakha's* prohibition of quietism. On the other hand, if Lloyd and the community took no precautions, then they would be guilty of quietism and hence of offering a deficient response to the threat. A more moderate response would be to establish a citizens' patrol that works closely with the local police.

Objection: The police may not be willing or able to work with community in this way.

Response: It would be better to try this route before resorting to vigilantism.

Q10.26. In Case 10.11, Rabbi Lloyd appears to hold that the neighbors have an obligation to defend themselves, given Muslim terrorists' verbal threats against them. Is the threat immediate enough to justify the rabbi's plan morally?

No. Based on the evidence, there is no immediate threat to the rabbi's community. So his call to arms is an excessive response to the perceived threat.

Objection: It is better to be prepared for the worst.

Response: Then the community may precipitate the very response it hopes to prevent.

NOTES

1. Letter from Thomas Jefferson to the Danbury Baptist Association, 1 January 1802; retrieved 7 August 2007 from http://www.usconstitution.net/jeffwall.html. Also see Stephen Prothero, *Religious Literacy: What Every American Needs to Know—But Doesn't* (San Francisco: HarperSanFrancisco, 2007).
2. Ralph B. Potter, *War and Moral Discourse* (Richmond, VA: John Knox Press, 1969), p. 61.
3. Gen. 1.
4. Gen. 6–9.
5. Gen. 12.
6. Exod. 19–24; Deut. 29–30.
7. 2 Sam. 6–7.
8. Based on *Fraternal Order of Police v. City of Newark,* U.S. Court of Appeals, 3rd Cir, Case # 97-5542.
9. Qur'an 19:51; hereafter Q followed by chapter number and verse number.
10. Gen. 12:1–3 (RSV).
11. Deut. 6:4–5 (KJV).
12. Exod. 20:2–14.
13. Mark 12:28–34 (KJV).
14. Q4:157, 171.
15. Ruqaiyyah Maqsood, *Islam* (Chicago: NTC Publishing, 1994), Ch. 5. On *ibadah,* see Q51:56. On *ihsan,* see Q2:25, 62, and 82. On the five articles of faith, see Q2:285 and 4:130.
16. Mustanisir Mir, *Dictionary of Qur'anic Terms and Concepts* (New York: Garland, 1987), q.v. "jihad." Also see Q5:35; 8:74, 75; and 9:41, 44.
17. Maqsood, *Islam,* Ch. 6.
18. Q37:35; Q47:19
19. Q50:39–40.

20. Q6:141.
21. Q2:183–185, 187.
22. Q3:97.
23. Albert C. Outler, *John Wesley* (New York: Oxford University Press, 1964).
24. Luke 15:11–32.
25. Exod. 21:23–25 (RSV). Also see Lev. 234:19–20 and Deut. 19:21.
26. Shabbath 31a.
27. Matt. 7:12; Luke 6:31.
28. Matt. 5:38 (NIV).
29. Matt. 5–7.
30. Matt. 5:3–12.
31. Matt. 5:17–20.
32. Matt. 5:27–30.
33. Matt. 5:43–48.
34. Matt. 7:7–14.
35. Matt. 7:15–20.
36. Maqsood, *Islam,* Ch. 4.
37. Based loosely on the film *A Stranger among Us,* starring Melanie Griffith and directed by Sidney Lumet (1992).
38. Matt. 22:15–22. Martin Luther King, Jr., "Letter from Birmingham Jail," in *Why We Can't Wait* (New York: Signet, 1963).
39. Based on a report in *Religion & Ethics Newsweekly,* 2 January 2004; retrieved 26 May 2005 from web.lexis-nexis.com/universe.
40. David R. Smock, *Religious Perspectives on War,* rev. ed. (Washington, DC: U.S. Institute of Peace, 2002), p. 24.
41. Maqsood, *Islam,* Ch. 12.
42. Ibid., p. 24.
43. Frederick Forsyth, "Terrorism Rooted in 200-Year-Old Violent Sect," *Baltimore Sun,* 21 March 2004, pp. 1c, 2c.
44. Thomas Hobbes, *Leviathan* (1651), Ch. 32.
45. Augustine, *The City of God,* trans. Marcus Dods (New York: Random House, 1950); Thomas Aquinas, *Summa Theologica,* trans. Fathers of the English Dominican Province (New York: Benziger, 1948), 1 to 2.90–94.
46. Duane L. Cady, *From Warism to Pacifism* (Philadelphia: Temple University Press, 1989), p. 24. Cf. Michael Walzer, *Just and Unjust Wars* (New York: Basic Books, 1977).
47. Cady, *From Warism to Pacifism,* p. 13.
48. H. Richard Niebuhr, "The Grace of Doing Nothing," *The Christian Century,* 23 March 1932.
49. Cady, *From Warism to Pacifism,* p. 12.
50. Paul D. Hanson, "War and Peace in the Hebrew Bible," *Interpretation* 38 (1984), pp. 341–410.
51. Cady, *From Warism to Pacifism,* Ch. 4.
52. Lisa Sowle Cahill, *Love Your Enemies: Discipleship, Pacifism, and Just War Theory* (Minneapolis: Fortress Press, 1994).
53. Associated Press, 17 June 2002.
54. Michael J. Broyde, "Fighting the War and the Peace: Battlefield Ethics, Peace Talks, Treaties, and Pacifism in the Jewish Tradition"; retrieved 12 March 2004 from http://www.jlaw.com/Articles/war1.html. See also Hanson, "War and Peace in the Hebrew Bible."

55. Retrieved 13 March 2004 from Biblegateway.com.

56. Smock, *Religious Perspectives on War,* pp. 13, 14.

57. Cahill, *Love Your Enemies,* pp. 13, 150, 236.

58. See, for example, Tertullian (160–220 CE), *On the Crown,* in *Latin Christianity: Its Founder, Tertullian,* ed. Cleveland Coxe (Grand Rapids, MI: Eerdman's, 1951); Origen (185–254 CE), *On First Principles,* ed. G. W. Butterworth (New York: Harper, 1966); Menno Simmons (1496–1561), *Foundations of Christian Doctrine,* in *The Complete Writings of Menno Simons,* ed. John C. Wenger (Scottsdale, PA: Herald Press, 1955); John Howard Yoder (d. 2001), *The Politics of Jesus* (Grand Rapids, MI: Eerdman's, 1972); and Stanley Hauerwas, *A Community of Character: Toward a Constructive Christian Social Ethic* (Notre Dame, IN: University of Notre Dame Press, 1981).

59. See, for example, Erasmus (1466–1536), *The Complaint of Peace* (New York: Scholars' Facsimiles and Reprints, 1946); George Fox (1624–1691), *The Journal of George Fox,* ed. Rufus M. Jones (New York: Capricorn, 1963); Walter Rauschenbusch (1861–1918), *A Theology for the Social Gospel* (1917; Louisville, KY: Westminster John Knox Press, 1997); Dorothy Day (1897–1980), *The Long Loneliness: The Autobiography of Dorothy Day* (New York: Harper, 1952, 1981); Thomas Merton (1915–1968), *The Seven Storey Mountain* (New York: Harcourt, 1948).

60. Smock, *Religious Perspectives on War,* pp. 14, 15.

61. Ibid., pp. 14–18.

62. Broyde, "Fighting the War and the Peace."

63. Ibid.

64. Cahill, *Love Your Enemies,* pp. 14, 237.

65. John Calvin, *Institutes of the Christian Religion,* trans. Ford Lewis Battles (1536; Grand Rapids, MI: Eerdman's, 1995); Martin Luther, *Christian Liberty,* ed. Harold J. Grimm (Philadelphia: Fortress, 1957). See also Reinhold Niebuhr, "Must We Do Nothing?" *The Christian Century,* 30 March 1932.

66. Smock, *Religious Perspectives on War,* p. 24.

67. Ibid., p. 23.

68. James Turner Johnson, "Jihad and Just War," *First Things* 124 (June/July 2002), pp. 12–14.

69. Smock, *Religious Perspectives on War,* p. 21.

70. Maqsood, *Islam,* p. 86.

71. Osama bin Laden, *Messages to the World: The Statements of Osama Bin Laden,* trans. James Howarth, ed. Bruce Lawrence (London: Verso, 2005).

72. Johnson, "Jihad and Just War," p. 13.

73. Forsyth, "Terrorism Rooted in 200-Year-Old Violent Sect," p. 2c.

74. Johnson, "Jihad and Just War," p. 14.

75. Smock, *Religious Perspectives on War,* p. 23.

76. Ibid., p. 25.

77. Cahill, *Love Your Enemies,* Ch. 7.

78. Bernard of Clairvaux, "Letter to the People of the English Kingdom," in James A. Brundage, *The Crusades: A Documentary Survey* (Milwaukee, WI: Marquette University Press, 1962).

79. Cahill, *Love Your Enemies,* p. 120.

PART V

The Profession of Criminal Justice

CHAPTER 11
⌘

PROFESSIONS AND
PROFESSIONAL ETHICS

 CASE 11.1

Far from Home[1]

O n May 21, 1995, New York City police attending a ceremony in Washington, DC, got drunk in their hotel, took off their clothes, poured beer down an escalator rail, and then slid down the rail. Responding to complaints from hotel staff, guests, and the DC Metropolitan Police Department, the New York officers noted that they were far from their jurisdiction and that they were off duty.

Part of what is morally wrong with the behavior of the New York officers in Case 11.1 is their lack of professionalism. We expect police officers and other criminal justice experts to be professional on and off duty. This expectation recognizes certain rights and responsibilities that it does not recognize in nonprofessionals. The study of criminal justice ethics, therefore, needs to address two questions: (1) What is a profession? (2) What moral difference does it make that a job is a profession rather than a nonprofession? This chapter will address both questions.

Before proceeding, we should acknowledge the possible objection that not all jobs in criminal justice are professions. The variety of jobs within criminal justice run the gamut from obvious professions (lawyers and judges) to jobs that one would tend not to regard as a profession (clerks, congressional pages), with other sorts of jobs (court reporters, legislative aides) falling somewhere in between. In subsequent chapters we will divide the criminal field into three major areas: legislative, executive, and adjudicative. We will identify several jobs within each and say more about their professional qualities. We will see that as components of the overall system of criminal justice, every job in the field is morally significant in ways that make sense only if we consider it through the lens of professional ethics.

For the purposes of this chapter, we will focus on the example of policing, because police are the most public practitioners of criminal justice and there is much debate about whether policing is a profession. This debate exposes fruitfully both sides of the argument, thus allowing us to explore several possibilities concerning the nature and moral implications of a profession.

Q 11.1

In Case 11.1, would it be fair to condemn the officers' actions as unprofessional when they were far from home and off duty?

✦ WHAT IS A PROFESSION?

The question of whether jobs in American criminal justice are professions is an old and persistent one. In one view, professional is the opposite of amateur, and the difference is whether one is paid. If so, then American police, for example, first became professional in 1845, when New York made policing a full-time job.[2] In this same view, attorneys in Virginia in 1645 could not be professionals because it was illegal for attorneys to collect fees.[3] This definition is not helpful, however, because paying jobs are not always professions. We don't think of hamburger making or trash hauling as professions, for example, even though they are legitimate jobs. Thus, we need a different, more relevant definition of profession before we can determine whether criminal justice jobs satisfy that definition. To that end, we will consider the traditional definition of *profession* first and then offer an alternative definition that may fit contemporary criminal justice practice better.

Profession: A Traditional Definition

The idea of a profession comes from the Middle Ages, when law, the clergy, and academics were distinguished as professions from other jobs and careers.[4] Each profession began with a public declaration—a *profession* of vows to assume the job as a way of life, not just a means of making money. All three required university study and commitment to high ideals.

Today, the common view is that at least three criteria are necessary to a profession: extensive training, "a significant intellectual component," and offering an important service to society.[5] Criminal justice jobs in general offer an important service to society, and many people in the field undergo extensive training over their careers, but many others often forgo the sort of higher education that we usually associate with "a significant intellectual component."

For example, attempts to make policing more professional began in 1902 with the formation of the International Association of Chiefs of Police (IACP), under the presidency of Richard Sylvester, and developed dramatically under August Vollmer, police chief for Berkeley, California, from 1905 to 1932.[6] Both regarded policing as a technically difficult and socially significant task that required sophisticated physical and mental talents. For Vollmer, this meant a minimum requirement of a bachelor's degree for all police officers.[7] As we shall see, although policing is as significant a task as Sylvester and Vollmer held, the bachelor's degree may be too strict a requirement for police to be professionals.

Other features that some scholars have proposed include credentialing, a professional organization of members that governs itself, and professional autonomy of the individual practitioners.[8] Policing, for example, requires credentialing, but it does not govern itself, nor are the practitioners autonomous *in principle*. Nevertheless, police in the field must make quick decisions without consulting their superiors, so they may have a level of discretion that makes them autonomous *in practice*.

Q 11.2

In Case 11.1, do the officers have the excuse that there was no superior present to forbid them from acting unconventionally?

On these criteria, it is easy to see why lawyers, clergy, and professors are still considered to be professionals. Each of these meets all six of the criteria to some extent:

- Extensive training
- A significant intellectual component
- Offering an important service to society
- Credentialing
- Professional organization of members
- Autonomy of individual practitioners

It is also possible to see why, on these criteria, some people might not regard policing as a profession. In many agencies, a person can become a police officer right out of high school, without significant intellectual development, without being a member of a professional organization, and without professional autonomy. It seems intuitively obvious, however, that to be successful in policing today one has to be a professional. Thus, either our intuitions are wrong, or we must approach the definition of profession from a different angle.

Profession: An Alternative Definition

 # Case 11.2

When in Rome . . .

Three police officers from an American city are on vacation in Amsterdam, where prostitution and smoking hemp and marijuana are legal. Two of the friends express an interest in trying these vices while they are there; one protests that it would compromise their integrity as police officers.

In deference to our intuitions, let's take a different approach to defining a profession, one that reflects such jobs as policing more fairly and accurately. First, there are four types of definition: analytic, stipulative, dictionary, and ostensive. The traditional approach to defining *profession* works primarily with one or more of the first three types, but we might find the fourth type the most useful in our case.

Q 11.3

Does the dissenting officer in Case 11.2 exemplify the public's expectation of police integrity?

An **analytic definition** replaces the word one wants to define with a word or phrase that means the same thing. For example, "A bachelor is an unmarried man." "Bachelor" and "unmarried man" mean the same thing, and the word *is* acts as an equal sign: "Bachelor = unmarried man." This definition might be useful, for example, when someone just learning the English language understands what *unmarried* and *man* mean, but has not yet learned the meaning of *bachelor*.

Some proposed definitions of *profession* attempt the precision of an analytic definition. For example, ethicist Richard DeGeorge's famous definition of profession has four criteria:

1. It performs a needed service for society.
2. It involves advanced education and specialized knowledge.
3. Its members decide who can enter the profession and how, and the circumstances under which members may be booted from the profession.
4. Its members are held to a higher standard than the general public.[9]

Apparently DeGeorge holds that "Profession = a career that performs a necessary social service, requires advanced education, is regulated by its members, and is held to a higher standard than mere jobs." But as we have noted, the requirement for advanced education may be too strict, and one could imagine other criteria that would be necessary to a profession—for example, a sense of a calling to the task. So DeGeorge's analytic definition is not adequate.

Q 11.4

If the two willing officers in Case 11.2 have college degrees, do they meet DeGeorge's criteria for professionals?

To see the limited usefulness of an analytic definition, consider a young child's request for a definition of an orange. Initially, she may believe that an orange is any edible sphere: tomatoes, peaches, apples. But in time she learns to tell the difference between oranges and other similarly shaped fruit and vegetables. She probably does not learn this from an analytic definition. Such a definition might look like this:

> An orange = "the fruit of any of several southeast Asian evergreen trees of the genus *Citrus,* widely cultivated in warm regions and having fragrant white flowers and round fruit with a yellowish or reddish rind and a sectioned, pulpy interior, especially *C. sinensis,* the sweet orange, and *C. aurantium,* the Seville or sour orange."[10]

Even if the child listened to this whole definition, it would not help her learn what an orange is.

Defining a profession, especially as it pertains to criminal justice, is more like defining an orange than defining a bachelor. There may be an analytic definition that fits *profession,* but it would be of little use to those who simply want to know what a profession is.

To offer a **stipulative definition** is to define a word by consensus. In wood shop, the students and teacher may agree that *plane* refers to a tool for shaving wood. People in a geometry class or an aerodynamics class would find that particular definition of *plane* to be useless. It may be tempting to define *profession* in this way; we could simply agree that, for example, policing is a profession, without need for further demonstration. But this is too subjective. If policing is a profession, it is not just because we have taken a vote and decided it is so—no matter how we vote, there is a chance we might be wrong. We need more objective criteria for a profession, against which we can test the proposition that professions include policing.

Q 11.5

Does the dissenting officer's view of integrity in Case 11.2 appear to rest on a stipulative definition?

Let's return to the little girl and the orange to see the limited usefulness of a stipulative definition. If the girl asks her father, "Daddy, what's an orange?" she will not settle for the answer, "Honey, in our house we have taken a vote and decided that *orange* means a particular kind of fruit with a particular texture and taste." The child has no interest in creating a name for something; she wants to know what object exists that goes by that name.

A third type of definition is a **dictionary definition.** *The American Heritage Dictionary,* Second College Edition, has four entrees for *profession* and two entrees for *orange.* But we are not interested merely in how people use these words; like the little girl, we want to know what something is. A dictionary merely describes current usage of a term; it does not declare whether that usage corresponds to reality. Besides, how useful would it be to respond to the little girl's inquiry by telling her to consult the dictionary?

A fourth and underrated type of definition is **ostensive definition**—definition by example. Eventually the little girl will be able to distinguish oranges from other edible spheres because she will have experienced enough oranges and non-oranges to understand the difference. When and how this works are subjects for scholarly research but need not concern us here. The point is that the little girl did not arm herself with a formal definition of orange and then go looking for objects that fit the definition; she let the objects speak for themselves until she was able to distinguish oranges from non-oranges. Turning from medieval and DeGeorgian attempts to define profession, we might take the same tack as the little girl and look to examples of professionals for elements to include in our definition.

Q 11.6

In looking to define *profession,* can we find anything useful in the example of the officers in Case 11.2? If so, what?

Profession: An Ostensive Definition

 ## CASE 11.3

Only a Buck

Jennifer Hall, a state senator, proposes that the state add a dollar surcharge to every traffic fine. She projects that within a year this would raise enough funds to pay for the college education of every police officer in the state who wished to get a bachelor's degree. The senator's fiery opponent, Senator Maggie Oates, counters that the police don't deserve such special treatment to the exclusion of other state employees and that a traffic fine surcharge sufficient to cover all employees would be too large.

The senate agrees to put the question on a referendum in the next statewide election.

Let's return to our examples of nonprofessions: burger making and trash hauling. These are legitimate and useful jobs, and we would hope that people who choose these jobs execute their tasks well. But they are not professions—not by medieval standards, not by DeGeorge's definition, and not in our intuition or experience. What qualities do these jobs have or lack that would distinguish them from professions as we have experienced them?

Q 11.7

Could Hall refute Oates's argument in Case 11.3 by pointing out that police officers are responsible for enforcing traffic laws?

Simply put, professionals have greater rights and responsibilities than non-professionals. The responsibilities inform and stem from public demand; the rights inform and stem from public acceptance. When the hamburger maker is on duty, the people most concerned with his performance are his customers, his manager, and his co-workers. Customers expect to receive their order correctly and in a timely manner; the manager and co-workers expect the burger maker to show up on time, do as he is told while he is on duty, and not leave until his shift is over. That's it! Once the hamburger maker is off duty, his job responsibilities end. People who do not patronize or work at the burger joint probably have no expectations of or interest in the burger maker's conduct while he is on duty.

When the trash hauler is on duty, the people most concerned with his performance are the customers. They expect him to remove all of the trash on schedule, not to leave a mess, and not to damage the trashcans. People who are neither customers of the trash hauler nor neighbors on his beat probably have no expectations of or interest in the trash hauler's conduct while he is on duty. And when he is off duty, he has no job responsibilities.

Q 11.8

Regarding Hall's argument in Case 11.3, would it be appropriate to add a dollar tax to periodic trash hauling bills in order to offer trash haulers in the state a free college education?

The demands on many criminal justice positions are greater in quantity and quality. Even when citizens do not need help, most assume that the criminal justice system is on call around the clock to make their community safer and to respond quickly if called. Citizens presume that police, for example, know and obey the local laws and norms; are ever vigilant for wrongdoers; are in many cases willing to risk their lives to protect the innocent; are able to communicate with and handle all sorts of people; will respect all citizens even when the citizens are being disrespectful; will construct a strong case for prosecution of suspects; and are members of the criminal justice field all the time, even when off duty.

Q 11.9

Given the public's expectations of police officers, isn't it in the public's interest to have a better educated police force, as Hall recommends in Case 11.3? If so, isn't this worth an extra dollar per traffic fine?

By the same token, many people in criminal justice have many more rights than hamburger makers or trash haulers. While on duty, the hamburger maker has the right to take some breaks, to expect clear directions from management, to be treated with respect from co-workers and customers, and to have the company honor its contractual commitments and obey the labor laws. Trash haulers have similar rights. Police officers, for example, have these rights too. But in addition, they have the right under certain circumstances to enter and search homes; to chase, stop, frisk, arrest, and interrogate people; and to use deadly force to protect themselves and other innocent people.

Two scenarios capture these differences well. First, imagine that at separate times and in separate places, the hamburger maker, the trash hauler, and the police officer each gets into a public, drunken brawl while off duty. Imagine further that the local newspaper reports each brawl. Chances are that there will be no headline that says "Off-duty burger maker in drunken brawl" or "Off-duty trash hauler in drunken brawl," because neither has betrayed the public's trust in his conduct while on duty. But the headline that fails to note the officer's professional status has failed to include a significant part of the story—the officer has betrayed the public's trust even if he was on his own time.

A second, more poignant scenario is the public's response to the death of an officer, especially in the line of duty. Local news media will make this death a top story. There will be a communitywide outpouring of grief and sympathy, and the funeral will be a major event attended by police from other agencies, local dignitaries, and many civilian onlookers. If the funeral procession should tie up traffic for a while, there will be few complaints. That such a loss is so profound suggests the importance of the police to the community. Nothing like this public grief accompanies the death of our hamburger maker or trash hauler.

Of course, nothing like this public grief accompanies the death of most judges or lawyers either, and they are more widely held to be professionals than police. Our point here is that one aspect of the *policing* profession is the public grief at the death of an officer; this aspect is not a necessary condition for all professions.

Q 11.10

As Oates's argument in Case 11.3 implies, should the public show as much interest in the behavior and well-being of the burger maker and the trash hauler as it does in those of the police?

In addition to the different rights and responsibilities of nonprofessionals versus professionals, consider two other related characteristics that we don't look for in jobs but we find readily among the professions. First, successful and happy professionals appear to be answering a call—being a lawyer, clergyman, professor, or police officer is not simply what they do, but who they are and where they belong. Professional education at its best allows prospective professionals to decide whether and why this is where they should cast their lot. On the other hand, mere jobs tend to be means to some other end. One is not *called* to make hamburgers or haul trash, but in taking such a job one is better able to do what one prefers to do with the other parts of one's life. Second, in this same vein, money plays a different role in jobs than in professions. A major mark of success on a job is that one has earned the money one expected to earn: the job is a means, and money is the end. A major mark of success in a profession is that one has put one's talents to the best use possible in serving the client. Money makes it possible for the professional to answer the call: money is a means, and professional success is the end.

To be sure, people may be drawn to a profession because of pay, but they appear to be the exception and are apt to find their jobs unfulfilling. Also, hamburger makers, trash haulers, and people with other jobs may commit themselves to doing their professional best and find as much fulfillment in good work as they find in receiving a paycheck. But in the public's mind, there is nothing wrong with the burger maker or trash hauler saying that he is in it for the money, whereas there is something unsettling about the professional who claims money as his primary motive.

Our examples suggest that policing is more a profession than a job. Policing, as with any profession, carries greater responsibilities and rights than mere jobs do, and the most successful police appear to be answering a call to the vocation, with money being a means to answering that call. Some people will demand more proof that policing is a profession. Some of these people might cling dogmatically to the medieval or DeGeorgian definitions; others might be unhappy with an ostensive definition of profession, rather than an analytic, stipulative, or dictionary definition. But even the skeptic must admit that the moral demands on police officers are as high as or higher than on other recognized professions—including medicine, law, academics, and the clergy. Thus, for the purposes of a book on criminal justice ethics, it makes sense to act *as if* policing were a profession, even if not everyone will agree. This becomes clearer with a look at the moral implications of a profession, which the next section undertakes.

✦ PROFESSIONAL ETHICS

CASE 11.4

The Maternal Rookie

Mary Worthington, a police rookie in her late 30s, chases a male teenage suspect into an abandoned warehouse and down a hall to a dead end. When the boy reaches the end of the hall, he draws a handgun from his waistband and turns toward Worthington. She already has her gun drawn and sees immediately that the boy has a gun too. The law, department policy, and Worthington's training would support her shooting the suspect. Instead, she holsters her gun and shouts, "Put that gun down, boy, before I slap you silly! Does your momma know that you play with guns?" Fortunately for Worthington, the boy complies, mutters that he is sorry, and starts to cry.

When Worthington reports this to her supervisor, he berates her for having acted recklessly. She responds that she has a son about the same age, that her maternal instincts kicked in when she thought about shooting the boy, and that everything turned out OK. Still, she agrees that things could have turned out badly and that she had the right to shoot. She promises to be less reckless if she ever faces similar circumstances.

Although we might praise Worthington for her courage in Case 11.4, we might not consider her behavior virtuous. The virtuous professional habitually knows the good and does the good. The criminal justice professional is accountable to the community and to her colleagues for demonstrating this virtue; the professional demonstrates this virtue to herself through her integrity. Her accountability and integrity come from her promise to uphold the U.S. Constitution, and thereby to protect and sustain the community and its citizens.

In habitually knowing and doing the good, the virtuous professional integrates into her life the cardinal virtues of courage, justice, temperance, and prudence, along with other virtues necessary to good professional practice, some of which we discuss below as professional obligations. We've acknowledged Worthington's courage in Case 11.4, but she did not act prudently, and some could argue that she made intemperate use of her gun.

Q 11.11

In Case 11.4, did Worthington act with integrity?

The virtuous professional knows that good moral decision making depends on a proper balance of concern for consequences, rules, and duties. Worthington acted solely on the basis of consequences in Case 11.4, ignoring rules and duty.

The virtuous professional recognizes the special importance that Americans in their moral discourse put on law, rights, and justice, and she recognizes the often incorrect presumption that definitions of these values reflect the U.S. Constitution.

The virtuous professional is aware of religion's importance in American ethics and in the professional's interaction with the community and with colleagues. Thus, the virtuous professional is sensitive to, if not conversant with, Christian, Jewish, and Muslim reliance on scripture, tradition, reason, and experience for making moral decisions as adherents to their God.

Q 11.12

In Case 11.4, did Worthington balance all concerns properly?

___

The virtuous professional has responsibilities and rights that go well beyond those of a mere job. A brief discussion of the moral implications of this premise will add to our understanding of the ethics of criminal justice. This discussion is in two parts: an account of the professional's relationships and a list of basic professional obligations that reflect and inform these relationships.

Professional Relationships

 CASE 11.5

The Neighborhood Cop Who Discouraged Pressing Charges

George's house has a basement that is accessible only through an outside door. One evening George hears a commotion in the basement and rushes out to find that a number of juveniles have broken the lock on the door and are rummaging through the junk in the basement. Upon seeing George, all but one of them escape and flee down the street, but George is able to shut the door and capture the straggler. While George holds the door shut, he shouts to his girlfriend, who is in the house, to call the police. Officer Smith arrives in his patrol car soon after the call.

When George explains the situation, Smith tells him to let go of the basement door. A boy of about 13 breaks from the entrance, and Smith grabs him immediately. Smith and the boy obviously know each other, as Smith asks the boy, "What are you up to this time, Joe?" When Joe does not answer, Smith asks George what he wants to do next.

George presumes he should press charges, but Smith discourages this. He explains that the juvenile justice system wouldn't do much to ensure justice and that pressing charges might only inflame the locals—kids and parents alike. What's more, he notes, the boy's father will deal with the boy more harshly than the justice system would. Smith then asks what George hopes to accomplish by pressing charges. Caught off guard by the question and still keyed up over the incident, George blurts out that he would like to achieve two things: discouraging the boy and his cronies from ever doing this again (at least to George) and getting his broken lock replaced. Smith promises to take care of these two concerns quickly, puts the boy in the back seat of his cruiser, and drives off.

Within the hour, Smith returns with a new lock for George's basement door. He also notes the displeasure with which the boy's father greeted the boy when Smith took him home. Smith then gives George his contact information and asks whether George is content with how Smith has handled the matter. George admits to being impressed with what he takes to be a wise resolution to the case. Satisfied, Smith drives off.

Years later, George would offer this example to a group of sergeants as evidence of good community policing. George is surprised, therefore, when the first response from the group is, "How far along was Smith in his shift that night?"

Case 11.5 invites at least two questions. The professional has responsibilities, but to whom? The professional has rights, but with regard to whom? One answer to both questions lies in the relationships that the professional has with clients, colleagues, the profession, and herself/himself.

Clients[11]

The first and most important professional relationship is with the client. This relationship invites two questions: Who is the client? What is the proper allocation of responsibility for decision making in the professional–client relationship?

The primary client of the police officer, for example, is the community, both collectively and individually. Collectively, the community expects the officer to keep it safe and secure. Individually, the people in the community challenge the police officer with different personalities in different circumstances—lawbreakers; victims; and citizens needing nonlegal help, such as directions, getting a cat out of a tree, or emergency medical assistance.

Arguably, the community is the primary client for most areas of criminal justice, but not necessarily all areas. An attorney's client, for example, is the individual whom the attorney represents. In criminal cases, this client's interest may directly oppose the community's expressed interest. For example, suppose a defense attorney believes that his client—a defendant on a murder charge—is guilty but that the attorney can get his client freed on a legal technicality. It is in the community's interest that the client be sent to prison if he is guilty, and it is in the client's interest that he be released, even if he is guilty. In this case, it appears that the attorney should act in favor of the client against the interests of the community.

Q 11.13

In Case 11.5, is Joe a client of Smith's as much as George is?

The professional must also consider third parties whom her actions might affect. A typical example for police is whether to shoot at a suspect and risk hurting bystanders. Another example is whether to engage in an auto pursuit of a dangerous suspect on a public thoroughfare.

> ### Q 11.14
>
> In Case 11.5, might Smith be endangering the neighborhood by not charging Joe?

The client also has moral responsibilities to the professional. In its interaction with police, the community must, for example, respect officers, unless they act in ways not deserving of respect; not hinder the officer's work; help the officer when asked; remain vigilant for suspected wrongdoers; and use the 911 system responsibly.

The other question in the professional–client relationship concerns allocation of responsibility. This is a central issue in Case 11.5, between George and Officer Smith. In serving the client, the professional must make and act on decisions. Who is primarily responsible for making those decisions? Three general models for allocation of responsibility for decision making are the paternal model, the agent model, and the contract model.

The **paternal model** makes the professional responsible for the decision. The client pays the professional to use her expertise to make decisions. If the decision is bad, the onus falls solely on the professional. On this model, for example, Officer Smith in Case 11.5 should have decided whether or not to arrest Joe, and Smith should not have asked George whether or not to press charges. If the arrest were bad, Smith, not George, would bear full responsibility for it.

The **agent model** makes the client responsible for the decision. The professional's job is to lay out the options for the client and to give the client the best advice possible, but only the client can make the final decision. If it is a bad decision, the onus falls solely on the client. In Case 11.5, Smith may have this model in mind when he asks George to decide whether or not to press charges, advises him that pressing charges is a bad idea, and convinces him to settle for a new lock.

The **contract model** makes the decision a joint responsibility of the professional and the client, assuming the client is physically and mentally able to participate in making the decision. There is no easy formula for dividing this responsibility between the parties, but generally there should be agreement up front about each party's role. This agreement may be codified, a matter of common sense, or made on the spot. In Case 11.5, Smith appeals to George's common sense by noting the futility of pressing charges. But if George has no prior relevant experience, it may be unfair of Smith to put so much responsibility on George.

Of these three models, the contract model is best whenever applicable, because it correctly recognizes each side as a full participant in the contract and it satisfies the Aristotelian principle of finding the mean between the extremes of overburdening one party or the other. In policing, this model may apply less frequently than in other professions, because the suspect or criminal is a client too. In this adversarial relationship, the professional must make most of the decisions regardless of the client's wishes, so the paternal model becomes the most useful of the three models.

Colleagues

A second relationship for the professional is with colleagues. Colleagues include superiors, peers, subordinates, support staff, and other related agencies and organizations. Superiors include people both in and out of the direct chain of command. Peers include partners and others of comparable rank. Subordinates may be in or out of the chain of command. Support staff—including administrative assistants, dispatchers, and maintenance people—are usually lower in the organizational hierarchy than the professional who receives the support. Other related agencies and organizations include local, state, and federal criminal justice agencies; unions; vendors; and municipal authorities such as a city office of human resources.

The Profession[12]

A third relationship is with the profession at large. Professions with autonomous associations, such as the American Bar Association or the American Medical Association, have at least three sorts of responsibilities. First is to develop and implement regulations for entrance into the profession, proper behavior within the profession, and means of dealing with professional violations. This often includes accreditation by a body of one's peers. Second is continued education and research to keep the profession up-to-date and to foster steady improvement. Third is public relations.

Some areas of criminal justice practice have no national association. For example, there is no nationwide professional association for police officers comparable to the American Bar Association for lawyers or the American Medical Association for doctors. Still, police must contribute to the profession. In terms of self-governance, this may include police departments seeking accreditation from the Commission on Accreditation for Law Enforcement Agencies (CALEA). In terms of education and research, there are many opportunities for offering or taking in-service training, specialty certification, and personal enrichment. Since the police officer has dedicated his life to the profession, he ought to take judicious advantage of these opportunities for improvement. In terms of public relations, just about every public act of a police officer either adds to or detracts from the image of law enforcement, which the New York police officers in Case 11.1 seem to have forgotten. The virtuous police officer will be mindful of the PR value of everything he does.

Q 11.15

In Case 11.5, did Smith's response reflect well on the profession of policing?

Oneself

A fourth relationship is with oneself. The professional's primary commitment is to her client, but she also has personal interests worth her consideration. These include physical and mental well-being, healthy relationships with family and friends, and religious and political beliefs. Some of the most difficult tasks facing the professional involve a clash of personal and professional interests, as Case 11.6 demonstrates.

Professional Obligations: The Basics

CASE 11.6

Florida Hurricanes

I n a large Florida city, the police and sheriff's departments require all of their sworn personnel to be on duty during hurricanes. Today a hurricane has hit the city dead-on, and Officer Simms has arrived for duty, leaving her husband and children at home in the next town. Listening to her police radio, she hears that an emergency response team is on the way to her neighborhood after a tornado reportedly tore through it. She tries to call her supervisor to ask for permission to go home, but she is unable to reach him, so she leaves her post to be with her family.

Within the week, she is fired for dereliction of duty because she left her post without permission.

Case 11.6 offers a powerful example of the clash between professional and personal responsibilities. For the most part, rights and responsibilities in professional relationships are reciprocal and complementary. For example, if the professional has a *responsibility* of confidentiality to the client, then the client has a *right* to confidentiality from the professional. If the client has a *duty* to be honest with the professional, then the professional has a *right* to have the client be honest. Two general categories of professional responsibilities are obedience and trustworthiness.

Q 11.16

In Case 11.6, did Simms's retreat violate the local citizens' rights to police protection?

Obedience

Any professional must obey the community's laws, the profession's rules, and superiors' orders, unless the professional has moral reasons for being disobedient. In policing, for example, the list of authorities to obey or heed is extensive. At least 10 come to mind.

- The *U.S. Constitution.* Every police officer promises to uphold the Constitution, the supreme law of the United States. But rarely may the officer interpret the Constitution as he wishes. Instead, the courts mediate his connection to the Constitution through decisions concerning legally acceptable and unacceptable police practice. As we saw in Part III, this poses a moral problem for the officer who believes that a judicial decision is unconstitutional. The virtuous officer will weigh the consequences of disobeying the court order, taking into account the community's safety and security, and come to the most moderate conclusion possible.
- The body of *criminal and civil laws.* As enforcers of law, police have a special duty to obey them. Moral problems arise for the police officer when the law appears to be a bad one or it seems useful or necessary to break one law in order to enforce a more important one.
- An agency's *code of conduct* or code of ethics. As we noted in Chapter 4, this may include a vision statement, a mission statement, statements of principles and standards, and specific rules. Generally, principles and standards are too abstract for determining compliance directly, but they act as the justification for the rules, which should be specific enough to determine compliance. For example, a basic principle is that one should perform one's duties. But this principle does not specify what those duties are. In deference to this principle, law enforcement has a standard that police have a duty to protect and serve the community, but the standard gives no specific guidelines for that protection or service. Under this standard, one rule might be that service to the public includes responding to a call for help within five minutes. Another rule might be for the officer always to state his badge number when a citizen requests it. It will be easy to determine whether these rules have been obeyed. Police and the community benefit from a clear understanding and acceptance of the department's vision and mission, as long as the police officers live up to those ideals. Otherwise, the vision and mission statements become empty sentiments, leaving the community cynical about the police department's sense of purpose.
- The department's *general and special orders.* As a rule, police are bound to obey these orders unless they are unlawful or superseded by more recent orders or by exigent circumstances. Suppose a department prohibits using squad cars to transport civilians who are not suspects or under arrest. Now suppose a patrol officer sees a young boy looking frantically for his dog and helps find the dog. If the boy and the dog are far from home and the trip home is dangerous because it involves crossing the interstate, wouldn't the officer be doing a good thing by driving them home? Also, the fact that an order does not spell out every possible instance of disobedience does not let the cop off the hook. For example, in Case 4.2, "Towing the Boat," the officer should have known that unauthorized use of a squad car includes using the car to tow a boat, even though no rule said this specifically.

- The *community's norms* that affect the police officer as a professional and as a citizen. In the proverbial case of the free cup of coffee, if the community supports merchants giving officers free coffee and there is no law or department policy against it, then why not allow it?
- *Tradition.* People often express this by saying "We've always done it that way" or "If it ain't broke, don't fix it." Sometimes the tradition is a bad one, and it may take courage to put a stop to it. A persistent issue is professional courtesy—police officers expecting to get out of a speeding ticket simply by showing their badges. Tradition alone does not make this morally right.
- *Experience.* Some aspects of the profession cannot be taught, although the rookie may benefit from a veteran's war stories. Beyond the formal training a professional receives, experience is often the best teacher. Departments may recognize this through Field Training Officer programs or by pairing a veteran with a rookie on patrol.
- *Intuition,* or "gut feeling." The experienced officer does not need to keep consulting laws, rule books, or training manuals to do his job well. Even the rookie has a moral conscience, unless he is sociopathic, and probably does the good instinctively. A virtuous police officer is sensitive to wrongdoing and may rely on this for moral direction.
- *Reason.* This is the fundamental tool for sound moral decision making and a primary focus of this book. Obedience here is to the laws of logic, tempered by intuition and experience.
- *Religious beliefs.* Police operate under a principle of separation of church and state. Nevertheless, the virtuous police officer will acknowledge her religious beliefs, if any, and the religious beliefs of her community, and be appropriately deliberate in working those into her moral decision making as a professional.

Trustworthiness

In addition to obedience, the professional has a fiduciary responsibility to the profession, the agency, the client, and the community. The professional acts on behalf of the clients in ways they cannot act themselves. For example, when a police officer arrests a suspect, it is not for the officer's sake but for the sake of the people on whose behalf the officer has the power to act, thus contributing to their safety and security.

In recognizing the professional as a fiduciary, we trust him to know the good and to do the good—to have integrity and to be accountable. In addition to all of the moral values and characteristics noted so far, we can, with ethicist Michael Bayles, identify at least seven specific obligations of professional trustworthiness.[13]

First is *competence.* It is not controversial to claim that a professional must be competent—but how competent? Is the professional duty-bound to be excellent at the profession, or is merely adequate good enough? Does the client have a right to expect "A" work from the professional, or should the client be satisfied with "C" work?

> ### Q 11.17
>
> In Case 11.4, did Worthington act competently when she verbally challenged the teenage assailant rather than using her gun on him?

Second is *diligence.* The professional should make a good effort and take care in fulfilling her agreement with the client. This is not the situation in Case 11.6 with the mom who went AWOL.

A third obligation of trustworthiness is *honesty.* Two questions arise: What is honesty? Is it always a virtue? Generally, to be honest is to say what one believes. Note that one could be honest and still tell a falsehood. One could also be dishonest and tell the truth. In the first case, imagine that Cpl. Juan is beginning his shift as Cpl. Olson is ending hers. Cpl. Juan has forgotten his flashlight, so he asks to borrow Olson's. She agrees and tells him to get it from her locker, which she has left unlocked. She then heads for home. On the way home, she sees the flashlight lying on the floor of her car, but before she can call Juan, he has checked her locker and found no flashlight. Did Olson lie to Juan? That would be an unfair accusation, even though Olson made a mistake. Now imagine that when Olson agreed to let Juan use her flashlight, she believed the light was in her car, but she unkindly decided to tell Juan it was in her locker. When she gets into the car, the light is not there and she remembers that she left the light in her locker after all. By this time, Juan has retrieved the light from Olson's locker and headed out for patrol. As far as he is concerned, Olson told him the truth, but we know that she lied, even though the trick was on her.

Many say that honesty is a virtue or that "honesty is the best policy,"[14] but is it always? A virtue is the mean between the extremes of deficiency and excess. In police work, might there be times where a lie is more virtuous than the truth? Undercover or sting operations are a normal and acceptable part of police work, in which the operation itself is dishonest and maintaining the dishonesty may be necessary to protect the operative and to achieve success. A harmless case of dishonesty involves an officer's lying to lure a retiring comrade to a surprise party. Neither of these cases appears to stray far from the mean, given the circumstances

These cases don't require moral scrutiny, but compare these to more controversial sorts of cases. For example, in Case 9.3, "Improbable Cause," lying might be the only way for the officer to make a case against an obvious offender, but the lie would violate lawful procedures. In these cases, would the end justify the means? In Case 6.1, "The Hit and Run Son," the father flirts with dishonesty in order to protect his son from harsher penalties that the son faced if they were completely honest. The father's protectiveness is understandable, but as a police chief he has duties that his son's predicament does not override. These appear to be cases of deficient honesty at best.

On the other side of the mean is *excessive* honesty, or inappropriate candor. Whereas honesty is a matter of saying what one believes when asked to speak, *candor*, a fourth obligation of trustworthiness, is saying everything one believes about the subject. It would be inappropriately candid to tell a stranger that you think his hat looks stupid, even if that's the truth. It would be inappropriately candid for a police officer testifying in court to offer an elaborate answer to a question for which the right response is "a simple yes or no." In other words, candor whose purpose is to be cruel or candor that subverts a moral purpose is morally wrong. Professionals and clients should expect candor from each other, but is this expectation always justified? The professional may feel that a full account would hurt the client. As noted previously, in policing, unlike in other professions, the client is often an adversary—a suspect or a convict. Sometimes the most practical way to deal with this client is to avoid candor and perhaps to lie, thus relying on the paternal model rather than the contract model of decision making.

A fifth obligation is *loyalty*. In the public image of policing, this may be the most ubiquitous obligation. Stories abound about the "thin blue line" and the whistle-blower who crosses that line. Often the professional has competing loyalties. Loyalty to the client may interfere with loyalty to a colleague or, as in Case 11.6, to one's family. In policing, the professional promises loyalty to the Constitution and to the community she serves; all other loyalties are subordinate. Failure to understand this or failure to act on this understanding is a symptom of and may be a cause of police corruption.

Q 11.18

Does Simms's act in Case 11.6 constitute corruption?

A sixth obligation is *discretion*. For the professional, this has two meanings: keeping a client's confidence, and the ability to make professional choices on one's own without having to run every decision by a superior. In policing, absence of discretion in the latter sense would pose two dangers. Police work would be much less efficient, and police would be susceptible to legalism—the belief that one should follow the rules at all costs. With the freedom of discretion comes the strong responsibility to use it well—to consider and balance consequences, rules, or duties in fulfilling the task.

Q 11.19

Did Officer Smith in Case 11.5 use his discretion wisely?

A seventh obligation is two-sided: *beneficence/nonmaleficence*. At the very least, the professional should try not to harm the client; otherwise, the professional is guilty of maleficence—wrongdoing. But the professional can intend to avoid harm without trying to do good for the client. Suppose that Officer Smith in Case 11.5 was interested only in avoiding having to write an arrest report so late in his shift. At the same time, imagine that he did not want to leave a dissatisfied citizen, because that might come back to haunt him. It is fair to say that he acted toward George with nonmaleficence, but not necessarily with beneficence—a desire to do some good for George. On the other hand, the marriage counseling police officer in Case 10.1 clearly meant to do some good for the troubled couple—the officer was acting beneficently. Note that the duty to be beneficent is both collective and individual. Although the marriage counseling officer acted as an individual, his department might also have been committed collectively to community policing through school outreach programs or police athletic leagues, for example. Of course, both the department and the individual need to balance opportunities to do good for some people against duties to others that may be more pressing. The maternal rookie in Case 11.4 appears to have been acting beneficently, but her duty probably was to be more careful about her own safety and about following protocol in a situation in which someone has a gun on her.

Professional Ethics as a Balancing Act

For the virtuous criminal justice professional, life is a series of balancing acts. She should try always to strike a balance between professional life and personal life in fulfillment of her responsibilities and exercise of her rights; among consequences, rules, and duties in her moral decision making; among the legal, political, and religious interests of community members and colleagues; and among the competing notions of law, justice, and rights as they allegedly stem from the U.S. Constitution.

Moral discourse often refers to our "moral compass," noting that for the virtuous person this compass points to true north and orients her accordingly. A better metaphor might be the *moral gyroscope*. A compass merely points us in a certain direction and leaves us to decide whether to go that way. A gyroscope is an internal device that when properly calibrated keeps the device in balance. The virtuous criminal justice professional should think of her moral conscience as a moral gyroscope, which she should keep in good working order.

Summary

This chapter has discussed the nature of a profession and the moral implications of this designation for criminal justice professionals. These implications include several moral obligations of trustworthiness, knowing and being faithful to all professional relationships, and knowing and properly availing oneself of the various authorities under which the professional operates.

The virtuous professional habitually knows and does the good. In doing the good, he fulfills his responsibilities and exercises his rights so that he and the community are the better for it.

Next, we will examine each of several criminal justice professions more closely, focusing on moral problems that are either unique or of special significance.

Answers to Case Study Questions

Q11.1. In Case 11.1, would it be fair to condemn the officers' actions as unprofessional when they were far from home and off duty?

Yes. First, the act is clearly not professional. Second, professionals wear the moral mantle of their profession all the time—even when they are off duty. Third, the distance from one's jurisdiction is not relevant to the morality of the misdeed.

Q11.2. In Case 11.1, do the officers have the excuse that there was no superior present to forbid them from acting unconventionally?

No. The absence of a superior did not give the officers the right to act unconventionally. Consider how many times there is no superior immediately available to an officer who is on duty. This does not relieve the officer of fulfilling his duty anyway.

Q11.3. Does the dissenting officer in Case 11.2 exemplify the public's expectation of police integrity?

Yes. Integrity requires moderation, and indulgence in the vices would be immoderate even if they were legal.

Q11.4. If the two willing officers in Case 11.2 have college degrees, do they meet DeGeorge's criteria for professionals?

No. The college degrees of the two willing officers are not enough to make them professionals. For DeGeorge, a college degree is a necessary but not sufficient condition for professionalism.

Q11.5. Does the dissenting officer's view of integrity in Case 11.2 appear to rest on a stipulative definition?

No. The dissenting officer appears to operate from a definition of integrity that goes beyond mere stipulation. His definition appears to lean toward the analytic—an identification of integrity with having all of the cardinal virtues: courage, justice, temperance, and prudence, the latter two of which the willing officers appear to lack.

Q11.6. In looking to define *profession*, can we find anything useful in the example of the officers in Case 11.2? If so, what?

Case 11.2 is useful in defining profession, because the case clearly offers an example of one officer who thinks as a professional and two who do not. The officer who thinks as a professional recognizes the higher standard to which police are held: Even when they are on vacation and in another country, they should act morally. The other two officers do not have the proper regard for the moral expectations of them as police officers.

Q11.7. Could Hall refute Oates's argument in Case 11.3 by pointing out that police officers are responsible for enforcing traffic laws?

In Case 11.3, Hall would have a good argument against Oates if Hall noted that police officers enforce traffic laws. There is a direct connection between those who enforce traffic laws and revenue from the tickets involved in such enforcement. There is no direct connection between revenue from tickets involved in law enforcement and state employees who have nothing to do with traffic enforcement. This observation would weaken Oates's analogy between police officers and other state employees who have nothing to do with enforcing traffic laws.

Q11.8. Regarding Hall's argument in Case 11.3, would it be appropriate to add a dollar tax to periodic trash hauling bills in order to offer trash haulers in the state a free college education?

No. Given Hall's argument in Case 11.3, it is tempting to argue that if adding a dollar surcharge to traffic fines is appropriate for helping police officers pay for higher education, then adding a dollar tax to trash hauling bills is appropriate for helping trash haulers pay for higher education. But the analogy is weakened by the different services offered by the two groups and by the education required to offer those services. Thus, on this analogy alone, the argument for the tax on trash hauling bills would not hold up.

Q11.9. Given the public's expectations of police officers, isn't it in the public's interest to have a better educated police force, as Hall recommends in Case 11.3? If so, isn't this worth an extra dollar per traffic fine?

Given the public's expectations of police officers, it is in the public's interest to have a better educated police force, as Hall recommends in Case 11.3. Thus, an extra dollar per traffic fine is worthwhile as long as it will contribute successfully to police education.

Q11.10. As Oates's argument in Case 11.3 implies, should the public show as much interest in the behavior and well-being of the burger maker and the trash hauler as it does in those of the police?

Oates implies that the public should show as much interest in the behavior and well-being of the burger maker and the trash hauler as of the police. But this premise fails to distinguish between a job and a profession, which is crucial to Hall's argument.

Q11.11. In Case 11.4, did Worthington act with integrity?

No. To act with integrity is to act with courage, justice, temperance, and prudence. It is fair to say that Worthington's act in Case 11.4 was foolhardy, rather than courageous and imprudent. One might also argue that she made intemperate use of her police powers.

Q11.12. In Case 11.4, did Worthington balance all concerns properly?

No. Worthington did not give her own concerns enough weight compared with her concern for the suspect.

Q11.13. In Case 11.5, is Joe a client of Smith's as much as George is?

Yes, because Joe is also a member of the community that Smith is sworn to protect. However, this doesn't mean that Smith must allow Joe to decide whether or not charges should be pressed. That decision belongs to Smith and George.

Q11.14. In Case 11.5, might Smith be endangering the neighborhood by not charging Joe?

Yes. Smith may be endangering the neighborhood by not charging Joe, because (1) Joe may have broken into other houses and planned to break into more and (2) Joe and his friends may take Smith's failure to arrest Joe as a precedent that will only encourage them to commit more burglaries.

Q11.15. In Case 11.5, did Smith's response reflect well on the profession of policing?

It depends. Smith's response reflects well on the profession of policing if Smith's motive was to maintain a safe and secure neighborhood. If, on the other hand, Smith's motive was to avoid writing an arrest report, then his response reflected poorly on the profession. The point is that we cannot answer on the basis of consequences alone.

Q11.16. In Case 11.6, did Simms's retreat violate the local citizens' rights to police protection?

Yes. The public has the right to expect protection from the police and to expect that police will obey lawful orders. Thus, Simms's retreat violated the citizens' rights to police protection.

Q11.17. In Case 11.4, did Worthington act competently when she verbally challenged the teenage assailant rather than using her gun on him?

No. She failed to follow proper procedure, but luckily everything turned out all right.

Q11.18. Does Simms's act in Case 11.6 constitute corruption?

No. A corrupt act involves choosing evil over good. Simms's act in Case 11.6 involves choosing between two conflicting duties—professional and familial. Although Simms made a wrong choice from the professional point of view, it is difficult to condemn her choice as corrupt. Perhaps her act was intemperate and unjust, but not every act against virtue is an act of corruption.

Q11.19. Did Officer Smith in Case 11.5 use his discretion wisely?

As suggested previously, if Smith's motive was to benefit the community, then he appears to have used his discretion wisely. If, on the other hand, his motive was to get out of filing a report, then he did not use his discretion wisely, because it was contrary to the purpose of such discretion.

NOTES

1. Steve Vogel, "Live From D.C., It's NYPD Blue," *Washington Post*, 19 May 1995, p. 1A.
2. Retrieved 20 June 2005 from realpolice.net/police_history.htm.
3. David Pake, "The Legal Profession and Its Ethical Responsibilities: A History," in *Ethics and the Legal Profession*, ed. Michael Davis and Frederick A. Elliston (Buffalo, NY: Prometheus, 1986), pp. 29–49.

4. Stephen Barker, "What Is a Profession?" *Professional Ethics* 1.1 and 2 (1992), pp. 73–99.

5. Michael Bayles, *Professional Ethics,* 2nd ed. (Belmont, CA: Wadsworth, 1995), p. 8.

6. Realpolice.net/police_history.htm.

7. Ibid.

8. Bayles, *Professional Ethics,* p. 8.

9. Richard DeGeorge, *Business Ethics* (New York: Macmillan, 1990), pp. 382–3.

10. Retrieved 20 June 2005 from www.answers.com.

11. Bayles, *Professional Ethics,* Ch. 4.

12. Ibid., Ch. 7.

13. Bayles, *Professional Ethics,* pp. 79–99.

14. Miguel de Cervantes, *Don Quixote,* Ch. 2.

CHAPTER 12

ETHICS IN THE LEGISLATURE

 CASE 12.1

The Consistent Candidate

U.S. Senator Malcolm won his first term 12 years ago, on the promise of fighting for "family values," including, in his words, maintaining the sanctity of marriage by preventing homosexuals from marrying. A recent poll shows that a vast majority of his constituents think that he is doing a fine job overall, but they believe homosexuals have the constitutional right to marry. The voters feel so strongly about this that in the upcoming election they will vote for Malcolm's opponent, a vocal supporter of gay rights, if Malcolm does not reverse his position on marriage.

To complicate matters, if Malcolm's opponent wins, this could put the opponent's party in the majority for the first time in many years. Thus, many influential members of Malcolm's party have encouraged him to change his marriage stance publicly, while reminding him that he can change his mind again after he has secured another six years in the Senate.

Malcolm believes that (1) anyone participating in a homosexual marriage should be criminally prosecuted; (2) to reverse his position would thus be a lie; (3) to lie in this way would be immoral, especially coming from someone who is campaigning on his moral credentials; (4) to act immorally would violate his oath to protect the Constitution; and (5) his constituents and the country will suffer a great deal if his party loses the majority in the Senate.

Case 12.1 offers one example of the many moral challenges a legislator faces, which can emerge when the legislator's personal views clash with the public will. How the legislator should act is a question of professional ethics. The previous chapter set a foundation for addressing this question by identifying eight criteria for distinguishing a profession from a job.

- Significant service to society
- Greater rights and responsibilities

- Self-governance
- Autonomy
- A calling
- Money as a means, professional fulfillment as the end
- Extensive training
- Credentialing

Some of these criteria are more relevant than others to the profession of criminal justice, and some pertain to one criminal justice field more than to others.

This chapter covers the field of legislation as it pertains to criminal justice. This is a good place to start for at least three reasons. First, although the study of criminal justice often focuses on police, the judiciary, and corrections and parole, criminal law is the starting point for all their endeavors, and legislators are responsible for making the law. Second, the Constitution gives the U.S. legislature primary responsibility for establishing the scope and limits of criminal justice in the United States.[1] Third, the U.S. Constitution governs all fields of criminal justice and all criteria for assessing the degree to which the fields are professions, because the Constitution is "the supreme law of the land."[2]

The field of legislation includes legislators—senators and representatives—primarily; legislative staff secondarily, but not insignificantly; and lobbyists, political action committees (PACs), and journalists somewhat less directly. In ethical terms, there is enough similarity between the federal legislature and state and local legislatures to limit our discussion here to the federal legislature. Additional support for this focus comes from the 14th Amendment to the U.S. Constitution: "No State shall make or enforce any law which shall abridge the privileges or immunities of citizens of the United States."[3] In other words, federal law should trump state law whenever the two conflict.

In terms of professional criteria, the most pertinent to the legislators' role in criminal justice are the first six of the eight previously listed. The criterion of extensive training is less relevant, and the criterion of credentialing is not relevant at all.

The first part of this chapter examines the ethics of legislators, with regard to their role in criminal justice, in light of each of these professional criteria. The second part of this chapter examines the ethics of staff, lobbyists, PACs, and journalists with regard to their roles in legislation.

→ THE LEGISLATOR

To the extent that legislators are professionals, they will meet most, if not all, of the criteria for a profession. They must also have regard for their various professional relationships, and they must understand and fulfill their professional obligations. Let's examine all of this by using the professional criteria—in descending order of importance to the profession—as our organizing principle, inserting observations about relationships and obligations where appropriate.

Significant Service to the Community

Of all the criteria that distinguish a profession from a mere job, none is more obvious or important to legislation than offering significant service to the community. Many jobs also offer significant services, but such service is not a necessary condition for being a job. Such service, however, *is* a necessary condition for being a profession.

In terms of professional relationships, the legislator's constituency is the client. All other professional relationships—to oneself, to third parties, to colleagues, and to the profession at large—are subordinate to serving the constituency well. In a republican system such as ours, the individual legislator serves his or her constituency mainly by representing its interests. This observation presents two questions: Who count as constituents? What does representing their interests entail? Let's take each of these questions in turn.

Constituents

In Case 12.1, who are Sen. Malcolm's constituents? It is tempting to presume that they are those who voted for him. After all, without their support Malcolm will not be a senator when this term expires. Yet, if the matter were that simple, Malcolm would not be so torn among maintaining his moral stance, representing the wishes of those who vote for him, and being a loyal party member. Nor would he be so concerned about the welfare of the country as a whole.

When Sen. Malcolm takes his professional oath, he declares his primary allegiance to the U.S. Constitution. If Lincoln was correct in declaring that the United States government is "of the people, by the people, for the people,"[4] then Malcolm's constituency is everyone whom the Constitution governs, and his main job is to protect it. This is somewhat abstract, however, and although voters should insist that Malcolm's professional activities obey the Constitution, the voters will be more interested in having Malcolm raise and satisfy their specific concerns in the legislative chamber.

In a republican system, the people who voted for Malcolm cannot claim exclusive right to his professional attention. Everyone eligible to vote in the United States expressly or tacitly agrees to abide by the decision of the majority. Thus, every voter in the senator's district is a constituent of the senator, even those who did not vote for him.

The voters are not the only ones whom Malcolm's professional actions affect. Everyone in Malcolm's district stands to benefit or suffer from legislative acts affecting the district. Thus, voters and nonvoters alike who live in Malcolm's district may rightly claim to be his constituents.

No district exists in isolation: whatever affects one district may have a ripple effect on other districts. Thus, for example, in Case 12.1, a law permitting gay marriage would affect not only Malcolm's state, but also surrounding states whose citizens might travel to Malcolm's state to get married. Such legislation in Malcolm's state would also breathe new life into a nationwide debate about legalizing gay marriage. It follows that while Malcolm serves his constituency first, he also serves the larger community of which his constituency is part.

We could push this point into ever widening circles, until we come back to the point that Malcolm serves the country in its guise as a constitutional system. What is of greater interest, however, is that the variety of stakeholders in the legislator's business has the potential to create conflicts for the legislator, as in Case 12.1, where Malcolm needs to choose among the interests of himself, his constituents, and his political party. The right choice depends on the legislator's proper representation of the constituents' interest, to which we turn next.

Q 12.1

Do Malcolm's fellow party members have as much of a claim on Malcolm's professional services as those eligible to vote for him?

Representing Constituents' Interests

Legislative representation is a double task: representation and legislation. Specific elements of each are relevant to the study of criminal justice ethics.

In both tasks, the legislators must keep the constituents in the loop, so that the legislators can represent the community's interests knowledgeably. Keeping constituents in the loop means informing them and educating them about the constitutional scope and limits of legislative rights and responsibilities, which we discuss later in this chapter. Keeping constituents in the loop also means informing them and educating them about pending legislation—how the law will be worded and what impact it may have on the community specifically and criminal justice in general. Finally, keeping constituents in the loop means providing them adequate access to the legislator so that they can express their interests and acquire the information they need to be well informed.

Q 12.2

In Case 12.2, does Malcolm have a duty to tell his constituents about the party's pressure on him to renounce his objection to homosexual marriage?

In both tasks, representing and legislating, legislators face the question, Which is the more important task for the legislator, to "secure the blessings of liberty" as the Constitution's Preamble promises, or to ensure security at the cost of certain liberties?[5] Some might regard this question as simple to answer: In the post–September 11 era of heightened security concerns, there can be no assurance of liberty without a strong defense against terrorism and other such threats. Others would see the significance of this question in apparent threats to constitutional liberties, such as warrantless searches in violation of the Fourth Amendment or denying an arrestee a speedy and public trial in violation of the Sixth Amendment. Since September 11, 2001, the federal government has allegedly committed such violations in the name of homeland security. The power to prevent such violations rests with the legislature—through "the power of the purse" and impeachment—as does the ultimate responsibility for not exercising that power. The more important emphasis for the legislator, liberty or security, depends in part on the moral dimensions of representation and in part on the moral dimensions of legislation.

Q 12.3

In Case 12.1, does Malcolm's aversion to homosexual marriage appear to be a matter of national security for him? Does it appear to be a matter of liberty?

Concerning the task of representation, as it pertains to criminal justice, recall our discussion in the previous chapter about proper allocation of responsibility for decision making between the professional and the client. There are three basic models for this allocation: paternal, agency, and contract. The paternal model has the professional make the decisions. In this model, the legislator is primarily a trustee and leader: the voters vote him into office and then trust him to make law for them without much further consultation. In Case 12.1, the paternal model would have Malcolm vote for or against a proposed law as he sees fit, regardless of his constituents' pleas. The paternal model would also have Malcolm participate in legislative oversight of the criminal justice process, including executive and judicial activity, without consulting with his constituents.

The agency model has the client make the decisions. On this model, the legislator is a delegate or servant: the constituents tell him how they want him to vote on a law and he votes accordingly, regardless of his personal views. Or the constituents tell the legislator how they want him to act in legislative oversight and he acts accordingly, regardless of his personal views. In Case 12.1, the agency model would have Malcolm honor his constituents' wishes regardless of his moral position.

The contract model has both parties make the decisions together. In our initial discussion of these models, we decided that the contract model is the best in principle because it distributes the burden for decision making among the concerned parties, rather than overburdening one party or the other. We also acknowledged that the contract model will not always work; that is, it will not always be the least deficient and least excessive means to fulfill a moral responsibility.

Debate over the proper model for the legislator and the community tends to focus on the agency and paternal models, while underemphasizing the value of the contract model.[6] This impoverishes the debate, so we should include all three models as we explore their applications to legislative activity.

In cases where the paternal model is most appropriate, the client may not have the intellectual ability or the will to participate in making the decision. For example, the economic consequences of illegal immigration in the United States are so complicated that it may be difficult for anyone but economists to decide reasonably which legal approach would result in the greatest good for the greatest number of people in the country. When voting on this issue, the legislator may have to rely on the economists, without waiting for the ordinary citizen to weigh in. At the same time, the ordinary citizen, while having an emotional response to the issue, may concede that the final decision belongs to the legislator alone. Another example finds the legislator participating in a debate over a highly sensitive national security issue that must be resolved immediately. For the legislator to put off such a decision while waiting for the constituents to make their decision would be irresponsible.

Sometimes the agency model is the best choice. For example, in 1965 the U.S. Congress approved a pair of charters: the National Endowment for the Humanities (NEH) and the National Endowment for the Arts (NEA). These charters provide government financial support for the humanities and the fine arts, but leave decision making about grant recipients to the people in those fields; the legislator has no direct say in those decisions.

In spite of the occasional propriety of the paternal model or the agency model, we will find that the best model as a rule is the contract model. On this model, the legislator and the constituents recognize their professional relationship as a cooperative agreement in which each side promises to do its part to make the relationship successful. On the legislator's side, this means paying close attention to the interests of the constituency and honoring those interests unless the legislator can show cause why those interests should be ignored. On the constituents' side, this means staying informed on the issues that the legislator faces and communicating interests to the legislator on a regular basis. It also means voting in every election and coming to the voting booth well informed.

Q 12.4

With which model of decision making does Malcolm appear to be most comfortable in Case 12.1? Which model do the voters appear to prefer?

The task of representation includes more than just making laws and overseeing the execution and adjudication of those laws. But our interest is primarily in the lawmaking and legislative oversight that are fundamental to criminal justice. Concerning legislation, the Preamble to the U.S. Constitution lays out the legislator's task:

> We the people of the United States, in Order to form a more perfect Union, establish Justice, insure domestic Tranquility, provide for the common defense, promote the general Welfare and secure the Blessings of Liberty to ourselves and our Posterity, do ordain and establish this Constitution for the United States of America.

Ideally, any law the legislator makes should honor these goals. Thus, any law that threatens tranquility, the general welfare, or liberty, for example, is contrary to the constitutional purposes of lawmaking and should be voted down or overturned. In addition to making laws, the legislature should monitor the publication and effect of laws, and should oversee and manage those responsible for executing and adjudicating the laws.

There is nothing too controversial about what we have just observed, even if it highlights an ideal rather than the typical practice of legislators. But once we have agreed in a preliminary way about the representative and legislative tasks of the legislator, we need to acknowledge the many disagreements about what morally good representation and morally good legislation mean. One way to frame this disagreement is to distinguish between conservatives and liberals, a distinction that has crystallized into a two-party system. As George Washington was stepping down from the presidency, he issued a farewell address in which he encouraged his successors not to divide into parties, because party members would be forced to divide their loyalties between the government as a whole and the party in particular. [7] This advice went unheeded, however, as John Adams—a strong supporter of national government—took office as the second president, in opposition to Thomas Jefferson and like-minded supporters who favored a weak national government and strong states' rights. Six years earlier, British political philosopher Edmund Burke (1729–1797) published *Reflections on the Revolution in France*, in which he defined conservatism. In response, American immigrant and philosopher Thomas Paine (1737–1809) wrote *The Rights of Man* (1791), in which he attacked Burke's conservatism and defended liberalism. This pair of "isms" has underscored conventional thinking about the two-party system in U.S. politics ever since.

The conservative, according to Burke, is someone who takes the lessons of history seriously and will consult history whenever possible before making an important decision about the future. One example of this view is Spanish-American philosopher George Santayana's oft-quoted claim that "Those who cannot remember the past are condemned to repeat it."[8] Another example comes from U.S. Senator Robert Byrd (D-WV), who opposed President George W. Bush's request for a congressional resolution authorizing an attack on Iraq in 2002.[9] Byrd noted that he had voted for the Gulf of Tonkin resolution in 1964 on false information that Pres. Johnson gave to Congress, thereby enabling him to escalate the war in Vietnam, which the United States eventually lost. Byrd expressed fear that Congress would make a similar mistake if it supported Pres. Bush's request, thus failing to learn an important historical lesson. At that point in the 2002 debate, Sen. Byrd appeared to be one of the most conservative members of the Senate, in the original sense of the word *conservative*. Note that Pres. Johnson was a Democrat and Sen. Byrd is a Democrat, which reminds us that the distinction between conservative and liberal does not necessarily parallel the distinction between Republican and Democrat, contrary to common stereotypes.

Today we can recognize four related meanings of *conservative*, each of which is reflected in discussions about the proper role of the legislator.[10] The first is the traditional, Burkean meaning. Second is the association of conservatives with a particular moral agenda. Generally, on this view, conservatives want to maintain traditional moral values—such as limiting marriage to heterosexual couples—and argue against greater moral permissiveness and thus against laws that might grant that permissiveness. Third is the association of conservatives with resistance to change in general. Fourth is the association of conservatives with the view that the federal government should be no larger than is necessary to provide for the common defense and that most decision making about laws should be left up to the individual states or to small jurisdictions.

The liberal, according to Thomas Paine, is someone who disregards the past in favor of a vision of the future. On the current U.S. Supreme Court, Justice Stephen Breyer appears to be a liberal of this sort when he claims that his task is to make judicial decisions in favor of "active liberty," and that active liberty is an evolving concept.[11] Parallel to the four meanings of *conservatism* today, we may recognize four related meanings of *liberalism*. First is Thomas Paine's meaning. Second is the association of liberals with a particular moral agenda. Generally, on this view, liberals tend to be more morally permissive than conservatives—wishing to give homosexuals the right to marry, for example—and to favor codifying that permissiveness in new laws or by overturning old ones. Third is the association of liberals with the view that change is good, sometimes even for its own sake. Fourth is the association of liberals with the view that a robust federal government can solve social problems by enacting the proper laws.

Q 12.5

In Case 12.1, does Malcolm appear to be a conservative?

Although the conservative–liberal distinction is useful for identifying basic views of a legislator and for framing debates about the proper role of legislation, the distinction is somewhat forced. To be sure, there are those who claim to be loyal to the conservative cause and those who claim to be loyal to the liberal cause, but it is becoming more difficult to decide what the cause is. Consider, for example, the North American Free Trade Agreement (NAFTA) Implementation Act, which the U.S. House of Representatives passed on November 17, 1993.[12] This agreement among Canada, the United States, and Mexico removed tariffs on imports and exports between the countries. It received strong support from many self-proclaimed conservatives and liberals, and it received strong opposition from others bearing both labels. As another example, consider the much more recent debate over the proper legal response to the 12 million-plus people who are in the United States illegally. Some legislators—both conservatives and liberals—argue that the country should enact a law or laws making it easier for these immigrants to remain in the United States and to achieve legal status. Other legislators—both conservatives and liberals—argue that the country should remove these immigrants from the United States as quickly as possible. The point for us is that while the labels *conservative* and *liberal* carry a lot of emotional and rhetorical weight, they should be used carefully when trying to determine the scope and limits of legislative ethics.

To sum up our look at the professional criterion of significant service to the community, as this criterion pertains to legislation, we may note the following about the virtuous legislator. The virtuous legislator

- Owes her first allegiance to the U.S. Constitution.
- Recognizes that her primary client is her community.
- Does not limit her community to those who voted for her. Rather, she recognizes the variety of individuals and groups who have an interest in her professional activities, recognizes the potential for conflicts among these interests, and works to minimize those conflicts.
- Will, all else being equal, in case of conflicting interests, show a preference for her constituency.
- Balances the twin tasks of representation and legislation.
- Whenever possible, applies the contract model for allocation of responsibility in decision making between the professional and the client. She will act paternally as little as possible and never use the agency model as an excuse for making a bad decision.
- To facilitate the contract model of decision making, works to inform and educate her constituents about the scope and limits of her professional rights and responsibilities, the constituents' rights and responsibilities, the workings of the legislature, and the details of pending legislation.
- Works to honor the goals of the Preamble to the Constitution.
- Does not let the conservative–liberal distinction overpower her reason or her responsibility to the community to serve its interests.

We turn next to the second professional criterion as it pertains to legislation

Greater Responsibilities and Rights

 ## CASE 12.2

The Lawbreaking Lawmaker

U.S. Representative William Jefferson (D-LA) was recently indicted in federal court on 16 corruption-related counts.[13] The specific charges included bribery, racketeering, money laundering, and obstruction of justice. On June 9, 2007, Jefferson pleaded not guilty to the charges.

Jefferson has been a U.S. Representative since 1991. The charges cover a five-year period from 2000 to 2005. The issue heated up when the FBI raided Jefferson's congressional office. This was the first raid involving a member of the executive branch of government searching the office of a member of the legislative branch.[14] The next day, the FBI searched Jefferson's home and found $90,000 in his freezer.

The legislature's initial response was to defend its independence from the executive branch. For example, on May 24, 2006, Republicans joined Democrats in decrying the FBI raid, claiming that the Bush administration overstepped its bounds in the search of Jefferson's office.[15] This defensive tone changed soon after, however, when on June 16, 2006, House Democrats voted to remove Jefferson from the House Ways and Means Committee, from which Jefferson had allegedly built his criminal enterprise.[16] On December 10, 2006, Jefferson won reelection in spite of all the media attention about his alleged crimes. On June 6, 2007, the *New York Times* reported that the House Ethics Committee would open an "inquiry into the conduct of [Jefferson] who relinquished his sole committee assignment in the wake of his indictment on corruption charges."[17] On June 7, 2007, a *New York Times* editorial called for Speaker of the House Nancy Pelosi to propose an independent office to oversee ethics enforcement in the wake of Jefferson's indictment.

Using Case 12.2 as a backdrop, we may recall that the second professional criterion of importance to legislation is the greater level of responsibilities and rights that the professional has compared to those with a mere job. While the charges against Jefferson, if true, are morally offensive, most of us would find them less disturbing if Jefferson were not a professional. We would feel less betrayed, for example, if we learned that a hamburger maker was stealing money from the cash register. As a legislator, Jefferson has more power and authority than a simple job would give him, including especially the power to make laws, and with this power and authority come greater rights and responsibilities. Thus, to exceed those rights or fail in fulfilling those responsibilities adds a certain moral outrageousness to already objectionable behavior.

In terms of responsibilities, we can identify a quick list of the more important ones. In terms of rights, we may consider these in light of the public's duties in its interaction with the legislator.

Responsibilities

If we think of responsibilities in terms of professional obligations of trustworthiness, we may recall our discussion of these obligations in the previous chapter and note seven of those that are especially relevant to the legislator's role as lawmaker.

The first of the seven basic obligations is *competence*. To become a legislator, one has only to be at least 25 years old for the House or 30 years old for the Senate; have been a U.S. citizen for seven or nine years, respectively; live in the state that one hopes to represent; and receive a sufficient number of votes.[18] To remain a legislator once elected, one has only to avoid being expelled by at least two-thirds of the legislative body.[19]

At present, William Jefferson remains in Congress having satisfied all of these criteria, but there remains the sense that, if the federal charges against him are true, he has failed in this position. At the least, he has failed to perform competently. One way to define the competent legislator is to review the Constitution and the codes of ethics for the House and Senate. Together these form a job description of sorts, according to which one may decide whether a legislator is acting competently.

Article 1, sec. 8 of the U.S. Constitution lists 17 specific powers of Congress and ends with an "elastic clause" giving Congress the responsibility "to make all laws which shall be necessary and proper for carrying into execution the foregoing powers, and all other powers vested by this Constitution in the government of the United States, or in any department or officer thereof." Among the 17 specific powers are the responsibility to manage U.S. finances and monetary policies, to set weights and measures, to establish rules for naturalization, to establish a post office, to manage international relations, and to declare war and manage the military. None of these enumerated powers comes with an explanation of how one is to exercise them competently, but they make it possible for us to establish a set of expectations on which to decide whether a legislator is acting competently in those areas. In Jefferson's case, we might argue that if the charges are true, he spent too much time on his personal enterprises to give proper attention to his legislative duties.

The House of Representatives has rules of conduct that are more specific to Jefferson's alleged incompetencies.[20] Of 18 specific rules, 5 cover general behavior:

1. Members shall act always "in a manner that shall reflect creditably on the House."
2. Members "shall adhere to the spirit and the letter of the Rules of the House."
10. A member "who has been convicted . . . of a crime for which a sentence of two or more years' imprisonment may be imposed should refrain from participation in the business of [any] committee and . . . should refrain from voting on any question at a meeting of the House."
13. Members must take an oath of confidentiality before reviewing classified information.
14. Members "may not, with the intent to influence on the basis of partisan political affiliation an employment decision or employment practice of any private entity—(a) take or withhold . . . an official act; or (b) influence . . . the official act of another."

Allegedly, Jefferson has violated Rules 1, 2, and 14, and may soon be subject to rule 10.

Of the 18 specific House rules, 7 regulate financial gain from the legislator's official position:

3. A member may not receive compensation "the receipt of which would occur by virtue of influence improperly exerted from his position in congress."
4. A member may not accept gifts.
5. A member may not accept an honorarium for a speech, publication, "or any other similar activity."
6–7. These rules provide strict regulations for designation and use of campaign funds.
12. A member may not "participate personally and substantially as an employee of the House in contact with an agency of the executive or judicial branches

with respect to nonlegislative matters affecting any nongovernmental person in which the employee has a significant financial interest."

15. Members may not use any funds "for a flight on a non-governmental airplane that is not licensed by the Federal Aviation Administration to operate for compensation or hire."

Allegedly, Jefferson has violated rules 3, 4, 6, 7, and 12.

The remaining House rules do not pertain to Jefferson directly, nor do the Senate rules, but they round out the picture of a competent legislator. The remaining House rules concern proper and improper employment of others, use of earmarks, and use of the terms *House of Representatives, Congress of the United States,* and *official business.*

The general headings of the U.S. Senate's code of ethics concern financial transactions and disclosures, conflicts of interest, campaign activities, employment practices, and interventions with other government agencies.[21]

In summary, we have been considering the obligation of competence that is one of seven major obligations that define a legislator's responsibilities. At the least, the competent legislator exercises his constitutional powers well and complies with the rules of his legislative house.

The second of the seven basic obligations is *diligence.* Two common complaints in this area are that legislators often begin running for reelection the day after winning an election and that legislators don't put in a full workweek, even when Congress is in session. The obligation of diligence requires legislators to put most of their professional energy into representing their constituents' interests, followed by engaging in the oversight necessary to running the government smoothly and ethically. To fulfill these requirements, legislators must seek and understand the information necessary for them to do their job well. Thus, there would appear to be little time to run for reelection and no time to waste by putting in less than a full workweek.

A third obligation is *honesty.* Legislative candidates should be honest with the voters and themselves about their qualifications and abilities. They also should be honest about their opponents' apparent shortcomings, being careful, for example, not to make unwarranted accusations. The legislator in office should be honest with her constituents and with her colleagues about her goals, her views, her accomplishments and failures, and her whereabouts. She also should be honest about upcoming legislation, including the bill's full content, its chances of passing, and its likely effects. Finally, the legislator should live an honest life in general, even concerning matters that have nothing directly to do with legislating or representing the constituents' interests.

Q 12.6

If Jefferson admitted to corruption, would he satisfy the professional criterion of honesty?

A fourth obligation is *candor*. A person is honest who, when speaking, says what he believes. He might keep silent sometimes in order to maintain his honesty. A person is candid who reveals everything he believes. On the whole, we expect our legislators to be candid—to tell us everything they are thinking about legislative matters that affect us. This is a reasonable expectation to the extent that we are participants in a democratic government. Nevertheless, there may be times where national security, for example, requires the legislator to be less than candid. The virtuous legislator will know where to draw this line and will draw it as rarely as he has to, to function morally.

A fifth obligation is *loyalty*. In our previous discussion about the makeup of the legislator's constituency, we recognized the legislator's duty to the Constitution, the voters, the district or state she represents, and the political system in general. We also noted the relationship the legislator has with her party. And we should acknowledge the relationship that the legislator has with herself and her family and friends. In general, the legislator should be loyal in all of these relationships, but this demand is incomplete in two ways: It does not recognize the moral limits of loyalty, and it does not take into account the possibility of conflicting loyalties. In Case 12.1, we find Sen. Malcolm torn among his loyalty to his party, the voters, and himself. Apparently he cannot be loyal to all three at the same time. In Case 12.2, we would not expect the House of Representatives to show loyalty to William Jefferson by permitting him to continue as if there were no indictments against him. The House's first loyalty is to the American citizens, and Jefferson has allegedly shown disloyalty to them. While the House may want to proceed slowly against Jefferson on the ground that he is presumed innocent until proven guilty, the indictments are strong enough to restrict morally any loyalty the House might show to Jefferson. In short, while legislators have an obligation to be loyal to all who have a stake in their profession, they also have a duty to limit that loyalty when there are conflicts of interest or when other moral responsibilities trump the obligation of loyalty.

A sixth obligation is *discretion*. In professional ethics, *discretion* has at least two meanings: keeping a client's confidence, and the freedom to make a professional decision on one's own. In the first sense, for example, we recognize a priest's duty not to reveal what someone has said to him during the act of confession. In the second sense, for example, we recognize a police officer's freedom to write a speeding ticket or give the speeder a verbal warning to slow down.

Unlike the priest, the attorney, or the psychiatrist, whose first loyalty is to an individual client, the legislator's first loyalty is to a group of people. Thus, the second meaning of *discretion* is more applicable to the legislator than the first sense. Once we have voted the legislator into office, it is difficult to remove him before the next election; thus, he has a lot of discretion by default. How he votes and what resources he consults in preparation for a vote are entirely up to him. In the light of our comments about a legislator's competence, diligence, honesty, candor, and loyalty, we should demand that the legislator use his discretion fairly, wisely, and effectively. At the same time, we must acknowledge that the precise definition of these adverbs is open to debate.

The seventh professional obligation of trustworthiness is b*eneficence/nonmaleficence,* or doing good/not doing harm. It is obvious that a legislator should never knowingly act to harm her constituents or her colleagues, but the moral complexity of her professional activities may have her harming someone by helping someone else. Imagine the following scenario, for example. A bill is before Congress making it illegal to buy prescription drugs from countries outside the United States. This law will help U.S. drug makers by limiting competition and thus increasing profits. This increase in profits will increase money available for research into new and more effective drugs, which could potentially benefit thousands of people. The law will also cause the price to rise on certain drugs by so much that many current users who buy these drugs from Canada will no longer be able to afford them and may die prematurely. The legislator faces the dilemma that whichever way she votes on this law, the legislature's decision will harm someone.

Also, it is not enough for a legislator to avoid doing harm. Imagine that Sen. Malcolm in Case 12.1 decides simply to abstain from voting for the rest of his term. Imagine further that had he voted, his vote would have made no difference to the outcome of any legislative decision. Malcolm could then make a plausible claim that he had done no harm during his term. But his constituents would have the justifiable claim that he failed in his professional task by never doing anything good for his constituents. There is nothing controversial about insisting that a legislator seek to do good things when making law. The challenge is to decide what constitutes the good and how to distribute the benefits as widely as possible.

In addition to beneficence and nonmaleficence, the legislator must avoid *malfeasance,* which is defined simply as a public official's wrongdoing.

Rights

With the greater responsibilities of a profession over a job come greater rights. All of these rights are conferred, rather than inalienable; some are positive, and some are negative. The Constitution confers on legislators a number of rights that no other profession or person has. Most important, for our purposes, is the right to make law.

In one sense, this right is negative, because people who are not legislators must only refrain from interfering with the legislator's exercise of this right. The non-legislator does not have to take any action to ensure that the legislator exercises that right. In another sense, the legislator's right to make law is positive, because the law's legitimacy lies in the constituent's obligation to obey it. Without this obligation, lawmaking would be meaningless.

Thus, rights that mark the legislator's work as a profession rather than a job will sometimes impose or arise from duties on the part of the constituents. For constituents to perform these duties well, they should understand the rights and responsibilities of the legislator, stay informed about issues before the legislator, communicate with the legislator regularly in a way that reflects the constituents' role in the democratic process, and vote. Constituents may or may not be professionals in their own right, but their regular and intelligent contribution is essential to the legislator's professional success.

> **Q 12.7**
>
> Did the voters in Case 12.2 act prudently when they voted in December 2006 to keep Jefferson in office?

In terms of the professional criterion of greater rights and responsibilities, the virtuous legislator is competent, diligent, honest, candid, loyal, discretionary, nonmaleficent, and beneficent in a way that is neither excessive nor deficient. The virtuous legislator also exercises well his right to make law.

Self-Governance

A third criterion that distinguishes a profession from a job is self-governance. This has two meanings. In one sense, it refers to the body of professionals that governs all members of the profession. In another sense, it refers to the autonomy of the individual. We will look at autonomy as a separate criterion. Article I of the Constitution gives each chamber of Congress the right and responsibility to govern itself. The Constitution also gives the executive and judicial branches of government the right and responsibility to check and balance the power of the legislature, by vetoing a legislative decision or declaring a legislative act unconstitutional, respectively.

Some features of self-governance that stand out with regard to the ethics of legislation include the following.

Financial Misdeeds and Conflicts of Interest

First, in terms of ethics, both the House of Representatives and the Senate emphasize avoiding financial misdeeds and conflicts of interest.[22] This is apparent from the codes of ethics that we previously identified and from the time that ethics committees devote to these concerns. The allegations against Jefferson in Case 12.2 support this emphasis, but we must (1) identify some of the forces that require it and (2) acknowledge other moral challenges that require careful self-governance of the legislature.

Two primary forces in combination justify close attention to financial misdeeds and conflicts of interest: self-interest and improper influence. As Case 12.2 demonstrates, the power and access that come with being a legislator make it easy for people of poor moral character to benefit at the cost of others. The right to self-govern makes this even easier, because there is no external oversight. There is nothing wrong with finding fulfillment in and otherwise enjoying the practice and benefits of one's profession, as long as the clients get the service they deserve and the professional meets all other professional obligations. Thus, there is nothing automatically wrong with self-interest, even an interest in being financially comfortable. The problem with self-interest arises when it interferes with fulfilling one's professional responsibilities. Adequate self-governance must discourage such self-interest and must deal with it convincingly when it occurs.

In addition to the challenges of self-interest, legislators' power and access expose them to all manner of people interested in exploiting the legislators through emotional and intellectual influence. Lobbyists and political action committees are two of the more obvious groups of people who aim to influence legislative activity. As with self-interest, such influence is not necessarily morally bad. Imagine, for example, a lobbyist representing a group of pediatricians who are hoping for legislation that will make excellent health care available to all children in the United States. To make her case, the lobbyist compiles a catalog of children who have died from medical problems that are easily treatable for those with adequate health care. The catalog includes photographs and brief biographies that the lobbyist hopes will play on the legislator's emotions. As an added thrust, the lobbyist reminds the legislator of his young children and the devastation he would feel if his children died—especially if adequate health care could have saved them. The lobbyist's attempt to influence is obvious and commendable. Only the most heartless legislator could ignore such a plea, although there may be other factors in the pending legislation that deserve the legislator's attention as well, such as cost. In short, there is nothing apparently wrong with such influence, and those responsible for legislative self-governance need not guard against such influence.

On the other hand, consider the issues of influence in Case 12.2. Allegedly, Jefferson let himself be influenced by people willing to pay him a great deal of money for acting immorally and illegally. It also appears that Jefferson influenced others to pay him under the same circumstances. This violation of the community's trust, the profession's rules, and the law is of major concern for self-governance. As we have noted, this may explain why so much of legislative self-governance focuses on preventing and punishing such abuses.

Q 12.8

Does Jefferson's alleged corruption in Case 12.2 suggest a failure in the House of Representatives' self-governance?

Other Moral Challenges to Self-Governance

There are moral challenges to legislative self-governance besides financial misdeeds and conflicts of interest. Consider the following four tensions, each of which calls for the legislature in general and the legislators individually to decide how to manage its challenge to self-governance.

First is the tension between private morality and public morality. In Case 12.1, we saw Sen. Malcolm's personal moral position against homosexual marriage in conflict with the community's desire to permit it. Although proper legislative self-governance should not prevent a legislator from voting his conscience, the moral challenge that this tension poses requires certain guidelines.

Second is the tension between federal legislation and states' rights. The argument over the extent to which the federal government should be able to dictate to individual states is as old as the Union. Slavery was the most enduring example of this argument, until the 13th Amendment outlawed slavery. Many U.S. citizens believed that each state should decide for itself whether to permit slavery; many other citizens felt that the federal government should ban slavery nationwide. In principle, the Civil War was supposed to have settled this argument in favor of a strong federal government; in practice, the debate continues. Take, for example, federal speed limits. Some years ago, Montana's lawmakers objected to federal speed limits as being too slow for the state's long, straight highways. The federal response was to threaten the state with loss of federal funds for interstate highways. Many federal legislators have expressed strong support for a state's right to govern itself. There may be no chance of resolving this issue to everyone's satisfaction, but proper self-governance requires that legislators have the means to deal with this issue constructively.

A third tension is between statutory law and common law. The Constitution calls itself the supreme law of the land and leaves it to legislators to make the law. There is, however, a rich history in the United States of common law or judge-made law. This comes from decisions that judges make in cases where the legal code is either unclear or declared unconstitutional. The decision sets a precedent that may influence subsequent judicial decision making and will maintain its lawlike status unless it is overturned by the legislature or by a future judicial decision. Consider *Roe v. Wade* (1973), which established the law granting a woman the right to seek abortion "on demand" anywhere in the United States, up to the point in her pregnancy where the fetus is viable. This decision overturned anti-abortion laws at the time and set a precedent that has withstood several state and federal challenges over the years, leaving the legislature out of the loop. The moral questions here are, To what extent will the legislature allow common law to stand, and how should the legislature work with the courts in maintaining the proper balance of statutory law and common law?

Q 12.9

In Case 12.1, should Malcolm encourage his colleagues in Congress to let the courts decide the issue of homosexual marriage, thus relieving the legislature of having to make law that is sure to displease a large number of constituents?

A fourth tension that poses a moral challenge to the legislature in terms of self-governance is between U.S. law and international law. The general view is that each country is sovereign and is thus free to make any laws it wishes, as long as this does not interfere with another country's sovereignty. However, humanitarian concerns or a country's practices that have ill affects on other countries may require international legislation that trumps the legislative decisions of individual countries. For example, some countries mistreat their citizens so badly that human decency requires intervention, especially by countries that have the means to intervene successfully. Consider the Nazi holocaust in World War II Germany or, more recently, the rampant genocide in the Darfur region of Sudan. It would be morally wrong for other countries to dismiss these as problems wholly internal to the country.

Global warming is another contemporary example of the tension between federal law and international law. A total of 169 nations have signed the Kyoto Protocol calling for reductions in greenhouse gas emissions that contribute to global warming.[23] Some of the signatory nations, including the United States, have refused to ratify the protocol.[24] Although no court of international law has taken this case of failure to ratify, one can imagine a future international endeavor to force countries to reduce polluting emissions, given their global consequences. As a matter of self-governance, the legislature needs to decide how to respond to the tension between federal law and international law.

Managing Self-Governance

The legislature's primary instruments of self-governance are its code of conduct and its committees and subcommittees responsible for managing and enforcing the code. In articulating the elements of its self-governance, the legislature should also consider the Constitution, the law, tradition, experience, common sense, and community norms. How to incorporate these elements should be a matter of ongoing conversation among legislators and between the legislature and the public.

When an individual legislator deserves punishment from his colleagues, this punishment may take any of a number of forms:[25]

- Verbal reprimand
- Written reprimand
- Public censure
- Loss of committee membership
- Loss of seniority
- Exclusion—refusal to seat a member who has been elected
- Expulsion—requiring at least a two-thirds majority vote

Proper self-governance requires a clear statement of the criteria for each of these forms of punishment and the means of imposing it.

Q 12.10

Which of the punishments listed would be most fitting for Jefferson, in Case 12.2, if he is guilty of the charges against him?

In terms of the professional criterion of self-governance, the virtuous legislator avoids financial misdeeds; avoids conflicts of interest wherever possible, and manages unavoidable conflicts by acting with the public good primarily in mind; discourages and avoids improper influence; and acts in self-interest only when it is appropriate to do so. The virtuous legislator also seeks and usually finds the proper balance in the tensions between private and public morality, federal law and states' rights, statutory law and common law, and federal law and international law.

Autonomy

So far, we have examined three primary professional criteria as they apply to the legislator: significant service to the community, greater rights and responsibilities than a mere job offers, and self-governance. A fourth criterion for a profession is autonomy. Whereas self-governance pertains primarily to the legislature as a whole, autonomy pertains primarily to the individual legislator. This reflects the great amount of personal independence that the legislator has in deciding, for example, when to show up for work, how to exercise his authority, whether and how to prepare for a vote, and how to vote. Although he must answer to the voters in the next election, the legislator in the interim has a great deal of freedom.

A primary feature of this autonomy is the importance of discretion and its proper use, which we have already discussed.

Another feature of this autonomy is its application in the important legislative roles of compromising, bargaining, and making practical decisions contrary to one's ideals. In this vein, we find Sen. Malcolm struggling in Case 12.1 to reconcile his moral ideals with the competing interests of his constituents and his party leaders. No one can force Sen. Malcolm's final decision. The responsibility for making the right decision, as difficult as it may seem, rests squarely on his shoulders.

Yet another feature of the legislator's autonomy is the need to maintain his independence against the onslaught of special interest groups. We have discussed this elsewhere in terms of proper and improper influence.

In terms of the professional criterion of autonomy, the virtuous legislator uses discretion wisely. To that end, he also acts neither deficiently nor excessively when compromising, bargaining, or making practical decisions.

Calling

A fifth criterion for a profession is a sense of calling in contrast with the other reasons that one might take a job, such as the need for money. The legislator's proper calling is to public service. Legislators who feel called to the position demonstrate this calling by frequently sacrificing their own interests in favor of their constituents. Sometimes, this may mean carrying out the wishes of the constituency in opposition to the legislator's personal feelings. At other times, it may mean acting paternally against the express wishes of the constituency, but with their well-being in mind.

By this same criterion, we tend to condemn legislators, such as Jefferson in Case 12.2, who are in the profession primarily for personal reward or because it appears that they couldn't find a job that they would rather do.

In terms of the professional criterion of the sense of a calling, the virtuous legislator puts public service ahead of self-interest except where putting herself first would be less deficient and less excessive than doing otherwise.

Money as Means

The idea of a calling as a criterion for professionalism closely relates to the role of money as a means rather than an end, the sixth professional criterion. In our discussion of professional criteria, we noted that a professional tends to see money as a means to practicing the profession well, while a person taking a job may reasonably regard the job as a means to making money.

It would appear that Jefferson, in Case 12.2, unprofessionally accepted his voters' acclaim in order to line his own pockets. We object not only to his breaking the law but also to his doing it for financial reasons, when he should be tending to the needs of his constituents instead.

In terms of the professional criterion of money as a means, the virtuous legislator does not treat the profession primarily as a means to financial success, but sees the value of his salary and benefits as necessary to practicing his profession well.

Extensive Training

A seventh professional criterion is extensive training. There is no formal requirement for a legislator to undergo training before assuming office. As noted previously, the Constitution requires only that the legislator be of a certain age, have been a U.S. citizen for a certain number of years, and be a resident of the state she represents. Nevertheless, the work of a legislator is so complex in quantity and quality that the effective legislator will study legislation, law, and the conditions and contexts surrounding a bill, and will find the legislative chamber to be a laboratory for continuous training in the Constitution and the legislative process.

In terms of this criterion, the virtuous legislator need not have a formal education, but should engage in ongoing study and training to the extent that this engagement helps her practice her profession well.

✦ Staff, Lobbyists, PACs, and Journalists

Case 12.3

Quid Pro Quo

U.S. Representative Sylvia Warden and her chief of staff are attending a fund-raising dinner for a colleague in the House. Warden spies Jill Solt, a lobbyist who represents Amigo Oil and Gas. Amigo is a major company that stands to benefit or suffer greatly from a bill that is before the committee that Warden chairs. Warden tells her chief of staff to walk over to Solt and hint that a major campaign contribution to Warden's colleague could mean a positive committee decision for Amigo, but only if the contribution is in the colleague's hands before the committee discusses the bill.

Case 12.3 reminds us that several people play important roles in the legislator's professional life. These roles may be supportive, or they may be confrontational, but all are important to a discussion about legislative ethics. Among these roles, the ones with the greatest impact are legislative staff, lobbyists, PACs, and journalists. Let's look at each more closely.

Staff

The legislator would find it difficult to fulfill her responsibilities without an intelligent and dedicated staff. Campaign staff help organize her campaign strategy, volunteers, appearances, and public relations. Office staff help her manage her office, communicate with constituents and colleagues, and acquire the information necessary to make informed decisions and votes. While it is debatable whether staff members are professionals in the sense that our seven criteria suggest, it is clear that staff have a crucial role to play in the legislator's professional activities. To that extent, therefore, the ethics of staff is of interest to the study of professional ethics in criminal justice.

A good first place to turn for understanding staff ethics is the staff section of the legislature's code of ethics. The House code, for example, emphasizes the following staff rights and duties:[26]

- "House employees are public servants, paid with United States Treasury funds. They must perform official duties commensurate with the compensation they receive. Employees are not paid to perform nonofficial, personal, or campaign duties on behalf of a Member or anyone else."
- Staff may not "discriminate on the basis of race, color, religion, sex (including marital or parental status), handicap, age, or national origin in hiring, pay, or working conditions."
- Staff may not hire or promote a relative.
- Staff may not promise a federal job or threaten to fire someone from a federal job "in order to obtain a political contribution or to coerce political activity."
- Staff may not be required to divide, share or "kick back" salaries.
- Staff may not "spend personal money to benefit a Member or the operation of a Member's office."
- Staff may engage in campaign activities or secondary employment, as long as they do so on their own time and in a manner that does not compromise their staff position.

Q 12.11

If the staff member in Case 12.3 obeys Warden's order, does the staff member violate the House staff code of ethics?

Our extensive discussion of ethics thus far allows us to make some more observations about the ethics of legislative staff. First, a staff member's primary loyalty is to the legislator or legislative committee that has hired the staff member. With this obligation of loyalty come the obligations to be obedient, honest, candid, diligent, competent, and nonmaleficent. These obligations end when the legislator or legislative committee requests or requires the staff member to act illegally or immorally.

Also, the duty to be honest, competent, and nonmaleficent extends to the staff's dealing with people other than the legislator, including other government employees, lobbyists, PACs, journalists, and the public at large. In those dealings, the staff may not have to be candid, diligent, or obedient, if doing so will jeopardize a morally appropriate relationship with the legislator or legislative committee.

In short, the virtuous staff member recognizes his role as a public servant, with a particular obligation of loyalty to the legislative member or the committee for which the staff member works; does not engage in unfair or nepotistic hiring practices; does not use threats or bribes; manages his salary and other finances properly; and does not engage in campaigning or secondary employment while he is on duty as a staff member. He is honest, competent, and nonmaleficent toward everyone; and candid, diligent, and obedient to the legislator or committee for which the staff member works.

Lobbyists

Whether lobbying is a profession is a discussion for another time. For our purposes, it is enough to note the integral role that lobbyists play in the legislative process and to identify the virtuous lobbyist in that process. A lobbyist's primary task is to represent the interests of a client to a key legislator or group of legislators. This may mean simply educating the legislator about the details of pending legislation—including who would be affected and how—or it may mean trying to convince a legislator to vote contrary to his expressed intentions. In either case, the lobbyist may act ethically or unethically.

We can get a sense of what it means for a lobbyist to act ethically from the American League of Lobbyists' *Code of Ethics.*[27] Under nine articles, the code requires the virtuous lobbyist to be honest, but not necessarily candid; compliant with laws and rules; informed; civil; diligent; discreet; and straightforward about fees and expected workload. The virtuous lobbyist also avoids conflicts of interest whenever possible and manages unavoidable conflicts to the advantage of the client, unless it would be immoral or illegal to do so.

Some argue that regardless of the lobbyists' virtues, lobbyists should not have access to the legislator that ordinary constituents do not have. It is a common sight, for example, to see lobbyists lining the passageways to congressional chambers as legislators enter the chambers. These lobbyists may whisper something in a legislator's ear or hand the legislator a piece of paper containing information that the lobbyist considers crucial to an upcoming debate or vote. How much impact this has on a legislator's decision is debatable, but the lobbyist clearly has an advantage that non-lobbyists don't have in terms of access to the legislator.

The ideal response might be to ban lobbying altogether, but this is neither practical nor, in the end, the most beneficial option. There is nothing in the Constitution that forbids such access to lobbyists, so enacting such a prohibition could be time-consuming and ultimately unconstitutional. Also, the virtuous legislator may learn a great deal from a lobbyist without having to commit to supporting the lobbyist's effort. Thus, it makes more sense to allow the lobbying to continue, but only under regulations and oversight that will discourage the unethical lobbyists and encourage the virtuous lobbyist.

Q 12.12

In Case 12.3, if the lobbyist for Amigo Corp. refuses to honor the staff member's request, but also refuses to tell anyone about the request, has the lobbyist handled the situation morally well?

Political Action Committees

Political action committees, or PACs, play a role in the legislative process similar to the lobbyist's role. PACs exist to influence elections and to promote legislation. Examples of PAC categories include agriculture, retail services, communications, city/county, organized labor, and health care.

Under the Federal Election Campaign Act of 1971, an organization is a PAC if it accepts more than $1,000 "for the purpose of influencing a federal election."[28] Corporations and unions may not contribute to PACs, and individuals may contribute a maximum of $5,000.

Because of their similarity to lobbyists, we may borrow from the American League of Lobbyists' Code of Ethics to identify the marks of a virtuous PAC, or more precisely, members of a PAC. Thus, the virtuous PAC member is honest, but not necessarily candid; compliant with laws and rules; informed; civil; diligent; discreet; and straightforward about finances.

Journalists

Since journalists serve a much broader and more varied function than simply being involved in legislation, it may seem out of place to bring up journalist ethics in the context of legislation. But journalists have a clear and important role to play in legislation that may contribute to or detract from legislative ethics and that requires virtue on the journalist's part.

The ways in which a journalist can contribute to legislative ethics include keeping legislative activity and individual legislators' activities in the public eye, educating the public about the legislative process, and encouraging public response through letters to the editor and op-ed pieces.

In this sense, journalism includes objective news reports and potentially more subjective editorials. Objective reports should be based on confirmed facts that "speak for themselves"; that cite their sources; and that are clear, concise, and complete, but not extraneous or irrelevant. Editorials should be clearly labeled as such, should make their premises and conclusion clear, and should encourage the readers', listeners', or viewers' responses.

> **Q 12.13**
>
> Suppose the chief of staff in Case 12.3 calls a newspaper reporter anonymously and tells the reporter about Warden's demand. Would it be morally appropriate for the reporter to publish an article detailing the case?

SUMMARY

This ends our discussion of legislative ethics. We have identified key features of the virtuous legislator, in his or her contributions to criminal justice. We have also identified the virtuous staff member, virtuous lobbyist, virtuous PAC, and virtuous journalist, in their relationships with the legislator. Our next step is to examine ethics in law enforcement.

ANSWERS TO CASE STUDY QUESTIONS

Q12.1. Do Malcolm's fellow party members have as much of a claim on Malcolm's professional services as those eligible to vote for him?
No. Malcolm's duty to represent the voters' interests is much greater than his duty to satisfy party members.

Q12.2. In Case 12.2, does Malcolm have a duty to tell his constituents about the party's pressure on him to renounce his objection to homosexual marriage?
Not necessarily. As long as Malcolm is able to act with discretion and autonomy, there may be nothing to gain from revealing the party's request to Malcolm's constituents.

Q12.3. In Case 12.1, does Malcolm's aversion to homosexual marriage appear to be a matter of national security for him? Does it appear to be a matter of liberty?
No and maybe. Although, he may believe that his constituents should have the liberty to avoid dealing with homosexual marriage, it would be difficult for him to argue validly that the issue is a matter of national security.

Q12.4. With which model of decision making does Malcolm appear to be most comfortable in Case 12.1? Which model do the voters appear to prefer?
Malcolm appears to be most comfortable with the paternalistic model. The voters appear to prefer the agency model.

Q12.5. In Case 12.1, does Malcolm appear to be a conservative?
Yes, in the sense of having a specific moral agenda.

Q12.6. If Jefferson admitted to corruption, would he satisfy the professional criterion of honesty?
No. The professional criterion of honesty regards it as a virtue. A moment of honesty does not make a person virtuous.

Q12.7. Did the voters in Case 12.2 act prudently when they voted in December 2006 to keep Jefferson in office?
Prudence is the cardinal virtue of acting properly based on available knowledge. To act less than prudently is to "leap before you look"—that is, to act without having sufficient knowledge to justify the act. To be excessively prudent is to fail to act when one has sufficient knowledge to act. The voters in Case 12.2 had good reason to suspect Jefferson of corruption, even though he had not been formally indicted, let alone convicted. It would be unwise to reelect a corrupt legislator. Thus, the voters acted imprudently.

Q12.8. Does Jefferson's alleged corruption in Case 12.2 suggest a failure in the House of Representatives' self-governance?
Not necessarily. Representatives properly have a great deal of autonomy. The virtuous legislator will put this autonomy to good use in pursuit of the public good; the vicious legislator may use it to engage in self-serving acts. Once the legislature finds out about Jefferson, however, not to respond appropriately would be a failure in self-governance.

Q12.9. In Case 12.1, should Malcolm encourage his colleagues in Congress to let the courts decide the issue of homosexual marriage, thus relieving the legislature of having to make law that is sure to displease a large number of constituents?
No. The Constitution requires the legislature to make law. If someone wants to challenge a specific law's constitutionality, this challenge should go before the court, whose decision will set a legal precedent. But the legislator should take the lead on the issue.

Q12.10. Which of the punishments listed would be most fitting for Jefferson, in Case 12.2, if he is guilty of the charges against him?
Expulsion. Anything less would undermine the morally desirable character of the legislature and would reflect poorly on the profession.

Q12.11. If the staff member in Case 12.3 obeys Warden's order, does the staff member violate the House staff code of ethics?
Not obviously, although the staff member would not be serving the public well, contrary to the code's reminder that the staff member is a public servant paid with U.S. funds. Also, if the staff member is on duty, he may not engage in any campaign activities, according to the code of ethics.

Q12.12. In Case 12.3, if the lobbyist for Amigo Corp. refuses to honor the staff member's request, but also refuses to tell anyone about the request, has the lobbyist handled the situation morally well?

No. Neither the representative nor the staff member should have the chance to make this immoral request again. If the lobbyist keeps the request to herself, she will have failed to bring it to light, thus violating the spirit, if not the letter, of Article IX of the American League of Lobbyists' Code of Ethics: Lobbyists should not "undermine public confidence and trust in the democratic governmental process" or "show disrespect for governmental institutions."

Q12.13. Suppose the chief of staff in Case 12.3 calls a newspaper reporter anonymously and tells the reporter about Warden's demand. Would it be morally appropriate for the reporter to publish an article detailing the case?

No. Unless the reporter can verify the allegation, reporting it on the strength of an anonymous phone call would be tantamount to engaging in hearsay or spreading gossip, neither of which satisfies the reporter's duty to report the facts objectively.

NOTES

1. Art. 1, sec. 1.
2. Art. 6.
3. Sec. 1.
4. Abraham Lincoln, "The Gettysburg Address," 19 November 1863.
5. Griffin Trotter, *The Ethics of Coercion in Mass Casualty Medicine* (Baltimore: Johns Hopkins University Press, 2007), p. 20.
6. The Hasting Center, *The Ethics of Legislative Life* (Hastings-on-Hudson, NY: The Center, 1985), p. 29.
7. George Washington, "Farewell Address," 1796.
8. George Santayana, *Life of Reason: Reason in Common Sense* (New York: Scribner's, 1905), p. 284.
9. Robert Byrd, "This Is Another Gulf of Tonkin Resolution," *Albion Monitor,* 4 October 2002; retrieved 15 June 2007 from http://albionmonitor.com.
10. The first three meanings come from Michael Kinsley, "What's Too Conservative?" *Washington Post,* 4 November 2005, p. A23.
11. Stephen Breyer, *Active Liberty: Interpreting Our Democratic Constitution* (New York: Vintage, 2006).
12. Retrieved 17 June 2007 from http://clerk.house.gov/evs/1993/roll575.xml.
13. *New York Times,* 5 June 2007, p. A1.
14. *New York Times,* 21 May 2006, p. A22.
15. *New York Times,* 24 May 2006, p. A1.
16. *New York Times,* 16 June 2006, p. A28
17. *New York Times,* 6 June 2007, p. A14.
18. Art. 1, secs. 2 and 3.
19. Art. 1, sec. 5.
20. U.S. House of Representatives, "Rules of the House of Representatives—110th Congress: Rule 23—Code of Official Conduct," 2007.

21. United States Senate Select Committee on Ethics, "An Overview of the Senate Code of Conduct and Related Laws," March 2007.

22. Hastings Center, *Ethics of Legislative Life,* p. vii.

23. United Nations Framework Convention on Climate Change, "Kyoto Protocol: Status of Ratification, 10 July 2006"; retrieved 25 June 2007 from [[check]]unfccc.int/files/essential_background/Kyoto_protocol/application/pdf/kpstats/pdf.

24. United States Energy Information Administration, "Country Analysis Briefs," November 2005; retrieved 25 June 2007 from www.eia.doe.gov/emeu/cabs/USA/full.html.

25. Hastings Center, *Ethics of Legislative Life,* pp. 16–17.

26. U.S. House of Representatives, *Ethics Manual* (c. 1997); retrieved 25 June 2007 from www.house.gov/ethics/ethicschap5.html.

27. Updated 9 October 2006; retrieved 26 June 2007 from www.alldc.org/ethicscode.cfm.

28. FECA Publ. L 92-225, 86 Stat. 3; enacted 1972-02-07; 2 USC par. 431 et. seq.

CHAPTER 13

ETHICS IN LAW ENFORCEMENT

CASE 13.1

Serpico[1]

Frank Serpico (b. 1936) became a patrol officer with the New York City Police Department in 1960, which in his own words fulfilled a lifelong dream. Within a few years he became a plainclothes detective working on vice racketeering. During this assignment he encountered a number of detectives accepting illegal cash gifts, but he refused to accept graft himself.

At first, Serpico tried to mind his own business, without reporting the graft to anyone. But after his colleagues tried to pressure him into "dirtying his hands," he reported the graft to NYPD officials in 1967. Finding the officials' responses frustrating and inadequate, he went public with his charges in 1970, resulting in a front page article in the *New York Times*.

Responding to the *Times* article, New York Mayor John Lindsay appointed a commission, headed by Whitman Knapp, to look into the corruption of the police department. In February 1971, Serpico was shot while on a drug raid and his fellow police were unusually slow to help, apparently out of anger at Serpico's "snitching." In October and December of 1971, Serpico testified before the Knapp Commission, at one point saying,

> Through my appearance here today . . . I hope that police officers in the future will not experience the same frustration and anxiety that I was subjected to for the past five years at the hands of my superiors because of my attempt to report corruption. . . . We create an atmosphere in which the honest officer fears the dishonest officer, and not the other way around. . . . The problem is that the atmosphere does not yet exist in which honest police officers can act without fear of ridicule or reprisal from fellow officers.

In 1972, Serpico received New York City's Medal of Honor, and a month later he retired.

Case 13.1 invites us to review and continue our discussion of law enforcement ethics. Law enforcement is a major function of the executive branch of government, which the Constitution covers in Article II. A thorough discussion of executive ethics might start with the office of the President of the United States, including his vice president, cabinet, and staff, then move to state governors, county councils, and city and town mayors. Presidents, governors, councils, and mayors bring to the criminal justice system important management functions that are necessary to executing the will of the people as expressed through legislation. These functions pose many moral challenges and call for executives with integrity. Because an adequate discussion of ethics at these executive levels would be so extensive, our discussion here will focus on law enforcement as a key representative of the executive branch of government.

Q 13.1

In Case 13.1, if Serpico reported the police corruption only because he feared for his life, did he do a morally good thing?

We will divide this examination into two major parts: police and corrections. This is an unusual pairing for a book on criminal justice ethics; the two areas are usually discussed in separate chapters and often fall on either side of a discussion of judicial ethics. We can justify uniting the police and corrections on two grounds. First, both are functions of the executive branch of government (although probation officers sometimes answer directly to the court). As such, both involve enforcement of the legislative will, which is supposed to reflect the will of the people.

Second, many of the moral issues that police officers face are similar to the issues that corrections officials face, and that neither legislative nor judicial professionals face. For a preliminary and obvious example, consider the use of deadly force. Perhaps the most challenging moral decision that a law enforcement official could face is whether to respond immediately with deadly force. No other field in criminal justice includes this potential decision in its day-to-day practice. Legislators may have to decide whether to make certain crimes capital crimes, and judges and juries may have to decide whether to impose the death penalty, but these do not require on-the-spot decisions that could end a person's life. This example represents many life-or-death decisions that police and corrections officials face and that unite the two professions in a moral environment with many similarities. We turn now to a closer look at each profession.

→ POLICE

Law enforcement occurs in two places in the general flow of the criminal justice system.[2] The first is between the enactment of a law and a judicial decision about whether someone has broken the law. The second occurrence is when a court decides that someone has broken a law and the court puts that person into the corrections system. We shall use the term *police* to refer to the professionals involved directly in the first occurrence. These include federal law enforcement officials from the U.S. Departments of Justice, Treasury, Homeland Security, Health and Human Services, Defense, Transportation, and other cabinet-level departments that have a law enforcement function. Our use of *police* will also include sheriffs, marshals, and constables at the state and local levels.

We have raised the question of whether policing is a profession and have argued that the moral demands on policing distinguish it as a profession, even if police do not have to meet all of the professional criteria to enter the field. Recall the eight basic professional criteria:

- Significant service to society
- Greater rights and responsibilities
- Self-governance
- Autonomy
- A calling
- Money as a means, professional fulfillment as the end
- Extensive training
- Credentialing

To the extent that police are professionals, they will meet most, if not all, of these criteria for a profession. They must also have regard for their various professional relationships, and they must understand and fulfill their professional obligations. Taking an approach similar to our examination of legislative ethics, let's examine police ethics by using the professional criteria as our organizing principle, inserting observations about relationships and obligations where appropriate.

Q 13.2

In Case 13.1, does Serpico appear to regard policing as a profession?

Significant Service to Society

Of all the criteria that are necessary to a profession but not to a job, the most important to policing is the offering of significant service to the community.

In terms of professional relationships, the police officer's clients are the people in his jurisdiction. All other professional relationships—to oneself, to third parties, to colleagues, and to the profession at large—are subordinate to serving this community well. Moral problems may arise at any point in a police official's work: keeping the peace; preventing crime; investigating crime; apprehending, arresting, and processing suspects; writing and submitting reports; testifying in court; dealing with colleagues; supervising personnel. These observations present two questions: Who are the members of the community? What does it mean for the police to meet the community's expectations? Let's address each of these.

The Client

CASE 13.2

The Funeral of Za Chue Xiong[3]

Tens of thousands of Hmong—an Asian people from Laos, Thailand, and North Vietnam—fled to the United States, especially the Minneapolis–St. Paul area, after the Vietnam War ended in 1975. Hmong funeral practices continue to arouse controversy. The typical Hmong funeral lasts for three days and includes the slaughtering and cooking of cows and chickens. One such funeral, for 88-year-old Za Chue Xiong, brought complaints from the funeral home's neighbors about "congested parking and strong odors," and it brought police to the funeral home to arrest the funeral director for violations of safety codes.

Protesting the arrest, one spokesperson for the grieving family noted that the funeral "ceremonies are considered sacred, and proper burial is necessary to help the deceased find his or her soul in the afterworld." Also, "the cow is very important in the Hmong culture. Sons and daughters need to slaughter cows so that the deceased can have enough animals in the afterlife and live a better life." Another spokesperson said, "the neighbors who complain aren't sympathetic to the culture behind the funerals. It's a basic human right to have a place and ceremony to respect your culture. It's really no different than Catholics or Lutherans who have their own traditions or ceremonies. I would think the neighbors would respect all cultural rites."

Case 13.2 is an example of a common challenge that police officers face in increasingly diverse communities. In the United States, police officers are peace officers. Their main responsibility is to keep the community members in their jurisdiction safe and secure, both collectively and individually. Collectively, the community includes a well-defined area and a set of generally clear laws, rules, and orders that guide the officer in the policing of that community. Individuals and different groups of people within the community offer the police different personalities in different circumstances—lawbreakers; victims; and citizens needing nonlegal help, such as directions, getting a cat out of a tree, or emergency medical assistance. This diverse clientele poses a number of challenges, some of which we have already identified but bear repeating.

One challenge concerns allocation of responsibility for decision making between the professional and the client. We have identified three models of decision making: paternal, agency, and contract. The paternal model makes the professional responsible for the decision. The agent model makes the client responsible for the decision. The contract model makes the decision a joint responsibility of the professional and the client, assuming the client is physically and mentally able to participate in making the decision.

Q 13.3

Which model of decision making for police and community does Case 13.2 exemplify? Is this the best model for the situation?

We have argued that, all else being equal, the contract model is the most desirable of the three models, because it correctly recognizes each side as a full participant in the contract and it satisfies the Aristotelian principle of finding the mean between the extremes of overburdening one party or the other. But sometimes the situation calls for one of the other two models. For example, an officer must sometimes act paternally, as when the client—a criminal, perhaps—refuses to work with the officer; or when two clients are at odds—a criminal and his victim, for example; or when the client, a victim or witness, is too distraught to participate in decision making. Other times, the client regards the officer as a mere agent, as when the client declares "I pay your salary!"

A second challenge that a diverse citizenry poses for the police comes from ethnic and cultural differences that may be at odds with the officer's values and may put citizens at odds with each other, as in Case 13.2. Police should respect all people, even criminals, and treat them with dignity. Police may also have to minimize others' disrespect or mistreatment of people. At the same time, the police officer must distinguish between behaviors that may be peculiar, but are not illegal, and those that demand legal action. These tasks are easier where the police officer understands the significance of cultural diversity, the diverse elements of her community, and the proper means for handling such diversity. The virtuous police officer will be able to find the proper balance between tolerating or celebrating diverse cultural practices, on the one hand, and preventing illegal or socially harmful practices, on the other.

A third, similar challenge that a diverse citizenry poses for the police comes from the variety of religious views and the strong influence of these views on many people's behavior. We discussed this at length in an earlier chapter. Here it is enough to note that the virtuous police officer is aware of religion's importance in American ethics and in the officer's interactions with the community and with colleagues. Thus, the virtuous officer is sensitive to, if not conversant with, his community's major religions and their reliance on scripture, tradition, reason, and experience for making moral decisions.

Q 13.4

In Case 13.2, do the police officers appear to be violating the mourners' First Amendment right to freedom of religion?

Meeting the Community's Expectations

As an attempt to capture clearly and concisely what it means for police to meet their clients' expectations, the New York Police Department statement of Mission and Values captures nicely the service that police should offer the community.[4]

> The Mission of the New York City Police Department is to enhance the quality of life in our City by working in partnership with the community and in accordance with constitutional rights to enforce the laws, preserve the peace, reduce fear, and provide for a safe environment.

In terms of values, NYPD's mission statement says the following:

> In partnership with the community, we pledge to:
>
> - Protect the lives and property of our fellow citizens and impartially enforce the law.
> - Fight crime both by preventing it and aggressively pursuing violators of law.
> - Maintain a higher standard of integrity than is generally expected of others because so much is expected of us.
> - Value human life, respect the dignity of each individual and render our services with courtesy and civility.

In sum, the professional criterion of significant service to the community calls for the virtuous police officer to foster proper allocation of responsibility for decision making with the members of the community, preferring the contract model where possible but using the paternal or agency model where necessary. The virtuous officer seeks to keep the peace and enforce the law while staying within the bounds of the Constitution and respecting the members of the community in all their diversity. Finally, the virtuous officer maintains his integrity, even when off duty, which reflects the next professional criterion—greater responsibilities and rights.

Q 13.5

In Case 13.1, did Serpico appear to satisfy the criterion of significant service to the community?

Greater Rights and Responsibilities

As defenders of the Constitution, police officers must protect rights, enforce the jurisdiction's laws, and promote justice in a way that coheres with the concept of democracy. Perhaps the most crucial parts of the Constitution for law enforcement are the Fourth, Fifth, and Sixth Amendments, which protect suspects against unreasonable search and seizure and self-incrimination, and guarantee arrestees due process, the right to confront their accusers, and the right to a speedy trial. Moral problems arise when the professional is unclear about what these obligations and rights entail, or when the professional feels confident about them but faces a citizenry that disagrees with her. Note that law enforcement is more concerned with distributive justice (who gets the professional's services) and commutative justice (fulfilling the social contract) than with retributive justice (punishment). The obligation to refrain from administering retributive justice puts a significant limit on the scope of the officer's responsibilities and rights, which we examine next.

Responsibilities

In addition to obeying the Constitution and the law, the officer has a fiduciary responsibility to the community. He acts on behalf of the community members in ways they cannot act themselves. For example, when he arrests a suspect, it is not for the officer's sake but for the sake of the people on whose behalf the officer has the power to act, thus contributing to their safety and security.

In recognizing the officer as a fiduciary, we trust him to know the good and to do the good—to have integrity and to be accountable. More specifically, we trust him to meet the following seven basic obligations of professional trustworthiness: competence, diligence, honesty, candor, loyalty, discretion, and beneficence/nonmaleficence.

The *competent* police officer knows the Constitution and laws as they apply to her professional practice and her jurisdiction. The police officer must be competent in all areas of policing that she practices, including, for example, patrolling, responding to calls, investigating, interrogating, reporting, testifying, relating with the community, and supervising sworn and unsworn personnel. The criteria for such competence often will appear in statutes, codes of conduct, general orders, and special orders. Proof of competence may come from colleagues' compliments, commendations, and public expressions of satisfaction with the work the officer is doing. Competence will also show in the safety of the community.

Q 13.6

Does Case 13.1 offer any examples of incompetence?

Just as an officer should be competent in all areas of policing that she practices, she should also be *diligent* in these areas. These may include vigilant patrolling, timely responses to calls, thorough investigation of crimes, careful and fruitful interrogation, filing complete and accurate reports, testifying well in court, continuous devotion to community relations, and fair and steady supervision of subordinates. A major challenge to the officer may be the temptation to cut corners—to get the bad guy at all costs. Another temptation may be to give up on a difficult case when there is still a chance for a successful solution. The diligent police officer will not give in to such temptations.

Q 13.7

In Case 13.1, does Serpico appear to be diligent?

A third obligation of trustworthiness is *honesty*. Recall our previous discussion about the nature of honesty and whether it is always a virtue. Generally, to be honest is to say what one believes, but not necessarily to reveal everything one believes. Honesty is a virtue when it is the mean between the extremes of deficiency and excess, but in virtuous police work there may be times where it is more reasonable for an officer to lie or to deceive. As we noted earlier, undercover or sting operations are a normal and acceptable part of police work, in which necessary elements of the operation are dishonest and maintaining the dishonesty may be necessary to protect the operative and to achieve success. The use of confidential informants (CIs) may also require deception on the CI's part or the officer's part, both to protect the CI and to maintain the integrity of the police operation.

While conceding that honesty may not always be the best policy in police work, we must insist that the officer be honest unless he can offer a morally sound reason for being otherwise. Thus, the community and the officer's colleagues generally have the right to expect the officer to deal with them honestly, both professionally and personally.

A fourth obligation closely related to honesty is *candor*. Where honesty is a matter of saying what one believes when one says or writes something, candor is a matter of revealing everything one believes about the subject. It is possible to be honest without being candid, but it is not possible to be candid without being honest. Generally, community members and the officer's colleagues should expect candor from the officer and from each other in matters relating to the officer's professional duties. Thus, it was better for Serpico to reveal what he knew about police corruption than to keep quiet about it. However, the officer must also know when to avoid candor. When the contract model or agency model of allocation of responsibility is appropriate, so is candor. When the paternalism model is appropriate, candor may not be. When it is not good to be honest, it is not good to be candid. When candor may hurt an innocent person, such as revealing a pending witness's name and whereabouts, candor may be wrong. Where candor may be counterproductive, as in undercover operations, it may be wrong.

A fifth obligation is *loyalty*. As we noted earlier, this may be the most ubiquitous obligation in the public image of morally good policing. Stories, such as Frank Serpico's in Case 13.1, abound about the "blue wall of silence" and the whistle-blower who crosses that line. It is worth taking a moment to consider whistle-blowing in more detail, by defining what it is and when it is morally appropriate.

In the conventional sense, to "blow the whistle" is to be an employee or member of an organization who goes public with information about the organization that the organization would rather keep from the public. Some experts describe this as *external* whistle-blowing, in contrast to blowing the whistle on one constituent of an organization to another constituent of that organization. The major difference between external and internal whistle-blowing is the former's "airing dirty laundry," whereas the latter keeps the information "in-house." Both raise issues of loyalty, since they involve "snitching" on one's colleagues, although sometimes loyalty to one's agency or to its morally good members may require turning in the bad members.

Whistle-blowing is morally good when it is the least deficient and least excessive response to the problem it is trying to solve. Generally, its goal must be to prevent harm or to bring a harmful act to the attention of the proper authorities. In Case 13.1, Serpico regarded the corruption as harmful to the safety and trust of the public. Generally, too, the whistle-blower must have attempted less drastic methods first, where feasible. Before Serpico blew the whistle publicly, he approached the NYPD command staff, giving them a chance to set things right without hurting the agency's image. Whether Serpico gave command a sufficient chance to solve the problem is a matter of debate, but in Serpico's mind, the agency was not going to take the issue any farther. Thus, the best option—the least deficient option—was to go public, which he did successfully through the *New York Times* article. Among the more excessive options, for example, would have been for Serpico to threaten the offending officers with physical harm or death if they didn't confess their actions and quit the force. If Serpico's version of the situation is correct, it appears that blowing the whistle as he did was the most moderate option.

Note that to call an act of whistle-blowing morally good may mean that it is morally permissible or morally obligatory.[5] Some argue that it is morally obligatory when

- Harm to the public is clearly imminent.
- Only the whistle-blower is willing to go public with the information.
- Only the whistle-blowing can prevent the harm.
- There is a reasonable chance that the whistle-blowing will prevent the harm.

An interesting question is whether a person must blow the whistle when she faces harmful consequences for doing so, such as loss of her job. In such circumstances, she may have the right but not the obligation to blow the whistle.

Q 13.8

In Case 13.1, if Serpico knew that his life would be in danger after going public about police corruption, would it have been morally permissible for him not to blow the whistle?

One last point about loyalty: Often the police officer has competing loyalties. Loyalty to a community member may interfere with loyalty to a colleague or loyalty to one's family. In policing, the professional promises loyalty to the Constitution and to the community she serves; all other loyalties are subordinate. Failure to understand this and to act on this understanding is a symptom of and may be a cause of police corruption. Some forms this sort of corruption may take are accepting graft or gratuities in one's official capacity, engaging in shakedowns, drinking alcohol or having sex while on duty, or sleeping while on duty in violation of department rules.

Q 13.9

In Case 13.2, suppose the police officers were Hmong and thus refused to arrest the funeral director. Would be this a morally admirable case of loyalty?

A sixth professional obligation of trustworthiness is *discretion.* For the police officer, this refers primarily to the ability to make professional choices on one's own, without having to run every decision by a superior. In policing, absence of discretion would pose two dangers: police work would be much less efficient, and police would be susceptible to legalism—the belief that one should follow the rules at all costs. With the freedom of discretion comes the strong responsibility to use it well—to consider and balance consequences, rules, or duties in fulfilling the task.

Discretion in the sense of keeping confidences also has its place in policing. A complainant or confidential informant may offer valuable information in exchange for an officer's promise to keep the source anonymous. An officer's colleague may confide in him about a domestic crisis. An investigator may be privy to embarrassing information about a suspect, information that has nothing to do with the investigation. In general, each of these examples would require the officer's keeping a confidence, unless public interest overrode that requirement and betraying the confidence would be legal.

A seventh professional obligation is *beneficence/nonmaleficence.* At the very least, the professional should try not to harm the client; otherwise the professional is guilty of maleficence, or wrongdoing. But the officer can intend to avoid harm without trying to do good for the client. Suppose that the officers in Case 13.2 arrested the funeral director because they did not want to irritate the superior who ordered the arrest. Suppose further that they failed to explain to the mourners why the director was under arrest and what might come of it, thus failing to put the mourners at relative ease over the incident. It is fair to say that the officers acted with nonmaleficence, but not necessarily with beneficence—a desire to do some good for the mourners. On the other hand, Serpico, in Case 13.1, appeared to be seeking some good for the citizens of New York and the upstanding members of the NYPD.

Rights

We have said a great deal about the professional responsibilities of an officer. With these responsibilities come rights that distinguish policing as a profession rather than a job. As we have noted, police officers have the right under certain circumstances to enter and search homes; to chase, stop, frisk, arrest, and interrogate people; and to use deadly force to protect themselves and other innocent people. Some of these rights complement duties on the community's part. For example, as we've noted, the community in its interaction with law enforcement must respect the law, respect the police, not hinder and sometimes assist the police in their work, respond honestly to an officer's inquiries, and use the 911 system responsibly.

In terms of the professional criterion of greater responsibilities and rights, the virtuous police officer puts her professional relationships in proper priority, giving preference to the Constitution's and community's interests over the interests of third parties, her colleagues, or herself. The virtuous police officer is competent, diligent, appropriately honest, candid, discreet, and loyal, and seeks not only to avoid harm but also to do good. Finally, the virtuous police officer is aware of the scope and limits of her rights and the community's role in helping her exercise those rights, and she exercises them only to the extent that they make her a more effective professional.

Self-Governance

CASE 13.3

The Backup [6]

Late one night, State Trooper Nicks is patrolling the interstate when he notices a car swerving in and out of traffic. Nicks signals the car to pull over, which it does without hesitation. Nicks approaches the car on the driver's side. The driver has rolled down the window and a strong smell of alcohol emanates from the car. The driver responds readily to Nicks's request for the driver to step out of the car and submit to a field sobriety test. The driver fails the test.

Looking into the car, Nicks sees in plain sight a gun and a small plastic bag containing what might be marijuana. In response to Nicks's inquiry about both, the driver admits that the gun is unregistered and that the bag contains marijuana. Nicks arrests the driver, puts him in handcuffs, puts him in the back seat of Nicks's car, and then calls for backup so Nicks can search the car further and see to its impounding.

Soon a second trooper, Lumpett, shows up and stands outside Nicks's car where Lumpett can plainly see the suspect handcuffed and seated in the back of the well-lit car. As Nicks proceeds to search the suspect's car, an elderly man, quite agitated, pulls in behind Lumpett's car (parked behind Nicks's car), gets out of the car, and walks to Lumpett to ask for directions to a place not easily found from their present location. The elderly man has a map in his hands and Lumpett, producing a flashlight, shines it on the map and attempts to explain the best way for the man to get to his destination.

In the meantime, the suspect, whose hands were originally cuffed behind him, has managed to get his hands in front of him and to get out of Nicks's car. Before Lumpett can catch him, the suspect escapes over the guardrail and into a nearby neighborhood. Soon the suspect is recaptured and taken to the barracks.

At the barracks, Nicks's sergeant reminds him of the arresting trooper's duty to transport an arrested suspect back to the barracks. He is reminded further of the penalty—suspension without pay—for failure to discharge this duty. There is no departmental policy holding a backup trooper to the same duty.

Case 13.3 is a useful introduction to the third criterion for a profession: self-governance. Obvious examples of self-governance are the American Bar Association's oversight of lawyers and the American Medical Association's oversight of physicians. Each association sets the criteria for entrance into the profession, standards of professional practice, and punitive responses to violation of those standards. Each association is also responsible for ongoing research toward improvement of the profession. The police do not have the same degree of self-oversight, which is one reason there is ongoing debate about whether policing is a profession. Police must answer to the U.S. Constitution, the laws of their jurisdiction, and the norms of the community they serve. Also, law enforcement professionals have no national organization, as lawyers and physicians do. Nevertheless, the typical structure of police organizations, together with their basic governing elements, leave much of the day-to-day oversight to the police themselves, thus raising moral issues that we ordinarily associate with self-governance. Let's look at the structure and elements, and then at some specific issues pertaining to self-governance.

Q 13.10

In Case 13.3, was the suspect's escape due to a failure in self-governance?

Structure and Elements of Governance

The police agency is a hierarchical structure that includes superiors, peers, subordinates, support staff, and related agencies and organizations. Superiors include people both in and out of the direct chain of command. Peers include partners and others of comparable rank. Subordinates may be in or out of the chain of command. Support staff are usually lower in the organizational hierarchy than the officer; they include administrative assistants, dispatchers, and maintenance people. Related agencies and organizations include local, state, and federal law enforcement agencies; unions; legal agencies such as the district attorney's office, the medical examiner's office, and the courts; vendors; and municipal authorities such as a city office of human resources.

In all of these relationships, the police officer carries the basic moral obligations of competence, diligence, honesty, candor, loyalty, discretion, and beneficence/nonmaleficence. In addition, the ethical officer will routinely display the cardinal virtues of courage, justice, temperance, and prudence. Virtue theory requires that these moral characteristics be a part of the agent's character, but the governing structure of the organization can either encourage or discourage virtue depending on the governing elements in place.

Q 13.11

In Case 13.3, is it fair to say that the suspect escaped because Lumpett was insufficiently diligent?

First, the agency should have a clear and appropriate vision, mission, and statement of goals and objectives. Administrators should ensure that everyone in the agency is familiar with these statements, supports them, and has a chance to participate regularly in the monitoring, fulfillment, and improvement of the statements.

Second, the agency should have a clear, relevant, and comprehensive code of conduct. This should identify permissions, obligations, and prohibitions, the sanctions for violating the code, and the means of appeal.

Third, the head of the agency should issue only general and special orders that support the vision, mission, and goals of the agency; that obey the law; and that enable the police to serve the community well.

Fourth, the agency should have a process in place to monitor, sustain, and improve the agency's ability to maintain the peace and to prevent or respond effectively to crime. A recent strategy that has gained in both acceptance and notoriety is CompStat (short for Computer Statistics).[7] This process began in the New York City Police Department in 1994 under Commissioner William Bratton and Deputy Commissioner Jack Maple. It has since sprung up in other agencies, with mixed reviews. The general idea of CompStat is to statistically pinpoint trouble spots in a jurisdiction on a frequent and regular basis and to direct police resources to those spots to reduce the trouble.[8] Where the emphasis has been on developing and applying strategies and tactics for crime reduction, CompStat has been an effective tool. Unfortunately, some agencies, whether out of desperation or lack of imagination, have treated CompStat as a numbers game whose primary purpose is to bring the crime statistics down by any means necessary. Since one could do this by underreporting crime or by reclassifying serious crimes to lesser offenses, the possibility for poor use or abuse of CompStat is obvious. The police agency that governs itself well will use CompStat or some other system with a similar purpose in a way that is beneficial to the agency and to the community. This agency will solicit steady input from all representatives whom the system concerns, and will make improvements wherever necessary.

Fifth, the agency should have an internal affairs unit that is easily accessible to the community and to the officers; handles issues expeditiously, fairly, and in accordance with clearly established rules; and has as its primary goal the integrity of the agency and the profession.

Issues of Self-Governance

The issues that arise for the agency in its self-governance fall into two major categories: external relations and internal relations. We have devoted a great deal of discussion to interaction with the community—the central factor in external relations. The agency should also have in place a clear plan and system for interaction with the media, usually centering around a public information officer; religious organizations; and advocacy groups that are not residents of the agency's jurisdiction, but that feel the need to advocate for some or all of those residents. In all of these relations, the agency must maintain its integrity; the integrity of the profession; and the liberty, safety, and security of the community.

One challenging issue in external relations is the value and role of a citizen review board (CRB). Some CRBs exist only to offer a community perspective on police work and police–community relations. Other CRBs have the power to handle citizens' complaints about police and to subpoena witnesses, take testimony, and recommend punitive action. Some agencies welcome CRBs as an enhancement to police self-governance and community relations; some agencies accept CRBs reluctantly as the price of doing business in a litigious society; and some agencies reject CRBs as unnecessary at best and counterproductive at worst. Whether or not CRBs are valuable depends on their role and the needs of the agency and its community; no one size fits all. Whatever an agency and community decide about forming a CRB and what its powers should be, the emphasis must always be on the liberty, safety, and security of the community members. If the CRB is an ill fit in its community, or if a CRB is merely window dressing on the part of the mayor, commissioner, or county executive, for example, then the CRB's formation and existence will be irrelevant or harmful and it should be disbanded.

The self-governance issues that arise from internal relations include recruiting and hiring, training, retention, professional support and development, promotion, discipline, and dismissal.

The agency that takes its professionalism seriously will seek to recruit and hire those with a talent and passion for the profession. This will require emphasis on the integrity and nobility of policing, the important service that policing offers, and the possibilities of self-sacrifice. The recruitment process should not overemphasize potential personal gain, because this may attract candidates who are in it solely for themselves. Those who develop and implement the recruitment strategy need to remember that sometimes what appears to be a failure in retention—an ability to keep a critical mass of professionals—may actually have been a failure in recruitment. A wise investment in personnel up front should make their governance much easier than if the agency takes whoever walks through the door.

Much training of the recruit is for the specific tasks of police work, such as answering calls for service, subduing, arresting, and processing suspects, writing reports, testifying in court, and following the proper protocols and chain of command. But if the recruit is to be a professional, he will also need education that promotes and provides constitutional literacy, legal scholarship, historical understanding of the profession, effective moral decision making, and fruitful human relations. Since many of these are perishable skills, education in these areas should be available to the professional from the first day of basic training until the end of the professional's career.

Here we should especially mention the value of a good field training officer (FTO) program. Many recruits develop a lasting impression of the proper way to practice their profession from the first veteran they see in action. If the recruits' exposure is uncontrolled, their first exposure may be to a cynical or lazy veteran who is the antithesis of a virtuous professional. To avoid this danger, many agencies have developed a program in which recruits pair up with a veteran who is able to add experience, wisdom, and intuition to the training mix, thus giving the recruit a rich and promising head start in what the agency hopes will be a long and successful career. At one time, the ideal FTO was a highly professional and seasoned official. Today, the apparent lack of glamour has many good FTO candidates opting out, leaving the task to young, inexperienced officers. An agency interested in virtuous self-governance will do its best to reverse this trend and match recruits with the best FTOs.

When an agency has invested wisely in a recruit, the agency will want to retain that person. To do this, the agency should provide adequate salary and benefits; excellent opportunities for advancement and promotion; educational incentives; ready access to answers concerning legal and agency procedures; and technical, moral, and legal support in cases of informal and formal complaints against the officer.

When it is necessary to discipline or fire an officer, the agency should have a clear, comprehensive, and fair process in place. Readily available intervention opportunities should make disciplinary action and firing a rare last resort.

Virtuous officers involved in the self-governance of the agency see to the development, management, and constant improvement of relations external and internal to the police agency. In general, this means the officers display courage, justice, temperance, and prudence, always with an eye toward avoiding deficient or excessive responses to moral challenges and opportunities.

With regard to external relations, virtuous officers put the community's liberty, safety, and security first. Virtuous officers also treat other external constituents, such as the media and advocacy groups, with respect and honesty, and work with them to the extent possible for the good of the community.

With regard to internal relations, virtuous officers involved in self-governance see to effective and ethical recruitment, hiring, training, retention, promotion, and discipline.

So far in our discussion of self-governance, we have emphasized the role of the agency. The individual officer also plays a major role in effective self-governance, which for him involves professional autonomy. This is the next professional criterion.

Autonomy

Autonomy is the fourth professional criterion that pertains to policing. In principle, individual officers are far from autonomous, because law enforcement agencies are hierarchical and often paramilitary, thus having a strong chain of command. In practice, a police officer is often on his own when he has to make quick decisions, many with moral import. While the officer may eventually have to answer to a superior, a CRB, or a court, it is the autonomy of the moment that concerns us here.

Q 13.12

In Case 13.1, was Serpico's decision to blow the whistle a morally good autonomous act? How about Lumpett's decision to help the elderly man in Case 13.3?

Much of what there is to say about the moral implications of autonomy is a repeat of what we have said in other contexts. The virtuous officer acting autonomously will be courageous, just, temperate, and prudent. He will obey the Constitution, the laws of his jurisdiction, and the rules and orders of his superiors, unless he has a morally compelling reason to disobey. He will be competent, diligent, appropriately honest, candid, loyal, discreet, and beneficent/nonmaleficent. He will treat all people whom he engages—both external and internal to the agency—with respect for their constitutional rights and human dignity. He will strive for constant improvement, always with the goal of serving his community well.

Q 13.13

In Case 13.2, is it fair to say that the police officers in the funeral home acted with proper autonomy?

In addition to reminding ourselves of these earlier conclusions, we can add a few observations that are relevant to the officer's autonomy. First, the officer should strive to improve his agency and the profession at large. It is not enough for him to simply show up for work, behave while on duty, and not leave until his shift is over. There may be few opportunities for officers in certain ranks to make these sorts of contributions, but the officer at all ranks should look for such opportunities and take advantage of them whenever possible. These opportunities will include, for example, staying informed about the latest developments in scholarship on good policing, offering constructive suggestions to and asking pertinent questions of superiors, and keeping the community informed about the work that the police are doing and about opportunities for community–police interaction.

Second, the virtuous officer acting autonomously will refrain from destructive behaviors and comments, especially those intended to hurt morale or subvert the attempts of others to improve the agency and its services. This means, for example, avoiding cynicism, gossip, and the "poor-me's." It does not mean ignoring problems or wrongdoing. The virtuous police officer will be vigilant for destructive behavior and attitudes and will seek constructive solutions either on his own or in concert with others.

Q 13.14

In Case 13.3, is Nicks receiving unfair treatment for his role in the suspect's escape?

In his nonprofessional life, the virtuous officer acting autonomously will behave ethically. As a professional, he bears the mantle of his profession all the time; ill behavior off-duty reflects poorly on him as a professional and on the profession itself.

A Calling

The fifth criterion for a profession is a sense of calling in contrast with the other reasons that one might take a job, such as the need for money. The police officer's proper calling is to protect the community's liberties, safety, and security. Police officers with a sense of calling demonstrate this by frequently sacrificing their own interests, and sometimes their lives, in pursuit of the community's well-being.

By this criterion, we tend to condemn police officers who are in the profession primarily for personal reward or because it appears that they couldn't find a job that they would rather do.

Money as Means

The idea of a calling as a criterion for professionalism closely relates to the role of money as a means, the sixth professional criterion. In our discussion of professional criteria, we noted that a professional tends to see money as a means to practicing the profession well, whereas a person taking a job may reasonably regard it as a means to making money. To be sure, many police officers enter the profession for the money. Indeed, many agencies imprudently recruit candidates on the basis of money and other personal benefits they can gain rather than on the nobility of public service.

In an occupation requiring professional skills and attention, basing the work primarily on self-benefit is apt to cause problems for the individual and for the organization. Although many big agencies offer commendable salaries, the officer who is working primarily to make money will always want more. If this officer sees a need for improvement in service to the community or to the agency, but no corresponding improvement in salary, the money-seeking officer may find no incentive to improve. Also, this officer may be hard to retain when other opportunities for a better salary present themselves.

Extensive Training

Extensive training is the seventh professional criterion. Earlier we noted that in many agencies a person can become a police officer right out of high school, without significant education or intellectual development. We have also noted, however, that police work can be complex, both in the various tasks that an officer faces and in the variety of people and groups of people with whom the officer must deal.

At its most complex, police work requires the officer to have a good grasp of law, psychology, sociology, religion, politics, and ethics. The officer will also benefit from a good working knowledge of history, culture, and languages other than English. It is no wonder, therefore, that many law enforcement agencies are increasing their education requirements either for entrance into the profession or for promotion.

Q 13.15

In Case 13.2, "The Funeral of Za Chue Xiong," does it appear that the police officers could have benefited from better training?

Credentialing

Credentialing is the eighth and final professional criterion that we intend to discuss concerning police officers.

For the police officer, the physical form of the credential—a certificate, license, or badge—is less important than the powers conferred upon her at the moment she is sworn in. Upon becoming a police officer, which includes an oath to protect, preserve, and defend the U.S. Constitution, the professional acquires credentials of which she should be proud. As we have said elsewhere, an important consequent of this credentialing is that the officer puts on the mantle of the profession, which she then wears 24 hours a day until her retirement. Even after retirement, she may proudly display a retirement badge, carry her service gun, and offer her professional services as a consultant or private investigator. Thus, in a sense, the virtuous police officer never has to give up her professional credentials completely, not even in retirement.

We turn now to the corrections officer, who also works under the auspices of the executive branch of government as a law enforcement professional.

✦ CORRECTIONS

CASE 13.4

Sheriff Joe and the Abortions

Sheriff Joe Arpaio of Maricopa County, Arizona, is famous for his strict jail polices.[9] Inmates sleep in tents or cells without heat or air conditioning. They eat meals costing pennies a day. All inmates, including women, spend most days on chain gangs. Male inmates must wear pink underwear and pink jumpsuits. And until recently, Arpaio would not allow female inmates to get abortions because this required transportation from the jail to an abortion facility.

This abortion policy changed on January 23, 2007, when the Arizona Court of Appeals upheld a lower court's ruling that declared Arpaio's policy unconstitutional.[10] Arpaio had argued that the jail should not have to transport inmates for elective medical procedures because (1) such transportation presents unnecessary liability and security risks and (2) these risks put an undue burden on the jail's resources. The court found no evidence for Arpaio's premises and added that under the 14th Amendment and *Roe v. Wade,* all female inmates have a right to an abortion.

Arpaio vowed to appeal the court's decision.

Case 13.4 invites us to shift our attention from police ethics to the ethics of corrections. Corrections officials include prison guards, wardens, and other prison staff, parole boards, and probation officers. Corrections officials face many of the same problems as police officers For example, both face similar moral issues that neither legislative nor judicial professionals face, as in the use of deadly force.

On the other hand, there are some significant differences between police ethics and corrections ethics. There are also some important differences between the ethics of corrections within the prison system and the ethics of corrections in probation and parole. Thus, we will find it useful to divide this discussion of ethics in corrections into two parts: a look at ethics in corrections, with emphasis on ethics in the prisons, and a specific look at ethics in probation and parole.

> ### Q 13.16
>
> In Case 13.4, if Arpaio had based his argument on the claim that abortion is immoral, would he have had a stronger reason for refusing to transport inmates to abortion clinics?

Ethics in Corrections

As with police, the moral rights and responsibilities of corrections officers distinguish them as professionals. Both the American Correctional Association and the American Jail Association refer to corrections officers as professionals in their codes of ethics and set their standards high accordingly.[11] The similarities between the professions are evident in the corrections officers' fulfillment of the same seven criteria for a profession that police officers meet.

Before reviewing the criteria, we should note the difference between a prison and a jail, and hence the difference between prison officials and jail officials. In general, jails are short-term prisons used to hold suspects before and during trial and to hold convicted offenders serving a short sentence or waiting to be transferred to a prison. Thus, while jails may play a role in law enforcement, they do not always play a role in corrections. Because of this difference, some might wish to distinguish the ethical problems that jails present from the ethical problems that prisons present. However, the difference is not great enough for our purposes to warrant a separate discussion. Therefore, we will use the term *prison* to cover both prisons and jails.

Significant Service to the Community

In terms of the seven professional criteria, police and corrections officials both offer a *significant service to the community.* But they differ with regard to their clients and the allocation of responsibility for decision making.

The corrections official's primary client is the prisoner or the person on parole or probation, not the community at large. The official must see to the prisoner's proper restraint, health, and safety, or to the parolee's/probationer's fulfillment of the conditions of parole/probation. To be sure, by seeing to the convict's imprisonment or overseeing the parolee or probationer, the corrections' official helps maintain the liberty, safety, and security of the community, but the day-to-day work of the corrections official has more to do with the individual in the corrections system. Even corrections officials whose administrative duties do not routinely put them in direct contact with the offender must put the proper treatment of the offender first.

The punitive nature of corrections makes it likely that the person undergoing it would rather be free from scrutiny and restraint. Thus, the most appropriate model for allocation of responsibility for decision making is often the paternal model, much like the situation of a police officer and a suspect, as opposed to a police officer and a non-suspect. When the offender is willing to cooperate, the official may want to apply the contract model to their joint decision making as long as it effective. This may help the offender maintain a sense of dignity and make him a participant rather than an adversary in his own punishment. Nevertheless, the rights of the offender are quite limited and the responsibilities are well defined; even the most cooperative offender must recognize the official's primary authority for making decisions.

The punitive nature of corrections also relates to debates about the purpose of punishment and the proper ways of fulfilling that purpose. If we can agree on the proper purpose of punishment and we can determine that a corrections official is seeing to the proper fulfillment of that purpose, then we can conclude that the official is doing a good job. What one believes about the proper purpose of punishment relates to what sort of justice one believes corrections is supposed to promote. This text has been using *retributive justice* as shorthand for the type of justice that others may call restorative, transformative, or corrective. The purpose of punishment may be rehabilitative, "an eye for an eye," vengeance, prevention, setting an example, or any combination of these. Some will argue that capital punishment is a morally proper means to fulfilling some of these purposes; others will argue that capital punishment is never morally acceptable and that punishment must always be humane.

In terms of virtue, punishment should always be just and never "cruel and unusual," which means giving the recipient what he deserves, no more and no less. It is fairly easy to identify deficient and excessive extremes; thus, it would be unjust to punish a shoplifter with execution, and it would be unjust to punish a serial killer with a "slap on the wrist." We can reject both of these cases as unjust, even if we don't agree on the proper purpose of punishment. As we move from the extremes toward a relatively more moderate middle, we encounter greater disagreement about the justice of specific punishments. Should "victimless" crimes, such as prostitution or violating a state's motorcycle helmet law, ever result in imprisonment for the perpetrator? Should a 14-year-old convicted murderer be jailed with adults? Is punishment calculated to shame the inmate ever morally proper? There is no ready formula for answering these questions to every reasonable person's satisfaction. Nevertheless, it is to the advantage of the corrections official to be aware of the ongoing debate about the proper nature of punishment and to refer to the scholarship on that debate as time permits. This will help the professional develop and maintain a clear sense of purpose, which in turn should help the official serve the offender and the community better.

Greater Responsibilities

Like police officers, corrections officials have *greater responsibilities* than we ordinarily ascribe to a job. The corrections official must be competent, diligent, honest, candid, loyal, discreet, and beneficent/nonmaleficent.

How the corrections official meets these obligations differs in some important ways from how a police officer meets them. On this point there is much to learn from the codes of ethics of the American Corrections Association (ACA) and the American Jail Association (AJA). Between them they paint a picture of the virtuous corrections official who works for the good of the inmates, the professionals, the profession, the public, and himself.

Concerning the inmate, the official

- Treats the inmate with compassion and respects the inmate's individuality, dignity, civil rights, and legal rights.
- Promotes a secure environment for the inmate, which, according to the AJA, "will keep the inmate involved in activities designed to improve his/ her attitude and character."
- Refrains from getting personally involved with any inmate.

The official treats her colleagues with respect; appoints, promotes, and dismisses subordinates according to published rules and procedures; and reports professional corruption or other wrongdoing to the proper authorities. The official also seeks to support and improve the profession at large through membership and participation in a professional association and by taking advantage of relevant educational and training opportunities. Finally, the official should always act in a way that is a credit to the profession, even when the official is off duty.

The corrections official respects the right of the public to be safeguarded. In communications with the public, the official reports only what he should, being mindful of the scope and limits of inmates' privacy. According to the ACA, the official criticizes his agency or other professionals only when such criticism is "warranted, verifiable, and constructive." The official strives always to be a good citizen. And the official is polite and respectful to visitors to the prison.

Personally, the corrections official lives a life beyond reproach, distinguishes his personal views from his agency's views, and avoids inappropriate gains from professional practice.

Self-Governance and Autonomy

There is less opportunity for *self-governance* and *autonomy* in corrections than in police work, because the prison system and prison life are more regimented and are under greater routine scrutiny. The hierarchical system of relationships among the professionals is similar in both professions, but the external relations are different.

For one thing, the police officer's clients—the community members—are not an integral part of the police department's internal operations, unlike the corrections official's clients—the inmates. Also, the police officer's clients often have more of a role to play in police governance—through citizen review boards, for example—whereas the corrections officer's clients (inmates) have at best a small role in the officers' governance.

Calling and Money as Means

It is easy to find people in the corrections profession who, like police officers, entered with a sense of *calling* and the view that *money is a means* to answer that call effectively. One may also find people entering corrections as a job, especially in the lower ranks of prison work, because the entrance requirements may be modest and the job may be relatively easy to learn. In time, however, the person who plans to make a career of corrections, whether inside or outside of prison, will have to rise to the professional demands of the position, which is a point that we expand on next.

Extensive Training

Finally, there are similarities between police officers and corrections officials with respect to *extensive training*. In many corrections systems, a person can enter the field right out of high school, without significant education or intellectual development. But similar to police work, corrections work can be complex, both in the various tasks that an official faces and in the variety of people and groups of people with whom the official must deal. Thus, similar to police work, effective corrections work requires the official to have a good grasp of law, psychology, sociology, religion, politics, and ethics. In addition, it is helpful for corrections officials to understand theories of punishment Also, as with the police officer, the corrections official will benefit from a good working knowledge of history, culture, and languages other than English.

The Ethics of Parole and Probation

 ## CASE 13.5

The Sex Offender

Nineteen-year-old Todd Schmitt had consensual sexual relations with his 15-year-old girlfriend, whom he believed to be 16. When her father found out about the relationship, he called the police, who arrested Schmitt for statutory rape. In Schmitt's state, the legal age of majority is 18 years; if an adult has consensual sex with a minor who is at least two years younger, this constitutes statutory rape regardless of the minor's consent.

In court, the judge believes Schmitt's claim that he thought his girlfriend was 16, and the judge believes that the sex was consensual. The judge also notes that these points are irrelevant to the charge. The judge finds Schmitt guilty and sentences him to three years of supervised probation. Soon after, Schmitt is added to the local sex offender registry, which is visited frequently by many community activists.

Schmitt's case is assigned to probation officer Rodney Thorn, who has a heavy caseload of probationers and parolees. Thorn is relieved to discover that Schmitt's crime was more a technicality than the act of a troublesome delinquent, so Thorn looks forward to a relatively easy relationship with Schmitt. Things heat up quickly, however, as community activists issue an onslaught of voice mails and e-mails demanding to know what Thorn is doing to protect the community.

Case 13.5 invites us to compare prison officials with parole officers and probation officers. Note that it is not unusual for a person to be both a probation officer and a parole officer. Both roles require supervision of the client and involve the power to recommend rescinding the client's release. In many jurisdictions, the officer has limited or full police powers, has a badge, and may carry a gun or other concealed weapons.

Prison officials and probation/parole officials have most of their professional rights and responsibilities in common. The big difference is in the location and physical freedom of the primary client. For parole officers and probation officers, the client is not in prison. The probationer has received a conditional release from the court before being imprisoned; the parolee has received a conditional release from prison before completing his sentence. This freedom of the client presents moral challenges unique to this area of corrections.

The most significant challenge is the possible conflict between the community's interests and the client's, as Case 13.5 depicts. The parole or probation officer's first task is to help the offender assimilate into the community and to receive the help needed not to offend again. The community member's first concern might be to kick the offender out of the community.

Q 13.17

In Case 13.5, are the community activists behaving virtuously?

Another challenge for the parole or probation officer is how to manage heavy caseloads. A simple solution in principle would be for the corrections system to lighten those loads by employing a sufficient number of officers and support staff. In fact, the caseload issue is a common one, and the harried officer cannot wait for it to be resolved. The moral problem is, Who gets the officer's attention first? Is it the one who is most likely to benefit from the officer's attention? Is it the one who is closest to having his probation or parole revoked? Is it the one whom the officer likes the best? This question becomes more complicated when we add the community's demands on the officer's time.

Q 13.18

If Thorn's caseload makes it impossible for him to respond effectively to the community's concerns about Schmitt, would it be morally sufficient for him not to respond to the activists at all?

Beyond these examples, relying on the moral similarities among law enforcement officers, and recalling the points we have already made in this chapter, we offer the following image of the virtuous probation/parole officer.[12] She

- Fulfills all responsibilities and exercises all rights with courage, justice, temperance, and prudence.
- Commits to serving the client well, but always with the liberty, safety, and security of the community in mind.
- Is competent, diligent, appropriately honest, candid, discreet, and loyal, and seeks not only to avoid harm but also to do good.
- Understands the workings of and respects the criminal justice system, including the U.S. Constitution, the applicable laws, and the people in the system.
- Pursues further education and training in an effort to stay abreast of current theories and to constantly improve.
- Treats colleagues—including subordinates, peers, and superiors—with proper respect.
- Reports the wrongdoing of clients or colleagues, when the officer is unable to solve the problem alone and when the officer has reasonable evidence of the wrongdoing.
- Refrains from unfair discrimination in all professional dealings.
- Refuses to accept gifts or gratuities in exchange for professional services.
- Lives a life that reflects well on the profession, even when off duty.

SUMMARY

The virtuous corrections officer and the virtuous police officer have in common the habitual ability to act courageously, justly, prudently, and temperately in all of their relationships. For both professions, the most important relationship is with the client, followed by the public at large, colleagues, the profession, and the self. Differences in the lives of the two professions reflect the clientele (inmates versus a free community), the physical environment (prison versus a neighborhood, city, or state), the specific service to the public (secure the inmates versus keep the peace and prevent or solve crime), and the role in the flow of the criminal justice process (in response to adjudication versus in response to legislation).

This chapter has explored the ethics of law enforcement, as a central feature of the executive branch of government. The previous chapter examined the ethics of the legislative branch. We have one branch of government left to consider—the judiciary—which we consider in the next chapter, on ethics in the courtroom.

ANSWERS TO CASE STUDY QUESTIONS

Q13.1. In Case 13.1, if Serpico reported the police corruption only because he feared for his life, did he do a morally good thing?
No. This would have constituted doing the right thing for the wrong reason—cowardice. The right reason is a virtuous reason. Among the virtues is courage, the mean between cowardice and foolhardiness. Thus, cowardice is a vice.

Q13.2. In Case 13.1, does Serpico appear to regard policing as a profession?
Yes. His biography suggests he had had a sense of calling to police work since he was a child. He had no interest in the money he could make illegally. And his testimony before the Knapp Commission suggests a desire to see the police profession brought back to health.

Q13.3. Which model of decision making for police and community does Case 13.2 exemplify? Is this the best model for the situation?
Paternalism. The police appear to be acting without consulting the community. It would seem that the matter was not so urgent that the officers couldn't have spoken with the mourners before officers arrested the funeral director. Plus, the community appeared to be upset at the arrest. So the paternal model was not the best model for this situation.

Q13.4. In Case 13.2, do the police officers appear to be violating the mourners' First Amendment right to freedom of religion?
Not directly. Freedom to practice religion does not necessarily mean freedom to practice it wherever one wants. As the case tells us, the number of mourners in the funeral home and the amount of time they were there violated safety codes, which law enforcement has a duty to enforce.

Q13.5. In Case 13.1, did Serpico appear to satisfy the criterion of significant service to the community?
Yes. The community is paying for a virtuous police force whose first interest is the liberty, safety, and security of the community. The officers Serpico turned in were failing to provide that service. Also, the Knapp Commission, which was a response to Serpico's revelation, provided the service of cleaning up the police force, at least for a time.

Q13.6. Does Case 13.1 offer any examples of incompetence?
Yes. The competent police officers prevent crime; the officers who accepted graft committed crime. Thus, the corrupt officers were incompetent. Also, if Serpico is

telling the whole story, the command staff responded incompetently to his warnings about corruption in the force. On the other hand, Serpico may not have given the command staff enough information to proceed with an investigation, in which case Serpico handled his communication with his superiors incompetently.

Q13.7. In Case 13.1, does Serpico appear to be diligent?

Yes—to the point of being unrelenting in his quest to bring the corrupt officers to justice.

Q13.8. In Case 13.1, if Serpico knew that his life would be in danger after going public about police corruption, would it have been morally permissible for him not to blow the whistle?

Yes, our answer to Q13.1 notwithstanding. At least it would have been permissible not to reveal the truth the way he did. The virtuous professional always seeks the mean between extremes. Extremes in this case would be doing nothing, on the one hand, out of cowardice or apathy, or knowingly sacrificing one's life to expose corruption, on the other, which would be foolhardy. If Serpico had good reason to believe that blowing the whistle would result in his death, he might, for example, have tried to blow the whistle anonymously or kept looking for a department administrator whom he could trust.

Q13.9. In Case 13.2, suppose the police officers were Hmong and thus refused to arrest the funeral director. Would this be a morally admirable case of loyalty?

No. We have encountered similar situations elsewhere in this text and have concluded that if one's religion prevents one from being an effective police officer, then one should consider a different profession.

Q13.10. In Case 13.3, was the suspect's escape due to a failure in self-governance?

No. The escape does not reflect a weakness in the system of police governance; it suggests a mistake that a helpful trooper made when he let a citizen in need distract him.

Q13.11. In Case 13.3, is it fair to say that the suspect escaped because Lumpett was insufficiently diligent?

Yes—although, more specifically, the suspect escaped because Lumpett chose between acting kindly to the elderly man and ignoring that man's request for help. So, it should be easy to forgive Lumpett's lapse.

Q13.12. In Case 13.1, was Serpico's decision to blow the whistle a morally good autonomous act? How about Lumpett's decision to help the elderly man in Case 13.3?

Assuming that Serpico acted from duty or a sense of service to the community or profession, we can applaud his autonomous use of discretion. It was morally good for Lumpett to help the man, but Lumpett should have made sure the suspect was secure first. Thus, Lumpett acted autonomously, but should have to take some sort of hit for the mistake.

Q13.13. In Case 13.2, is it fair to say that the police officers in the funeral home acted with proper autonomy?

No. It is apparent that they were following orders, but with a proper sense of autonomy they might have worked more closely with the mourners, thereby causing less upset.

Q13.14. In Case 13.3, is Nicks receiving unfair treatment for his role in the suspect's escape?

Not necessarily. Although it feels unfair that Nicks gets in trouble for Lumpett's mistake, the rule that requires the arresting trooper to transport an arrested suspect back to the barracks is not unreasonable.

Q13.15. In Case 13.2, "The Funeral of Za Chue Xiong," does it appear that the police officers could have benefited from better training?

Yes. The case suggests that the officers acted with inappropriate sensitivity to mourners in general and to a different ethnic group in particular.

Q13.16. In Case 13.14, if Arpaio had based his argument on the claim that abortion is immoral, would he have had a stronger reason for refusing to transport inmates to abortion clinics?

No. As a law enforcement official, Arpaio has a duty to obey the law, which includes respecting the legal rights of those under his authority. If Arpaio feels so strongly against abortion that it prevents him from doing his job, then he should let someone else do the job.

Q13.17. In Case 13.5, are the community activists behaving virtuously?

Not necessarily. It is reasonable to want to keep a community safe from sex offenders, and it is reasonable to call the proper authorities to express concern and seek pertinent information. But in Case 13.5, the activists seem to be harassing Thorn, which is both excessive and unproductive.

Q13.18. If Thorn's caseload makes it impossible for him to respond effectively to the community's concerns about Schmitt, would it be morally sufficient for him not to respond to the activists at all?

No. This would be a deficient response relative to other options. Thorn could, for example, put a message on his voice mail and e-mail that lets the community know about how low a threat Schmitt is and that would explain how Thorn is handling the situation. Thorn's message might also include a way for concerned citizens to contact Thorn's superior, if they felt the need to take their concerns further.

NOTES

1. A compilation of facts from Peter Maas, *Serpico: The Classic Story of the Cop Who Couldn't Be Bought* (New York: Viking, 1973); "Graft Paid to Police Here Said to Run into the Millions," *New York Times,* 25 April 1970), p. 1; and Mark Arnold, "Crusading Policeman: Francesco Vincent Serpico," *New York Times,* 11 May 1971, p. 27.

2. President's Commission on Law Enforcement and Administration of Justice, *The Challenge of Crime in a Free Society* (1967; Honolulu: University Press of the Pacific, 2005), pp. 7–12.

3. May Chow, "Long Weekend Rites Fuel Demand for Hmong Funeral Homes," *AsianWeek.Com,* 9 July 2004; retrieved 29 June 2007 from http://news.asianweek.com/news/view_article.html?article_id=9567c93e8ce9ab69c3656c39796caa0e.

4. "NYPD Mission," retrieved 6 May 2007 from www.nyc.gov/html/nypd/html/mission.html.

5. William Shaw and Vincent Barry, *Moral Issues in Business,* 10th ed. (Belmont, CA: Wadsworth, 2006), Ch. 6.

6. From the files of the Maryland State Police. Discussed at the Maryland State Police Command College, Camp Fretterd, MD, summer 2003. The names of the parties in the case have been changed to ensure anonymity.

7. Vincent Henry, "CompStat: The Emerging Model of Police Management," in *Critical Issues in Crime and Justice,* 2nd ed., ed. Albert R. Roberts (Thousand Oaks, CA: Sage, 2003), pp. 117–47.

8. Phyllis McDonald, *Managing Police Operations: The New York City Crime Control Model* (Belmont, CA: Wadsworth, 2002).

9. Peta Hellard, "America's Toughest Sheriff: A Serve of Slops and Pink Undies," *The Advertiser* (Adelaide, Australia), 24 March 2007, p. 8.

10. *Jane Joe v. Arpaio,* 1 CA-CV 05-0835. See Paul Davenport, "Court Rules against Arpaio Jail Policy on Abortions," Associated Press, 23 January 2007; and Gary Grado, "Sheriff Loses Bid to Halt Abortions for Inmates," *East Valley Tribune* (Mesa, AZ), 23 January 2007.

11. American Correctional Association, *ACA Code of Ethics* (1994), retrieved 2 July 2007 from http://www.aca.org/pastpresentfuture/ethics.asp; American Jail Association, *AJA Code of Ethics* (1993), retrieved 2 July 2007 from http://www.aja.org/aja/about/code.shtml.

12. Two representative codes of ethics worth reviewing come from the Probation Officers Association of Ontario, Inc., retrieved 3 July 2007 from www.poao.org/ethics.htm; and the Denton County, Texas, *Code of Ethics for Juvenile Probation Officers,* retrieved 3 July 2007 from dentoncounty.com/dept/juvenile/images/juvenile%20probation%20officer%20code%20of%20ethics.pdf.

CHAPTER 14

ETHICS IN THE COURTROOM

CASE 14.1

The Alford Plea

During a detective's interrogation of Uta Halberg, Halberg confessed to murdering her neighbor's child. However, Richard Helleck, the prosecutor in the murder case, could not use the confession as evidence in the trial, because nobody read Halberg her *Miranda* rights before or during the interrogation. With no other sufficient evidence, Helleck had to drop the case.

Recently, a low-level drug dealer has offered to present evidence to Helleck of Halberg's felonious involvement in drug sales, if Helleck will drop charges against the dealer. Helleck agrees, if the evidence is compelling. Upon receiving the evidence, Helleck believes that the drug dealer manufactured it, but if the dealer is convincing on the witness stand, the jury will probably convict Halberg.

If the jury convicts Halberg, she could receive up to 50 years in prison. Helleck presents Halberg and her attorney with the evidence and agrees to recommend 10 to 20 years in prison for Halberg if she pleads guilty to the drug charge. Halberg agrees to enter an Alford plea, meaning that she agrees that the evidence is convincing enough to convict her, but she denies the charge.

When Halberg goes before Judge Myra Kerr to enter the plea, Kerr is as skeptical as Helleck about the evidence, but Kerr is so glad to get Halberg off the street that the judge accepts the plea without further inquiry.

Case 14.1 exemplifies the challenge adjudicators face when the morally right thing to do may not be the legal thing to do. The Constitution's framers did not anticipate the judiciary's importance in America's criminal justice system. In *Federalist Paper* No. 78, Alexander Hamilton writes that "The judiciary is incontestably the weakest of the three branches of power," since "it can never successfully attack the other two" branches.[1] In this paper, Hamilton cites French political philosopher Montesquieu's claim that "Of the three powers above mentioned, the judiciary is next to nothing."[2]

It turns out, however, that there is no greater opportunity for moral complexity in criminal justice than in the courtroom. As the President's Commission on Law Enforcement and Administration of Justice puts it,

> The criminal court is the central crucial institution in the criminal justice system. It is the part of the system that is the most venerable, the most formally organized, and the most elaborately circumscribed by law and tradition. It is the institution around which the rest of the system has developed and to which the rest of the system is in large measure responsible. It regulates the flow of the criminal process under governance of the law. The activities of the police are limited or shaped by the rules and procedures of the court. The work of the correctional system is determined by the court's sentence.[3]

In the criminal justice profession, adjudication includes judges, lawyers, juries, and court reporters. There are other roles in the courtroom as well, such as the paralegal, the bailiff, and the court clerk. With the legislators and the law enforcers, the adjudicators have the responsibility of being distributively and commutatively just. In other words, each stakeholder should receive a proper share of the adjudicator's services, and that obligation comes from the social contract between the adjudicators and their clients, which Article III of the U.S. Constitution governs. In addition, adjudicators have a greater responsibility than the legislature or police for administering retributive justice.

As with law enforcers, it may be difficult for the adjudicator to apply the contract model of professional–client responsibility for decision making. Expedience or fairness may require the professional to act paternally, or the client may insist on treating the professional merely as the client's agent. What's more, the primary client differs from one area of adjudication to another. Thus, for example, the defense attorney's primary client is the defendant; the prosecutor's primary defendant is "the people," whose interests clash with the defendant's. Since different professional–client relationships may yield different sorts of moral problems, it will be useful to divide this chapter according to the professions: judge, attorney, jury, and court reporter.

Before considering each profession, we will look at the adversarial system of justice, because this system provides much of the moral force of professional adjudication.

Q 14.1

In Case 14.1, can one morally justify Helleck's act by arguing that the end justifies the means?

✦ THE ADVERSARIAL SYSTEM

There are two principal systems of adjudication worldwide. The adversarial system, which the United States has, is in the common law tradition of developing abstract legal principles from specific cases and judicial decisions. Its roots are British. The inquisitorial system is in the civil law tradition of identifying abstract rules and then applying them to specific cases. Its roots are Roman.

In the adversarial system, each party to the case gathers evidence and constructs arguments to try to prove its point to an impartial third party—a judge or jury. Ideally, a thorough presentation by both sides of the issue will allow the truth to emerge, giving the neutral finder of fact (the judge or jury) the chance to offer an appropriate disposition of the case. In practice, of course, the personality and ability of the various players in the trial may have a profound effect on its outcome, raising moral issues of unfairness, ineptness, and bias. In the inquisitorial system, the judge or tribunal of judges develops the case, attempting to engage in an impartial search for the truth.[4] Thus, in the adversarial system, each of the parties must be skilled at this sort of investigating and arguing, whereas the inquisitorial system rests primarily on the judge's skills. In the adversarial system, the judge's primary task is to produce and maintain a forum for each party to make its best case; in an inquisitorial system, the judge creates the case.[5]

The adversarial system in the United States has a constitutional foundation, especially Article III, the Fourth through Eighth Amendments, and the 14th Amendment. As the baseline, the Constitution permits legal punishment only for specific acts that a plaintiff (in civil cases) or prosecutor (in criminal cases) proves in court to have violated existing laws. Thus, no one in the United States can be punished without reason or punished without proof of having committed a crime. Nor can anyone in the United States be punished *ex post facto*—that is, for an act that was not a crime at the time it was committed.

Any attempt to punish a defendant must apply due process. The defendant is presumed innocent unless the plaintiff can prove guilt by a preponderance of the evidence or the prosecutor can prove guilt beyond a reasonable doubt. The defendant must receive notification of the specific charges before the trial starts and be able to hire an attorney to represent him. In a criminal case, the defendant has a right to have court provide an attorney if the defendant cannot afford one. Then, the defendant must be able to confront his accusers, present evidence in his behalf, and have an impartial jury weigh that evidence.

The plaintiff or prosecutor also has rights.[6] Within legal limits, he may submit a charge or appeal to a judge or group of judges, summon the defendant to court to respond to the charges, have the judge or judges make a decision, and have the decision enforced if the plaintiff or prosecutor wins.

The biggest practical problem due process presents is that it is not an efficient process—it favors the rights of the accused over the expeditious resolution of the case.[7] This has caused a huge backlog of cases in lower courts, leading at times to "assembly line justice."[8] Often in lower courts, prosecutors and defense attorneys seek to cut deals that deprive the parties of the full hearing in court to which they are entitled. In criminal cases, figures for the number of convictions resulting from plea bargains rather than trials are debatable, but they are generally greater than 90%. For example, of 33,217 convictions in federal courts between October 1, 2006, and March 31, 2007, a total of 31,816—or 95.8%—resulted from guilty pleas rather than trials.[9] Thus, much adjudication is administrative rather than judicial, which raises more constitutional concerns about the defendant's chance for a fair trial.

As we shall see, the adversarial system in general, its constitutional restraints, and the resulting backlog pose moral challenges to each of the adjudicating professions in different ways.

✦ THE JUDGE

The judge presides over the court, whether there is a hearing, a trial, or an appeal of a lower court's decision. He also signs warrants and may issue legal opinions on certain issues that do not require an appearance on the bench. In an adversarial system, the judge must be impartial, independent, and accountable. He must also realize that his decision could set a legal precedent that will serve as a premise in future legal cases.

A judge's jurisdiction may be as small as a local town or village or as large as the United States. The judge may sit in a trial court or on an appeals court. The judge may be elected to a limited term or appointed to a term for life, assuming "good behavior." In all cases, the judge is a professional, as we can see more clearly by considering the professional criteria we have discussed regarding the legislature and law enforcement.

Q 14.2

In Case 14.1, did Kerr show impartiality in her acceptance of Halberg's plea?

Significant Service to Society

As a professional, the judge offers a significant service to society. Although he works for the criminal justice system, his primary client is the person who has brought the matter before the court. This is not the judge's only client, however. He must see that the opposing side has the proper opportunity to present its case. He must see that the jury has what it needs to offer a reasonable verdict. Sometimes, after a defendant has been convicted, the judge will allow victims and their relatives or friends to describe in court what impact the crime has had on them. This may influence the convict's punishment. Also, to the extent that a judge's decision may enhance or decrease a community's sense of safety or may set the precedent for future legal decisions, the judge has the people in general as clients.

As legal ethicist Kenneth Kipnis points out, there are four primary advantages to having a responsible and informed judge oversee an adversarial proceeding.[10] First, the judge knows and applies legal standards that minimize the chance of a trial's being unfair. Second, the judge lacks bias that would tip the scale in favor of one party or the other. Third, the judge's authority "equalizes the power" of the two parties. Fourth, the outcome of the trial usually settles the matter, at least by the end of the appeals process, whereas the feud might continue unabated if the community had no impartial judge on whom to rely.

Q 14.3

In Case 14.1, has the judge served her primary client adequately?

Greater Responsibilities and Rights

The judge's position in the courtroom and in the criminal justice system carries with it professional responsibilities and rights that distinguish it as a profession.

The *competent* judge knows the law and the jurisdiction's legal system well. She is impartial toward all parties. She is mindful of the importance of her decision beyond the trial, because the decision may serve as a precedent in future cases. To this end, she is sensitive to the difference between adjudicating and legislating from the bench, and she never seeks to usurp the legislature's authority to make law.

The *diligent* judge remains current with relevant legal scholarship. She always has control of her courtroom and makes decisions in a timely manner. Also, she never lets extrajudicial activities, such as secondary employment or private consulting, conflict with her professional obligations.[11]

The judge's responsibility for *honesty* and *candor* is especially important when she explains her decisions. Writing on *The Responsible Judge,* Federal Judge John T. Noonan and philosopher Kenneth I. Winston argue that a full and reasonable explanation demonstrates the judge's accountability in three ways. It makes public the judge's impartiality; it demonstrates the integrity of the judicial enterprise; and it encourages the public's democratic responsiveness.[12] The authors note that the judge's argument will be especially effective if she bases it on the litigants' arguments, rather than introducing premises that suggest a personal agenda or bias.[13] Kenneth Kipnis adds that a full and public explanation of the judge's decision enables the public to criticize the judge's decision.[14]

The judge's first *loyalty* is to the integrity of the position. Thus, she will avoid conflicts of interest and improper political activity that may undermine her impartiality, and she will recuse herself from any trial or legal decision in which conflict of interest or its appearance is unavoidable.[15]

Recall that the obligation of *discretion* may call for the professional to keep certain confidences or it may refer to acting on one's own authority. Since most legal proceedings in the United States are public, there will be little need for the judge to maintain confidentiality about what she has learned on the bench. Nevertheless, she may have knowledge about colleagues, litigants, or jury members that is irrelevant to the proceedings and could be embarrassing or harmful. The discreet judge will know when it is better to keep these matters to herself.

As for acting on one's own authority, the judge must act within the law and the rules of procedure, but she has a lot of discretion in interpreting those laws and rules. She has the rights, for example, to set bail, to interfere in the give-and-take between the parties in a trial, to decide how to instruct the jury, to set aside a jury's verdict, to declare a mistrial, and to offer a wide range of punishments. A virtuous exercise of these rights gives litigants the fairest hearing possible and promotes the integrity of the profession and of the criminal justice system.

As in any profession, the judge has the obligations of *beneficence* and *nonmaleficence*. Although the judge's primary purpose is to achieve justice, she should do so with compassion and with respect for the dignity of all parties in a dispute.

Self-Governance and Autonomy

A mark of a profession generally is self-governance of the body of professionals. Judges are governed by the U.S. Constitution and the laws of their jurisdiction. Usually the jurisdiction's legal code prescribes limits on courtroom procedure and the punishment that a judge can impose on a convict. Also, if elected, a judge must answer to the electorate, and if appointed, he must answer to an administrative judge, judicial commission, or legislature. In spite of such oversight, however, judges tend to govern themselves, both collectively and individually. On the whole, history suggests that this process has gone well. It remains important, however, for judges to continue to police themselves, and for the public and legal scholars to stay informed about a judge's professional activities and to keep the judges accountable.

It also remains important for judges to contribute to the profession through contributions to scholarship and active membership in one or more professional organizations.

Calling and Money as Means

As with other professions, most judges appear to have a sense of calling to public service in general and to the bench in particular. To be sure, judges in some courts and jurisdictions can make a comfortable living, but many judges are paid much less than they would make if they were in private law practice.[16] Where money becomes the purpose of being a judge, the judge's impartiality and loyalty to the justice system come into question, thus hurting the judge's credibility and, by extension, the profession itself.

Extensive Training and Credentialing

The work of a judge is so sophisticated that one would expect every judge to have extensive training going into the profession and to undergo continued training while active in the profession. However, there are no educational criteria for judges. An elected judge has only to meet residency and age requirements for the position. Appointed judges have only to convince the person or group appointing her that she should get the job. The election or the appointment becomes the only credential that the judge needs to practice the profession.

We would hope that the voters or appointers would hold the candidate to a high standard of legal skill, knowledge, and wisdom, but forcing this would undermine the democratic nature of America's criminal justice system, which is under the people's authority.

Summary

We have examined the morality of the judicial profession. We have seen that among the many professional criteria and obligations that the virtuous judge meets, the most important are impartiality, diligence, respect for and knowledge of the law, and respect for all parties in a legal dispute. We have seen that he exercises his rights and fulfills his responsibilities always with the integrity of the professional and the criminal justice system in mind. Our next step in looking at courtroom ethics is to consider the lawyer.

✷ THE LAWYER

CASE 14.2

Malpractice

Stephen Foot is a malpractice attorney whose face and annoying advertisements are well known to the city's TV viewers. Foot has successfully settled thousands of malpractice cases over the past 20 years without once stepping into a courtroom.

One night a few months ago, Harold Kimes, a kind, upstanding elderly citizen of one of the city's poorer neighborhoods responded to a ruckus in his well-kept front yard by grabbing a pistol, running to the front door, and opening it to find a group of young teenagers trampling his garden, ripping out his bushes, and throwing rocks at his windows. Without warning, he fired a pistol shot well over the heads of the ruffians. Unfortunately, the slug ricocheted off a brick wall across the street, hitting one of the teenagers and killing him. Kimes was arrested for manslaughter, and Foot has offered to take the case *pro bono*. Kimes and his family have gratefully accepted.

As the trial is about to begin, the prosecutor offers Kimes a deal. Ordinarily in this city, anyone convicted of a crime with a handgun must receive a minimum sentence of five years in prison. The prosecutor will waive jail time if Kimes pleads guilty to involuntary manslaughter. Foot asks and receives 24 hours to consider the plea.

Shortly after receiving the plea, Kimes goes back to his holding cell, and Foot goes back to his office to discuss the plea offer with his law partner, Al Nosis. Nosis points out that if Foot wins the case, this could open up a whole new area of practice for the law firm—criminal defense. On the other hand, if Kimes takes the plea, Foot will have little to brag about. Foot convinces Kimes to turn down the plea offer, promising Kimes that they will win the trial.

After a two-week trial, the jury convicts Kimes of involuntary manslaughter. The jury did not know that the conviction carries a mandatory five-year prison sentence.

Foot appeals the decision on the ground that the jury did not know about the mandatory sentence, but the appeals court denies the appeal.

Case 14.2 reminds us that the adversarial system is at its best when each side in a dispute is able to present the best case possible. Such a presentation requires detailed knowledge of the law, judicial proceedings, and legal argument. Such a presentation, in other words, requires the skill of an attorney. It is a given that the lawyer is a professional, even if some lawyers do not live up to the title. We can examine the moral challenges by referring to the professional criteria as they relate to the lawyer's work.

Significant Service

The most significant services that a lawyer offers are as a counselor and as a representative.[17] The lawyer also may serve as a negotiator or as a non-adversarial representative, as in writing a will or registering a patent. The primary client is the person seeking counseling or representation. As a counselor, the lawyer offers advice about legal rights, statutory law, and ordinances. She should offer this advice as neutrally and objectively as possible, leaving it to the client to take the advice or not. As a representative, the lawyer argues on behalf of the client in the courtroom, acting as the client's fiduciary and zealous advocate, and thus showing strong bias in the client's favor.

At first blush, it appears that the preferable model for professional–client decision making is the agency model: The lawyer provides the professional expertise, and the client decides what to do with it. This may make it easier for virtuous lawyers to engage in acts that they consider immoral, such as attacking the character of a creditable witness. This model makes more sense when the case is a civil matter or the lawyer is a defense attorney. Often prosecutors will have to act paternally, because their client, the state, is not readily available to participate in decisions about the case. However, as usual, the preferred model is the contract model, in which both parties assume a degree of responsibility for decision making and for the success or failure of the professional transaction.

Q 14.4

In Case 14.2, which model of decision making does Foot employ? Was this the morally right choice of model?

We will have more to say about decision making in the context of the lawyer's responsibilities and rights.

Greater Responsibilities and Rights

As professionals, lawyers have considerable responsibilities and rights. These flow from the U.S. Constitution, through laws and professional codes of conduct. The American Bar Association (ABA) is "home base" for all lawyers in the United States.

The ABA establishes recommended standards for admission into the profession, standards for the curricula of law schools that seek ABA accreditation, and standards for disciplining lawyers. The ABA also has a lot of input into the selection of judges, usually by way of formal recommendations to those responsible for appointing judges. Thanks to the ABA, the scope and limits of a lawyer's obligations are clear, although specific moral challenges are ever present.

The *competent* lawyer in the United States has graduated from law school, passed the bar exam, and received a license to practice from authorities in his jurisdiction. He knows the law and rules of procedure and evidence well, especially in his area of practice, and he has the research skills necessary to come up to speed quickly in areas of knowledge that affect his client's case. If he is a trial lawyer, he knows the courtroom procedure well and uses it, within legal and regulatory bounds, to the advantage of his client.

The zealous advocacy that is key to good representation in an adversarial system requires an especially high degree of *diligence* on the lawyer's part. For the defense attorney, this presents some interesting challenges. As law professor Monroe Freedman suggests, the three hardest moral questions for the defense attorney are whether he should

- Cross-examine a reputable witness for the other side with the distinct purpose of discrediting the witness.
- Put a witness on the stand, knowing that the witness plans to commit perjury.
- Give the client legal advice if the knowledge the client acquires will tempt her to commit perjury.[18]

Kipnis adds that the defense attorney facing these questions runs the risk of being complicit in his client's wrongdoing.[19]

For the prosecutor acting as a zealous advocate for the people, one of the more tempting challenges is to achieve a conviction at all costs, rather than follow the trail of justice, no matter where it goes.

On both sides, the zealous advocates must remember that they are officers of the court. This imposes severe limits on what they may do legally or morally to make their clients' case. Thus, for example, it is wrong to make up evidence, to threaten a jury member with physical harm, or to offer a bribe to the judge.[20]

Q 14.5

In Case 14.2, does the prosecutor appear to be acting sufficiently zealously?

The lawyer has a duty to be completely *honest* and *candid* with her client about all matters relevant to the case. This will help the client participate in his own defense to the degree he is able.

It is rare that the lawyer must be candid with the opposing party, the judge, or the jury. Matters are more complicated with respect to honesty. In a civil case, the plaintiff needs to convince the judge or jury by a preponderance of the evidence that the defendant is guilty and should pay a penalty. In a criminal case, the prosecutor must convince the judge or jury beyond a reasonable doubt that the defendant has committed the crime. In both cases, the defendant begins under a presumption of innocence, and he needs only to keep sufficient doubt in the mind of the judge or jury. If the defendant knows that he is guilty, then it would seem that any effort to convince the court otherwise is a dishonest act. Yet one can consistently point out the weakness in the prosecution's case without necessarily declaring that the facts the prosecution is alleging are false.

A famous example of this challenge to honesty is the criminal trial of O. J. Simpson in 1995 for the murder of his ex-wife and her friend. At the close of the lengthy trial, Judge Lance Ito's 36-minute instruction to the jury made clear that the jury was to decide the case on whether the prosecution had proved its case beyond a reasonable doubt.[21] The jury was not to consider hunches or personal feelings. After only four hours of deliberations, the jury found Simpson not guilty. Afterward some jurors admitted that they thought Simpson had committed the murders, but all the jurors agreed that the prosecution had failed to prove it. On the surface, it appears that a gross act of dishonesty resulted in the release of a murderer. But the jury followed Ito's instructions, which were arguably fair given the rules of the adversarial system.

In terms of the professional obligation of discretion, the lawyer has a duty to the client to maintain *confidentiality*. Attorney–client privilege renders almost sacred the communication between the two, much like the communication between a priest and a confessant. Although common sense might view a client's statement as sufficient grounds for moral or legal retribution, the lawyer's duty is to work that statement into the purpose of representing the client's interests. To fail in this regard would be malpractice: a violation of the lawyer's duty to be competent and diligent. We may find some solace in the realization that everyone in the United States has a right to this sort of representation. Thus, to argue successfully for elimination of the attorney–client privilege, one would have to argue successfully for elimination of the adversarial system as it functions today.

The foregoing makes obvious the lawyer's obligation of *loyalty* to the client. The greatest obstacle to meeting this obligation is the ever present danger of conflict of interest. Unless the lawyer has only one client ever, the lawyer runs the risk of having two clients simultaneously with competing interests or two clients successively with competing interests. Kenneth Kipnis offers excellent examples of each.[22]

In the first example, three people are in a car that is hit by a bus. The two passengers are hurt and require expensive medical treatment; the driver is unhurt, but her car sustains some damage. The three hire a lawyer to sue the bus company. The bus company countersues, claiming the accident was the driver's fault. The jury finds the bus company and the driver equally liable for the two passengers' medical bills. Should the lawyer appeal on the driver's behalf, but to the passengers' detriment? Or should he counsel against appeal, thus hurting the driver but benefiting the passengers? Kipnis describes ways in which the lawyer might have handled this, had he foreseen these circumstances, but the fact remains that the lawyer now faces a genuine conflict of interest.

Kipnis's second example concerns a woman who seeks a divorce and wants to hire an attorney who once represented her husband and her. The attorney has had no contact with the husband for some time and considers their professional relationship over. The wife does not know anything about her husband's financial holdings, but the attorney is well aware of them as a result of his legal representation of the husband. The wife wants advice on how much alimony and marital property to request in her suit for divorce. If the lawyer takes the case, does he have a duty to keep confidential anything he learned about the husband's assets while the husband was a client? Since the husband and wife were married at the time, weren't these the wife's assets too? It is tempting to dismiss this case simply by telling the attorney not to represent the wife. But as things stand, there is a clear case of conflict of interest.

One more interesting case of conflict of interest that Kipnis notes involves representation of a corporate client.[23] For legal purposes, the corporation is an entity separate from its individual managers and shareholders. The corporation can be sued and it can sue, while leaving the assets of the individuals out of the process. At the same time, a lawyer for a corporation usually represents the managers and shareholders in their roles as corporate members. The problem, Kipnis notes, is when the interest of one of these individuals, acting in her corporate capacity, conflicts with the interest of another corporate agent, or conflicts with the interests of the corporation as a whole. In Kipnis's example, a corporate CEO has bribed an overseas company to get some of its business, which is a violation of the federal Foreign Corrupt Practices Act. The CEO anticipates personal legal trouble if these bribes become public, so the CEO wants legal help from the attorney. As the corporation's lawyer, the attorney feels he should turn in the CEO and try to put as much distance as possible between the corporation and the CEO. However, since the CEO came to the attorney in good faith, it is unclear whether the attorney can betray his confidence. A clear conflict of interest!

> ### Q 14.6
>
> Another form of conflict of interest is between a lawyer's personal interest and the client's. In Case 14.2, does Foot face such a conflict?

The lawyer's twin obligations of *beneficence* and *nonmaleficence* are obvious toward the client. The challenge is how far she may go in hurting someone else in order to protect her client. We have already seen the example of discrediting a witness that is averse to the client. The witness may have been subpoenaed against his will but has answered the summons as a matter of duty. To give the client the best defense against this witness, the lawyer may have to embarrass the witness on the record and bring up private matters that the witness had long put behind him. We have also seen the example of withholding information that could ease a family's grief, but that could hurt the client's defense. If these harmful acts are necessary to a zealous defense, then the lawyer should commit them, while making every effort to be as civil toward the "victims" as possible. Anything less zealous could constitute malpractice; anything crueler could violate basic human rights.

Self-Governance and Autonomy

The practice of law is the stereotypical example of a profession. This is partly because of the central and strong role that the ABA plays in its governance of the profession and its provision for the lawyer's autonomy. An interesting debate among professionals and scholars alike is whether professionals are doing enough to preserve the law's professional characteristics. This leads us to the next pair of professional criteria.

Calling and Money as Means

As with other professions, there is something unsettling about professionals who appear to be practicing for the money, not for the good that the profession can do. The Philadelphia Bar Association, for example, has complained that there is too much emphasis on the business of law and not enough on the profession. Thus, the association has proposed a series of steps for restoring professionalism to the practice:[24]

- Treat opposing counsel and witnesses with civility.
- Keep open lines of communication between clients and opposing parties.
- Respect others' schedules.
- Be punctual.
- Provide your adversary with whatever he deserves, without making it difficult for him.
- Grant reasonable extensions of time when they will not adversely affect your client's interests.
- Try to resolves differences through negotiation, expeditiously and without needless expense.

Note that the emphasis here is on the professional relationship with colleagues. Although the most significant professional relationship is with one's client, it is useful for the lawyer to pay attention to the other professional relationships as well and to engage in those relationships in a way that reflects well on the profession.

Training and Credentials

Again thanks to the ABA, the training and credentials of the professional lawyer are admirable. The individual lawyer's task is to keep up with training and education that will help her stay at the top of her game.

Summary

We have examined the ethics of the lawyer, noting especially the challenges that come with zealous advocacy for the client. The virtuous lawyer will serve the client and the adversarial system well, while maintaining a virtuous lifestyle in and out of the courtroom.

As we continue our look at ethics in the courtroom, our next stop is the jury.

✦ THE JURY

 ## CASE 14.3

The Activist Juror

Marcia Monfils is a staunch opponent of capital punishment. Her state has the dubious distinction of performing more executions per year than any other state in the union. At least once a year she is summoned to jury duty, but she has only sat on minor civil cases. This time, however, she has been called to a courtroom with a large number of other potential jurors for a trial on a capital charge. As the voir dire process begins, during which the judge and opposing parties select or disqualify potential jurors, the judge asks the usual questions about the jurors' familiarity with the case or with any party to the case. Monfils is unfamiliar with the case and the parties. Then the judge asks whether any juror has objections to the death penalty. Monfils decides not to answer, hoping that she might be impaneled so she can prevent the defendant, if guilty, from receiving the death penalty.

Sure enough, Monfils is impaneled, and the jury finds the defendant guilty of a capital crime. Per state law, the jury must next decide whether the defendant is to receive the death penalty or life in prison without parole. By a majority of 11 to 1, the jury initially leans toward execution, but Monfils convinces the others that she will never go along with them. Finally, anxious to be finished, the other 11 agree to the lesser penalty.

Monfils feels that she has struck a blow for justice.

It is a stretch to refer to jurors as criminal justice professionals. Yet as Case 14.3 reminds us, their function is very much part of the professional effort to ensure a fair trial. As with the judge, the jury's primary clients are the parties before the court, but the jury's actions also affect the community. Unlike with judges and attorneys, the jury's professional role is limited to the trial and is also limited by the lack of any requirement to know the Constitution or the laws, rights, and concepts of justice that come from it. Therefore, jurors face many of the same moral problems that other adjudicators face because of the rights and responsibilities of the profession, but they are much less prepared to deal with those problems.

The Sixth Amendment to the U.S. Constitution sets the stage for jury ethics in criminal cases:

> In all criminal prosecutions, the accused shall enjoy the right to a speedy and
> public trial, by an impartial jury of the State and district wherein the crime shall
> have been committed.

The Seventh Amendment addresses civil trials:

> In suits at common law, where the value in controversy exceeds twenty dollars, the right of trial by jury shall be preserved, and no fact tried by a jury, shall be otherwise re-examined in any court of the United States than according to the rules of common law.

Note that there is no constitutional guarantee of right to trial by a jury of *one's peers,* although one can find this right in the *Magna Carta,* which is an important ancestor of the U.S. Constitution:

> No freemen shall be taken or imprisoned or disseised [deprived] or exiled or in any way destroyed, nor will we go upon him nor send upon him, except by the lawful judgment of his peers or by the law of the land.[25]

We may dispense quickly with several professional criteria before considering the ethics of the jury. Other than being summoned, a juror is not expected to have a sense of *calling.* Jurors get paid very little for jury duty, if they receive pay at all, so it would be silly for someone to seek a spot on a jury in order to make *money,* either as an end or as a means. Jurors need no *training,* beyond the instructions they receive from the judge. Nor does one require *credentials* to be a juror, other than to be impaneled by a judge. There is a sense in which the jury is *self-governing* and the jurors have *autonomy* in their decision about a defendant's guilt, but this hardly rises to the level of professional self-governance. On the other hand, the criteria of a *significant service to the community* and *greater responsibilities* are relevant to the jury, so let's look at these criteria more closely.

Q 14.7

Does Case 14.3 present Monfils as an impartial juror in the sense that the Sixth Amendment promises?

Significant Service

There is debate about the value a jury adds to the criminal justice system. Political scientist Jeffery Abramson notes seven reasons for being skeptical about such value:[26]

- A fully impartial juror would need a pure conscience, which is an ideal that no one can achieve.
- Jurors tend not to measure up to the challenges of modern litigation.
- Attempts to balance juries demographically can slow down jury selection.
- Justice means treating like cases alike, but history shows that jurors don't do this.
- Defendants play to the emotions and prejudices of the jury, so the trial becomes theatrical, pushing the quest for justice aside.

- Jury democracy is not democratic because it allows an anonymous group of unelected people to ignore laws that a democratically elected legislature has enacted.
- The ideal juror is ignorant of the case before the trial. Thus, the better known the case is, the less observant and aware of current events the juror should be.

In spite of these concerns, Abramson defends the jury's role.[27] It is, he says, a deliberative body rather than a representative body, and therefore one of the last bastions of true democratic deliberation. It supports Aristotle's point that an advantage to democracy is its gathering up of the "collective wisdom" of the people.

Law professor Nancy King notes four advantages of a jury trial over a bench trial:[28]

- A jury protects litigants from abuse of judicial power.
- A jury brings community-based sense to fact-finding and to the application of law to facts.
- A jury helps to promote acceptance of case outcomes and legitimacy of the justice process.
- A jury increases lay participation in our democracy.

Q 14.8

Does Monfils's behavior in Case 14.3 work against defense of the jury's role in the adversarial system?

Greater Responsibilities and Rights

Jurors have a lot of responsibility and a lot of rights for the relatively brief time they serve. For the jury system to play its proper role in criminal justice, jurors must fulfill these obligations well and exercise these rights wisely. The professional life of a juror consists of six stages: the summons, the voir dire process, the trial, the deliberations, the verdict, and the post-trial.[29] Each of these stages provides moral challenges and opportunities, which we may consider in light of the professional obligations of trustworthiness.

There is no specific obligation of *competence* for the juror. In fact, depending on how weak a party's argument is, the attorney may hope for an incompetent jury that is easy to persuade through theatrics and fallacious reasoning. However, for the jury system to fulfill its role in criminal justice, the jurors should be able to follow and evaluate both parties' arguments, understand the judge's instructions, and engage thoughtfully with fellow jurors during deliberations.

In terms of *diligence*, the potential juror should answer the summons on the date and at the time that the summons specifies, unless she can show that other matters have a better claim on her time. During the voir dire process, she should listen carefully to the judge's questions. The impaneled juror should follow the trial closely, take careful notes where allowed, pay careful attention to the judge's instructions, and participate collaboratively during deliberations—neither monopolizing the conversation nor letting others do so.

One interesting problem in the context of diligence is the holdout juror, such as Monfils in Case 14.3.[30] The virtuous juror will not be excessively diligent, but will persist in the name of fairness and truth. How persistent should the juror be if she feels strongly about one side of the jury's argument but all the other jurors have the opposing view? In Case 14.3, Monfils' persistence has more to do with her political and philosophical views than with the law. By lying her way onto the jury and ignoring the rules for imposing capital punishment, Monfils's behavior as a juror is morally questionable. Compare her to the protagonist, known as Juror #8, in the movie *Twelve Angry Men*.[31] The story begins with #8 as the lone holdout against conviction of a young man for murdering his father. Juror #8 has not found the evidence convincing beyond a reasonable doubt. By the end of the movie, he has convinced the others of the flaws in the prosecution's case, and the jurors acquit the defendant. Monfils's position and the capitulation of her fellow jurors are harder to justify morally than #8's position. Perhaps the difference is one of reasonableness. Consider the two arguments:

Argument 1 (Monfils)

1. I have a duty to protest capital punishment.
2. The law requires jurors to impose capital punishment if the convict's crime meets certain criteria.
3. My duty trumps the law.
4. Therefore, I should not impose capital punishment, no matter how convincing the evidence.

Argument 2 (Juror #8)

1. I have a duty to uphold the law.
2. The law presumes a defendant's innocence unless the prosecution has proved guilt beyond a reasonable doubt.
3. The prosecutor has not proved guilt beyond a reasonable doubt.
4. Therefore, the law requires me to vote not guilty.

Monfils's argument is reasonable in form: It appears that if the premises are true, then the conclusion is true. But the third premise is not self-evidently true and thus requires a proof of its own. We have agreed that a law can be morally bad and that, therefore, there can be a moral duty to violate the law. Many will agree that capital punishment is bad, as is any law permitting or requiring it. Monfils, however, is not giving the jury the chance to debate this; she is short-circuiting the process by acting out a personal agenda. This violates her duty as a juror. Juror #8, on the other hand, offers an argument that is reasonable in form and that stays within the parameters of his duty as a juror. Thus, one could condemn Monfils's persistence as excessive and praise #8's persistence as virtuous at the same time. We will have more to say about this when we discuss jury nullification below.

The juror's obligation to be *honest* and *candid* pertains to all the stages in the juror's professional life cycle. A person who receives a summons to jury duty and who wishes to be excused should be honest about the reasons why. During the voir dire process, the potential juror should respond to all questions as candidly as necessary to help the judge and the adversaries decide whether to disqualify the juror. Also, the jurors should be honest with each other during deliberations. Each juror should feel free to "speak his mind" and should encourage others to do likewise. This will enhance the value of the collective wisdom that justifies the jury system.

In general, the professional obligation of *loyalty*, especially as it involves avoiding conflicts of interest, does not present a big problem for the juror. Perhaps the juror will answer the summons and deliberate diligently out of patriotic loyalty, but this sense of loyalty is not essential to fulfilling the juror's task. An effective voir dire process eliminates much of the risk of conflict of interest, and an impaneled juror who discovers such a conflict, real or apparent, may bring it to the attention of the jury foreman or the judge. If the judge decides there is no conflict or that there is no threat to a fair verdict, then the juror need not worry about it any further.

Q 14.9

In Case 14.3, does Monfils have a conflict of interest?

Although *beneficence* and *nonmaleficence* are always desirable, the juror's focus should be on justice. This means giving the defendant what he deserves and, by extension, giving the plaintiff what he deserves. At times this may be unpleasant or harmful, and someone will walk away the "loser," but it would be unfair to accuse the juror of acting maleficently if the verdict is just. Justice is a virtue, even if it may not always appear to be.

Note that the benefit of treating the defendant justly extends to all whom the justice system affects. Thus, one can act beneficently toward the whole while appearing to harm the individual. This is a classic example of utilitarian decision making.

Note, too, that the jurors should treat each other well, avoiding harm where possible.

Q 14.10

Is Monfils acting beneficently in Case 14.3?

Discretion refers both to confidentiality and to making decision on one's own authority. During the juror's tenure, issues of confidentiality may emerge during the trial if the judge orders the jurors not to discuss the case with anyone before deliberations and not to discuss the case with non-jurors during deliberations.

Issues of confidentiality also arise after the trial. Jurors in the United States have the legal right to publicly discuss jury deliberations after the trial, unlike their counterparts in Great Britain and Canada.[32] Since the juror's job is over once the trial has ended, denying her the right to speak about her experience would arguably violate her First Amendment freedom of speech. This does not settle the question of whether it is morally right to speak about the trial after the fact. On the one hand, such public discussion may have social benefit, promoting acceptance of case outcomes and legitimacy of the criminal justice process.[33] On the other hand, it would be unfair and possibly harmful to betray the confidences of fellow jurors.[34] So the virtuous juror will discuss deliberation publicly only to the extent that it is morally neither an excessive nor a deficient response to whatever prompted the disclosure.

The second meaning of discretion is the professional's ability to act on one's own authority. In this sense, discretion raises one of the most interesting issues in jury ethics—**jury nullification.** Jury nullification refers to the jury's right to render a not guilty verdict even if the prosecution has proved its case. Juries have used it only rarely in the United States.[35] The rationale for this right is the belief that in a democracy the people are the final arbiters of the law. The constitutions of California, Maryland, and Indiana specifically recognize this right.[36] None of the constitutions of the other 47 states denies this right.

Of course, the legal right of jury nullification does not necessarily make it morally right, so let's consider some moral pros and cons. Psychologist Norman J. Finkel notes that some critics mistakenly regard jury nullification as a wrong verdict.[37] Instead, says Finkel, nullification should be seen as a victory for common-sense justice over "black letter of the law justice." Besides, he continues:

- If we knew the verdict in advance, we would not need a trial.
- Since we cannot read minds, only the jurors know what constitutes reasonable doubt for them.
- Sometimes a jury must compromise because it doesn't get the option it wanted.
- A jury trial means that the jury has the discretion to convict or acquit.[38]

Social scientist Candace McCoy adds that the jury determines the truth in a trial, and the jury's interpretation of the proceedings is the final say. Thus, any verdict will be the legal truth, so the jury cannot be wrong even if it nullifies.[39]

On the other hand, Kleinig and Levine liken jury nullification to civil disobedience, and note that nullification allows a jury to acquit a bad person.[40] Thus, even if jury nullification may be good sometimes, it may not always be good.

McCoy points out that deontologists and consequentialists would disapprove of jury nullification because it fails to follow universal rules and may be concerned more with the good of the defendant than the greater good.[41] Sociologists Harry Kalven and Hans Zeisel add that a jury is "non-rule minded" because it will follow equity rather than rules.[42] If McCoy, Kalven, and Zeisel are correct, then virtue theory is the only basic theory that remains to defend jury nullification. Jury nullification is a virtuous act when it is precisely what the defendant deserves and any other option would be excessive or deficient relative to what the defendant deserves. Recall our example of Huck Finn and his attempt to help his friend Jim escape slavery (Case 3.1). Now imagine that Huck is on trial for violating Missouri's pro-slavery laws and that if Huck is found guilty he will be executed. Execution would be an excessively harsh response to Huck's act, especially given the evil of slavery; keeping Huck from being executed would be less excessive. So the jury that prevented his execution rather than endorsing it would be taking the more virtuous path, even if this required jury nullification.

Q 14.11

In Case 14.3, could Monfils argue that her stance during the sentencing phase of the trial was analogous to a virtuous act of jury nullification?

Regarding jury nullification, another question is whether a judge should be required to notify the jury of its right to nullify. So far, the courts considering this question have answered in the negative. Moreover, it is common for judges to include the instruction to the jury that if the prosecution has proved its case, the jury must find the defendant guilty. Given the right of nullification, this instruction is false.[43] According to Kleinig and Levine, however, such instruction is likely to continue indefinitely.[44]

Social psychologist Shari Seidman Diamond offers an interesting twist by suggesting that attorneys should be able to argue for or against nullification before the jury.[45] Scheflin adds that there has not been a case in which "counsel's attempt to argue nullification indirectly resulted in contempt or disciplinary action."[46] So attorney-generated arguments might be a good alternative to requiring a judge's instructions to permit jury nullification.

Summary

We have been discussing jury ethics. We have noted the jury's profession-like rights and responsibilities, while agreeing that jurors do not have to meet many of the criteria for a profession. We have focused on the advantages of a jury trial over a bench trial, especially in a democracy; the scope and limits of the juror's obligations of diligence and confidentiality; and the jury's right to nullify.

Our next and final topic concerning ethics in the courtroom is the ethics of the court reporter.

✦ THE COURT REPORTER

The court reporter is an officer of the court whose task is to produce an official transcript of a trial, as well as transcripts of depositions, hearings, arbitration, and other proceedings requiring a legal, written record. To produce this transcript requires special and advanced technical and technological skills. The transcript provides both a public record and the record for any appeal of a verdict. Once the court reporter has signed and notarized a transcript, it becomes the final word on the proceeding; thus, he must listen carefully and attentively and produce a virtually error-free transcript. Often he must do this in "real time," meaning that he must produce a transcript immediately.

Court reporters recognize themselves as a profession. Their primary organization, the National Court Reporters Association, is the umbrella for state court reporting associations.[47] To demonstrate their status as a profession, one has only to consider their work in light of the criteria for a profession.

Significant Service to the Community

In terms of professional criteria, the court reporter provides an important service to society by preparing and verifying the official record of court proceedings. An official reporter, one who works in the courtroom, works under a judge, but has the parties to the case as his primary clients. The freelance reporter, one who works outside the courtroom either as an independent contractor or as an employee of an agency, has as a client whoever is paying for his transcription.

In both cases, the general model of professional–client decision making is the paternal model, since the reporter must record exactly what he hears, regardless of what his client would like him to say he heard.

Greater Responsibilities

In terms of professional responsibilities, court reporting calls for a high degree of *competence.* To enter the profession, a reporter must be able to write down at least 225 words per minute, must have the ability to pay close attention for long periods of time, and must have strong language and editing skills.

The court reporter must be *diligent,* as the required attention to detail and accuracy attests.

Because the primary task of the court reporter is to produce a verbatim record of what she hears, she must be *honest* and *candid* in that record. This poses an interesting problem in choosing between what she hears literally and what the speaker means to say. Suppose for example, that a literal transcription of a witness's comment would be "Jeet yet?" The reporter, recognizing the speaker's accent, understands the witness to be asking, "Did you eat yet?" What should the reporter put in print? There is also the problem of whether to include every utterance. From time to time, a magazine or newspaper, for example, will publish a transcript or excerpt of a transcript that includes "uh" and other pauses and interjections that do not necessarily add to the point of the speech. There may also be an occasional "[expletive deleted]," which seems to have put the transcriber or editor in the position of censor. As the expert, the virtuous court reporter will know how much to include and how much to leave out in order to fulfill her obligation to produce a proper transcript.

The court reporter's *loyalty* is first to the truth as she reports it. She should also be loyal to her clients by avoiding conflicts of interest or the appearance of such conflict. A conflict may arise, for example, when someone she is close to is a party to a legal proceeding and the reporter is supposed to record the proceeding. The other side of the dispute might worry about the reporter's objectivity. The NCRA requires reporters to bring possible conflicts to the attention of the parties and to reach an agreement on how to proceed. The official court reporter will have to abide by the judge's decision; the freelance reporter may have to let another reporter take the job.

The court reporter has little *discretion* in what she reports on the record, but she has a lot of discretion in what to disclose about what she has heard off the record. Suppose, for example, that she is taking a deposition in a heated divorce case with both parties present. Suppose further that in between moments of on-the-record testimony the parties hurl accusations at each other that would make good gossip but that are legally irrelevant. The discreet professional would keep this information private, because she acquired it while "on duty" and it has nothing to do with doing her job well. To reveal that information would be unprofessional and might hurt her professional reputation.

Finally, the court reporter has a duty to be *beneficent* and *nonmaleficent*, but like other professionals in the courtroom, her first concern is justice. Generally, she should treat all parties and personnel with civility, dignity, and respect for their rights. However, she should also let the truth that emerges from the proceedings take her wherever it leads, even if that is hurtful to one or the other party.

Self-Governance and Autonomy

The NCRA has a lot of influence over the standards for entrance into the profession, although some of the reporter's rights and responsibilities are set by statute. The freelance reporter has more autonomy than the official reporter in choosing which jobs to take, but even the official reporter has the final say in what goes into the transcript.

The virtuous reporter needs little supervision. He knows what is expected of him and what he has to do to meet those expectations, and he meets those expectations in an accurate and timely manner.

Training and Credentials

Most court reporters undergo extensive training to get into the profession and then undergo continuous education and training to stay current in techniques, new technologies, the law, specialized terminology, business practices, and methods for maintaining one's personal and professional well-being.

Also, in most cases the court reporter must have some form of certification that indicates her educational and professional achievements.

Calling and Money as Means

Court reporting can be a lucrative career, and anecdotal evidence suggests that many people are drawn to it for that reason. However, the same anecdotal evidence suggests that those who survive the rigorous training and entrance requirements have a justly deserved sense of pride in their capabilities and their contribution to the criminal justice system. In any event, the reporter's professional contribution to the criminal justice process is obvious and indispensable, as are the professional rights and responsibilities that come with it. In short, she is a professional whether she feels called to it or not.

SUMMARY

This chapter has examined ethics in the American courtroom by discussing several professional roles within the adversarial system of justice. These roles include the judge, the lawyers, the court reporter, and, by analogy, the jury. All are there to ensure justice for the parties to the criminal trial or civil lawsuit. All the roles provide a significant service to the community, carry great responsibilities and unusual rights, and have a degree of self-governance and autonomy. The roles differ, however, in the training and credentialing required, and in the extent to which the professional has a sense of calling to the role. The virtuous professional in the courtroom will be competent, diligent, and appropriately honest and discreet. He will be loyal, but the object of this loyalty may vary by role; for example, the lawyer has a strong loyalty to his client, whereas the judge must treat the adversarial parties impartially. The virtuous professional in the courtroom will be candid, but the proper degree of candor may vary by role; for example, the judge should be candid in her reasons for her findings, but a jury need not reveal anything about its deliberations. Finally, the virtuous professional will not harm anyone unnecessarily but will allow justice to prevail even if that means upsetting someone.

Our next and final step is to consider the future of criminal justice ethics.

ANSWERS TO CASE STUDY QUESTIONS

Q14.1. In Case 14.1, can one morally justify Helleck's act by arguing that the end justifies the means?

Not necessarily. This would be a consequentialist argument. A consequentialist might argue that Helleck did the right thing by pressuring Halberg to take the plea. However, a consequentialist could also argue that Helleck's misuse of his authority hurt the legal profession and the criminal justice system, so the outcome was worse than if Helleck had declined the drug dealer's offer.

Note that no other basic moral theory supports Helleck. A regularian would note that Helleck violated a basic norm: The prosecution should pursue justice, not a conviction at any cost. A deontologist would argue that Helleck could not argue for making his tactic a universal duty, because this would illogically make legal justice a matter of unjust coercion. A virtue theorist would note that Halberg did not deserve punishment for a crime she didn't commit.

Q14.2. In Case 14.1, did Kerr show impartiality in her acceptance of Halberg's plea?

No. Kerr acted with a bias against Halberg by denying her the chance to respond freely to what Kerr suspected was a false charge.

Q14.3. In Case 14.1, has the judge served her primary client adequately?

No. Her primary client is Halberg, who deserves her "day in court." The judge also failed Helleck, by making it too easy for him to short-circuit the prosecutorial process.

Q14.4. In Case 14.2, which model of decision making does Foot employ? Was this the morally right choice of model?

The paternal model. Foot decided that his defendant should go to trial rather than take the plea, and he gave Kimes little chance to do otherwise.

Q14.5. In Case 14.2, does the prosecutor appear to be acting sufficiently zealously?

Yes. There appears to be little that the community would gain by the defendant's serving jail time. Thus, if the prosecutor can dispense with the case before having to take it to trial, he will have served the public adequately.

An interesting objection to this answer is legal historian and law professor John H. Langbein's argument that a plea bargain of any sort denies the defendant his Sixth Amendment right to trial by jury. Thus, Langbein would hold that the prosecutor was insufficiently zealous because he avoided a trial.[48]

Q14.6. Another form of conflict of interest is between a lawyer's personal interest and the client's. In Case 14.2, does Foot face such a conflict?

Yes. He is more interested in bolstering his business than in representing his client's interests.

Q14.7. Does Case 14.3 present Monfils as an impartial juror in the sense that the Sixth Amendment promises?

No. She is using the defendant's case as an instrument toward her political and philosophical goals. Although it may be good that Monfils spared a person from execution, this was not due to impartiality on her part.

Q14.8. Does Monfils's behavior in Case 14.3 work against defense of the jury's role in the adversarial system?

Yes. It demonstrates how jurors may use the system to the juror's advantage regardless of the interests of the adversarial parties.

Q14.9. In Case 14.3, does Monfils have a conflict of interest?

Yes. The criminal justice system's interest in an impartial and objective decision clashes with Monfils's interest in scoring a political and perhaps moral victory.

Note that Monfils might argue that her sole interest is in achieving justice, even if there are different means to that end; thus, there is no conflict of interest.

Q14.10. Is Monfils acting beneficently in Case 14.3?

Yes and no. She has done something good for the defendant by sparing him from execution. But some might protest that she has harmed the public by acting against its interests in seeing justice done.

Q14.11. In Case 14.3, could Monfils argue that her stance during the sentencing phase of the trial was analogous to a virtuous act of jury nullification?

Yes, if nullification can be virtuous. The basic argument in jury nullification is that either the law is bad or the defendant does not deserve the punishment that conviction requires. This is the same sort of argument that Monfils brought to the sentencing phase of the jury's deliberations.

NOTES

1. *Independent Journal* (New York), 14 June 1788.
2. Charles de Secondat, Baron de Montesquieu, *Spirit of the Laws,* Vol. I (1748), p. 186.
3. President's Commission on Law Enforcement and Administration of Justice, *The Challenge of Crime in a Free Society* (1967; Honolulu: University Press of the Pacific, 2005), p. 125.
4. David E. Schrader, *Ethics and the Practice of Law* (Englewood Cliffs, NJ: Prentice-Hall, 1988), p. 13.
5. Kenneth Kipnis, *Legal Ethics* (Englewood Cliffs, NJ: Prentice-Hall, 1986), p. 29.
6. Kipnis, *Legal Ethics,* p. 23.
7. President's Commission, *Challenge of Crime,* p. 125.
8. Ibid., p. 128.
9. U.S. Sentencing Commission Preliminary 2007 Datafile USSCFY07, 1 October 2006–31 March 2007; retrieved 17 July 2007 from http://www.ussc.gov/sc_cases/Quarter_Report_2Qrt_07.pdf.
10. Kipnis, *Legal Ethics,* p. 24.
11. West Virginia Code.
12. John T. Noonan and Kenneth I. Winston, *The Responsible Judge* (Westport, CT: Praeger, 1993), p. 309.
13. Ibid., p. 96.
14. Kipnis, *Legal Ethics,* pp. 32–3.
15. Noonan and Winston, *Responsible Judge,* p. 278.
16. "Judges Behaving Badly," *Economist,* 30 June 2007, pp. 36–8.
17. Kipnis, *Legal Ethics,* 34–5.
18. Monroe H. Freedman, "Professional Responsibility of the Criminal Defense Lawyer: The Three Hardest Questions," in *Ethics in the Legal Profession,* ed. Michael Davis and Frederick A. Elliston (Buffalo, NY: Prometheus, 1986), pp. 328–39.
19. Kipnis, *Legal Ethics,* Ch. 5.
20. Ibid., p. 36.
21. Lance Ito, Instructions to the Jury, 29 September1995; retrieved 8 July 2007 from http://www.lectlaw.com/files/cas62.htm.
22. Kipnis, *Legal Ethics,* Ch. 3.
23. Ibid., pp. 55–62.
24. Philadelphia Bar Association, "Working Rules of Professionalism," 1990; retrieved 7 July 2007 from www.law.stetson.edu/excellence/litethics/philadelphiabar.htm.

25. Magna Carta, 1215, #39.

26. Jeffrey Abramson, *We the Jury: The Jury System and the Ideal of Democracy* (Cambridge, MA: Harvard University Press, 1994), pp. 3, 4, 17.

27. Ibid., p. 9.

28. Nancy J. King, "Ethics for the Ex-Juror: Guiding Former Jurors after the Trial," in *Jury Ethics: Juror Conduct and Jury Dynamics,* ed. John Kleinig and James P. Levine (Boulder, CO: Paradigm, 2006), pp. 219–36.

29. John Kleinig and James P. Levine, eds., *Jury Ethics: Juror Conduct and Jury Dynamics* (Boulder, CO: Paradigm, 2006), p. vii. See also Paula Hannaford-Agor and G. Thomas Munsterman, "Ethical Reciprocity: The Obligations of Citizens and Courts to Promote Participation in Jury Service," in ibid., pp. 21–34.

30. Jeffrey Abramson, "Jury Deliberation, Fair and Foul," in Kleinig and Levine, pp. 181–208.

31. Reginald Rose wrote the play and the screenplay for CBS in 1954. Sidney Lumet directed the movie, starring Henry Fonda, in 1957.

32. King, "Ethics for the Ex-Juror," p. 219.

33. Ibid.

34. Ibid.

35. Kleinig and Levine, *Jury Ethics,* p. 9.

36. Alan W. Scheflin, "Mercy and Morals: the Ethics of Nullification," in ibid., p. 143.

37. Norman J. Finkel, "Juries' Duties, Obligations, and Rights: The Ethical/Moral Roots of Discretion," in Kleinig and Levine, pp. 53–82.

38. Ibid., p. 59.

39. Candace McCoy, "The Truth of Nullification: A Reply to Professor Scheflin," in Kleinig and Levine, p. 175.

40. Kleinig and Levine, *Jury Ethics,* Ch. 1.

41. McCoy, "Truth of Nullification," p. 176.

42. Cited in Kleinig and Levine, *Jury Ethics,* p. ix.

43. B. Michael Dann, "The Constitutional and Ethical Implications of "Must-Find-the-Defendant-Guilty" Jury Instructions," in Kleinig and Levine, pp. 93–118.

44. Kleinig and Levine, *Jury Ethics,* p. 9.

45. Shari Seidman Diamond, "When Ethics and Empirics Are Entwined: A Response to Judge Dann's Nullification Proposals," in Kleinig and Levine, pp. 119–30.

46. Scheflin, "Mercy and Morals," p. 143.

47. National Court Reporters Association, "NRA Code of Professional Ethics"; retrieved 5 May 2007 from www.ncraonline.org/AboutNCRA/cope.

48. John H. Langbein, "Torture and Plea Bargaining," in *The Philosophy of Law,* 5th ed., ed. Joel Feinberg and Hyman Gross (Belmont, CA: Wadsworth, 1994), pp. 349–58.

PART VI

CRIMINAL JUSTICE ETHICS IN THE FUTURE

CHAPTER 15

CRIMINAL JUSTICE ETHICS IN THE FUTURE

 CASE 15.1

Seeing through Walls[1]

On June 11, 2001, the U. S. Supreme Court issued its decision in the case of *Kyllo v. United States*, finding that use of a thermal imaging device to detect a possible marijuana growing operation constituted a search that the Fourth Amendment prohibits.

Danny Kyllo lived in a triplex in Florence, Oregon, where he was growing marijuana. Federal Agent William Elliott, suspecting Kyllo's operation, trained a thermal imager on the triplex, looking for unusually high infrared radiation that might indicate the use of heat lamps necessary to the growth of marijuana. "The scan showed that the roof over the garage and a side wall of petitioner's home were relatively hot compared to the rest of the home and substantially warmer than neighboring homes in the triplex." Elliott combined this information with informants' tips and Kyllo's utility bills to get a search warrant from a federal magistrate. Upon searching the home, Elliott found more than 100 marijuana plants and arrested Kyllo for manufacturing marijuana in violation of federal law.

Kyllo moved to have his arrest thrown out, arguing that the use of the thermal imager was an unreasonable invasion of his privacy. When the district court denied the motion, Kyllo entered a conditional plea of guilty and appealed the sentence. The Ninth Circuit Court of Appeals remanded the case to the district court, which concluded that the imager "is a non-intrusive device which emits no rays or beams and shows a crude visual image of the heat being radiated from the outside of the house"; it "did not show any people or activity within the walls of the structure"; "[t]he device used cannot penetrate walls or windows to reveal conversations or human activities"; and "[n]o intimate details of the home were observed." Thus, the court declared, the warrant was valid.

The Court of Appeals agreed. The U.S. Supreme Court overturned the conviction.

Writing for the majority, Justice Scalia agreed that a "naked-eye" surveillance of a publicly accessible area would not have constituted a search in the constitutional sense and thus would not have required a warrant. But the technological assistance of the thermal imager and other devices, such as satellites and sensitive sound equipment, "would leave the homeowner at the mercy of advancing technology—including imaging technology that could discern all human activity in the home." Scalia continued: "While the technology used in the present case was relatively crude, the rule we adopt must take account of more sophisticated systems that are already in use or in development."

Noting Justice Stevens's dissenting opinion that "There is, in my judgment, a distinction of constitutional magnitude between 'through-the-wall surveillance' that gives the observer or listener direct access to information in a private area, on the one hand, and the thought processes used to draw inferences from information in the public domain, on the other hand," Scalia responded:

> To begin with, there is no necessary connection between the sophistication of the surveillance equipment and the "intimacy" of the details that it observes—which means that one cannot say (and the police cannot be assured) that use of the relatively crude equipment at issue here will always be lawful. The Agema Thermovision 210 might disclose, for example, at what hour each night the lady of the house takes her daily sauna and bath—a detail that many would consider "intimate"; and a much more sophisticated system might detect nothing more intimate than the fact that someone left a closet light on. We could not, in other words, develop a rule approving only that through-the-wall surveillance which identifies objects no smaller than 36 by 36 inches, but would have to develop a jurisprudence specifying which home activities are "intimate" and which are not. And even when (if ever) that jurisprudence were fully developed, no police officer would be able to know *in advance* whether his through-the-wall surveillance picks up "intimate" details—and thus would be unable to know in advance whether it is constitutional.

Case 15.1 exemplifies the challenge that technology poses to the criminal justice professional of the future, one of many challenges to criminal justice ethics that lead us to wonder what the future of criminal justice ethics looks like.

Q 15.1

The Fourth Amendment reads, in part, "The right of the people to be secure in their persons, houses, papers, and effects, against unreasonable searches and seizures, shall not be violated." On this wording alone, who has the better moral argument in Case 15.1, Stevens or Scalia?

In one sense, the future looks the same as the present and the past. First and foremost a representative of the U.S. Constitution, the criminal justice professional will face the challenge of balancing constitutional liberties with the community's safety and security. All moral problems will require the professional to consider possible consequences, relevant rules, and professional duties, while making sure to act in a way that is neither deficient nor excessive. The professional will have to be familiar with the varieties of alleged moral authorities, including the Constitution, religion, and professional codes of conduct. Finally, the professional will have all of the relationships in the future that that she has today, each relationship bearing particular rights and responsibilities, including her relationship with herself, her clients, her colleagues, third parties, and her profession.

In another sense, the future promises challenges that the Founding Fathers probably never anticipated. Who in 1788, besides Ben Franklin perhaps, could have imagined thermal imaging devices that allowed someone to see through walls? Would such technology have affected the wording of the Fourth Amendment's protection from unreasonable search and seizure? Could the Founding Fathers have predicted the other scientific advances in medicine, war, and communications; the vast and constantly changing demographic challenges; the current geopolitical realities of terrorism and globalization; the environmental concerns? These and other developments will pose new and tougher challenges for the criminal justice professional both within the United States and in relation to other countries and peoples. Thus, the future bears a closer look.

It will be useful to organize our examination around three major factors in the moral challenges of the future: technology, demographics, and the media. We will find that the future we thus describe points to the need for more citizen involvement in the criminal justice system, more and better education for criminal justice professionals, and a greater commitment to public sector ethics.

→ TECHNOLOGY

The criminal justice system faces a future filled with new technologies and vast improvements on old technologies. Among some of the more interesting technologies on the near horizon are

- Surveillance technology, including night vision goggles, global positioning systems, and highly sensitive audio recording devices
- Advanced photography techniques
- Modern forensics or criminalistics
- DNA profiling and genetic fingerprinting
- Biometric information
- Robotics[2]

Some new technologies will enhance the criminal justice profession by permitting faster and more precise communication, better and more efficient research, and quicker and more exact solutions of criminal cases. These new technologies will also pose at least two significant moral challenges to the profession: It will be more difficult to fulfill the moral obligation of competence, and it will put people's privacy at greater risk.

Q 15.2

In Case 15.1, is it fair to claim that Agent Elliott acted incompetently when he failed to get a warrant before scanning Kyllo's house?

The minimum level of competence will rise considerably, forcing professionals to balance their time more carefully among learning these new technologies, applying them effectively, and going about the other business of their profession. Professionals will have to be familiar with new methods and tools for investigating criminal complaints; pursuing, apprehending, interrogating, convicting, and punishing criminals; and communicating with other agencies and with citizens about the criminal justice process and specific cases. Suppose, for example, that a technology exists that offers a nonlethal and highly effective alternative to a sidearm, but is expensive and difficult to master. Now suppose that a police officer in a small agency with no budget for buying or mastering this weapon shoots and kills a suspect with what once was considered justified deadly force. If the suspect's angry family members accuse the officer of excessive use of force, would he have as an excuse that he didn't know better and couldn't have afforded the less lethal weapon even if he knew how to use it? Not obviously. Arguably, the professional obligations of competence and avoiding unreasonable harm would require the officer to make use of this technology as soon as possible.

In this same vein, consider the "CSI effect," which exists today but points to more complications in the future. Popular media have glamorized the profession of crime scene investigation (CSI), making it appear as if investigators can easily and quickly solve any crime and identify any culprit with the slightest of evidence. Key to this expectation is the media hype about DNA analysis and matching. With the smallest trace of a person's DNA, some stories suggest, the investigator can pinpoint the criminal, the time the crime occurred, and anything else about the crime that will ensure a swift and certain conviction. Forensic experts responsible for DNA analysis will tell you that although the science is impressive, these popular notions have set expectations far too high. Word is spreading about juries who see anything less than a clear DNA match as cause for reasonable doubt about a defendant's guilt. Since many criminal trials are not serious enough to require expensive and time-consuming DNA forensics, the defense attorney can make good use of this on behalf of his client, while the prosecutor struggles to convince the jury that there are other ways to prove guilt besides the exotic and expensive methods that jurors have seen on TV dramas or read about in supermarket tabloids. It is hard to find moral fault with the defense attorney for using this phenomenon in zealous defense of his client; it also is easy to sympathize with the prosecutor who must struggle with a reality that is less exciting than fiction. But this doesn't let the prosecutor off the hook; she will simply have to try harder to build her cases and convince the jury. Note that this poses a moral problem for the jury as well. Any juror who will settle for nothing less than a DNA match to remove reasonable doubt about a defendant's guilt is putting an unfair burden on the prosecution and making it more likely that a morally guilty suspect will fail to receive legal justice. As forensic science becomes even more sophisticated, the criminal justice system will have a harder time overcoming the CSI effect and problems like it.

Another problem that new technologies pose for criminal justice professionals is the increased threat to citizens' privacy, as we see in Case 15.1. As the technology that enables invasion of privacy becomes more sophisticated, opportunities for invading privacy will increase, as may the temptation to use the technology unconstitutionally.

We should note that the concern for technology's threat to privacy is an old one. Moreover, not everyone agrees that there is a constitutional right to privacy, because the Constitution does not articulate such a right explicitly. Both these points emerge in an article written in 1890 by law partners Samuel D. Warren (1852–1910) and Louis D. Brandeis (1856–1941) that makes the case for such a right, noting that scientific and communications advances of the time make articulating this right all the more important.

> Recent inventions and business methods call attention to the next step which must be taken for the protection of the person, and for securing to the individual what Judge Cooley calls the right "to be let alone." Instantaneous photographs and newspaper enterprise have invaded the sacred precincts of private and domestic life; and numerous mechanical devices threaten to make good the prediction that "what is whispered in the closet shall be proclaimed from the house-tops." For years there has been a feeling that the law must afford some remedy for the unauthorized circulation of portraits of private persons; and the evil of invasion of privacy by the newspapers, long keenly felt, has been but recently discussed by an able writer. The alleged facts of a somewhat notorious case brought before an inferior tribunal in New York a few months ago, directly involved the consideration of the right of circulating portraits; and the question whether our law will recognize and protect the right to privacy in this and in other respects must soon come before our courts for consideration.[3]

Brandeis became a U.S. Supreme Court Justice in 1916, and during his tenure, which ended in 1939, he often argued for this right to privacy. It was not until 1965, however, that the Court expanded this right in *Griswold v. Connecticut,* to be followed eight years later by *Roe v. Wade.* Griswold recognized, if not conferred, the right of married couples to buy and use contraceptives. *Roe* recognized the right of a woman to an abortion "on demand" during the first trimester of her pregnancy. The Court predicated both decisions on the right to privacy, which was not an issue before 1890.

Perhaps the greatest moral challenge that this right poses, besides the question of whether the right actually exists in the Constitution, is the threat that current government security measures pose to it. For example, after the terrorist attacks on September 11, 2001, Pres. George W. Bush authorized the National Security Agency (NSA) to eavesdrop on people in the United States without obtaining a warrant.[4] Many people have suggested that Bush acted contrary to the Fourth Amendment, and several people have filed suit to reverse Bush's decision. This highlights the challenge that judges face when balancing constitutional liberties with the safety and security of the community. It also raises an interesting question about the proper relationship of the three branches of government. More than one judge has agreed that NSA agents should have to get warrants before they can eavesdrop on Americans. But Pres. Bush has argued that his roles as president and commander in chief of the military give him the right, if not the duty, to expedite certain security measures, even if that means bypassing the ordinary constitutional protocols. Judges have the moral responsibility to weigh the president's argument against the Constitution, as the judges understand it. Then, since a judge's first loyalty is to the

Constitution, he must deny the president's position if it is unconstitutional. What such denial means—a written dissent, a criminal contempt citation, a cease-and-desist order—remains debatable.

→ DEMOGRAPHICS

CASE 15.2

Stem Cell Therapy: The Near Future

It is 2015. U.S. scientists have perfected and patented a procedure using embryonic stem cells to cure some of the more common fatal diseases, including Alzheimer's disease, Parkinson's disease, and most cardiopulmonary diseases and cancers. The procedure requires the destruction of human embryos and the use of drugs whose chemical compositions remain a trade secret. In several scientifically valid tests, the procedure has been 100% successful in eradicating all signs of the disease being treated.

News of this procedure generates a lot of excitement worldwide, as its potential sinks in. People could live much longer, healthier lives. They could enjoy a prolonged period of creativity and prosperity, potentially making contributions for the good of society. Health care costs would plummet, as far fewer people would face expensive, prolonged deaths from these diseases.

Soon, however, the downsides of this procedure become apparent. It is very expensive and will remain so for 20 years—the life of the patent. Insurance companies cannot afford to cover this procedure without raising insurance premiums so high that very few people could afford them. The patent holders have made clear their interest in making a profit from the procedure. The head of the U.S. Food and Drug Administration (FDA), a strong opponent of any procedure that destroys human embryos, refuses to grant approval, arguing that the drug's long-term effects are uncertain.

Citing complicated commerce laws, the patent holders sue the FDA in federal court, asking that the procedure be approved regardless of FDA consent.

Citing an overriding public health need, the American Association of Retired Persons (AARP) sues the patent holders in federal court, demanding that the procedure be made widely available to U.S. citizens.

Case 15.2 provides a backdrop against which to discuss demographic effects on criminal justice ethics in the future. As the case implies, two of the more significant concerns demographically are population growth and international relations. Population growth will be affected by people having the chance to live longer, healthier lives. But this may also lead to greater demands for increasingly limited supplies of life-sustaining and life-enhancing resources. This, in turn, may strain international relations as disagreements arise over who owns such resources and the extent to which these owners have an obligation to share those resources with humanity the world over. Let's look more closely at population growth and international relations as two demographic factors that might affect criminal justice ethics in the future.

Population Growth

If the present is a proper indicator, the U.S. population in the future will be larger, longer-lived, and more transitory. This will put greater demands on the criminal justice system for services, and it will make it harder to keep track of people. On a moral level, this will affect each of the criminal justice professions in different ways.

The Legislature

The U.S. population will grow not only in number but in diversity. With these increases will come more demands for existing public services as well as new public services. Increased demands require increased supplies or greater rationing of existing supplies, thus creating a need for new legislation and regulation to provide and oversee those services, and to see that the rights of all stakeholders are protected as well as possible. As states find it more difficult to deal with these demands, they will look more frequently to the federal government for help. Thus, as legal historian Lawrence Friedman notes, the legislature will have additional responsibilities, resulting in greater centralization of legislative power in Washington.[5] Friedman suggests that we are already moving toward a single country culturally and economically. He admits that this appears to contradict the evidence of increasing numbers of special interest groups, but he seems to regard these as the last gasp of distinct groups of people trying to keep their identities. Once, our concerns were primarily local, as were most of our communications and cultural experiences. With the Internet and other technological advances, more frequent interstate travel, more transient professionals, and nationwide worries such as terrorism, illegal immigration, health care, and global warming, our focus has broadened from local concerns to national concerns, and we turn more frequently to the federal government to protect our liberties and security.

Q 15.3

Assume that the procedure in Case 15. 2 could markedly increase the U.S. population, because people would live much longer than they do at present. From a strictly utilitarian point of view, would it be morally reasonable for the federal government to ban use of the procedure in order to control the population? How about from a virtuous point of view?

As the public clamors for more legislative action, the legislature will find it increasingly necessary to delegate some of its regulating responsibilities to boards, agencies, and administrations. Political scientist Louis C. Gawthorp adds that once public policy is made, there will also be a greater tendency to rely "on the private sector for the implementation of public policy."[6] This does not absolve the legislature of its responsibility to oversee these other bodies, because the legislature remains the primary lawmaking body in the United States. But it may make it more difficult for the legislature to remain in charge as it parcels out its tasks to other government bodies and to the private sector.

As the legislative task becomes more complicated, the virtuous legislator will have to be all the more ready to decide what laws to promote, how much federal money to spend, and what persons or agencies to task with fulfilling the legislative will—all of this while maintaining the proper balance between citizens' rights and their safety and security.

Law Enforcement

Future demands for law enforcement services will be greater in two respects. More professionals will be needed, and they will have to be better prepared to meet the increasingly complex and sophisticated challenges to the criminal justice system.

These demands will require greater and more creative efforts to recruit and retain well-educated and highly skilled professionals. Since many agencies already have difficulty meeting their recruiting goals, these future demands appear to make effective recruiting even more challenging. However, emphasizing the nobility and sophistication of law enforcement may make the profession more attractive as people seek to be part of an elite group. This move toward exclusivity has worked well for agencies such as the U.S. Marines, and there are no readily available examples of such appeals that have failed.

Note that a larger and more professional workforce in law enforcement will require greater financial support or more effective budgeting strategies to pay for higher salaries, more sophisticated technologies, and continued education and training. Since financial support is the public's concern, the moral burden for recruiting and retaining the law enforcement professionals of the future will fall on the public as well as on the law enforcement agencies.

In the face of growing demands for police services, the public will face a second burden. Police agencies will not be able to prevent crime all by themselves; they will need to incorporate the citizenry more fully and effectively in crime prevention.[7] Thus, the virtuous police officer and the virtuous citizen will have to work together steadily to determine how much responsibility for crime prevention to place on the police and how much to place on the citizenry. This reminds us that the moral burdens in the American criminal justice system fall on everyone whom the system benefits.

Q 15.4

Suppose the story in Case 15.1 was that Kyllo's neighbor, a civilian, had scanned Kyllo's house with a thermal imager, discovered the hotspot, and contacted Agent Elliott to tell him about the result. Suppose that Elliott then included the neighbor as a confidential informant in his request for a warrant, but made no mention of the imaging device. Would Kyllo have a reasonable argument that law enforcement treated him unfairly by violating his Fourth Amendment freedom from unreasonable search and seizure?

The increasing demands on law enforcement will also pose challenges specific to corrections. The greatest challenge will come from the increased number of inmates flowing in and out of the prison system.[8] Overcrowding in the prisons and unmanageable caseloads for probation and parole officers are present realities and point to a worsening situation. Since 1980, the U.S. prison population has quadrupled to 2 million. More than 95% of these will eventually leave prison, and more than 650,000 prisoners reenter society each year.[9] As legal scholars Henry Ruth and Kevin R. Reitz put it, these ex-prisoners are "unprepared for the daunting contrast between prison rigor and the sudden freedom of choice among life's joys, sorrows, demands, and responsibilities."[10] What's more, the link between unemployment or underemployment and recidivism is well established.[11] At the same time, there are decreasing funds available for giving prisoners the training and education they need to become gainfully employed after their release.[12] Thus, a major moral challenge facing corrections in particular and the public in general is whether and how to support ex-prisoners in their attempts to rejoin society. Are we willing to make the financial commitments necessary, even if this means taking money from other social and political projects? Are we willing to gamble on the rehabilitative aspect of punishment rather than simply give up on the offenders? These important questions require public dialogue and commitment. Since the public is unlikely to initiate this dialogue, corrections professionals will have to take the initiative.

Q 15.5

Suppose that all of the suits in Case 15.2 have been settled for the plaintiffs and the life-prolonging procedure is now widely available. Should prisoners who have received life terms receive the procedure, even if they don't want it?

The Courtroom

The moral impact of population growth on adjudication in the future is evident from four historical trends. These trends point to the judiciary's responsibility for promoting dialogue among professionals, and between professionals and the public, toward keeping the courtroom just and efficient.

The first historical trend is the *"liability explosion."*[13] As the United States becomes more litigious and the population grows, lawsuits over product liability and medical malpractice promise to multiply. This is all the more likely because of the vast numbers of new products hitting the market regularly and the increasing acrimony over the cost and quality of health care. This "liability explosion" already clogs the courts, encourages overregulation, and creates overcautious manufacturers and health care providers. Many a news story, for example, tells of doctors leaving medical practices or avoiding certain specialties because their malpractice insurance premiums are too high. It is difficult to assign blame for this suit-happiness, but it has to stop or the court system may grind to a halt. The virtuous judge and lawyer will discourage frivolous or unfair lawsuits, while encouraging litigation for legitimate redress of grievances. The virtuous citizen will use the courtroom only as a means to restoring justice and not as a get-rich-quick scheme. The virtuous legislator will encourage tort reform that seeks to give disputing parties what they deserve, no more and no less.

The second historical trend that challenges the judiciary is the *expansion of defendants' rights*.[14] Two landmark cases illustrate this trend. The case of *Gideon v. Wainwright* in 1963 established a defendant's right to a court-appointed attorney if the case is serious and the defendant cannot afford an attorney. The case of *Miranda v. Arizona* in 1966 established a suspect's right to resist police coercion and to be informed of that right prior to interrogation by police. Some critics have condemned these decisions as interfering with criminal justice by allowing criminals to escape punishment on a technicality when suspects are not informed of their rights. The greatest challenge that expansion of defendants' rights poses to courtroom ethics is how to find the proper mean between giving the prosecutor or plaintiff what she deserves and giving the defendant what he deserves. Given the power of the state in a criminal case, it is good for the defendant to have opportunities and resources that remove unfair advantages on the prosecutor's side. But what if the increasing number of defendants' rights now tips the scale unfairly in favor of the defendant? Given the likelihood that defendants' rights will continue to expand, and given the judge's and jury's discretion, the primary responsibility rests with the judge and jury to see that all rights in a case are honored and that all parties are given due respect and satisfaction.

Q 15.6

Does Scalia's decision in Case 15.1 constitute an *expansion* of defendants' rights?

A third historic trend that challenges courtroom ethics is *"plural equality."*[15] Since its inception, the United States has believed that "all men are created equal." For many years, this referred primarily to white Protestant men. However, court decisions and legislation have gradually included more categories of people, so that in true democratic fashion more and more people are sharing political and cultural power. In other words, more and more people are being accepted as "equal." Thus, African Americans and women who once were relegated to the political margins have taken their place front and center in politics. On the whole, plural equality is a positive trend, but there have been backlashes that promise legal and moral challenges in the future. Typically, the backlashes include claims of "reverse discrimination." As schools, businesses, and other organizations seek to give all eligible participants an equal chance, many of these organizations expressly encourage minorities to apply. This encouragement may simply be a verbal invitation, or it may involve a quota system whereby minorities or women will have an easier chance of acceptance than white males. Many people feel that the issue is overblown and that most organizations today emphasize an applicant's relevant qualities over any other consideration. Proponents of minority encouragement note that it is striking a balance of opportunity that should have been struck a long time ago. Opponents argue that such encouragement commits the same wrong it was meant to fix; only the victim has changed.

Plural equality is here to stay—and rightly so. Thus, judges and juries will have to ensure that plural equality receives the support it deserves without crossing the line into a new version of discrimination. This responsibility applies not only to parties in a case but also to personnel decisions among courtroom professionals and to jury selection.

A fourth challenge to courtroom ethics, for which expanding defendants' rights and plural equality offer strong evidence, is an apparent *judicial revolution*.[16] It is as if, notes Lawrence Friedman, we have "a wildly inventive and proactive court system, intent on imposing its progressive views on the country as a whole."[17] Americans first encountered this problem in 1803, when Justice Marshall dismissed William Marbury's complaint while declaring that the Court had the right to review all legislative and executive acts. So, it is an old problem: How much right do the courts have to make decisions that in effect legislate from the bench? Since there is nothing to indicate a solution anytime soon, the courtroom and the citizenry need to steel themselves for the continued debate. At the same time, Friedman notes, "the courts follow as much as they lead." Before the Supreme Court has a case to settle, it

> must have rights-conscious, rebellious, feisty human beings who have a sense of what is due to them, and are willing to struggle for their goals. And before you can have these rebels, you must have the right norms, the right zeitgeist [spirit of the times].[18]

In short, the question concerning a judicial revolution is, How much do the people in the United States want such a revolution? Thus, the responsibility for meeting this challenge belongs to all of us, not just to the judiciary.

International Relations

At least three features of the United States' international relations are relevant to the future of criminal justice ethics in America: terrorism, globalization, and international law.

Terrorism

Although terrorism is not just an international phenomenon, the focus has recently been and will continue to be on threats of terrorism from international groups seeking to hurt the United States. These perceived threats will affect criminal justice ethics in several ways, two examples of which follow.

First, as the legislature continues to grapple with legislation and funding requests that support security efforts in the United States and abroad, the virtuous legislator will have to balance security interests with other concerns, both foreign and domestic. Every minute and every dollar that the legislature spends on security issues are a minute and a dollar not spent on issues such as education, health care, and the environment, for example.

Second, police, especially patrol officers, are the frontline of defense against terrorism in the United States. Regarding this role, philosopher Edwin Delattre notes that what is most necessary in response to today's terrorism is to teach "newcomers to policing and law enforcement how to learn, and continue to gain access to, all the details of terrorism and terrorists they need to know to uphold and defend the Constitution in daily practice."[19] This education and its application will take time away from the work that police do ordinarily. It will also put police in a new and perhaps contentious relationship with federal agencies that are fighting terrorism. The virtuous police officer will have a steady struggle balancing her various responsibilities and making sure that she gets the education and resources she needs to do her job effectively. Also, police agencies and the citizenry will have to determine what they should do in support of the police officer and then do that as best they can.

Globalization

Economics and politics are becoming increasingly global. As columnist Thomas L. Friedman notes, an entrepreneur with a computer and access to the Internet and without any strong political or business ties can start an enterprise anywhere in the world and have that enterprise rapidly grow worldwide.[20] The World Bank supports this view, claiming that 70% of the structure of the world economy is in services that can be rendered from anywhere in the world to anywhere in the world.[21]

In addition, new forms of economic collaboration are in the works. For example, China is in detailed talks with several African countries about combining Africa's natural resources and China's economic resources.[22] The United States is beginning to court India's middle class, which comprises more than 300 million people, a vast number of whom have expressed interest in American goods and services.[23] One can imagine a time, therefore, where economic power trumps military power and the sovereign nation is no longer the fundamental geopolitical unit.

The upshot of this for criminal justice ethics in America is that professionals should prepare for these possible drastic changes to political and economic boundaries. There could be a time in the near future when American criminal justice professionals will need to think globally as a rule if they are to meet their moral challenges successfully. This might mean, for example, that the U.S. Congress will have to spend a larger share of its time on international relations, making sure that the United States gets a fair share of the global economic pie and that the United States does its fair share to contribute to the global marketplace. The fiscal implications of such legislation may make financial matters more difficult for law enforcement and the courts, forcing them to seek new ways of economizing or cut services. For the virtuous criminal justice professional to be competent and diligent, he will have to be aware of this economic globalization and its implications for his practice, and do everything he can not to render less service than his client deserves.

International Law

The growing influence of international law is a specific feature of globalization, along with the new economic and political realities. International law refers to legal relationships between nations. These relationships may depend on a particular treaty, such as the Geneva Convention, or on a formal organization, such as the United Nations. The latter concerns us here.

The United Nations, consisting of 50 nations at its founding in 1945, now includes almost all of the independent nations in the world—192 of them.[24] U.N. members agree to abide by the charters and rules of the United Nations and to regard the organization as the primary arbiter in international disputes. In terms of international law, the most important U.N. institution is the International Court of Justice (ICJ) in The Hague. The ICJ identifies its role as "to settle in accordance with international law, legal disputes submitted to it by states and to give advisory opinions on legal questions referred to it by authorized U.N. organs and specialized agencies."[25]

Q 15.7

Suppose that every member of the United Nations but the United States signs a resolution demanding that, out of respect for human rights, the United States allow people all over the world to have access to the procedure in Case 15.2. Suppose further that the United States refuses, on the grounds that the procedure is the property of its patent holders and the United States as a sovereign nation has the right, if not the duty, to protect its patent holders. Who has the better moral argument?

This arrangement looks good in theory and has often worked well in practice, but not always. At times the United States or its closest allies have ignored U.N. charters or decisions, and the future promises more U.N. resolutions that will not appeal to U.S. interests. For example, the United States has refused to sign the Kyoto Protocol to the United Nations Framework Convention on Climate Change,[26] and the United States refuses to allow its soldiers and government officials to be subject to the International Criminal Court, which was founded in 2002 with jurisdiction over genocide, crimes against humanity, and war crimes.[27]

In terms of international law, the primary moral challenge facing American criminal justice professionals in particular, and U.S. citizens in general, is to identify our responsibilities and rights in the international community as globalization evolves and international law becomes more important. To be sure, there is a lot to occupy the criminal justice professional within the American criminal justice system, but neither the country nor its legal system exists in political isolation. And since criminal justice professionals are the experts, they will have to take the lead in a national discussion on how best to participate internationally.

✦ MEDIA

The media serve four basic purposes in a democratic society: to inform, to provide a public forum for ideas and opinions, to entertain, and to serve the marketplace. With each advance in media technology come new and greater opportunities for achieving these purposes. At the same time, however, there is greater moral challenge to the criminal justice system, including both professionals and the citizenry.

The problems stem from a convergence of two phenomena: the profound *influence* that the media have on public opinion and, in turn, on the criminal justice profession's response to that opinion; and *information overload* that makes it increasingly difficult to evaluate content and put it to proper use. Let's look at these phenomena and then draw some conclusions about their moral significance.

Influence

There is much debate about the extent to which media reflect culture rather than create it, but it is obvious that much of what the public thinks it knows about the criminal justice system is what the media portray. It is also obvious that much of what the media portray is misleading.

One way media mislead is by presenting the extraordinary as if it were ordinary. For example, police activity rarely makes the news unless the police have done something very bad or unusually heroic. Similarly, fictional stories about police tend to magnify their vices and virtues. The bulk of a police officer's typical day simply isn't newsworthy. The result is that an undiscriminating audience gets an unrealistic sense of what police officers do and what the public has the right to expect from them. We have already seen this in our note about the CSI effect. It is easy to find similar examples of unrealistic images of the courtroom and corrections. This false perspective makes it more difficult for the public to participate in constructive dialogue about the place of criminal justice professionals in society.

Another way the media mislead is by scaremongering—emphasizing unusual natural and moral evils as if they were the norm. This may contribute to an irrational fear of crime, terrorism, and natural disaster that works against the public's sense of security and safety and forces the criminal justice system to respond to unfounded fears in much the same way it has to respond to false alarms. This is a waste of public services, and it causes unfounded discomfort and anxiety.

Yet another way the media mislead, especially through advertising, is by contributing to a consumer mentality that defines happiness in terms of material possessions, especially brand-name items with prestige. The vast amount of scholarship on this consumerism points to two primary results that affect the criminal justice system. First, many people who are unable to acquire these materials by legal means will seek to acquire them by any means necessary, thus raising the crime rate. Second, those who are able to acquire these material goods in socially acceptable ways often discover that these goods are not sufficient for happiness, thus adding to a frustrated and unhappy public.

The media also influence criminal justice professionals. As Lawrence Friedman points out, lawmakers tend to spend most of their lawmaking energy reacting to "public opinion, scandal, and incident," which is "mute testimony to the rampant power of the media, especially television."[28] This leads to an "avalanche of harsh laws, and the fact that a whole nation of people is crammed into prisons at the beginning of the twenty-first century."[29] Political Scientist Louis Gawthorp agrees, arguing that the criminal justice profession needs an "eschatological vision"—that is, a clear vision of what the future might hold and where we want the country to go.[30] To develop and sustain this vision, the criminal justice professional must be resistant to the whims of current popular sentiment, but still take seriously the people's interests and input in the interest of democratic governance.

Information Overload

The digital age has brought with it an explosion of media content: information and misinformation; opportunities for unfettered exchange of ideas and opinions; and new venues for uncensored visual and audio entertainment. Chances are that when the authors of the Bill of Rights guaranteed free speech, they had no inkling of a future with such a variety of "speech" and so little restraint. Had the authors known, would they have been apt to promote free speech so absolutely?

Perhaps not. Democracy requires a level of free exchange of information, ideas, and opinions that would suffer if people had to limit their give-and-take according to the subjective views of a person or group of people. Still, we readily impose some limits. For example, we condemn child pornography and shouting "fire!" in a crowded theater. Even today, then, we recognize that virtuous speech is not unconditionally free. So one challenge the future holds for the criminal justice system is whether and how to regulate the media.

Another problem that information overload presents is that it fragments audiences, thus making democratic exchange of information, ideas, and opinions more difficult. For example, before the digital age there were fewer media sources of the news and more consumers of any one source of news.[31] To be sure, there were more organizations publishing newspapers, and more people subscribing to those papers, than there are today. However, there were far fewer organizations broadcasting news on television or radio, and there was no Internet news, listserv, or blog. With more people accessing the same sources, there was more media content in common and thus greater chance for exchange among news consumers. Today, there are thousands of sources of news—real and alleged—available in print, on the Internet, and through audio and visual media such as CDs and DVDs. Each of these sources has its proponents, but no one source has the critical mass of users that a single news source, such as a newspaper or network broadcast, once had and which was crucial to the democratic exchange of ideas. Attorney Dusty Horwitt summarizes this problem neatly when he declares that "the Internet siphons audiences and revenue from media outlets that can give citizens a voice, causing them to shrink and further impairing the media's democratic power."[32] If the American criminal justice system depends on democratic input, then the problem of audience fragmentation is a problem for criminal justice.

Moral Significance

Media influence and information overload will continue to grow, as will the opportunities and moral problems they present to the criminal justice system. The responsibility for managing media sources and media content falls not only on the criminal justice professional, but also on the media professional and the media consumer.

The virtuous criminal justice professional will need to understand media's role in human behavior, especially criminal behavior, and the media's influence on the practice of criminal justice. With that understanding, the professional will have to remain as free as possible from undue influence, while using the media to stay informed about events and views that affect the professional's service to the community. The professional will have to take the lead in ensuring that speech remains as free as the Constitution requires, while carefully and rarely limiting expression that is especially harmful, such as child pornography and incitant rhetoric. Finally, the professional will have to take the lead in encouraging dialogue between the professionals and the citizenry and among the citizens themselves concerning the proper role of media in the criminal justice system.

To the extent that the media affect the criminal justice system, the virtuous media professional will understand and fulfill her responsibility to foster rather than hurt the democratic process. She will distinguish clearly between information and entertainment, being mindful of her audience and the extent to which the media influence her audience. And she will work with criminal justice professionals to ensure ongoing dialogue among all concerned about the proper role of media in the criminal justice system.

The virtuous media consumer will understand the value of his input to the democratic process and thus the importance of being well informed, as well as the responsibility he has for properly evaluating the media content he encounters. He too will seek ongoing and meaningful discussion about the proper role of media in the criminal justice system. In this quest, he will join with other citizens in holding criminal justice professionals and media professionals accountable for their contributions and failures regarding the public's liberty, safety, and security.

✦ Engagement, Education, and Ethics

If technology, demographics, and the media will affect criminal justice ethics in the ways we have anticipated, then there will be an even greater need for civic engagement, professional education, and public sector ethics. Let's say a little more about each of these.

The Need for Civic Engagement

Philosopher Peter Levine makes a strong argument for engaging the citizenry more fully in the political process, including legislation.[33] With all the emphasis we put on the moral responsibility of the criminal justice professional, it is helpful to remember that in a democracy, this responsibility does not fall solely on the professional.

Levine argues that since the health of the future will depend especially on the civic involvement of today's youth, we should engage these youth civically as soon and as well as possible.

Levine defines civic engagement as the effort to "enhance the commons [the goods and resources that are not privately owned] or to influence the state distribution and regulation in ways that benefit the underlying political structure."[34] The country needs civic engagement, Levine argues, because

- Civil society complements government professionals.
- The broader the participation, the greater the chance of equity.
- Democratic institutions need people to participate in them.
- Everyone has civic needs.
- Civic participation is valuable in itself.[35]

In addition, young people especially need to engage civically because "improving youth civic engagement is the most effective way to enhance civil society" and youth have an "autonomous culture with powerful effects."[36]

The relevance of this call for civic engagement to the future of criminal justice ethics is that it puts the onus on legislator and citizen alike to encourage people to be more civically engaged. This encouragement may involve direct efforts at engaging people through political associations or organized protests, for example. Or it may involve indirect efforts, such as support for educational and public policies that promote civic engagement.

The Need for Education

As we have seen, a person may not need extensive formal education to enter some of the criminal justice professions, such as law enforcement and corrections, but doing these jobs effectively requires technical skill, critical thinking, and practical wisdom. The professional may acquire much of this through practice, but there is always a place for relevant in-service training and continuing education.

The same holds for criminal justice professions that have advanced formal education as an entrance requirement, such as lawyers. Earning a law degree and passing the bar exam may be sufficient for entering the profession, but with all of the changes in law and the complex legal issues that emerge anew, lawyers have to continue studying and learning to stay on top of their professional game.

Much of what education has to offer the criminal justice professional is obvious: technical skills, knowledge about the law and the criminal justice system, a useful understanding of human behavior. Other necessary elements of professional knowledge, some of which we have alluded to, are less obvious but as important: constitutional literacy, information literacy, media literacy, and the basic tenets and practices of America's major religions.

In short, if the criminal justice professional is to render the best possible public service and to fulfill professional responsibilities and exercise professional rights as well as possible, then the professional has a moral obligation to pursue training and education routinely.

Note that a key feature of this education is research. This is a point that discussions of professional ethics in criminal justice often underplay or ignore. The profession is responsible for fostering and publishing research that will improve professional practice. Individual professionals are responsible for staying current with this research and contributing to it as they are able. The research itself should be thorough, well documented, and widely available for comment and improvement. There is much more to say about the ethics of research and its role in criminal justice ethics, but a fair treatment of the topic is beyond the scope of this book.

One final comment concerning education: To ensure an ethical criminal justice system, the citizenry also has a responsibility to study and learn. Citizens are the clients of the profession, and they must hold the professionals accountable. We have noted Aristotle's praise of democracy for its gathering of collective wisdom. Peter Levine takes this idea in a useful but slightly different direction, invoking philosopher John Dewey's argument that democracy itself is essentially collective learning and mutual education. Thus, we must think of the citizen's democratic engagement in the criminal justice system as primarily a learning activity.[37] This activity should (1) take place in the schools and in the community; (2) promote constitutional literacy and deeper understanding of the criminal justice system; and (3) involve not only theory but practice, in school government, service learning, and local governing bodies, for example. Without democratic involvement, as fostered through education, the future of criminal justice ethics is less hopeful.

Public Sector Ethics

It may seem redundant to declare that the future of criminal justice ethics requires public sector ethics. Isn't that what we have been arguing all along? Perhaps, but the question, as Gawthorp puts it, still remains: "Why are individuals being prepared to enter the public service without adequate training in ethical decision making?"[38]

Gawthorp argues persuasively that the tendency today is to replace public sector ethics with a simple legalism—the view that what's legal is what's moral—or with a sense of duty that leaves out compassion and a respect for moral gray areas. Adding to Levine's call for getting more citizens civically engaged, Gawthorp claims that "the character of democracy is derived solely from the body, mind, and spirit of the individual commitment to a common good," and "our sense of public sector ethics is inextricably linked to the moral essence of each individual citizen, as well as to the fabric of democracy."[39]

Though speaking specifically to policing, philosopher Edwin Delattre makes an interesting point that applies to a need for the study of ethics in the public sector generally: "the future of trustworthy policing depends on the recruitment and retention of sworn personnel and support staff who have learned . . . and made fundamental to their way of life" the fact that professionals must rise above the narcissism and childishness of today's young adults.[40] What's missing, Delattre argues is a "social stigma," both in society and in policing, that would tweak the moral conscience of someone about to do wrong.[41] As a means to this end, Delattre suggests better recruiting of police officers. This would include dropping residency requirements and requiring a college degree in a field or fields that are relevant to policing, have an ethics component, and are properly accredited.[42] As Delattre puts it, "our social conditions threaten to complicate the challenges for police. The capacities of police will have to rise to meet those challenges."[43]

Delattre may be overstating the case, but there are enough instances of police brutality and corruption to suggest that many police "have no shame." Whether this is due to lack of a proper understanding of ethics remains debatable, although as we have argued previously, a student of ethics will have a better chance of handling difficult moral cases than one who has not studied ethics. Still, there may be highly intelligent, well-trained police officers who have studied ethics but who have no moral conscience. Nothing short of careful vigilance and swift discipline can minimize the harm they can do.

In short, this interplay of the individual and the democratic whole requires the criminal justice professional to ask not only what she can do, but what she *should* do. Our point has been that in answering this question, she should be aware of her options and choose the one that is at the same time the least deficient and the least excessive.

Summary

This chapter has examined the future of criminal justice ethics from four vantage points: technology; demographics; the media; and the need for civic engagement, education, and public sector ethics. The future promises new and increasingly sophisticated challenges, given the steady introduction of new technologies, the growing population of the country and the world, and the influence of the media on human behavior and the criminal justice professions. The virtuous professional, and the virtuous citizen who must hold that professional accountable and who seeks to benefit from the criminal justice system, will seek continually to understand these challenges and ways to meet them constructively. The virtuous professional will take the lead in fostering this understanding through ongoing training, education, and research.

This book recognizes criminal justice practitioners as professionals. They include professionals in the three constitutional branches of government: legislative, executive, and judicial. This book's basic premise is the importance of the virtuous criminal justice professional to a healthy, robust, and effective criminal justice system. A sure sign of such a system is the assurance of the citizens' constitutional liberties, along with their safety and security.

The virtuous criminal justice professional recognizes and values the significance of his service to society. He accepts and fulfills his obligations of trustworthiness, including competence, diligence, honesty, candor, loyalty, discretion, beneficence, and nonmaleficence. He is drawn to the profession with a sense of calling, rather than with financial gain as his primary goal. And he commits to the level of training and education necessary to serving his clients well.

Thus, the virtuous professional recognizes the central role that ethics plays in fulfilling her role in the criminal justice system. She handles present challenges and meets new challenges with courage, justice, temperance, and prudence. She knows when to focus her moral attention on consequences, rules, or duties, and how to find the moral solution that is the least deficient and least excessive among the options. She knows the Constitution and its moral implications well, being especially aware of the different views concerning rights, justice, and law, and which views are most pertinent to the Constitution. She understands the influence of religion on the moral views of citizens and policy makers. And once again, she applies this knowledge in a way that honors her clients' constitutional rights while ensuring their safety and security.

Answers to Case Study Questions

Q15.1. The Fourth Amendment reads, in part, "The right of the people to be secure in their persons, houses, papers, and effects, against unreasonable searches and seizures, shall not be violated." On this wording alone, who has the better moral argument in Case 15.1, Stevens or Scalia?

Scalia. Except for the thermal imaging device, Kyllo's behavior in his house would have remained private and thus subject to search only by warrant.

Q15.2. In Case 15.1, is it fair to claim that Agent Elliott acted incompetently when he failed to get a warrant before scanning Kyllo's house?

No. He knew how to use the device, and he included the result of its use in what appeared to be a proper request for a warrant. In short, he acted competently.

On the other hand, now that the court has declared the imager's use unconstitutional without a warrant, it would be either incompetent or intentionally wrong to use the device unless there is a warrant permitting its use.

Q15.3. Assume that the procedure in Case 15.2 could increase the U.S. population markedly, because people would live much longer than they do at present. From a strictly utilitarian point of view, would it be morally reasonable for the federal government to ban use of the procedure simply in order to control the population? How about from a virtuous point of view?

No and no. Population growth can affect the greater good positively or negatively. While a larger population may strain natural and government resources, it may also provide the mind-power needed to solve many of the problems that plague humanity. Thus, banning the procedure might be a detriment to the common good.

From a virtuous point of view, banning the procedure would be an excessive response to the potential for population growth. First of all, it would be imprudent, because there may be demographic and natural reductions in birth rates that offset the growth in population. Thus, although the procedure *could* increase the population, it may not. It also may be unjust to deprive people of the opportunity to live longer and realize the liberty that health provides.

Q15.4. Suppose the story in Case 15.1 was that Kyllo's neighbor, a civilian, had scanned Kyllo's house with the thermal imager, discovered the hotspot, and contacted Agent Elliott to tell him about the result. Suppose that Elliott then included the neighbor as a confidential informant in his request for a warrant,

but made no mention of the imaging device. **Would Kyllo have a reasonable argument that law enforcement treated him unfairly by violating his Fourth Amendment freedom from unreasonable search and seizure?**

No. No government entity included the thermal imaging device in the warrant request, and only a government entity or its representative can violate the Fourth Amendment. The question remains whether Kyllo's neighbor morally violated Kyllo's privacy, which in turn might raise trespassing or "Peeping Tom" issues, but that is not Elliott's concern.

A more interesting question remains about the lengths to which a neighbor has the right or obligation to go in looking out for criminal activity.

Q15.5. Suppose that all of the suits in Case 15.2 have been settled for the plaintiffs and the life-prolonging procedure is now widely available. Should prisoners who have received life terms receive the procedure, even if they don't want it?

It depends. The virtuous answer would consider whether use of the procedure is just and temperate. In terms of justice, one could go either way. If the morally right purpose of the punishment is merely to get the prisoner out of society short of executing him, then there is no good reason for prolonging his life beyond its ordinary and expected course. If the morally right purpose of the punishment is to force the prisoner to contemplate his crime and, one hopes, to do so remorsefully, then the longer he is alive, the better.

In terms of temperance, using the procedure simply to extend the prisoner's term would be an intemperate use of a humanitarian procedure. Using the procedure to restore the quality of his life might be humanitarian, and thus temperate, in the same way giving him an emergency appendectomy might be of benefit.

There is also the question whether keeping him alive beyond his naturally allotted time would constitute cruel and unusual punishment.

Q15.6. Does Scalia's decision in Case 15.4 constitute an expansion of defendants' rights?

Yes and no. As a traditionalist, Scalia believes that he is recognizing a right that is as old as the Constitution. But until *Kyllo,* there had never been a need to articulate a right against unreasonable surveillance by a thermal imager. One might interpret Stevens's dissenting opinion as an effort not to expand a defendant's rights in such a case.

Q15.7. Suppose that every member of the United Nations but the United States signs a resolution demanding that, out of respect for human rights, the United States allow people all over the world to have access to the procedure in Case 15.2. Suppose further that the United States refuses, on the grounds that the procedure is the property of its patent holders and the United States as a sovereign nation has the right, if not the duty, to protect its patent holders. Who has the better moral argument?

The United Nations. In general, matters of life and death that affect the greater good trump commercial self-interest.

NOTES

1. *Kyllo v. United States* (99-8508) 533 U.S. 27 (2001) 190 F.3d 1041; retrieved 15 July 2007 from http://www.law.cornell.edu/supct/html/99-8508.ZO.html.

2. John Dempsey and Linda S. Forst, *An Introduction to Policing*, 4th ed. (Belmont, CA: Wadsworth, 2008), Ch. 14.

3. Samuel D. Warren and Louis D. Brandeis, "The Right to Privacy," *Harvard Law Review* 4, no. 5 (15 December 1890).

4. James Risen and Eric Lichtblau, "Bush Lets U.S. Spy on Callers without Courts," *New York Times*, 16 December 2005, p. 1A.

5. Lawrence M. Friedman, *Law in America: A Short History* (New York: Modern Library, 2004), p. 183.

6. Louis C. Gawthorp, *Public Service and Democracy: Ethical Imperatives for the 21st Century* (New York: Chatham House, 1998), p. 125.

7. David H. Bayley, *Police for the Future* (New York: Oxford University Press, 1994), p. 140.

8. Henry Ruth and Kevin R. Reitz, *The Challenge of Crime: Rethinking Our Response* (Cambridge, MA: Harvard University Press, 2003).

9. *The Power of Work: The Center for Employment Opportunities Comprehensive Prisoner Reentry Program* (New York: MDRC, 2006).

10. Ruth and Reitz, *Challenge of Crime*, p. 283.

11. *The Power of Work*, p. 8.

12. Ruth and Reitz, *Challenge of Crime*, p. 284.

13. L. M. Friedman, *Law in America*, p. 129.

14. Ibid., p. 145.

15. Ibid., p. 147.

16. Ibid., p. 152.

17. Ibid.

18. Ibid.

19. Edwin J. Delattre, *Character and Cops*, 4th ed. (Washington, DC: AEI Press, 2002), p. 386.

20. Thomas L. Friedman, *The World Is Flat: A Brief History of the Twenty-First Century*, expanded edition (New York: Farrar, Straus and Giroux, 2006).

21. World Bank, *The Global Citizen's Handbook: Facing Our World's Crises and Challenges* (New York: HarperCollins, 2007), p. 58.

22. William Wallis and Geoff Dyer, "China Promotes Africa Ties Ahead of Talks," *Financial Times*, 15 May 2007; retrieved 16 July 2007 from www.ft.com.

23. George W. Bush, "The President's Radio Address," 4 March 2006; retrieved 16 July 2007 from http://www.presidency.ucsb.edu/ws/print.php?pid=65342.

24. Retrieved 16 July 2007 from www.un.org.

25. Retrieved 16 July 2007 from www.icj-cij.org.

26. United Nations, "Kyoto Protocol: Status of Ratification," 10 July 2006; retrieved 16 July 2007 from http://unfccc.int/files/essential_background/kyoto_protocol/application/pdf/kpstats.pdf.

27. "United States Defends Position on International Criminal Court: Napper Addresses OSCE Human Dimension Implementation Meeting," 12 October 2004; retrieved 17 July 2007 from http://usinfo.state.gov/dhr/Archive/2004/Oct/13-40327.html.

28. L. M. Friedman, *Law in America*, p. 181.

29. Ibid., p. 180.

30. Gawthorp, *Public Service and Democracy*, p. 146.

31. Ben H. Bagdikian, *The New Media Monopoly* (Boston: Beacon Press, 2004).
32. Dusty Horwitt, "New Media: Good for Democracy?" *Baltimore Sun,* 20 July 2007, p. 17A.
33. Peter Levine, *The Future of Democracy: Developing the Next Generation of American Citizens* (Medford, MA: Tufts University Press, 2007).
34. Ibid., p. 8.
35. Ibid., pp. 14–37.
36. Ibid., pp. 70, 74.
37. Ibid., pp. 41–2.
38. Gawthorp, *Public Service and Democracy,* p. 19.
39. Ibid., pp. 36, 157.
40. Delattre, *Character and Cops,* p. 310.
41. Ibid., pp. 312–19.
42. Ibid., p. 322.
43. Ibid., p. 327.

GLOSSARY

A

absolutism The argument that at least some things are always morally evil or morally good. The opposing theory is **relativism.**

accountability The external test by which professionals demonstrate that they are fulfilling their promise to the people.

act utilitarianism The consequentialist theory that each act should result in the greatest good for the greatest number.

affirming the consequent The pure non sequitur fallacy that affirms the consequent in the second premise, where the first premise is a hypothetical sentence and the conclusion is the antecedent.

agency model The allocation of responsibility for decision making that makes the client responsible for the decision.

altruism The argument that one's interests are irrelevant as long as one is serving the interest of others.

ambiguity The fallacy in which something about the language of the argument is ambiguous.

amphiboly The fallacy in which the grammar of an entire sentence is ambiguous.

analytic definition A statement of meaning in which the word one wants to define is replaced with a word or phrase that means the same thing.

argument Any set of sentences in which one sentence (the conclusion) is claimed to be proven by the other sentences (the premises).

argumentum ad baculum Appeal to force or fear; a fallacious attempt to scare someone into accepting a conclusion.

argumentum ad hominem Argument against the person; a fallacious attempt to refute an argument by attacking the arguer.

argumentum ad ignorantiam Appeal to ignorance; an illogical argument that because one does not know something to be the case, it must not be the case.

argumentum ad misericordiam Appeal to pity; an attempt to refute an argument by appealing to pity, rather than to logic.

argumentum ad populum Appeal to the masses; an illogical argument that because so many people like something, it must be the best; or because so many people believe something, it must be true.

B

bad argument An argument in which a premise is false, a premise is irrelevant to the conclusion, or a premise simply restates the conclusion.

begging the question The fallacy in which the question is answered with the premise.

black and white thinking The fallacy that involves illogically jumping from one extreme to another when the truth is somewhere in between.

C

cardinal virtues Basic virtues. In Greek ethics: courage, temperance, justice, and prudence.

categorical imperative According to Kant, "Act only according to that the maxim *[the principle behind one's act]* whereby you can at the same time will that it should become a universal law."

causal responsibility An obligation for one's actions that one does not necessarily have control over.

circular argument. *See* **fallacy of petitio principii.**

coherence theory A sentence is true if it is coherent within one's system of belief, and a sentence is false if it is incoherent within one's system of belief.

commutative justice The form of justice concerning contracts. *Cf.* **distributive justice; retributive justice.**

complex question The fallacy in which the question does not permit all possible answers, thus forcing a conclusion.

conclusion Decision, judgment, or thesis; the sentence that an argument claims to prove.

conferred right   A right that somebody with sufficient authority confers on another.

consequentialism   The theory that an act is good if the *consequences* of the act are good.

contract model   The allocation of responsibility for decision making that makes the decision a joint responsibility of the professional and the client, assuming the client is physically and mentally able to participate in making the decision.

correspondence theory   The theory that a sentence is true if it corresponds to the facts; a sentence is false if it is contrary to the facts; and in the absence of facts one must suspend judgment about the truth of the sentence.

D

deductive   Arguments that claim certainty—that is, claim that because the premises are true, the conclusion is definitely true.

deontology   (from the Greek word *deon*, meaning "from duty") The theory that an act is good if the agent acted from *duty*.

determinism   The argument that something other than free will determines our actions.

dictionary definition   A statement of meaning that describes current usage of a term.

dilemma   A problem for which there appears to be no right answer or solution.

distributive justice   The form of justice concerning the proper distribution of goods and services among stakeholders. *Cf.* **commutative justice; retributive justice.**

E

egalitarianism   A form of distributive justice that calls for all stakeholders getting "an equal piece of the pie." *Cf.* **libertarianism; utilitarianism.**

egoism   The consequentialist theory that the only morally relevant consequences are the consequences "for me."

equivocation   The fallacy in which a word or short phrase in the argument is ambiguous.

ethic of care   Feminists' alternative to the ethics of justice, in which women approach a moral problem holistically and collegially, seeking to resolve the problem in the most caring way.

ethical egoism.   *See* **rational egoism.**

F

fallacy   An argument that, while logically incorrect, may be psychologically persuasive.

fallacy of inconsistency   The fallacy in which all the premises cannot be true at the same time.

fallacy of petitio principii   The fallacy of using as a premise what you are trying to prove in the conclusion.

false cause   The fallacy that because two things occur together, one must be the cause of the other.

formal non sequitur.   *See* **pure non sequitur.**

free will   The ability to do otherwise.

G

golden mean   Referring to Aristotle's virtue theory: the mean between the extremes of deficiency and excess. In other words, something is morally best—that is, virtuous—if it is the least deficient and the least excessive of the alternatives.

Golden Rule   *Do unto others as you would have them do unto you.* Sometimes appearing in its negative form: *Do not do unto others what you would not want others to do unto you.*

good argument   An argument in which the premises are true, the premises are relevant to the conclusion, and no premise simply restates the conclusion.

H

hasty generalization   The fallacy that involves drawing a conclusion based on insufficient evidence.

hedonism   (from the Greek word *edon*, which means "pleasure") The view that an act is morally good if it causes pleasure and morally evil if it causes pain.

I

inalienable right   A right that no one can take away or give away.

inductive   Describing an argument that claims probability—that is, claims that because the premises are true, the conclusion probably is true.

integrity   (1) The quality of having integrated the virtues into one's life. (2) The internal test by which professionals demonstrate to themselves that they are fulfilling their promise.

intellectual virtue   According to Aristotle, the ability to find the truth. Divisible into practical wisdom and theoretical wisdom.

invalid   Describing a bad argument; even if the premises were true, that would not demonstrate the truth or probability of the conclusion.

irrelevance   The fallacy in which the premises are logically irrelevant to the conclusion.

J

judicial activists   Those who argue that the Constitution is a living document that judges must interpret in the context of contemporary values and that the framers intended the Constitution to be adaptable to change.

judicial discretion   The power or right of a judge to act according to his or her judgment, not being restricted by the standards and rules.

jury nullification   The jury's right to render a not guilty verdict even if the prosecution has proved its case.

just war   A war that meets certain criteria for logical possibility and moral propriety.

L

legal positivism   The theory that human legislatures make law.

legal realism   The theory that judges make law.

lex talionis   Law of retaliation.

libertarianism   The form of distributive justice that claims the legitimate holder of goods has a complete claim to those goods, regardless of the interest of any other stakeholders. Opposed to **egalitarianism** and **utilitarianism.**

M

metaphorical theory   The truth is in the meaning of the metaphor, not in the literal meaning of the words or in the hearer's assent.

modus ponens   A valid argument of the form "If p, then q. p. Therefore, q."

moral reasoning   The process of drawing a morally significant conclusion from a set of premises.

moral responsibility   An obligation for one's actions over which one has control.

moral theology   The study of religious ethics.

moral virtue   According to Aristotle, the ability to control the nonrational soul.

N

natural law theory   The theory that some power higher than humans—God or nature—gives us our law.

negative right   A right the exercise of which no one else may interfere with.

non sequitur   The fallacy in which the premises "do not follow" logically from the conclusion.

O

objectivism   The argument that moral value is in the object of the judgment, not in the mind of the judge. The opposite of **subjectivism.**

ostensive definition   A statement of meaning that defines by example.

P

paternal model   The allocation of responsibility for decision making that makes the professional responsible for the decision.

performative theory   The view that when one says something is true, one *performs* the act of making it true (albeit subjectively).

positive right   A right that someone else has a duty to help the rights holder exercise.

practical wisdom   According to Aristotle, one of two forms of intellectual virtue: the capacity to grasp changeable truth.

pragmatic theory   The theory that a sentence is true if it works to believe that it is true—that is, if there is some helpful consequence to accepting the sentence as true. A sentence is false if it is harmful to believe that the sentence is true. And if there is no practical value to believing the sentence, then it is neither true nor false, but nonsense.

premise   Any sentence that an argument offers as proof of the conclusion; reasons, evidence, support, or justification.

principle of double effect   The principle that when doing something right requires doing something usually considered wrong, the wrong becomes right.

principles   Statements that help explain the application of a standard in a particular professional context, but that do not describe their own scope or limits.

psychological egoism   The argument that human psychology is naturally egoist.

pure non sequitur   The fallacy of non sequitur in which the argument is bad because of its structure rather than its language. *See* **affirming the consequent.**

R

rational egoism   The argument that accepts the possibility of self-sacrifice but holds that we *should* be egoists; we should tend only to our business and not "stick our noses" into anyone else's.

regularianism   The theory that an act is good if the act obeyed a rule.

relativism   The argument that there are no moral absolutes, because all of morality is relative to a culture, a time, or personal interest. The opposite of **absolutism.**

retributive justice   The form of justice that is concerned with the proper response to acts of commutative or distributive injustice.

right   The freedom to do something or refrain from doing something.

rule utilitarianism   The theory that each act should follow a rule that is in the best interest of the greatest number.

rules   Statements that are specific about what should or should not be done, making it possible to decide readily whether one has obeyed or disobeyed them.

S

"sinning bravely"   Choosing the lesser of two evils, with the faith that one is operating under an umbrella of God's grace.

social contract theory   The theory that people create governments by contracting with each other to recognize a sovereign—a monarch, a group of aristocrats, or a democratic body—and to agree to a set of laws.

sound   Describing a valid argument with all true premises.

standards   General statements of moral value, widely open to discretion and evaluation.

stipulative definition   A statement of meaning that defines a word by consensus.

strict constructionists   Those who argue that judicial decisions should rest on the intent of the framers of the Constitution and that their intent came from absolute and thus unchangeable values.

subjectivism   The argument that moral value is in the mind of the judge, not in the object of that judgment. The opposite of **objectivism.**

T

teleology   (1) The theory that everything in nature has a purpose unique to its species and that to understand anything is to understand its purpose. (2) An alternative name for **consequentialism.**

theoretical wisdom   The ability to grasp unchangeable truth.

tu quoque   "You do it too!" A form of the argumentum ad hominem that someone's argument is bad because he or she is hypocritical.

U

unsound   Describing a valid argument with at least one false premise.

utilitarianism   (1) The consequentialist theory that what is morally good is based on utility, and therefore all action should be directed toward achieving the greatest happiness for the greatest number of people. (2) The theory of distributive justice that is opposed to **libertarianism** and **egalitarianism.**

V

valid   Describing a good argument. If the premises are true, then the conclusion must certainly be true (in a deductive argument) or as probable as the argument claims (in an inductive argument).

veil of ignorance   John Rawls's technique for invoking the Golden Rule to make morally significant decisions. That is, we should do unto others as we would have them do unto us while pretending that we do not know who we are until we have acted.

W

Wesleyan Quadrilateral   Recognition of four sources of religious moral authority: scripture, tradition, experience, and reason. Named for John Wesley (1703–1791), founder of Methodism.

INDEX